Praise for *Becoming Supernatural*

"From a gifted scientist and passionate teacher, this unique and practical guide shows us—step by step—how to move beyond the limits of the known and into an extraordinary new life."

— **Tony Robbins**, #1 *New York Times* best-selling author of *Unshakeable*

"I have long been a fan of Dr. Joe Dispenza's work. In Becoming Supernatural, *you will learn exactly how you can transcend the limitations of your past—including health challenges—and, quite literally, create a new body, a new mind, and a new life. This information is thrilling, life changing, and incredibly practical."*

— **Christiane Northrup, M.D.**, *New York Times* best-selling author of *Goddesses Never Age*

"Dr. Joe Dispenza is a doctor, a scientist, and a modern-day mystic. . . . In a style that is simple, straightforward, and easy to understand, [he] has woven into a single volume the paradigm-altering discoveries of quantum science and the deep teachings that adepts of the past dedicated their entire lifetimes to master."

— **from the foreword by Gregg Braden**, *New York Times* best-selling author of *Human by Design* and *The Divine Matrix*

"Becoming Supernatural takes the idea of realizing your full potential to a crazy new level. Joe Dispenza has done an outstanding job of creating a 21st-century operator's manual for the human body and brain by combining his vast experiential wisdom with compelling case studies, exciting scientific research, and the exercises his students have used to do everything from healing their bodies to dramatically altering the course of their lives. He's a man on a mission, and while the idea of Becoming Supernatural is a BIG promise, this book delivers hands down!"

— **Cheryl Richardson**, *New York Times* best-selling author of *Take Time for Your Life*

"In this provocative, fascinating book, Dr. Joe Dispenza shows that we are so much more than just our linear minds. As our savvy guide, Dr. Dispenza takes readers further than ordinary awareness to understand the infinite quantum field of consciousness which goes beyond the senses and beyond space and time. I recommend this book to everyone who wants to explore the extraordinary nature of consciousness and healing."

— **Judith Orloff, M.D.**, author of *The Empath's Survival Guide*

BECOMING
SUPERNATURAL

ALSO BY DR. JOE DISPENZA

YOU ARE THE PLACEBO:
*Making Your Mind Matter**

BREAKING THE HABIT OF BEING YOURSELF:
*How to Lose Your Mind and Create a New One**

EVOLVE YOUR BRAIN:
The Science of Changing Your Mind

*Available from Hay House
Please visit:

Hay House USA: www.hayhouse.com®
Hay House Australia: www.hayhouse.com.au
Hay House UK: www.hayhouse.co.uk
Hay House India: www.hayhouse.co.in

BECOMING SUPERNATURAL

*How Common People Are
Doing the Uncommon*

DR. JOE DISPENZA

HAY HOUSE, INC.
Carlsbad, California • New York City
London • Sydney • Johannesburg
Vancouver • New Delhi

Published and distributed in the United States by: Hay House, Inc.: www
.hayhouse.com® • *Published and distributed in Australia by:* Hay House
Australia Pty. Ltd.: www.hayhouse.com.au • *Published and distributed in the
United Kingdom by:* Hay House UK, Ltd.: www.hayhouse.co.uk • *Distributed in
Canada by:* Raincoast Books: www.raincoast.com • *Published in India by:* Hay
House Publishers India: www.hayhouse.co.in

Cover design: John Dispenza
Interior design: Karim J. Garcia
Interior illustrations: John Dispenza
Illustrations on pages 32, 35, 49, 56, 60, 72, 94, 100, 101, 103, 105, 116, 118, 123, 133,
    267: Icon made by John Dispenza from www.flaticon.com
Images on pages 174, 175, 177, and 305 and on page 22 of the insert: Courtesy of the
    HeartMath® Institute
Photograph on page 263: Reprinted with permission from Simon Baconnier et al.,
    "Calcite microcrystals in the pineal gland of the human brain: First physical
    and chemical studies," *Bioelectromagnetics* 23, no. 7 (October 2002): 488–495.
Photograph on page 282: © Steve Alexander
Images on pages 1, 5, 6, 23, and 24 of the insert: Courtesy of Dr. Konstantin Korotkov
Indexer: Joan D. Shapiro

Library of Congress Cataloging-in-Publication Data

Names: Dispenza, Joe, 1962- author.
Title: Becoming supernatural : how common people are doing the uncommon /
    Joe Dispenza.
Description: Carlsbad, California : Hay House, Inc., 2017.
Identifiers: LCCN 2017029723 | ISBN 9781401953096 (hardback)
Subjects: LCSH: Energy medicine. | Mind and body. | Self-care, Health. |
    BISAC: BODY, MIND & SPIRIT / New Thought. | BODY, MIND & SPIRIT /
    Inspiration & Personal Growth. | BODY, MIND & SPIRIT / General.
Classification: LCC RZ421 .D57 2017 | DDC 615.8/51--dc23 LC record available at
    https://lccn.loc.gov/2017029723

Hardcover ISBN: 978-1-4019-5309-6

10 9 8 7 6 5 4 3
1st edition, October 2017

Printed in the United States of America

For my brother John,
who has always been a true mystic

CONTENTS

Foreword by Gregg Braden xi

Introduction: Getting Ready to Become Supernatural xvii

Chapter 1:   Opening the Door to the Supernatural 1

Chapter 2:   The Present Moment 27

Chapter 3:   Tuning In to New Potentials in the Quantum 61

Chapter 4:   Blessing of the Energy Centers. 85

Chapter 5:   Reconditioning the Body to a New Mind 113

Chapter 6:   Case Studies: Living Examples of Truth 143

Chapter 7:   Heart Intelligence. 155

Chapter 8:   Mind Movies/Kaleidoscope 179

Chapter 9:   Walking Meditation. 205

Chapter 10:   Case Studies: Making It Real 213

Chapter 11:   Space-Time and Time-Space. 219

Chapter 12:   The Pineal Gland 255

Chapter 13:   Project Coherence: Making a Better World 287

Chapter 14:   Case Studies: It Could Happen to You. 307

Afterword: Being Peace 317

Acknowledgments 323

Endnotes. 327

Index 335

About the Author 347

FOREWORD

Throughout human history there have been accounts of everyday people having experiences that catapult them beyond the limits of what was thought to be possible. From the multi-century lifespan of Li Ching-Yuen, the martial artist whose 256-year-long life began in 1677 and included 14 wives and over 200 children before he died in 1933, to the spontaneous healing of myriad diseases documented by the Institute of Noetic Sciences (IONS) through 3,500 references from over 800 journals in 20 languages, the evidence clearly tells us that we're not what we've been told in the past, and even more than we've allowed ourselves to imagine.

As the acceptance of expanded human potential gains mainstream momentum, the question has shifted from "What is possible in our lives?" to "How do we do it? How do we awaken our extraordinary potential in everyday life?" The answer to this question forms the foundation for this book: Becoming Supernatural: How Common People Are Doing the Uncommon.

Dr. Joe Dispenza is a doctor, a scientist, and a modern-day mystic. He's also a synthesizer of information with a vision that extends beyond the confines of a single scientific discipline. Drawing from diverse fields of rock-solid science, such as epigenetics, molecular biology, neurocardiology, and quantum physics, Joe crosses the traditional boundaries that have separated scientific thinking and human experience in the past. In doing so he opens the door to a bold new paradigm of self-actualized empowerment—a way of thinking and living based upon what we sense is possible in our lives, as well as what we accept as scientific fact. This new frontier of realized potential is redefining what it means to be a fully enabled, fully capacitated human. And it's a frontier that holds promise for everyone from homemakers, students, and skilled laborers to scientists, engineers, and health-care professionals.

The reason for such a wide appeal is that Joe's work today parallels a proven model that masters have used successfully with their students for centuries. The idea for the model is simple—once we have a direct experience of a greater potential, it frees us to embrace that potential in our everyday lives. The book you hold in your hands, Becoming Supernatural, is the first-of-its-kind manual that does precisely this: it leads us on a step-by-step journey to achieving our greatest potential in body, health, relationships, and life purpose and allows us to make that journey at our own pace.

It was in the walls of a cave on the Tibetan plateau that I saw for myself how the same model was used by one of the great yogic masters of the past to free his students of their own limited beliefs. The legacy of his teaching remains today, preserved in the native rock that provided both the home, and the classroom, for the master eight centuries ago.

In the spring of 1998 I facilitated a group pilgrimage into the highlands of Western Tibet. Our route led us directly to the remote cave of the 11th-century poet, mystic, and yogi, Ujetsun Milarepa, known in his day simply as Milarepa.

I first learned of the legendary yogi while I was a student of a Sikh mystic that became my yoga teacher in the 1980s. For years I studied the mystery surrounding Milarepa's life—how he had come from a privileged family yet chose to renounce his worldly possessions; the brutal and tragic circumstances of losing his family and loved ones to mass violence; and how his revenge, and subsequent suffering, led to his retreat high in the Himalayan mountains, where he discovered his extraordinary potential as a devoted yogi. I wanted to see for myself the place where Milarepa breached the laws of physics to demonstrate to himself, and to his students, that we are confined in our lives only by the limits of our own beliefs. Nineteen days into my journey, I had the opportunity to do just that.

After acclimating to single-digit humidity and elevations of more than 15,000 feet above sea level, I found myself precisely at the place where Milarepa stood before his students 800 years before. With my face only inches away from the cave's wall, I was staring squarely into the unsolved mystery that modern scientists have never been able to explain or duplicate. It was in this exact place that Milarepa first placed his open hand against the rock at about shoulder level, and then continued to push his hand further into the wall in front of him, as if the stone did not exist! When he did so, the rock beneath his palms became soft and malleable, giving way to the pressure of his push. The result was a perfect impression of the yogi's hand left in the rock for his students then, and throughout the centuries, to see. Scanning our lights across the walls and ceiling of the cave, we could see even more hand impressions making it clear that Milarepa had offered this demonstration on more than one occasion.

As I opened my palm and pushed it into the impression, I could feel my fingers cradled in the form of the yogi's, precisely in the position that his hand had assumed eight centuries earlier. The fit was so perfect that any doubt I had about the authenticity of the handprint quickly disappeared. It was a feeling that was both humbling and inspiring at the same time. Immediately, my thoughts turned to the man himself. I wanted to know what was happening to him when he engaged the rock. What was he thinking? Perhaps more importantly, what was he feeling? How did he defy the physical "laws" that tell us a hand and the rock can't occupy the same place at the same time?

As if he was reading my mind, my Tibetan guide answered my questions before I even asked him. "The geshe's [great teacher's] meditation teaches that he is part of the rock, not separate from it. The rock cannot contain him. To the geshe, this cave represents a place of experience, rather than a barrier of limitation. In this place he is free and can move as if the rock does not exist." My guide's words made perfect sense. When Milarepa's students saw their teacher accomplish something that traditional beliefs said was not possible, they were faced with the same dilemma in their day that faces each of us today when we choose to free ourselves from our own limiting beliefs.

The dilemma is this: The thinking that was embraced by the family, friends, and society of the student's day thought of the world in terms of limits and boundaries. This included the belief that a cave wall is a barrier to the flesh of a human body. As Milarepa pushed his hand into the rock, however, his students were shown that there are exceptions to such "laws." The irony is that both ways of seeing the world are absolutely correct. Each depends upon the way we choose to think of ourselves in a given moment.

As I pressed my hand into the impression that the yogi left for his students long ago, I asked myself: Are we confined in our lives today by the same limiting beliefs that Milarepa's students experienced in their day? And if so, how do we awaken the power to transcend our own limiting beliefs?

I've found that when something is true in life, that truth shows up in many ways. For this reason it comes as no surprise that the scientific documentation from Joe's classroom discoveries leads to the same conclusion that Milarepa, and mystics throughout the centuries, arrived at in the past—that the universe "is" as it is, our bodies "are" as they are, and the circumstances of our lives exist as they do because of consciousness itself and the way we think of ourselves in our world. I've shared the story of Milarepa to illustrate this seemingly universal principle.

The key to the yogi's teaching is this: when we experience for ourselves, or witness in another person, something that we've once believed to be impossible, we are freed in our beliefs to transcend those limitations in our own lives. And this is precisely why the book you're holding has the potential to change your life. By showing you how to accept your future dream as your current reality, and to do so in a way that your body believes is happening "now," you discover how to set into motion a cascade of emotional and physiological processes that reflect your new reality. The neurons in your brain, the sensory neurites in your heart, and the chemistry of your body all harmonize to mirror the new thinking, and the quantum possibilities of life are rearranged to replace the unwanted circumstances of your past with the new circumstances that you've accepted as the present.

And that's the power of this book.

In a style that is simple, straightforward, and easy to understand, Joe Dispenza has woven into a single volume the paradigm-altering discoveries of quantum science and the deep teachings that adepts of the past dedicated their entire lifetimes to master—he shows us how to become supernatural.

Gregg Braden
New York Times best-selling author of
Human by Design and *The Divine Matrix*

INTRODUCTION

Getting Ready to Become Supernatural

I realize that writing this book is a risk for me and my reputation. There are certain people in the world—including some in the scientific community—who might call my work pseudoscience, especially after *Becoming Supernatural* makes its debut. I used to be overly concerned about those critics' opinions. In the early days of my career, I always wrote with skeptics in mind, trying to make sure they would approve of my work. On some level, I thought it was important to be accepted by that community. But one day when I was standing in front of an audience in London and a woman holding the microphone was telling her story about how she overcame her disease—how she healed herself through the practices I've written about in other books—I had an epiphany.

It became very clear that those skeptics and rigid scientists who hold their own beliefs about what is possible aren't going to like me or my work no matter what I do. Once I had that realization, I knew that I'd been wasting a lot of my vital energy. I was no longer interested in convincing that particular culture—especially those studying the normal and natural—about human potential. I was totally passionate about anything *but* normal, and I wanted to study the supernatural. I got very clear that I should give up my futile efforts to convince that community of anything and instead direct my energy to a whole other part of the population that *does* believe in possibility and *does* want to listen to what I have to share.

What a relief it was to fully embrace that idea and to let go of any attempt to make a difference in that other world. As I listened to the sweet lady in London, who wasn't a monk or a nun or an academic or a scholar, I knew that in telling her story to the audience, she was helping others see some part of themselves in her. Those hearing her journey might then believe it would be possible for them to accomplish the same. I'm at the point in my life where I am okay with people saying anything about me—and I certainly do have my flaws—but I now know, more than ever, that I am making a difference in people's lives. I say that with utter humility. I have labored for years in taking complex scientific information and making it simple enough for people to apply to their lives.

In fact, in the last four years my team of researchers, my staff, and I have gone through extensive strides to scientifically measure, record, and analyze these transformations in people's biology to prove to the world that common people can do the uncommon. This book is about more than just healing, although it includes stories of people who have made significant changes in their health and have actually reversed diseases—along with the tools you need to do the same. These accomplishments are becoming quite common in our community of students. The material you are about to read lives outside of convention and is not usually seen or understood by most of the world. The content of this book is based on an evolution of teachings and practices that have culminated in our students' ability to delve deeper into the more mystical of these. And of course, I am hoping it will bridge the world of science with the world of mysticism.

I wrote this book to take what I've always thought was possible to the next level of understanding. I wanted to demonstrate to the world that we can create better lives for ourselves—and that we are not linear beings living linear lives, but dimensional beings living dimensional lives. Hopefully, reading it will help you understand that you already have all the anatomy, chemistry, and physiology you need to become supernatural sitting latent within you, waiting to be awakened and activated.

In the past, I hesitated to talk about this realm of reality because I feared it might divide an audience based on their own personal beliefs. However, I have wanted to write this book for a long time now. Over the years, I have had profoundly rich mystical experiences that have changed me forever. Those inner events have influenced who I am today. I want to introduce you to that world of dimension and show you some of the measurements we took and the studies we did in our advanced workshops around the world. I started collecting data on our students in these workshops because we witnessed significant changes in their health, and I knew they were changing their biology during the meditations—in real time.

We have thousands and thousands of brain scans that prove those changes were not just imagined in their minds but actually took place in their brains. Several of the students we measured accomplished those changes within four days (the length of our advanced workshops). The scientific teams I've assembled have taken brain scan recordings using quantitative electroencephalogram (EEG) measurements before and after workshops as well as real-time measurements during the meditations and practices themselves. I was not only impressed with the changes, but shocked by them—they were that dramatic.

The brains of our students function in a more synchronized and coherent fashion after participating in the advanced retreats around the world. This increased order in their nervous systems helps them get very clear about a future they can create, and they are able to hold that intention independent of the conditions in their external environment. And when their brains are working right, *they* are working right. I will present scientific data that shows how much their brains improved in just a few days—which means you can do the same for your brain.

At the end of 2013, something mysterious started occurring. We started seeing brain scan recordings that puzzled the researchers and neuroscientists who came to our events to study my work. The high amount of energy in the brain that we were recording while a student was in certain meditations had never been recorded up until this point. And yet we were seeing these off-the-charts readings again and again.

When we interviewed the participants, they reported that their subjective experience during the meditation was very real and mystical, and that this either profoundly changed their view of the world or dramatically improved their health. I knew in those moments that these participants were having transcendental experiences in their inner world of meditation that were more real than anything they had ever experienced in their outer world. And we were capturing those subjective experiences objectively.

That has become a new normal for us now, and as a matter of fact, we can often predict when these high amplitudes of energy in the brain will occur, based on certain indicators and signs that we have seen for years now. In these pages, I want to demystify what it is to have an interdimensional experience as well as provide the science, biology, and chemistry of the organs, systems, and neurotransmitters that make this happen. It is my hope that this information will give you a road map for how to create such experiences for yourself.

We have also recorded amazing changes in heart rate variability (HRV). That's when we know a student is opening their heart and maintaining elevated emotions like gratitude, inspiration, joy, kindness, appreciation, and compassion, which cause the heart to beat in a coherent fashion—that is, with rhythm, order, and balance. We know that it takes a clear intention (a coherent brain) and an elevated emotion (a coherent heart) to begin to change a person's biology from living in the past to living in the future. That combination of mind and body—of thoughts and feelings—also seems to influence matter. And that's how you create reality.

So if you're going to truly believe in a future that you are imagining with all your heart, let's make sure it's open and fully activated. Why not, through practice and quantitative feedback, get good at doing it and make it a skill?

So we partnered with the HeartMath Institute (HMI), a sharp group of researchers based in Boulder Creek, California, who helped us measure the responses of thousands of our participants. It is our desire for our students to develop the ability to regulate an internal state independent of the conditions in their external environment and to know when they are creating heart coherence and when they are not. In other words, when we measure those internal changes, we can tell a person that they created a more balanced pattern in the heart measurement and that they are doing a great job and should keep doing exactly what they are doing. Or we can let them know they are not making any biological changes and then give them the proper instruction and provide several opportunities to practice getting better at the process. That's what feedback does; it helps us know when we are doing something correctly and when we aren't.

When we can change some feeling or thought inside of us, we can see changes outside of us, and when we observe that we did it correctly, we will pay attention to what we did and do it again. That action creates a constructive habit. By demonstrating how others perform such feats, I want to show you how powerful you can be.

Our students know how to influence the autonomic nervous system (ANS)—the system that maintains health and balance by automatically taking care of all our bodily functions while we have the free will to live our lives. It is this subconscious system that gives us our health and gives life to our bodies. Once we know how to gain access to this system, we can not only make our health better, but we can also transform unwanted self-limiting behaviors, beliefs, and habits into more productive ones. I'll present some of the data we have been collecting for years.

We've also taught our students that when they create heart coherence, their hearts create a measurable magnetic field that projects beyond their body. That magnetic field is an energy, and that energy is a frequency, and all frequency carries information. The information carried on that frequency can be an intention or thought that can influence the heart of another person at a different location by moving it into coherence and balance. I will show you evidence that a group of people sitting in a room together can influence others sitting at some distance *in the same room* to go into heart coherence at the exact same time. The evidence clearly shows that we are bound by an invisible field of light and information that influences us and others.

Given that, imagine what can happen when we all do this at the same time to change the world. That's exactly what we are up to as a community of individuals who are passionate about making a difference in the future of this Earth and the people and other life forms that inhabit it. We have created Project Coherence, in which thousands of people come together at the exact same time on the exact same day to increase the frequency of this planet and of everyone who lives here. Sound impossible? Not at all. More than 23 peer-reviewed articles and more than 50 peace-gathering projects show such events can lower incidents of violence, war, crime, and traffic accidents and at the same time increase economic growth.[1] My wish is to show you the science of how you can contribute to changing the world.

We have also measured the energy in the room during our workshops and watched how it changes when you have a community of 550 to 1,500 people raising their energy together and creating heart and brain coherence. We have seen significant changes time and time again. Although the instrument we use to measure this is not approved by the scientific community in the United States, it has been acknowledged in other countries, including Russia. In every event, we're wonderfully surprised by the amount of energy certain groups have been able to demonstrate.

We have also assessed the invisible field of vital energy surrounding the body of thousands of students to determine whether they can increase their own light field. After all, everything in our material universe is always emitting light and information—including you. When you are living in survival mode under the burden of the hormones of stress (such as adrenaline), you draw from this invisible field of energy and turn it into chemistry—and as you do so, the field around your body shrinks. We discovered a very advanced piece of equipment that can measure the emission of photons (particles of light) to determine whether a person is building a field of light around them or diminishing their own light field.

When more light is emitted, there's more energy—and hence more life. When a person has less light and information surrounding their body, they are more matter and thus emit less vital energy. Extensive research proves that the body's cells and various systems communicate not only by the chemical interactions we are familiar with, but also by a field of coherent energy (light) that carries a message (information) that causes the environment within and all around the cell to give instructions to other cells and biological systems.[2] We've measured the amount of vital energy that our students' bodies emit because of the inward changes they've made doing our meditations, and I want to show you what changes they can create in only four days or less.

Other centers in your body besides the heart are also under the control of the autonomic nervous system—I call them *energy centers*. Each has its own frequency, its own intent or consciousness, its own glands, its own hormones, its own chemistry, its own individual little brain, and so its own unique mind. You can influence these centers to function in a more balanced and integrated fashion. But to do that, you must first learn how to change your brain waves so you can enter this subconscious operating system. In fact, moving from beta brain waves (where the thinking brain is constantly analyzing and putting much attention on the outer world) to alpha brain waves (which indicate you're calmly placing more attention on the inner world) is key. By consciously slowing your brain waves down, you can more readily program the autonomic nervous system. Students who've done my various meditation practices over the years have learned how to change their brain waves as well as sharpen the type of focus it takes to be present long enough to produce measurable effects. We've discovered an instrument that can measure those changes, and again, I'll show you some of the research.

We've also measured several different biological markers related to changing gene expression (a process known as making epigenetic changes). In this book, you will learn that you are not in fact beholden to your genes, and that gene expression is changeable—once you begin to think, act, and feel differently. During our events, students leave their familiar lives for four to five days to instead spend time in an environment that doesn't remind them of who they think they are. In doing so, they separate themselves from the people they know, the things they own, the automatic behaviors they demonstrate in their daily lives, and the places they routinely go, and they begin to change their inner states through four different types of meditations—walking, sitting, standing, and lying down. And through each one of these, they learn to become someone else.

We know it's true because our studies show significant changes in our students' gene expression, and they've then reported significant changes in their health. Once we can show someone measurable results proving they truly have altered neurotransmitters, hormones, genes, proteins, and enzymes through thought alone, they can better justify their efforts and prove to themselves that they really are transforming.

As I share these ideas with you in this book, walking you through the process and explaining the science behind the work that we're doing and why, you'll be learning a lot of fairly detailed information. But don't worry: I will review certain key concepts in different chapters. I do this intentionally to remind you of what you have already learned so we can build a bigger model of understanding in that moment. At times the material I present may be challenging. Because I've taught this material to audiences for years, I know it can be a lot. I'll be reviewing and reminding you of what you've learned so you do not have to go back in the book to search for the information, although you can always review the earlier chapters if you feel you need to. Of course, all of this information will prime you for your own personal transformation. So the better you can wrap your mind around these concepts, the more easily you can surrender to the meditations at the end of most of the chapters, using them as tools to have your own personal experience.

What's Inside This Book?

In **Chapter 1**, I tell three stories that will give you a basic understanding of what it means to *become supernatural*. In the first story, you'll meet a woman named Anna who developed several serious health conditions because of a trauma that keep her anchored to the past. The emotions of stress triggered her genes, and the corresponding hormones created some very challenging health conditions for her. It is a very tough tale. I intentionally chose this story and included all its details because I wanted to demonstrate to you that no matter how bad things can get, you have the power to change them—just as this amazing woman did. She applied many of the meditations in this book to modify her personality and heal herself. To me, she is the living example of truth. But she's not the only one who has kept overcoming herself on a daily basis until she became someone else. She joins a whole student body of participants who have done the same—and if they can do it, so can you.

I also share two of my own personal stories here—experiences that have changed me at a very deep level. This book is as much about the mystical as it is about healing and creating new opportunities in our lives. I share these stories because I want to prime you for what is possible when we leave this realm of space-time (the Newtonian world we learned about in high school science class) and activate our pineal gland so we can move into the realm of time-space (the quantum world). Many of our students have had similar mystical and interdimensional experiences, which seemed as real as this material reality.

Because the second half of the book delves into the physics, neuroscience, neuroendocrinology, and even genetics of how this happens, I hope these stories will pique your curiosity, acting as teasers to open your mind to what's possible. There's a future you—a you who already exists in the eternal present moment—who is actually calling himself or herself to the more familiar you who is reading this book. And that future you is more loving, more evolved, more conscious, more present, more kind, more exuberant, more mindful, more willful, more connected, more supernatural, and more whole. That is who's waiting for you to change your energy to match his or her energy on a daily basis so you can find that future you—who actually exists in the eternal now.

Chapter 2 covers one of my favorite topics. I wrote it so you could fully comprehend what it means to be in the present moment. Since all potentials in the fifth dimension known as the quantum (or the unified field) exist in the eternal present moment, the only way you can create a new life, heal your body, or change your predictable future is to get beyond yourself.

This elegant moment—which we have witnessed in thousands of brain scans—arrives when a person finally surrenders the memory of themselves for something greater. So many people spend the majority of their lives unconsciously choosing to live by the same routines on a regular basis, or they automatically romance their past, feeling the same way every day. As a result, they program their brain and body to be in a predictable future or a familiar past, never living in the present moment. It takes practice to get there but it's always worth the effort. Finally finding the sweet spot of the generous present moment is going to require you to exercise a will that is greater than any of your automatic programs, but I'll encourage you every step of the way.

The chapter starts off with a basic review of some scientific principles so we can establish a common terminology to develop models of understanding throughout the book. I'm going to make it pretty simple. Talking about brain function (that is, the mind), nerve cells and networks, different parts of the nervous system, chemicals, emotions and stress, brain waves, attention and energy, and a few other subjects is necessary to get you where you want to go. I have to establish the language to explain why we are doing what we are doing before I teach you how to do it in the meditations that appear throughout the book. If you want more explicit, in-depth information, I invite you to read any of my previous books (including *Breaking the Habit of Being Yourself* and *You Are the Placebo*).

Chapter 3 is your introduction to the quantum world—the fifth dimension. I want you to understand that there is an invisible field of energy and information that exists beyond this three-dimensional realm of space and time—and that we have access to it. In fact, once you are in the present moment and you've entered this realm, which exists beyond your senses, you are now ready to create your intended reality. When you can take all your attention off your body, the people in your life, the objects you own, the places you go, and even time itself, you will literally forget about your identity that has been formed by living as a body in this space and time.

It is in this moment that you, as pure consciousness, enter the realm called the quantum field—which exists *beyond* this space and time. You can't enter this immaterial place with your problems, your name, your schedules and routines, your pain, or your emotions. You can't enter as some body—you must enter as no body. In fact, once you know how to move your awareness from the known (the material physical world) to the unknown (the immaterial world of possibility) and you become comfortable there, you can change your energy to match the frequency of any potential in the quantum field that already exists there. (Spoiler alert: Actually, *all* potential futures exist there, so you can create whatever you want.) When a vibrational match occurs between your energy and the energy of that potential you select in the unified field, you will draw that experience to you. I'll show you how it all works.

Chapter 3 ends with a brief description of a meditation I have developed to help give you an actual experience of the quantum. Each of the teaching chapters from this point on will also end with a brief description of a different meditation. If you want to follow along as I guide you, you can purchase a CD or download an audio recording of any of these meditations from my website, **drjoedispenza.com**. Of course, you can also opt to try any of the meditations in this book on your own, without listening to a recording. For this purpose, I have made free detailed descriptions available giving the steps of each of these meditations on my website at **drjoedispenza.com/bsnmeditations**.

If you are meditating on your own, I recommend you listen to music while you do so. The best type of music is without vocals, and I prefer slow and trancing. It's best to use music that stops you from thinking and that doesn't evoke past memories. You'll find a suggested music list on my website, mentioned earlier.

In **Chapter 4**, I introduce you to one of the most popular meditations in our community. It's called the Blessing of the Energy Centers. Each center is under the control of the autonomic nervous system. I will give you the science of how you can program these centers for health and the greatest good during a meditation. If you have been doing my introductory level meditations where you have been placing your attention on different parts of your body and the space around your body, I want you to know that all of your training was for this meditation. Practicing that has helped you sharpen your skill to focus your attention and change your brain waves so you can enter the operating system of the autonomic nervous system. Once you are there, you can program the operating system with the right orders to heal you, balance your health, and improve your energy and your life.

In **Chapter 5**, I introduce you to a breath that we use at the start of many of our meditations. This breath enables you to change your energy, run an electrical current through your body, and create a more powerful electromagnetic field around you. As I will explain, most people's energy is stored in the body because they have conditioned their body to become the mind from years of thinking, acting, and feeling the same way. It is this process—related to living in survival mode—that causes most of the creative energy to be rooted in the body. Therefore, we must have a way to pull that energy out of the body and deliver it back to the brain, where it will be available for a higher purpose than mere survival.

I'll give you the physiology of the breath so you can put more intention behind it when you begin to free yourself from the past. Once you start to liberate all that energy back into the brain, then you will learn how to recondition your body to a new mind. I'm going to show you how to teach your body emotionally how to live in the future-present reality instead of the past-present reality where we spend most of our time. Science tells us that the environment signals the gene. Since emotions are the chemical end products of experiences in our environment, when you embrace elevated emotions in your meditations, you will not only raise your body's energy, but you will also start to signal new genes in new ways—*ahead of the environment.*

There's nothing like a good story or two. In **Chapter 6**, I give you a few examples of students who applied themselves to the meditations in the previous chapters. These case histories should serve as teaching tools to help you fully understand the material I have presented so far. Most of the people you will read about are no different from you—they're common people who have done the uncommon. Another reason I share these stories is so you can personally relate to these people. Once you have the thought *If they can do it, so can I,* you will naturally believe in yourself more. I always tell our community, "When you chose to prove to yourself how powerful you really are, you have no idea who you will be helping in the future." These people are proof that it's possible for *you.*

In **Chapter 7**, I introduce what it means to create heart coherence. Like brain coherence, the heart functions in the same organized way when we are truly present, when we can sustain elevated emotional states, and when we feel safe enough to fully open up to possibility. The brain *thinks*, but the heart *knows*. This is the center of oneness, wholeness, and unity consciousness. It is where opposites meet, representing the union of polarities. Think of this center as your connection to the unified field. When it is activated, you go from selfish states to selfless states. When you can maintain internal states independent of conditions in your external environment, you are mastering your environment. It takes practice to get good at keeping your heart open, and if you do, it will keep beating longer.

Chapter 8 shares one of the other favorite activities we do at our advanced workshops: combining a kaleidoscope with videos called Mind Movies that our students make of their future. We use the kaleidoscope to induce a trance because when you are in trance you are more suggestible to information. Suggestibility is your ability to accept, believe, and surrender to information without any analysis. If you do this properly, it is indeed possible to program your subconscious mind. So it makes sense that when you use the kaleidoscope to change your brain waves—with your eyes open instead of closed in a meditation— you can lower the volume of the analytical mind to open the door between the conscious mind and the subconscious mind.

And when you follow that with a Mind Movie—with scenes of yourself or pictures of what the future you want looks like—you program yourself into that new future. So many of our students have created amazing new lives and opportunities when they took the time to make their Mind Movie and then watch it with the kaleidoscope. Some students are already on their third Mind Movie because everything in their first two has already happened!

In **Chapter 9**, I introduce the walking meditation. This meditation incorporates both standing and walking. I find this practice such a valuable tool in helping us literally walk into our future. Many times we can have an amazing seated meditation and connect to something bigger than us, but when we open our eyes and come back to our senses, we go unconscious again and return to a series of unconscious programs, emotional reactions, and automatic attitudes. I developed this meditation because I want our community to be able to embody the energy of their future—and do it with their eyes open as well as closed. In time as you practice this, you might naturally begin to think like a wealthy person, act like an unlimited being, and feel an expansive joy for existence because you installed the circuits and conditioned your body to become that person.

Chapter 10 shares another set of case studies to engage your level of understanding with allegory. These fascinating stories will help you connect the dots so you can hear the information from another angle and read about people who have experienced it firsthand. I hope they will inspire you to do your practice with more conviction, certainty, and trust so you can experience the truth for yourself.

Chapter 11 opens your mind to what's possible in the interdimensional world beyond the senses. In quiet moments, I often find my mind drifting to the mystical—one of my favorite topics. I love those transcendental experiences that are so lucid and real that I can never go back to business as usual because I know too much. During those inner events, the level of awareness and energy is so profound that when I come back to my senses and my personality, I often naturally think to myself, *I got this all wrong.* The *this* I'm referring to is the way reality really is, not how I've been conditioned to perceive it to be.

In this chapter, I take you on a journey from this realm of spacetime—where space is eternal and we experience time as we move through space—to the realm of time-space—where time is eternal and we experience space (or spaces, or various dimensions) as we move through time. It is going to challenge your very understanding of the nature of reality. All I can say is that if you hang in there, you will get it. It might take you a few readings to fully understand it, but as you study the material and contemplate it, your contemplation builds the circuits in your brain in preparation for the experience.

Once you are beyond your associations to this material world and you are in the unified field—chock-full of infinite possibilities— biological systems exist for taking that energy that's beyond the vibration of matter and turning it into imagery in the brain. That's where the pineal gland comes in, the subject of **Chapter 12**. Think of your pineal gland—a tiny gland perched in the central back area of your brain—as an antenna that can transduce frequencies and information and turn them into vivid imagery. When you activate your pineal gland, you are going to have a full-on sensory experience *without your senses.* That internal event will be more real to you in your mind while your eyes were closed than any past external experience you've ever had. In other words, in order to lose yourself fully in the inward experience, it has to be so real that *you are there.* When this happens, this little gland transmutes melatonin into some very powerful metabolites that cause you to have that type of experience. We will study the properties of this gland and then you will learn how to activate it.

Chapter 13 introduces you to one of our most recent endeavors: Project Coherence. When we witnessed the measurements of so many of our students going into heart coherence at the exact same time on the exact same day during the exact same meditation, we knew that they were affecting each other nonlocally (energetically, as opposed to physically). The energy they were emitting in the form of elevated emotions carried their intention that the greatest good happen to everyone gathered in the room. Imagine a large body of people all elevating their energy and then placing the intention on that energy that lives be enriched, bodies be healed, dreams come true, futures be realized, and the mystical become common in our lives.

When we saw how our students were able to open the hearts of others, we knew it was time to start doing global meditations to help change the world. Thousands and thousands of people from all over the world have joined in and participated in changing and healing this planet and the people on it. After all, aren't we doing this work to make the world a better place? I'll give you the science of how this all works—and I do mean science. Enough peer-reviewed studies on the power of peace-gathering projects have been published to prove it works, so instead of just studying history, why not *make* history?

The book finishes with **Chapter 14**, which shares some pretty wild case studies of some of the mind-blowing mystical experiences people have had doing this work. Once again, I share them so you can see that even the most mystical adventures can be yours if you work at it.

So, are you ready to become supernatural?

Chapter 1

OPENING THE DOOR
TO THE SUPERNATURAL

As spring was ending and the first glimpse of summer was approaching, what first appeared to be a typical Sunday afternoon in June 2007 turned out to be anything but typical for Anna Willems.

The French doors from the living room to the garden were open wide, and the thin white curtains danced lightly in the breeze as scents from the garden floated inside. Streams of sunlight shone brightly all around Anna as she lounged comfortably. A chorus of birds chirped and trilled outside, and Anna could hear the distant melody of children's laughter and playful splashing coming from a neighbor's swimming pool. Anna's 12-year-old son reclined on the sofa, reading a book, and she could hear her 11-year-old daughter in the room directly above her, singing to herself as she played.

A psychotherapist, Anna worked as a manager and board member for a major psychiatric institution in Amsterdam whose profits totaled more than 10 million euros annually. She often caught up on professional reading on the weekends, and on this day she was sitting in her red leather chair reading a journal article. Little did Anna know that what looked like the perfect world to anyone peering into her living room that day would become a nightmare within minutes.

Anna felt a bit distracted, noticing that her attention wasn't fully engaged in the material she was attempting to study. She set her papers down and paused, suddenly wondering again where her husband had gone. He had left the house early that morning while she was taking a shower. Without saying where he was headed, he had simply disappeared. The children had told her that their father had said good-bye, giving each of them a big hug before he left. She'd tried to reach him on his cell phone many times, but he hadn't returned her calls. She tried one more time—no answer. Something definitely felt odd.

At 3:30 P.M. the doorbell rang, and when Anna opened the front door, she found two police officers standing outside.

"Are you Mrs. Willems?" one of them asked. When she confirmed that she was indeed Mrs. Willems, the officers asked if they could come in and talk to her. Concerned and a bit confused, she complied. Then they delivered the news: Earlier that morning, her husband had jumped off one of the tallest buildings in the center of the city. Not surprisingly, the fall was fatal. Anna and her two children sat in shock and disbelief.

Anna's breath momentarily stopped, and as she then gasped for air, she started to shake uncontrollably. The moment seemed frozen in time. While her children sat paralyzed in shock, Anna tried to hide her pain and stress for their sakes. An intense pain suddenly shot through her head, and she simultaneously felt a deep, hollow ache in her gut. Her neck and shoulders instantly stiffened as her mind frenetically raced from thought to thought. The hormones of stress had overtaken her. Anna was now in survival mode.

How Stress Hormones Take Over

From a scientific standpoint, living in stress is living in survival. When we perceive a stressful circumstance that threatens us in some way (one for which we cannot predict or control the outcome), a primitive nervous system called the sympathetic nervous system turns on and the body mobilizes an enormous amount of energy in response to the stressor. Physiologically, the body is automatically tapping into the resources it will need to deal with the current danger.

The pupils dilate so we can see better; the heart rate and respiratory rate increase so we can run, fight, or hide; more glucose is released into the bloodstream to make more energy available to our cells; and our blood flow is shunted to the extremities and away from our internal organs so we can move quickly if we need to. The immune system initially dials up and then dials down as adrenaline and cortisol flood the muscles, providing a rush of energy to either escape or fend off the stressor. Circulation moves out of our rational forebrain and is instead relayed to our hindbrain, so we have less capacity to think creatively and instead rely more on our instinct to instantly react.

In Anna's case, the stressful news of her husband's suicide threw her brain and body into just such a state of survival. In the short term, all organisms can tolerate adverse conditions by fighting, hiding, or fleeing from an impending stressor. All of us are built for dealing with short-term bursts of stress. When the event is over, the body normally returns to balance within hours, increasing its energy levels and restoring its vital resources. But when the stress doesn't end within hours, the body never returns to balance. In truth, no organism in nature can endure living in emergency mode for extended periods of time.

Because of our large brains, human beings are capable of thinking about their problems, reliving past events, or even forecasting future worst-case situations and thus turning on the cascade of stress chemicals by thought alone. We can knock our brains and bodies out of normal physiology just by thinking about an all-too-familiar past or trying to control an unpredictable future.

Every day, Anna relived that event over and over in her mind. What she didn't realize was that her body did not know the difference between the original event that created the stress response and the memory of the event, which created the same emotions as the real-life experience all over again. Anna was producing the same chemistry in her brain and body as if the event were actually happening again and again. Subsequently, her brain was continuously wiring the event into her memory bank, and her body was emotionally experiencing the same chemicals from the past at least a hundred times each day. By repeatedly recalling the experience, she was unintentionally anchoring her brain and body to the past.

Emotions are the chemical consequences (or feedback) of past experiences. As our senses record incoming information from the environment, clusters of neurons organize into networks. When they freeze into a pattern, the brain makes a chemical that is then sent throughout the body. That chemical is called an emotion. We remember events better when we can remember how they feel. The stronger the emotional quotient from any event—either good or bad—the stronger the change in our internal chemistry. When we notice a significant change inside of us, the brain pays attention to whoever or whatever is causing the change outside of us—and it takes a snapshot of the outer experience. That's called a memory.

Therefore, the memory of an event can become branded neurologically in the brain, and that scene becomes frozen in time in our gray matter, just as it did for Anna. The combination of various people or objects at a particular time and place from that stressful experience is etched in our neural architecture as a holographic image. That's how we create a long-term memory. Therefore, the experience becomes imprinted in the neural circuitry, and the emotion is stored in the body—and that's how our past becomes our biology. In other words, when we experience a traumatic event, we tend to think neurologically within the circuitry of that experience and we tend to feel chemically within the boundaries of the emotions from the event, so our entire state of being—how we think and how we feel—becomes biologically stuck in the past.

As you can imagine, Anna was feeling a rush of negative emotions: tremendous sadness, pain, victimization, grief, guilt, shame, despair, anger, hatred, frustration, resentment, shock, fear, anxiety, worry, overwhelm, anguish, hopelessness, powerlessness, isolation, loneliness, disbelief, and betrayal. And none of those emotions dissipated quickly. As Anna analyzed her life within the emotions of the past, she kept suffering more and more. Because she couldn't think greater than how she constantly felt, and since emotions are a record of the past, she was thinking in the past—and every day she felt worse. As a psychotherapist, she could rationally and intellectually understand what was happening to her, but all her insights couldn't get beyond her suffering.

People in her life started treating her as the person who had lost her husband, and that became her new identity. She associated her memories and feelings with the reason she was in her present state. When anyone asked her why she felt so bad, she told the story of the suicide—each time reliving the pain, anguish, and suffering over again. All along, Anna kept firing the same circuits in her brain and reproducing the same emotions, conditioning her brain and body further into the past. Every day, she was thinking, acting, and feeling as if the past were still alive. And since how we think, how we act, and how we feel is our personality, Anna's personality was completely created by the past. From a biological standpoint, in repeatedly telling the narrative of her husband's suicide, Anna literally couldn't get beyond what had happened.

A Downward Spiral Begins

Anna could no longer work and had to take a leave of absence. During that time, she found out that her husband, although a successful lawyer, had made a mess of their personal finances. She would have to pay off significant debts that she had previously been unaware of—and she didn't have the money to even begin. Not surprisingly, even more emotional, psychological, and mental stress began to add up.

Anna's mind went in circles, constantly flooded with questions: *How will I take care of our children? How will all of us deal with this trauma in our future and how will it affect our lives? Why did my husband leave without saying good-bye to me? How could I not know that he was so unhappy? Did I fail as a wife? How could he leave me with two young children and how will I manage to raise them by myself?*

Then judgments crept into her thoughts: *He shouldn't have committed suicide and left me in this financial mess! What a coward! How dare he leave his children without a father! He didn't even write a message for the children and me. I hate him for not even leaving a note. What a jerk to leave me and make me raise these kids alone. Did he have any idea what this might do to us?* All these thoughts carried a strong emotional charge, further affecting her body.

Nine months later, on March 21, 2008, Anna woke up paralyzed from the waist down. Within hours she was lying in a hospital bed, a wheelchair beside her, diagnosed with neuritis—inflammation of the peripheral nervous system. After several tests, the doctors could not find anything structural as the cause of the problem so they told Anna that she must have an autoimmune condition. Her immune system was attacking the nervous system in her lower spine, breaking down the protective layer that coats the nerves and causing paralysis in both of her legs. She could not hold her urine, had difficulty controlling her bowels, and had no feeling or motor control in her legs and feet.

When the fight-or-flight nervous system is switched on and *stays* on because of chronic stress, the body utilizes all its energy reserves to deal with the constant threat it perceives from the outer environment. Therefore, the body has no energy left in its inner environment for growth and repair, compromising the immune system. So because of her repeated inner conflict, Anna's immune system was attacking her body. She had finally physically manifested the pain and suffering she'd emotionally experienced in her mind. In short, Anna could not move her body because she wasn't moving forward in her life—she was stuck in her past.

For the next six weeks, Anna's doctors treated her with huge doses of intravenous dexamethasone and other corticosteroids to reduce inflammation. Because of the added stress and the types of drugs she was taking—which can further weaken the immune system—she also developed an aggressive bacterial infection for which her doctors gave her huge doses of antibiotics. After two months, Anna was released from the hospital and had to use a walker and crutches to get around. She still could not feel her left leg and found standing very difficult. She couldn't walk properly. Although she could hold her bowels a bit better, she still couldn't control her urine. As you can imagine, this new situation was adding to Anna's already high stress levels. She had lost her husband to suicide, she could not work very much to support herself and her children, she was in serious financial crisis, and she had been living in a hospital paralyzed for more than two months. Her mother had to move in to help.

Anna was an emotional, mental, and physical wreck, and although she had the best doctors and the latest medications from a reputable hospital, she was not getting any better. By 2009, two years after the death of her husband, she was diagnosed with clinical depression—so she started taking even *more* medication. Consequently, Anna's moods swung widely from anger to grief to pain to suffering to hopelessness to frustration to fear to hatred. Because those emotions influenced her actions, her behavior became somewhat irrational. At first, she fought with almost everybody around her except her children. But then she started to have conflicts with her youngest daughter.

The Dark Night of the Soul

In the meantime, many more physical problems started showing up and Anna's journey became even more painful. The mucous membranes in her mouth started to develop large ulcerations that spread into her upper esophagus as the result of another autoimmune disease called erosive lichen planus. To treat it, she had to use corticosteroid ointments in her mouth, in addition to more pills. These new medications caused Anna's saliva production to stop. She couldn't eat solid foods, so she lost her appetite. Anna was living with all three types of stress—physical, chemical, and emotional—at the same time.

In 2010, Anna found herself in a dysfunctional relationship with a man who traumatized her and her children with verbal abuse, power games, and constant threats. She lost all her money, her job, and her feeling of safety. When she lost her house, she had to move in with her abusive boyfriend. Stress levels continued climbing. Her ulcerations started to spread to other mucous membranes, including her vagina, her anus, and further down her esophagus. Her immune system had totally collapsed and now she was experiencing several different skin conditions, food allergies, and weight problems. Then she started having problems swallowing and developed heartburn, for which the doctors prescribed still more medications.

Anna started a small psychotherapy practice at home in October. She could only handle seeing clients for two sessions a day in the morning after her children went to school, three days a week. In the afternoon, she was so tired and sick that she would lie in bed until her children returned from school. She tried to be there for them as much as possible, but she had no energy and didn't feel well enough to leave the house. Anna hardly saw anyone. She had no social life.

All the circumstances in her body and in her life constantly reminded her of how bad things were. She automatically reacted to everyone and everything. Her thinking was chaotic and she could not concentrate. She had no vitality or energy to live anymore. Often, when she exerted herself her heart rate exceeded 200 beats per minute. She found herself sweating and gasping for breath all the time, and she felt an enormous pain in her chest on a regular basis.

Anna was passing through her darkest night of the soul. Suddenly, she understood why her husband had taken his life. She wasn't sure she could go on anymore and started thinking of committing suicide herself. She thought, *It can't get any worse than this . . .*

And then it did. In January 2011, Anna's medical team found a tumor near the entrance of her stomach and diagnosed her with esophageal cancer. Of course, this news severely increased Anna's stress levels. The doctors suggested a rigorous course of chemotherapy. No one asked her about emotional and mental stress; they only treated the physical symptoms. But Anna's stress response was fully turned on and it couldn't turn off.

It's amazing how this can happen to so many people. Because of a shock or trauma in their lives, they never get beyond those corresponding emotions, and their health and their lives break down. If an addiction is something that you think you can't stop, then objectively it looks as though people like Anna become addicted to the very emotions of stress that are making them sick. The rush of adrenaline and the rest of the stress hormones arouses their brain and body, providing a rush of energy.[1] In time, they become addicted to the rush of that chemistry—and then they use the people and conditions in their lives to reaffirm their addiction to the emotion, just to keep feeling that heightened state. Anna was using her stressful conditions to re-create that rush of energy, and without realizing it, she became emotionally addicted to a life she hated. Science tells us that such chronic, long-term stress pushes the genetic buttons that create disease. So if Anna was turning the stress response on by thinking about her problems and her past, her thoughts were making her sick. And since stress hormones are so powerful, she had become addicted to her own thoughts that were making her feel so bad.

Anna agreed to start chemotherapy, but after her first session she had an emotional and mental breakdown. One afternoon after her kids went to school, Anna collapsed on the floor crying. She had finally reached the bottom. It occurred to her that if she continued this way, she would not survive for long and she would leave her children alone without either parent.

She started to pray for help. She knew in her heart that something needed to change. In utter sincerity and surrender, she asked for guidance, support, and a way out, promising that if her prayers were answered, she would be thankful and grateful every day for the rest of her life and she would help others to do the same.

Anna's Turning Point

The choice to change became Anna's quest. She first decided to stop all the treatments and all the medications for her various physical illnesses, although she continued to take her antidepressants. She didn't tell the doctors and nurses that she was not coming back for treatment. She simply did not show up anymore. No one ever called her to ask why. Only her family doctor contacted Anna to express concern.

On that cold winter's day in February 2011 when Anna was on the floor crying for help, she made a choice with a firm intention to change herself and her life, and the amplitude of that decision carried a level of energy that caused her body to respond to her mind. It was that decision to change that gave her the strength to rent a house for herself and her children and move away from the negative relationship she was in. It was as if that moment redefined her. She knew she had to start all over.

When I first saw Anna, it was one month later. One of the few friends she had left had reserved a seat for Anna at a Friday evening talk that I was giving. Her friend made Anna an offer: If she liked the evening lecture, she could stay for a full two-day weekend workshop. Anna agreed to go. The first time I saw her, she was sitting in a packed conference room on the left side on the outer aisle, her crutches leaning against the wall near where she sat.

As usual, I was carrying on that night about how our thoughts and feelings affect our bodies and our lives. I lectured about how stress chemicals can create disease. I touched on neuroplasticity, psychoneuroimmunology, epigenetics, neuroendocrinology, and even quantum physics. I will go into more detail on all of these later in this book, but for now it's enough to know that the latest research in these branches of science point to the power of possibility. That night, filled with inspiration, Anna thought, *If I created the life I have now, including my paralysis, my depression, my weakened immune system, my ulcerations, and even my cancer, maybe I can uncreate everything with the same passion I created it with.* And with that potent new understanding, Anna decided to heal herself.

Immediately after her first weekend workshop, she started meditating twice a day. Of course, sitting and doing the meditations was difficult at the beginning. She had a lot of doubt to overcome, and some days she did not feel mentally and physically well—but she did her meditations anyway. She also had a lot of fear. When her family doctor called to check up on her because she'd stopped her treatments and medications, he told Anna that she was being naïve and stupid and that she would get worse and die soon. Imagine the memory of an authority figure telling you that! Even so, Anna did her meditations every day and began to move beyond her fears. She was often consumed with financial burdens, her children's needs, and various physical limitations, yet she never used those conditions as an excuse to not do her inner work. She even attended four more of my workshops during that year.

By going within and changing her unconscious thoughts, automatic habits, and reflexive emotional states—which had become hardwired in her brain and emotionally conditioned in her body—Anna was now more committed to believing in a new future than believing in her same familiar past. She used her meditations, combining a clear intention with an elevated emotion, to change her state of being from biologically living in the same past to living in a new future.

Every day, Anna was unwilling to get up from her meditations as the same person who sat down; she decided that she wouldn't finish until her whole state of being was in love with life. To the materialist, who defines reality with the senses, of course, Anna had no tangible reason to be in love with life; she was a depressed, widowed single parent who was in financial debt and had no real job, she had cancer and suffered from paralysis and ulcerations in her mucous membranes, and she was in a poor living situation with no partner or significant other and no energy to tend to her children. But in the meditations, Anna learned that she could teach her body emotionally what her future would feel like *ahead of the actual experience.* Her body as the unconscious mind did not know the difference between the real event and the one she was imagining and emotionally embracing. She also knew through her understanding of epigenetics that the elevated emotions of love, joy, gratitude, inspiration, compassion, and freedom could signal new genes to make healthy proteins affecting her body's structure and function. She fully understood that if the stress chemicals that had been coursing through her body had been turning on unhealthy genes, then by fully embracing those elevated emotions with a passion greater than the stressful emotions, she could turn on new genes—and change her health.

For a year, her health didn't change very much. But she kept doing her meditations. In fact, she did all the meditations I designed for students. She knew it had taken several years to create her current health conditions, and so it would take some time to re-create something new. So she kept doing the work, striving to become so conscious of her unconscious thoughts, behaviors, and emotions that she would not let anything she did not want to experience slip by her awareness. After that first year, Anna noticed that she was slowly starting to get better mentally and emotionally. Anna was breaking the habit of being herself, inventing a whole new self instead.

Anna knew from attending my workshops that she had to move her autonomic nervous system back into balance because the ANS controls all the automatic functions that happen beyond the brain's conscious awareness—digestion, absorption, blood sugar levels, body temperature, hormonal secretions, heart rate, and so on. The only way she could slip into the operating system and affect the ANS was to change her internal state on a regular basis.

So first, Anna began each meditation with the Blessing of the Energy Centers. These specific areas of the body are under the control of the ANS. As I mentioned in the Introduction, each center has its own energy or frequency (which emits specific information or has its own consciousness), its own glands, its own hormones, its own chemistry, its own individual little mini-brain, and therefore its own mind. Each center is influenced by the subconscious brain sitting under our conscious thinking brain. Anna learned how to change her brain waves so she could enter the operating system of the ANS (located in the midbrain) and reprogram each center to work in a more harmonious manner. Every day, with focus and passion, she rested her attention in each area of her body as well as the space around each center, blessing it for greater health and the greater good. Slowly but surely, she began to influence her health by reprogramming her autonomic nervous system back to balance.

Anna also learned a specific breathing technique I teach in our work to liberate all the emotional energy that is stored in the body when we keep thinking and feeling the same way. By constantly thinking the same thoughts, Anna had been creating the same feelings, and then by feeling those familiar emotions, she would think more of the same corresponding thoughts. She learned that the emotions of the past were stored in her body, but she could use this breathing technique to liberate that stored energy and free herself from her past. So every day, with a level of intensity that was greater than her addiction to past emotions, she practiced the breath and got better and better at doing it. After she learned to move that stored energy in her body, she learned how to recondition her body to a new mind by embracing the heart-centered emotions of her future *before* her future unfolded.

Since Anna also studied the model of epigenetics I teach in our workshops and lectures, she learned that genes don't create disease; instead, the environment signals the gene to create disease. Anna understood that if her emotions were the chemical consequences of experiences in her environment, and if she lived every day by the same emotions from her past, she was selecting and instructing the same genes that might be causing her poor health conditions. If she could instead embody the emotions of her future life by embracing those emotions before the experience actually happened, she could change her genetic expression and actually change her body to be biologically aligned with her new future.

Anna did an additional meditation that involved resting her attention in the center of her chest, activating the ANS with those elevated states to create and maintain a very efficient type of heart rate we call a *coherent* heart rate (which I will explain in detail later in the book) for extended periods of time. She learned that when she felt resentment, impatience, frustration, anger, and hatred, those states induced the stress response and caused the heart to beat incoherently and out of order. Anna learned in my workshops that once she could sustain this new heart-centered state, just as she had gotten used to feeling all those negative emotions on a regular basis, in time she could feel these new emotions more fully and deeply. Of course, it took quite a bit of effort to trade anger, fear, depression, and resentment for joy, love, gratitude, and freedom—but Anna never gave up. She knew that those elevated emotions would release more than a thousand different chemicals that would repair and restore her body . . . and she went for it.

Anna then practiced a walking meditation I designed in which she walked as her new self every day. Instead of sitting down and meditating with her eyes closed, she started these meditations standing up with her eyes closed. While standing, she got into the meditative state that she knew would change her state of being, and then while still in that state, she opened her eyes, staying in a meditative state, and walked as her future self. By doing so, she was embodying a new habit of thinking, acting, and feeling on a regular basis. What she was creating would soon become her new personality. She never wanted to go unconscious again and return to her old self.

Because of all this work, Anna could see that her thought patterns had changed. She was no longer firing the same circuits in her brain in the same way, so those circuits stopped wiring together and starting pruning apart. As a result, she stopped thinking in the same old ways. Emotionally, she began to feel glimpses of gratitude and pleasure for the first time in years. In her meditations, she was conquering some aspect of her body and her mind every day. Anna calmed down and became much less addicted to the emotions derived from stress hormones. She even started to feel love again. And she kept going—overcoming, overcoming, and overcoming every day on her way to becoming someone else.

Anna Grabs Ahold of Possibility

In May 2012, Anna attended one of my four-day progressive workshops held in upstate New York. On the third day, during the last of four meditations, she completely surrendered and finally let go. For the first time since she had started meditating, she found herself floating in an infinite black space, aware that she was aware of herself. She had moved beyond the memory of who she was and became pure consciousness, totally free of her body, of her association to the material world, and of linear time. She felt so free that she no longer cared about her health conditions. She felt so unlimited that she couldn't identify with her present identity. She felt so elevated that she was no longer connected to her past.

In this state, Anna had no problems, she left her pain behind, and she was truly free for the first time. She wasn't her name, her gender, her disease, her culture, or her profession—she was beyond space and time. She had connected to a field of information called the quantum field, where all possibilities exist. Suddenly, she saw herself in a brand-new future, standing on a huge stage, holding a microphone, and talking to a crowd as she told them the entire story of her healing. She wasn't imagining or visualizing this scene. It was as if she got a download of information, a glimpse of herself as a totally different woman in a new reality. Her inner world appeared much more real to her than her outer world, and she was having a full-on sensory experience without using her senses.

The moment Anna experienced this new life in the meditation, a burst of joy and light came into her body and she felt relief on a deep, visceral level. She knew she was something or someone greater, much grander than her physical body. In this state of intense joy she felt such delight and such immense gratitude that she burst into laughter. And at that moment, Anna knew she was going to be okay. From then on, she developed so much trust, joy, love, and gratitude that her meditations became easier and easier, and she began to go much deeper.

As Anna moved out of her past, she felt this new energy opening her heart further and further. Instead of seeing her meditations as something she *had* to do every day, she started looking forward to them. It became her way of life—doing the work became her habit. Her energy and vitality returned. She stopped taking antidepressants. Her thought patterns completely changed and her feelings were different. She felt like she was in a new state of being, so her actions changed drastically. Anna's health and life improved tremendously that year.

The next year, she attended several more events. By keeping connected to the work, Anna started to develop relationships with more people in our community and she received more and more support to keep her going on her journey back to health. Like many of our students, she sometimes found it challenging not to take a few steps back into the old programs and the old patterns of thinking, feeling, and acting once she returned home after a workshop. But even so, she kept doing her meditations every day.

In September 2013, Anna's doctors gave her a very thorough medical checkup that included many different tests. One year and nine months after her cancer diagnosis and six years after her husband's suicide, Anna's cancer had completely healed and the tumor in her esophagus had vanished. Her blood tests showed no cancer markers. The mucous membranes in her esophagus, vagina, and anus were completely healed. Only a few minor problems remained: The mucous membranes in her mouth were still slightly red, although she no longer had any ulcerations, and because of the medication she had taken for the ulcerations, she still didn't produce saliva.

Anna had become a new person—a new person who was healthy. The disease existed in the old personality. By thinking, acting, and feeling differently, Anna reinvented a new self. In a sense, she had become reborn in the same life.

In December 2013, Anna came to an event in Barcelona with the friend who had introduced her to my work. After hearing me tell the participants a story about a remarkable healing of another student in our community, Anna decided it was time to share her story with me. She wrote it all down and gave the letter to my personal assistant. Like many letters I get from students, the first line read, "You are not going to believe this." After I read what she'd written, the next day I asked Anna to come up onstage and share her story with the audience. And there she was, a year and a half after the vision she'd had during her meditation in New York (unbeknownst to me), standing on a stage talking to an audience about her journey healing herself.

After the Barcelona event, Anna was inspired to work on her mouth even more. About six months later, I was lecturing in London and Anna attended. I spoke in detail about epigenetics. Suddenly a light went on for Anna. *I've healed myself of all these medical conditions—including cancer,* she thought. *I should be able to signal the gene for my mouth to produce more saliva.* A few months later, during another workshop in 2014, Anna suddenly felt saliva dripping in her mouth. Ever since then, Anna's mucous membranes and her saliva production have returned to normal. The ulcerations never came back.

Today, Anna is a healthy, vital, happy, stable person with a very sharp and clear mind. Spiritually, she has grown so much that she goes very deep in her meditations and has had many mystical experiences. She is living a life full of creation, love, and joy. She has become one of my corporate trainers, regularly teaching this work to organizations and companies. In 2016, she founded a successful psychiatric institution, employing more than 20 therapists and practitioners. She is financially independent and earns enough money to live a rich life. She travels around the world, visits beautiful places, and meets very inspiring people. She has a very loving and joyful partner, as well as new friends and new relationships that honor both her and her children.

When you ask Anna about her past health problems, she will tell you that having those challenges was the best thing that ever happened to her. Think about it: What if the worst thing that ever happened to you turns out to be the best thing that has ever happened to you? She often tells me that she loves her present life, and I always respond, "Of course you do, you *created* your life every day by not getting up from your meditations until you were in love with that life. So now, you get to love your life." It was through the course of her transformation that Anna had, in effect, become *supernatural*. She had overcome her identity, which was connected to her past, and she literally created a new, healthy future—and her biology responded to a new mind. Anna is now the living example of truth and possibility. And if Anna healed herself, so can you.

Getting Mystical

Healing all sorts of physical conditions may be a very impressive benefit of doing this work, but it's not the only one. Because this book is also about the mystical, I want to open your mind to a realm of reality that will be just as transformative as healing but that works on a deeper and different level. Becoming supernatural can also involve embracing a greater awareness of yourself and who you are in this world—and in other worlds as well. Let me share some stories about this from my own life to illustrate exactly what I mean and to show you what is possible for you too.

One rainy winter evening in the Pacific Northwest, as I sat on my couch after a very long day, I listened to the branches of the tall fir trees outside my window filtering the gusts of wind through their canopies. My children were in bed, deep asleep, and at last I had a moment to myself. As I got comfortable, I began to review all the things I needed to accomplish the following day. By the time I'd made my mental list, I was too exhausted to think so I just sat still for a few minutes, my mind empty. As I watched the shadows from the flames in the fireplace flicker and dance on the walls, I began to move into trance. My body was tired but my mind was clear. I wasn't thinking or analyzing anymore; I was simply staring into space, being in the present moment.

As my body relaxed more and more, I slowly and consciously let it fall asleep as I simultaneously kept my mind conscious and awake. I wouldn't let my attention narrow in on any object in the room but instead kept my focus open. This was a game I often played with myself. I liked the practice because every once in a while, if everything lined up, I had very profound transcendental experiences. It was as if a door of sorts opened somewhere between wakefulness, sleep, and normal dreaming and I slipped into a very lucid mystical moment. I reminded myself to not expect anything but to simply stay open. It took a lot of patience to not rush it or get frustrated or try to make something happen but instead to slowly slip into that other world.

That day, I had finished writing an article about the pineal gland. After spending several months researching all the magical derivatives of melatonin that this little alchemical center had up its sleeve, I was over-joyed about linking the scientific world and the spirit world. For weeks, my entire mind had been consumed with thinking about the role of the pineal metabolites as a possible connection to the mystical experiences most ancient cultures knew how to elicit, such as Native American sha-manic visions, the Hindu experience of *samadhi*, and other similar rituals involving altered states of consciousness. Some concepts that had been loose ends for years had suddenly clicked for me, and my discoveries left me feeling more whole. I thought I was one step closer to understanding the bridge to higher dimensions of space and time.

All the information I had learned inspired me to a deeper awareness about what is possible for human beings. Yet I was still curious to learn more—curious enough to move my awareness to where the pineal gland existed in my head. I casually thought, speaking to the gland, *Where are you, anyway?*

As I rested my attention in the space the pineal gland occupies in my brain, and as I was drifting off into the blackness, suddenly, out of nowhere, a vivid image of my pineal gland appeared in my mind as a three-dimensional round knob. Its mouth was wide open in a spasm and it was releasing a white milky substance. I was shocked by the intensity of the holographic image, but I was too relaxed to be aroused or react, so I simply surrendered and observed. It was so real. I *knew* what I was seeing before me was my own tiny pineal gland.

In the next instant, a huge timepiece appeared right in front of me. It was one of those old-fashioned pocket watches with a chain, and the vision was incredibly vivid. The moment I put my attention on the timepiece, I received very clear information. I suddenly *knew* that linear time as I believed it to be—with a definite past, present, and future—was not the way the world really works. Instead, I understood that everything is actually happening in an eternal present moment. In this infinite amount of time there exist infinite spaces, dimensions, or possible realities to experience.

If there is only one eternal moment happening, then it makes sense that we would have no past in this incarnation, let alone no past lives. But I could see every past and future like I was looking at an old-fashioned piece of movie film with an endless number of frames—with the frames representing not single moments but windows of limitless possibilities that existed as scaffolding and went on in all directions forever. It was much like looking into two mirrors opposite one another and seeing infinite spaces or dimensions reflected in both directions. But to understand what I was seeing, imagine that those infinite dimensions are above and below you, in front and behind you, and to your left and to your right. And each one of those limitless possibilities *already existed*. I knew that by putting my attention on any one of these possibilities, I would actually experience that reality.

I also realized I wasn't separate from anything. I sensed oneness with everything, everyone, every place, and every time. I can only describe it as the most familiar unfamiliar feeling I have ever had in my life.

The pineal gland, as I soon understood I was being shown, serves as a dimensional timepiece that, when activated, we can dial in to any time. When I saw the hands of the timepiece move forward or backward, I understood that, like a time machine set to any particular time, there is also a reality or a dimension to experience in a particular space. This amazing vision was showing me that the pineal gland, like a cosmic antenna, had the ability to tune in to information beyond our physical senses and hook us up to other realities that already exist in the eternal moment. While the download of information I received seemed limitless, no words exist that can completely describe the magnitude of this experience.

Experiencing My Past and Future Selves Simultaneously

As the hands of the watch moved backward to a past time, a dimension in space and time came to life. I immediately found myself in a reality relevant to me personally—although amazingly, that past moment was still occurring in the present moment I was experiencing while sitting on my couch in the living room. I next became aware that I was in a physical space at that specific time. I observed myself as a young child—again, while simultaneously having the experience of being the adult me on the couch. The child version of me was about seven years old and had a very high fever. I remembered how much I loved fevers at that age because I could go deep within and have the kind of abstract dreams and visions that often come with the delirium produced by high body temperatures. This specific time, I was in my room in bed with the covers up to the bridge of my nose and my mother had just left the room. I was happy I was alone.

The moment she closed the door, I somehow innately knew to do exactly what I had just been doing in my living room as an adult—continuously relaxing my body and remaining somewhere between sleep and wakefulness as I stayed present to whatever came up. Up to this point in my present life, I had completely forgotten about the memory of this childhood experience, but when I lived it again in that moment, I saw myself in the midst of a lucid conscious dream, comprehending possible realities like the squares on a chess board.

As I observed myself as this young boy, I was deeply moved by what he was attempting to understand, and I wondered how he could grasp such complicated concepts at his age. In that moment as I watched him, I fell in love with that little guy—and the second I embraced that emotion, I somehow felt a simultaneous connection to both that point in time and the one I was experiencing as my present time back in Washington State. I had such a strong knowingness that what I was doing then and what I am doing now were happening at the same time, and that those moments were significantly connected. In that split second, the love I felt for him as my present self was drawing that young boy to the future I was living now.

Then the experience got even stranger. That scene faded away and the watch appeared again. I became aware that the hands of the timepiece could also move forward. Filled with a sense of wonder, and without any trepidation or fear, I simply observed the watch move forward in time.

Instantaneously, I was standing barefoot in my backyard in Washington in the cold night. It's difficult to explain what time it was because it was the same night I was in my living room, but the me who was outside the house was the me from the future in that now. Again, words are limited here, but the only way I can explain this experience is that the future personality called Joe Dispenza had changed immensely. I was so much more evolved, and I felt *amazing*—euphoric, in fact.

I was so aware—or should I say, as that person I *am* so aware. By *aware*, I mean superconscious, as if all my senses were heightened 100 percent. Everything I saw, touched, felt, smelled, tasted, and heard was amplified. My senses were so elevated that I was acutely aware of and paying attention to everything around me, wanting to experience the moment completely. And because my awareness increased so drastically, so did my consciousness and therefore my energy. Feeling so full of this intense energy caused me to be more conscious of everything I sensed simultaneously.

I can describe this feeling only as consistent, unwavering, highly organized energy. It was nothing like the chemical emotions we normally feel as human beings. In fact, in that moment I knew I couldn't even feel those normal human emotions. I had evolved beyond them. I did, however, feel love, although it was an evolved form of love that was not chemical but electric. I felt almost as though I was on fire, passionately in love with life. I was in an incredibly pure form of joy.

I was also walking around my backyard in the middle of winter with no shoes and no jacket—yet I was so aware of the feeling of the cold that it was actually intensely enjoyable. I didn't have an opinion about how ice cold the ground under my feet was; I just loved having my feet touch the frozen grass on the earth, and I felt very connected to both the feeling and the grass. I understood that if I entertained the typical thoughts and judgments I normally would have about being cold, it would cause me to create a sense of polarity, dividing the energy I was experiencing. If I judged it, I would lose the feeling of wholeness. The amazing feeling of energy that I was experiencing inside my body was so much greater than the conditions in my surrounding environment (the cold). And as a result, I effortlessly embraced the cold with zeal. It was simply life! In fact, it was so pleasurable that I didn't want the moment to end. I wanted it to last forever.

I walked as this upgraded version of myself with strength and knowingness. I felt very empowered and calm, yet overflowing with joy for existence and love for life. Passing through my garden, I intentionally walked on huge basalt columns that were laid on their sides, stacked like huge stairs to create levels to sit at the fire pit. I loved the experience of walking barefoot on those huge pieces of stone. I truly honored their magnificence. As I continued walking, I approached a fountain that I had built, and I smiled at the memory of my brother and me creating such a marvel.

Suddenly, I saw a tiny woman in a glowing white garment. She was no more than two feet tall, and she was standing a little behind the fountain with another woman of normal size who was dressed similarly and was also radiant and full of light. The other woman stood in the background observing, seemingly acting as the tiny woman's protector.

When I looked at the tiny woman, she turned to me and gazed into my eyes. I felt an even stronger energy of love, as if she were sending it to me. Even as this evolved version of myself, I realized I had never felt anything like that before. The feelings of wholeness and love amplified exponentially, and I thought to myself, *Wow—is there even more love than the love I was just experiencing moments ago?* It wasn't at all a romantic love. It was more of that exhilarating, electrifying energy, and it was being awakened from inside of me. I knew she was acknowledging that there was indeed even more love within me to experience. I also knew she was more evolved than I was. When I felt that electricity, it carried a message to look toward the kitchen window, and I instantly remembered why I was there.

I turned and looked into the kitchen, where my present self, a few hours before I went to the couch to relax, was busy washing dishes. From the backyard, I smiled. I was so in love with him. I saw his sincerity; I saw his struggles; I saw his passion; I saw his love; I saw his mind busy, as always, constantly attempting to dovetail concepts into meaning; and among other things, I saw some of his future. Like a great parent, I was proud of him and had nothing but admiration for who he was in that moment. As I was feeling that intense energy increase inside of me while I observed him, I witnessed him suddenly stop washing the dishes and look out the window, staring out and panning the backyard.

While I was still my future self, I was able to remember the moment as my present self, and I remembered that I had indeed stopped and looked outside in that instant because I felt a spontaneous feeling of love in my chest, and I sensed that I was being watched or that someone was outside. I further recalled that while I was washing a glass, I actually leaned forward to minimize the glare in the window from the kitchen light above me and peered into the darkness for a few minutes before returning to the remaining items in the sink. My future self was doing to my present self what the beautiful luminous lady had done to me moments before. Now I understood why she was there.

And like looking at the child in the previous scene, once again, the love that my future self was feeling for my present self somehow connected me to my future self. My future me was there to call my present self to that future, and I knew that it was love that made that bond possible. The evolved version of me had such a sense of knowing. The paradox is that it is all me living at the same time. In fact, there is an infinite number of me's—not just the one in the past, the one in the present, and the one in the future. There are so many more possible me's in the realm of infinity, *and* there is not just one infinity but multiple infinities. And all of this is happening in the eternal now.

When I came back to physical reality as we know it on the couch, which paled in comparison to the other dimensional world I was just in, my first thought was *Wow! My view of reality is so limited!* The rich inner experience provided such a sense of clarity and the understanding that my beliefs—that is, what I thought I knew about life, God, myself, time, space, and what is even possible to experience in this infinite realm— were so very limited, and I hadn't even realized it until that moment. I knew I was like an infant with little comprehension of the magnitude of how big this thing we call reality is. I understood, without fear or anxiety, what the phrase "the unknown" meant for the first time in my life. And I knew I would never be the same person again.

I'm sure you can imagine that when something like this happens, trying to explain it to your family or friends suggests some chemical imbalance in the brain. I was hesitant to talk about the event to anyone because I didn't even have the words to describe the experience and I didn't want to jinx it from happening again. For months, I was very preoccupied with reviewing the entire process that I thought may have created the experience. I was also mystified about the concept of time and couldn't stop thinking about it. Aside from the paradigm shift about the eternal moment in time, I discovered something more. I realized after the transcendental event that night, when I came back to the world of three dimensions, that the whole experience had transpired in about 10 minutes. I had just lived two extensive events, and it should have taken much more time for that entire experience to unfold. This time dilation further piqued my interest in committing more of my energy to investigating what had happened to me. Once I understood more, I hoped I might be able to reproduce the experience.

For days after that important night, the center of my chest was electric in the same way I had felt when that beautiful tiny woman activated something within me. I kept thinking, *How can this feeling still be lingering inside of me unless something real happened?* When I put my attention on the center of my chest, I noticed the feeling amplify. Understandably, I wasn't very interested in any social interaction during this period because the people and conditions in the outer world distracted from that feeling in my inner world, and the special feeling diminished. In time, it finally faded completely, but I never stopped thinking about the idea that there is always more love to experience and that the energy I had embraced in that realm still lived within me. I wanted to activate it again but I didn't know how.

For a long time, even though I tried and tried to reproduce the experience, nothing happened. I now realize that the expectation of the same outcome, combined with the frustration of trying to force it to happen, is the worst combination for creating another mystical experience (or anything, for that matter). I became lost in my own personal analysis, trying to figure out how it occurred and how I could make it happen again. I decided to add a few new approaches. Instead of trying to re-create the experience in the evening, I decided to wake up early in the morning and meditate. Since melatonin levels are the highest between 1:00 A.M. and 4:00 A.M., and the mystical chemical metabolites of melatonin are the very substrates responsible for creating a lucid event, I decided I would practice my inner work at 4 every morning.

Before I share what happened next, I want to ask you to keep in mind that this was an unusually difficult time in my life. I was deciding whether it was worth it for me to continue to teach. I'd experienced a fair amount of chaos in my life after appearing in the 2004 documentary *What the Bleep Do We Know!?* I was considering stepping away from the public world and disappearing into a simpler life. It seemed so much easier to just walk away.

Living a Past Incarnation in the Present Moment

One morning about an hour and a half after I started my meditation in a seated position, I finally reclined. I put some pillows under my knees so I wouldn't fall asleep too quickly, allowing me to linger between wakefulness and sleep. As I lay down, I simply put my attention in the place the pineal gland occupies in my head. But this time, instead of trying to make something happen, I just let go and said to myself, *Whatever . . .* Apparently, that was the magic word. I know what that means now. I surrendered, got out of the way, let go of any specific outcome, and simply opened up to possibility.

The next thing I knew, I was experiencing myself as a stout man in a very hot region of the world that seemed to be in what we now call Greece or Turkey. The terrain was rocky, the ground was parched, and stone buildings like those in Greco-Roman times were interspersed with many small tents made of brightly colored fabrics. I was wearing a one-piece, skirted burlap garment that fell from my shoulders to my mid-thighs, and I had a thick rope tied around my waist like a belt. I wore sandals roped up to my calves. I had thick curly hair and my body felt strong. My shoulders were broad and my arms and legs were muscular. I was a philosopher and a longtime student of some charismatic movement.

I was simultaneously the self in that experience and my present self observing me in that particular time and space. Again, I was way more conscious than normal—I was superconscious. All my senses were heightened and I was very aware of everything. I could smell the familiar musk of my body, and I could taste the salt of my perspiration dripping from my face. I loved the taste. I felt grounded in the physicality and strength of my body. I was aware of deep pain in my right shoulder but it did not consume my attention. I saw the brightness of the blue sky and the richness of the green trees and mountains, as if I were living in Technicolor. I heard seagulls in the distance, and I knew I was near a large body of water.

I was on a pilgrimage and mission of sorts. I was traveling about the country teaching the philosophy that I had studied and lived by my whole life. I was under the tutelage of a grand master whom I loved very deeply because of the care, patience, and wisdom he had given me for so many years. It was my time now to be initiated and to deliver a message to change the minds and hearts of the culture. I knew that the message I was disseminating was counter to the current beliefs of that time and that the government and religious orders of the day would challenge me.

The main message of the philosophy I studied would free people from living in any type of obligation to "some thing or some one" outside of them. It would also inspire individuals to demonstrate a code of principles that would empower them to have more enriched and meaningful lives. I was passionate about this idealism, and I worked daily to live in alignment with the doctrines. Of course, the message would omit the need for religion and for any dependence on governments, and it would free people from personal pain and suffering.

As the scene came to life, I had just finished addressing a crowd in a relatively populated village. The gathering was just breaking up when suddenly, several men quickly moved through the masses to arrest me. Before I could even try to escape, I was seized. I knew that they had planned their strategy well. If they had begun to move about while I had been talking to the crowd, I would have spotted them. They timed it perfectly.

I surrendered without resistance, and they took me to a prison cell where I was left alone. Locked in a small stone cube with narrow slits for windows, I sat there knowing my destiny. Nothing I could do would prepare me for what was about to happen. Within two days, I was taken to the center of the city where hundreds of people gathered—many of them the same people who had listened to me speak just a few days earlier. But now, they eagerly anticipated the chance to watch my trial and impending torture.

I was stripped to a small cloth undergarment and then strapped to a large horizontal stone slab with large grooves notched into the corners through which ropes slid. The ropes had metal cuffs on the ends that were fastened to my wrists and ankles. Then it began. A man standing to my left started to crank a lever that moved the slab slowly from a horizontal position forward to a more vertical position. As the stone block moved upward, the ropes pulled my limbs tighter in all four directions.

When I made it to about 45 degrees, the real pain began. Someone who seemed to be a magistrate yelled out, asking me if I would continue teaching my philosophy. I did not look up or answer. He then ordered the man to crank the lever further. At a certain point, I started to hear audible noises and pops, evidence of my spine dislocating in certain areas. As the observer of this scene, I watched the look on my face as the pain increased. It was like looking into a mirror and seeing myself—I became acutely aware that it was me on that slab.

The metal cuffs around my wrists and ankles now tore into my skin and the sharp metal burned. I was bleeding. One of my shoulders dislocated and I heaved and grunted in pain. My body was convulsing and shaking as I tried to resist the tearing of my limbs by flexing and holding my muscles tight in resistance. Letting go would have been unbearable. Suddenly, the magistrate hollered out again, asking me if I would continue to teach.

I had a thought: *I will agree to stop teaching, and then when they let me down from this public display of torture, I will simply start again.* I reasoned that this was the right answer. It would appease the magistrate and stop the pain (and my death) while enabling me to continue my mission. I slowly shook my head from side to side in silence.

Then the magistrate pressed me to verbally say no, but I would not speak. He then motioned quickly to the tormentor on my left to push the crank even harder. I looked down at the man as he turned the gears with a clear intention to hurt me. I saw his face, and as we looked into each other's eyes, I as the observer instantly recognized this person as someone in my present life as Joe Dispenza: the same person but in a different body. Something clicked within me as I witnessed this scene. I recognized that this tormentor is still tormenting others—including me—in my current incarnation, and I understood that person's role in my life. It was an oddly familiar feeling of knowing, and it all made perfect sense.

As the slab accelerated upward, my lower back snapped and my body started to lose control. That was the moment that broke me. I wept from the blinding pain, and I also felt such a deep sadness consume my whole being. When the weight of the heavy stone was released, it fell quickly back to the horizontal position. I lay there quivering uncontrollably in silence. I was then dragged back to the small prison cell, where I lay curled up in the corner. For three days, I couldn't stop the flashbacks of my torture.

I was so humiliated that I never could speak in public again. The very thought of returning to my mission created such a visceral response in my body that I stopped even thinking about it. One night they released me, and without being noticed, head down in utter shame, I disappeared. I was unable to look anyone in the eye ever again. I felt like I had failed in my mission. I spent the rest of my life in a cave by the sea, trapping fish and living in silence as a hermit.

As I witnessed this poor man's plight and his choice to hide from the world, I understood that this was a message for me. I knew that in my present life I could not disappear and hide from the world again and that my soul wanted me to see that I had to continue my work. I had to make the effort to stand up for a message and never again retract from adversity. I also recognized that I hadn't failed at all—I had done my best. I knew that the young philosopher still lived in the eternal present moment as a myriad of possible me's and that I could change my future, and his, by never again being afraid to live for the truth instead of dying for it.

Each of us has myriad possible incarnations that exist in the eternal present moment, all waiting to be discovered. When the mystery of the self is unveiled, we can wake up to the understanding that we are not linear beings living a linear life but instead dimensional beings living dimensional lives. The beauty behind the infinite probabilities that await us is that the only way we can change those futures is to change ourselves in the present infinite moment.

Chapter 2

THE PRESENT MOMENT

If you want to experience the supernatural in your own life—by healing your body, creating new opportunities you could never have imagined before, and having transcendent, mystical experiences—you first need to master the concept of the present moment: the eternal now. There's a lot of talk about being present or being in the now these days. While most people understand the basics of what that means (not to think about the future or live in the past), I want to offer you a completely different understanding of the concept. It's going to require that you get beyond the physical world—including your body, your identity, and your environment—and even beyond time itself. This is where you turn possibility into reality.

After all, if you don't get beyond who you think you are and the way you've been conditioned to believe the world works, it's not possible to create a new life or a new destiny. So in a very real sense, you have to get out of your own way, transcend the memory of yourself as an identity, and allow something greater than you, something mystical, to take over. In this chapter, I'm going to explain how that works.

First, let's take a look at how the brain functions. When any neurological tissue in the brain or the body is activated, it creates mind. Consequently, from a neuroscientific understanding, mind is the brain in action. For instance, you have a specific mind to drive your car. You have another mind to take a shower. You have a different mind when you sing a song or listen to music. You use a specific level of mind to execute each of those complex functions because you've probably done each of these tasks thousands of times, so your brain turns on in a very specific way whenever you do any of them.

When your brain is in action as you drive your car, for example, you are in fact turning on a specific sequence, pattern, and combination of neurological networks. Those neural networks (or neural nets) are simply clusters of neurons that work together as a community—just like an automatic software program or a macro—because you've done that particular action so many times. In other words, the neurons that fire together to accomplish the task become more wired together.[1] As you consciously choose to perform the task of driving your vehicle, we could say that you are automatically selecting and instructing those neurons in your brain to turn on to create a level of mind.

For the most part, your brain is a product of the past. It has been shaped and molded to become a living record of everything you have learned and experienced up to this point in your life. Learning, from a neuroscientific standpoint, is when neurons in your brain assemble to form thousands of synaptic connections and those connections then assemble into complex, three-dimensional neurological networks. Think of learning as your brain getting an upgrade. When you pay attention to knowledge or information and it makes sense to you, this interaction with the environment leaves biological impressions in your brain. When you experience something new, your senses write the story neurologically in your brain and even more neurons come together to make even more enriched connections, upgrading your brain even further.

Experiences not only enhance the brain circuitry, but they also create emotions. Think of emotions as the chemical residue from past experiences—or chemical feedback. The stronger the emotional quotient from an event in your life, the more the experience leaves a lasting impression in your brain; that's how long-term memories are formed. So if learning means making new connections in your brain, memories are when you maintain those connections. The more you repeat a thought, choice, behavior, experience, or emotion, the more those neurons fire and wire together and the more they will sustain a long-term relationship.

In Anna's story in the previous chapter, you learned most of your experiences come from your interaction with your external environment. Since your senses plug you into the external environment and neurologically record the narrative in your brain, when you experience a highly charged emotional event—bad or good—that moment becomes embossed neurologically in your brain as a memory. Therefore, when an experience changes how you normally feel chemically and heightens your attention to what caused it, you will associate a specific person or thing with where your body is at a particular time and place. That's how you create memories by interacting with the outer world. It's safe to say that the only place the past actually exists is in your brain—and in your body.

How Your Past Becomes Your Future

Let's take a closer look at what happens biochemically inside your body when you think a thought or feel an emotion. When you think a thought (or have a memory), a biochemical reaction begins in your brain causing the brain to release certain chemical signals. That's how immaterial thoughts literally become matter—they become chemical messengers. These chemical signals make your body feel exactly the way you were just thinking. Once you notice you are feeling a particular way, then you generate more thoughts equal to how you're feeling, and then you release more chemicals from your brain to make you feel the way you've been thinking.

For example, if you have a fearful thought, you start to feel fear. The moment you feel fear, that emotion influences you to think more fearful thoughts, and those thoughts trigger the release of even more chemicals in the brain and body that make you continue to feel more fear. The next thing you know, you get caught in a loop where your thinking creates feeling and your feeling creates thinking. If thoughts are the vocabulary of the brain and feelings are the vocabulary of the body, and the cycle of how you think and feel becomes your *state of being*, then your entire state of being is in the past.

When you fire and wire the same circuits in your brain over and over again because you keep thinking the same thoughts, you are hardwiring your brain into the same patterns. As a result, your brain becomes an artifact of your past thinking, and in time it becomes easier to automatically think in the same ways. At the same time, as you repeatedly feel the same emotions over and over again—since as I just said, emotions are the vocabulary of the body and the chemical residue of past experiences—you are conditioning your body into the past.

So now let's look at what that means for you on a day-to-day basis. Given what you just learned about feelings and emotions being the chemical end products of past events, the moment you wake up in the morning and search for the familiar feeling called you, you are starting your day in the past. So when you start to think about your problems, those problems—which are connected to the memories of past experiences of different people or things at certain times and places—create familiar feelings such as unhappiness, futility, sadness, pain, grief, anxiety, worry, frustration, unworthiness, or guilt. If those emotions are driving your thoughts, and you cannot think greater than how you feel, then you are also thinking in the past. And if those familiar emotions influence the choices you are going to make that day, the behaviors you're going to exhibit, or the experiences you are going to create for yourself, then you're going to appear predictable—and your life is going to stay the same.

Now let's say after you wake up, you turn off your alarm, and as you lie there in bed, you check your Facebook, your Instagram, your WhatsApp, your Twitter, your texts, your e-mails, and then the news. (Now you are really remembering who you are as you reaffirm your personality and connect to your past-present personal reality.) Then you go to the bathroom. You use the toilet, brush your teeth, take a shower, get dressed, and then head for the kitchen. You drink some coffee and eat breakfast. Maybe you watch the news or check your e-mail again. It's the same routine you follow every day.

Then you drive to work using the same old route, and when you get there you interact with the same coworkers you saw the day before. You spend your day performing pretty much the same duties you performed yesterday. You might even react to the same challenges at work with the same emotions. Then after work, you drive home; maybe you stop at the same grocery store and buy the food you like and always eat. You cook the same food for dinner and watch the same television show at the same time while sitting in the same place in your living room. Then you get ready for bed in the same way you always do—you brush your teeth (with your right hand starting from the upper right side of your mouth), you crawl into the same side of the bed, maybe you read a little, and then you go to sleep.

If you keep doing these same routines over and over again, they will become a habit. A habit is a redundant set of automatic, unconscious thoughts, behaviors, and emotions that you acquire through frequent repetition. Basically, it means your body is now on autopilot, running a series of programs, and over time, your body becomes the mind. You've done this routine so many times that your body automatically knows how to do certain things better than your brain or conscious mind. You just switch on the autopilot and go unconscious, which means you'll wake up the next the morning and essentially do the same things all over again. In a very real sense, your body is dragging you into the same predictable future based on what you have been repeatedly doing in the same familiar past. You will think the same thoughts and then make the same choices that lead to the same behaviors that create the same experiences that produce the same emotions. Over time, you've created a set of hardwired neurological networks in the brain and you have emotionally conditioned your body to live in the past—and that past becomes your future.

If you were looking at a timeline of your day, starting with waking up in the morning and continuing until you go to bed that night, you could pick up that timeline of yesterday or today (your past) and place it in the space reserved for tomorrow (the future) because essentially the same actions you took today are the ones you are going to take tomorrow—and the day after that, and the day after that. Let's face it: If you keep the same routine as yesterday, it makes sense that your tomorrow is going to be a lot like your yesterday. Your future is just a rerun of your past. That's because your yesterday is creating your tomorrow.

Take a look at Figure 2.1. Each of those vertical lines represents the same thought that leads to the same choice that initiates an automatic behavior that creates a known experience that produces a familiar feeling or an emotion. If you keep reproducing the same sequence, in time all those individual steps merge into one automatic program. This is how you lose your free will to a program. The arrow represents an unknown experience dropping in somewhere between you driving to work in traffic, knowing you are going to be late again, and you trying to stop by the dry cleaner's on your way.

We could say that your mind and body are in the known—the same predictable future based on what you did in the same familiar past—and in that known, certain future there's no room for the unknown. In fact, if something new happened, if something unknown were to unfold in your life at that moment to change the same predictable timeline of your day, you'd probably be annoyed at the disruption of your routine. You'd likely consider it troublesome, problematic, and downright inconvenient. You might say, "Can you come back tomorrow? This is not the right time."

LIVING IN THE PROGRAM
Predictable Timeline of Your Known Reality

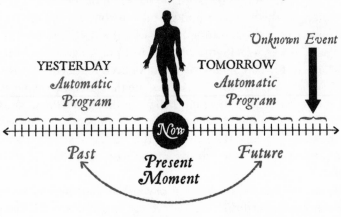

Figure 2.1

A habit is a redundant set of automatic unconscious thoughts, behaviors, and emotions that develop through repetition. It's when you've done something so many times that your body is programmed to become the mind. Over time, your body is dragging you to a predictable future based on what you've been doing in the past. Therefore, if you're not in the present moment, you're probably in a program.

The fact is, there's no room for the unknown in a predictable life. But being predictable is not how the unknown works. The unknown is unfamiliar, uncertain—but it's also *exciting* because it occurs in ways you cannot expect or anticipate. So let me ask you: How much room in your routine, predictable life do you have for the unknown?

By staying in the known—following the same sequence each day of thinking the same thoughts, making the same choices, demonstrating the same programmed habits, re-creating the same experiences that stamp the same networks of neurons into the same patterns to reaffirm the same familiar feeling called you—you are repeating the same level of mind over and over again. In time, your brain becomes automatically programmed to do any one of those particular sequences more easily and effortlessly the next time, and then the next time, and so on.

As each of these individual steps merge into one complete step, thinking a familiar thought of an experience of somebody or something at some place in some time will automatically create the anticipation of the feeling of the experience. If you can predict the feeling of any experience, you are still in the known. For instance, the thought of having a meeting with the same team of people you have worked with for years can automatically cause you to call up the emotion of what that future event will feel like. When you can predict the feeling of that future event—because you've had enough past experiences to make it known to you—you are probably going to be creating more of the same. And of course, you are right. But that's because *you* are the same. By the same means, if you are in the automatic program and you cannot predict the feeling of an experience in your life, you will probably be hesitant to engage it.

We need to look at one more aspect of thinking and feeling to get the full picture of what's happening when you keep living in the same state of being. This thinking-feeling loop also produces a measurable electromagnetic field that surrounds our physical bodies. In fact, our bodies are always emitting light, energy, or frequencies that carry a specific message, information, or intention. (By the way, when I say "light," I am not just referring to the light we see but to all spectrums of light—including x-rays, cell phone waves, and microwaves.) In the same way, we also receive vital information that is carried on different frequencies. So we are always sending and receiving electromagnetic energy.

Here's how that works. When we think a thought, those networks of neurons that fire in our brain create *electrical* charges. When those thoughts also cause a chemical reaction that results in a feeling or an emotion, as well as when a familiar feeling or emotion is driving our thoughts, those feelings create *magnetic* charges. They merge with the thoughts that create the electric charges to produce a specific electromagnetic field equal to your state of being.[2]

Think of emotions as *energy in motion*. When someone experiencing a strong emotion walks into a room, their energy (aside from their body language) is often very palpable. We have all felt another person's energy and intent when they were angry or very frustrated. We felt it because they were emitting a strong signal of energy that carried specific information. The same is true of a very sexual person, a person who is suffering, or a person who has a calm, loving energy: All those energies can be sensed and felt. As you might expect, different emotions produce different frequencies. The frequencies of creative, elevated emotions like love, joy, and gratitude are much higher than the emotions of stress, such as fear and anger, because they carry different levels of conscious intent and energy. (See Figure 2.2, which details some of the different frequencies associated with various emotional states.) You'll read more about this concept later in the book.

SCALE OF SOME EMOTIONS
WITH DIFFERENT ENERGIES

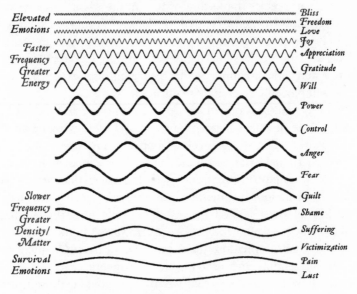

Figure 2.2

Emotions are energy in motion. All energy is frequency and all frequency carries information. Based on our own personal thoughts and feelings, we are always sending and receiving information.

So if we are re-creating the past day after day, thinking the same thoughts and feeling the same emotions, we are broadcasting the same electromagnetic field over and over again—sending out the same energy with the same message. From the perspective of energy and information, this means the same energy of our past continues to carry the same information, which then keeps creating the same future. Our energy, then, is essentially equal to our past. The only way we can change our lives is to change our energy—to change the electromagnetic field we are constantly broadcasting. In other words, to change our state of being, we have to change how we think and how we feel.

SIPHONING ENERGY OUT
OF THE PRESENT MOMENT

Electromagnetic
Field
All of the energy is comingled in this known timeline

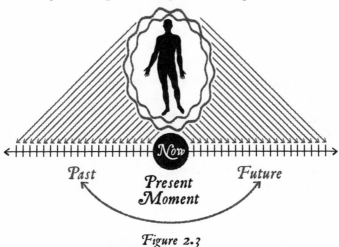

Figure 2.3

If where you place your attention is where you place your energy, the moment you put your attention on familiar feelings and memories, you are siphoning your energy into the past and out of the present moment. In the same way, if your attention is constantly on all the people you have to see, the places you have to go, the things you have to do at certain times in your known familiar reality, then you are siphoning your energy out of the present moment and into the predictable future.

If where you place your attention is where you place your energy (a key concept you'll read more about later in this chapter), then the moment you place your attention on a familiar emotion, your attention and your energy are in the past. If those familiar emotions are connected to a memory of some past event involving a person or an object at a particular place and time, then your attention and your energy are in the past as well. As a consequence, you are siphoning your energy out of the present moment into your past. By the same means, if you start to think about all the people you have to see, the things you have to do, and the places you have to go at certain times in your routine day, you are siphoning your attention and energy into a predictable known future. Take a look at Figure 2.3, which illustrates this point.

All of your energy is now completely comingled with those known experiences in that specific line of time. Your energy is creating more of the same and your body is going to follow your mind to the same events in your same reality. Your energy is being directed out of the present moment and into the past and the future. As a result, you have very little energy left to create an unknown experience in a new timeline.

Figure 2.3 also shows how the electromagnetic energy you emanate is a vibrational match with everything known to you. So as you start your day, when you have the thought of the toilet, the next thing you know there you are walking toward the toilet. Then you have the thought of the shower and you find yourself in the shower, adjusting the water temperature. You have the thought of the coffeemaker and you're projecting your attention and energy to the coffeemaker, and as you automatically walk to the kitchen to make your morning cup of java, once again your body is following your mind. And if you've done that for the last 22 years, your body is going to effortlessly coast right over there. Your body is always following your mind—but in this case, it's been repeatedly following your mind to the known. That's because that's where your attention—and therefore your energy—is.

So now let me ask you this: Could it ever be possible for your body to start following your mind to the *unknown*? If so, you can see that you would have to change where you put your attention, and that would lead to changing your energy, which would require you to change how you think and how you feel long enough for something new to happen. While it may sound incredible, this is indeed possible. It makes sense that just as your body has been following your mind to every *known* experience in your life (like the coffeemaker each morning), if you were to start investing your attention and energy into the *unknown*, your body would then be able to follow your mind into the unknown—a new experience in your future.

Priming Your Mind and Body for a New Future

If you are familiar with my work, you know that I'm in love with the concept of mental rehearsal. I am fascinated by how we can change the brain as well as the body by thought alone. Think about that for a moment. If you focus your attention on specific imagery in your mind and become very present with a sequence of repeated thoughts and feelings, your brain and body will not know the difference between what is occurring in the outer world and what is happening in your inner world. So when you're fully engaged and focused, the inner world of imagination will appear as an outer-world experience—and your biology will change accordingly. That means you can make your brain and body look as if a physical experience has already happened *without* having the actual experience. What you put your attention on and mentally rehearse over and over again not only becomes who you are from a biological perspective, it also determines your future.

Here's a good example. A team of Harvard researchers took a group of volunteers who had never before played the piano and divided the group in half. One half practiced a simple five-finger piano exercise for two hours a day over a period of five days. The remaining half did the same thing, but just by imagining they were sitting at the piano—without physically moving their fingers in any way. The before-and-after brain scans showed that *both* groups created a dramatic number of new neural circuits and new neurological programming in the region of their brains that controls finger movements, even though one group did so by thought alone.[3]

Think about this. The folks who mentally rehearsed the actions had brains that looked like the experience had already happened—even though they never lifted a finger. If you were to put them in front of a piano after five days of mental rehearsal, many of them would be able to play the exercise they imagined pretty well, even though they had never before tickled the ivories. By mentally imagining the activity every day, they installed the neurological hardware in preparation for the experience. They repeatedly fired and wired those brain circuits with their attention and intention, and over time the hardware became an automatic software program in their brains and it became easier to do the next time. So if they were to start to play after five days of mental practice, their behaviors would become easily aligned with their conscious intentions because they primed their brains for the experience *ahead of time*. That's how powerful the mind can be, once trained.

Similar studies show the same kinds of results with muscle training. In a pioneering study at the Cleveland Clinic, ten research subjects between the ages of 20 and 35 imagined flexing one of their biceps as hard as they could in five training sessions a week for 12 weeks. Every other week, the researchers recorded the subjects' electrical brain activity during their sessions and measured their muscle strength. By the end of the study, the subjects had increased their biceps' strength by 13.5 percent, even though they hadn't actually been using their muscles at all. They maintained this gain for three months after the training sessions stopped.[4]

More recently, a research team made up of scientists from the University of Texas at San Antonio, the Cleveland Clinic, and the Kessler Foundation Research Center in West Orange, New Jersey, asked subjects to visualize contracting their elbow flexor muscles. As they did so, they were instructed to *urge* the muscles to flex as strong and hard as possible—adding a firm intention to their strong mental energy—for 15-minute sessions, five days a week, for 12 weeks. One group of subjects was instructed to use what is called external or third-person imagery, imagining themselves performing the exercise by observing themselves in a scene in their heads separate from the experience (like watching a movie of themselves). A second group was instructed to use internal or first-person imagery, imagining that their bodies as they existed right then in real time were doing the exercise, making it more immediate and realistic. A third group, the control, did no practice. The group using external imagery (as well as the control group) showed no significant change, but the group using internal imagery showed a 10.8 percent increase in strength.[5]

Another team of researchers from Ohio University went so far as to wrap the wrists of 29 volunteers in surgical casts for one month, ensuring they wouldn't be able to move their wrists even unintentionally. Half the group practiced mental-imagery exercises for 11 minutes a day, five days a week, imagining they were flexing their immobilized wrist muscles while actually remaining completely still. The other half, the control group, did nothing. At the end of the month, when all the casts came off, the muscles of the imagery group were twice as strong as those of the control group.[6]

Each of these three muscle studies shows how mental rehearsal not only changes the brain, but can also change the body by thought alone. In other words, by practicing the behaviors in their mind and consciously reviewing the activity on a regular basis, the bodies of the subjects looked like they had been physically performing the activity—and yet they never did the exercises. Those who added the emotional component of doing the exercise as hard as possible to the intensity of the mental imagery made the experience even more real and the results more pronounced.

In the piano-playing study, the brains of the research subjects looked as though the experience they'd imagined had already happened because they had primed their brains for that future. In a similar way, the subjects in the muscle-flexing studies changed their bodies to look as if they had previously experienced that reality—just by mentally rehearsing the activity through thought alone. You can see why when you wake up in the morning and start thinking about the people you have to see, the places you have to go, and the things you have to do in your busy schedule (that's mentally rehearsing), and then you add an intense emotion to it like suffering or unhappiness or frustration, just like the elbow flexor volunteers who *urged* their muscles to flex without moving them at all, you are conditioning your brain and body to look like that future has already happened. Since experience enriches the brain and creates an emotion that signals the body, when you continuously create an inward experience that is as real as an outer experience, over time you're going to change your brain and body—just like any real experience would.

In fact, when you wake up and start thinking about your day, neurologically, biologically, chemically, and even genetically (which I will explain in the next section), it looks as though that day has already happened for you. And in fact, it has. Once you actually start the day's activities, just as in the experiments above, your body is naturally and automatically going to behave equal to your conscious or unconscious intentions. If you've been doing the same things for years on end, those circuits—as well as the rest of your biology—are more readily and easily activated. That's because not only do you prime your biology every day with your mind, but you also re-create the same physical behaviors in order to reinforce those experiences further in your brain and body. And it actually becomes easier to go unconscious every day because you keep mentally and physically reinforcing the same habits over again—creating the habit of behaving by habit.

Making Genetic Changes

We used to think that genes created disease and that we were at the mercy of our DNA. So if many people in someone's family died of heart disease, we assumed that their chances of also developing heart disease would be pretty high. But we now know through the science of epigenetics that it's not the gene that creates disease but the *environment* that programs our genes to create disease—and not just the external environment outside our body (cigarette smoke or pesticides, for example), but also the internal environment within our body: the environment outside our cells.

What do I mean by the environment within our body? As I said previously, emotions are chemical feedback, the end products of experiences we have in our external environment. So as we react to a situation in our external environment that produces an emotion, the resulting internal chemistry can signal our genes to either turn on (up-regulating, or producing an increased expression of the gene) or to turn off (down-regulating, or producing a decreased expression of the gene). The *gene itself* doesn't physically change—the *expression* of the gene changes, and that expression is what matters most because that is what affects our health and our lives. Thus, even though someone may have a genetic predisposition for a particular disease, for example, if their genes continue to express health instead of expressing that disease, they won't develop the condition and will remain healthy.

Think of the body as a finely tuned instrument that produces proteins. Every one of our cells (except red blood cells) makes proteins, which are responsible for the body's physical structure and physiological function. For example, muscle cells make specific proteins known as actin and myosin, and skin cells make the proteins collagen and elastin. Immune cells make antibodies, thyroid cells make thyroxine, and bone-marrow cells make hemoglobin. Some of our eye cells make keratin, while our pancreatic cells make enzymes like protease, lipase, and amylase. There isn't an organ or a system in the body that does not rely on or produce proteins. They are a vital part of our immune system, digestion, cellular repair, and bone and muscle structure—you name it, they're a part of it. In a very real way, then, the expression of proteins is the expression of life and is equal to the health of the body.

In order for a cell to make a protein, a gene must be expressed. That's the job of the genes, to facilitate making proteins. When the signal from the environment outside of the cell reaches the cell membrane, the chemical is accepted by a receptor outside of the cell and makes its way to the DNA inside the cell. Then a gene makes a new protein that's equal to that signal. So if the information coming from outside of the cell does not change, the gene keeps making the same protein and the body stays the same. Over time, the gene will begin to down-regulate; it will either shut off its healthy expression of proteins or it will eventually wear out, like making a copy of a copy of a copy, causing the body to express a different quality of proteins.

Different classifications of stimuli up-regulate and down-regulate genes. We activate experience-dependent genes, for example, by doing new things or learning new information. These genes are responsible for stem cells getting the instructions to differentiate, transforming into whatever type of cell the body needs at that particular time to replace cells that are damaged. We activate behavioral state–dependent genes when we are in high levels of stress or arousal, or in alternate states of awareness, like dreaming. You can think of these genes as the fulcrum of mind-body connection because they provide a link between our thoughts and our bodies, allowing us to influence our physical health through various behaviors (meditation, prayer, or social rituals, for example). When genes are altered in this way, sometimes within minutes, those altered genes can then be passed on to the next generation.

So when you change your emotions, you can change the expression of your genes (turning some on and others off) because you are sending a new chemical signal to your DNA, which can then instruct your genes to make different proteins—up-regulating or down-regulating to make all kinds of new building blocks that can change the structure and function of your body. For example, if your immune system has been subject to living in the emotions of stress for too long and has certain genes activated for inflammation and disease, you can turn on new genes for growth and repair and switch off the old genes responsible for disease. And at the same time, these epigenetically altered genes will begin to follow new instructions, making new proteins and programming the body for growth, repair, and healing. This is how you can successfully recondition your body to a new mind.

So as you read earlier in this chapter, this means that if you're living by the same emotions day in and day out, your body believes it's in the same environmental conditions. Then those feelings influence you to make the same choices, causing you to demonstrate the same habits that then create the same experiences that then produce the same emotions all over again. Thanks to these automatic, programmed habits, your cells are constantly being exposed to the same chemical environment (outside your body in your environment as well as outside the cells but within your body). That chemistry keeps signaling the same genes in the same way—and so you're stuck because when *you* stay the same, your *genetic expression* stays the same. And now you are headed for a genetic destiny because you don't have any new information coming from the environment.

But what if the circumstances in your life change for the better? Shouldn't that also change the chemical environment surrounding your cells? Yes, that happens, but not all the time. If you've spent years conditioning your body to this cycle of thinking and feeling, and then feeling and thinking, without realizing it you've also conditioned your body to become addicted to these emotions. So simply changing the external environment by, say, getting a new job doesn't necessarily break that addiction any more than someone addicted to drugs would be able to stop their cravings just by winning the lottery or moving to Hawaii. Because of the thinking-feeling loop, sooner or later—after the novelty of the experience is over—most people return to their baseline emotional state, and the body believes it is in the same old experience that created the same old emotions.

So if you were miserable in your old job but managed to get a new one, you might be happy for a few weeks or even a few months. But if you had spent years conditioning your body to be addicted to misery, you would eventually return to that old emotion because your body would crave its chemical fix. Your outer environment may have changed, but your body will always believe its internal chemistry more than its external conditions, so it remains emotionally locked into your old state of being, still addicted to those old emotions. That's just another way of saying you're still living in the past. And because that internal chemistry hasn't changed, you can't change the expression of your genes to make new proteins in order to improve the structure or the function of your body, so there's no change in your health or your life. That's why I say you have to think greater than the way you feel to make any real, lasting changes.

In the winter of 2016, at our advanced workshop in Tacoma, Washington, my team and I performed a study on the effect elevated emotions had on immune function, taking saliva samples from 117 test subjects at the start of the workshop and then again four days later at the workshop's conclusion. We measured immunoglobulin A (IgA), a protein marker for the strength of the immune system.

IgA is an incredibly powerful chemical, one of the primary proteins responsible for healthy immune function and the internal defense system. It's constantly fighting a barrage of bacteria, viruses, fungi, and other organisms that invade or are already living within the body's internal environment. It's so powerful that it's better than any flu shot or immune system booster you could possibly take; when it's activated, it's the primary internal defense system in the human body. When stress levels (and therefore the levels of stress hormones like cortisol) go up, this lowers levels of IgA, thereby compromising and down-regulating the immune system's expression of the gene that makes this protein.

During our four-day workshop, we asked our study participants to move into an elevated emotional state such as love, joy, inspiration, or gratitude for nine to ten minutes three times a day. If we could elevate our emotions, we wondered, could we boost our immune system? In other words, could our students up-regulate the genes for IgA simply by changing their emotional states?

The results amazed us. Average IgA levels shot up by 49.5 percent. The normal range for IgA is from 37 to 87 milligrams per deciliter (mg/ dL), but some people measured more than 100 mg/dL at the end of the workshop.[7] Our test subjects showed significant, measurable epigenetic changes without having any significant experiences in their external environment. By attaining states of elevated emotion even for just a few days, their bodies began to believe that they were in a new environment, so they were able to signal new genes and change their genetic expression (in this case, the protein expression of the immune system). (See Figure 2.4.)

OUR TACOMA, WA, SIgA & CORTISOL STUDY

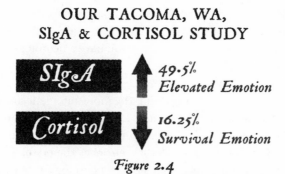

Figure 2.4

As we practice maintaining elevated emotions and changing our energy, we can literally up-regulate new genes that make new healthy proteins to strengthen our internal defense system. As we reduce our survival emotions, and minimize the need for our external protection system, we down-regulate genes for the production of stress hormones. (*SIgA* in the figure above stands for salivary immunoglobulin A; *cortisol* represents stress hormones. Both were measured in saliva.)

This means that you might not need a pharmacy or an exogenous substance to heal you—you have the power from within to up-regulate the genes that make IgA within a few days. Something as simple as moving into an elevated state of joy, love, inspiration, or gratitude for five to ten minutes a day can produce significant epigenetic changes in your health and body.

Where Attention Goes, Energy Flows

Since where you place your attention is where you place your energy, when you wake up in the morning and immediately start putting your attention and energy on all the people you have to see that day, the places you have to go, the objects you own, and the things you have to do in the three-dimensional world, your energy becomes fractured. All of your creative energy is flowing away from you, as Figure 2.5 illustrates, to all the things in the outer world that compete for your attention—your cell phone, your laptop, your bank account, your house, your job, your coworkers, your spouse, your kids, your enemies, your pets, your medical conditions, and so on. Take a glance at Figure 2.5. It is obvious that most people's attention and energy are directed to their outer material world. It begs the question: How much energy do you have left in your inner world of thoughts and feelings to create a new reality?

Consider for a moment that each of these people or things you give so much attention to is a known in your life because you've experienced it. As I mentioned earlier in the chapter, you have a neurological network in your brain for each one of those things. Since they are mapped in your brain, you perceive and so experience them from your past. And the more you keep experiencing them, the more automatic and enriched the neural circuits for each of them become because the redundancy of the various experiences keeps assembling and refining more and more circuits. That's what experience does; it enriches the brain. So you have a neurological network about your boss, a neurological network about money, a neurological network about your partner, a neurological network about your kids, a neurological network for your financial situation, a neurological network for your house, and neurological networks about all your physical-world possessions because you've experienced all of those people or things at different times and places.

WHERE YOU PLACE YOUR ATTENTION
IS WHERE YOU PLACE YOUR ENERGY

Outer World of Physical Reality

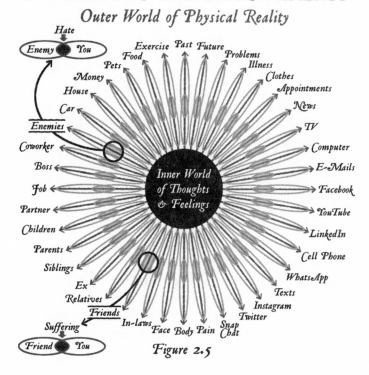

Figure 2.5

Every person, object, thing, place, or situation in our familiar physical reality has a neurological network assigned to it in our brain and an emotional component connected to it because we've experienced all these things. This is how our energy becomes bonded to our past-present reality. Therefore, as you place your attention on all these elements, your energy is flowing away from you and it leaves little energy in your inner world of thoughts and feelings to create something new in your life.

If you look at the magnified portions of the figure where the two ovals intersect, these represent how we use different elements in our outer world to reaffirm our emotional addiction. You may use your friends to reaffirm your addiction to suffering, you may use your enemies to reaffirm your addiction to hatred. It begs the question, *How much of your creative energy could you be using to design a new destiny?*

When your attention, and therefore your energy, is divided between all these outer-world objects, people, problems, and issues, there's no energy left for you to put on your inner world of thoughts and feelings. So there's no energy left for you to use to create something new. Why? Because how you think and how you feel literally creates your personal reality. Therefore, if you are thinking and feeling equal to everything that you know (that's the known), you keep reaffirming the same life. In fact, we could say that your personality is no longer creating your personal reality; now your personal reality is creating your personality. Your external environment is controlling your thoughts and feelings. There's a biological match between your inner world of thoughts and feelings and your outer-world, past-present reality made of people and objects at certain times and places. You are continuously keeping your life the same because you are keeping your attention (thoughts) and your energy (feelings) the same.

Finally, if how you think and how you feel broadcasts an electromagnetic signature that influences every area of your life, you are broadcasting the same electromagnetic energy and your life never changes. We could say that your energy is equal to everything in your past-present reality—and you are re-creating the past. That's not the only limitation that occurs, though. When you place all your attention and energy on the outer world and you keep reacting to the same conditions in the same way—in a state of chronic stress, which causes the brain to be in a constant state of arousal—your inner world becomes imbalanced and your brain begins to work inefficiently. And then you become less effective in creating anything at all. In other words, you become a victim of your life instead of the creator of your life.

Living by the Hormones of Stress

Now let's take a closer look at how we end up getting addicted to our negative emotions—or more precisely, what we call the hormones of stress. The moment we react to any condition in our outer world that tends to be threatening, whether the threat is real or imagined, our body releases stress hormones in order to mobilize enormous amounts of energy in response to that threat. When this occurs, the body moves out of balance—that's exactly what stress is. This is a natural and healthy response, because in antiquity, that chemical cocktail of adrenaline and cortisol and similar hormones were released when we were facing some danger in the outer world. Maybe a predator was chasing us, for example, and we had to make the decision to fight, run, or hide.

When we are in survival mode, we automatically become materialists, defining reality with our senses: by what we can see, hear, smell, feel, and taste. We also narrow our focus and put all our attention on matter—on our bodies existing in a particular space and time. The hormones of stress cause us to give all our attention to our outer world because *that's* where the danger lurks. Back in the days of early humans, of course, this response was a good thing. It was adaptive. It kept us alive. And once we had focused our attention on the cause and then the danger had passed, the levels of all those stress hormones went back into balance.

But in modern times, that's no longer the case. After just one phone call or e-mail from our boss or a family member that elicits a strong emotional reaction such as anger, frustration, fear, anxiety, sadness, guilt, suffering, or shame, we turn on the primitive fight-or-flight nervous system, causing us to react as if we were are being chased by a predator. The same chemistry automatically stays switched on because the external threat never seems to go away. The truth is that many of us spend the majority of our time in this state of heightened arousal. It's become chronic. It's as though the predator is not out there in the wild, making an occasional toothy appearance, but is instead living in the same cave as we are—a toxic coworker whose desk is right next to ours, for example.

Such a chronic stress response is not adaptive; it's maladaptive. When we're living in survival mode and those hormones of stress like adrenaline and cortisol keep pumping through our body, we stay on high alert instead of returning to balance. As in Anna's experience in Chapter 1, when this imbalance is maintained long-term, chances are we are headed for disease, because long-term stress down-regulates the healthy expression of genes. In fact, our bodies become so conditioned to this rush of chemicals that they become addicted to them. Our bodies actually crave them.

In this mode, our brains become overly alert and aroused as we try to predict, control, and force outcomes in an effort to increase our chances of survival. And the more we do this, the stronger the addiction becomes and the more we believe we *are* our bodies connected to our identities and our environment, living in linear time. That's because that's where all of our attention is.

When your brain is aroused and you are living in survival mode, and you have to keep shifting your attention to your job, to the news, to your ex, to your friends, to your e-mails, to Facebook, and to Twitter, you're activating each of these different neurological networks very quickly. (Review Figure 2.5.) If you keep doing this over time, the act of habitually narrowing your focus and shifting your attention compartmentalizes your brain and it no longer works in a balanced fashion. And when that happens, you are training your brain to fire in a disordered, incoherent pattern, which causes it to work very inefficiently. Like a lightning storm in the clouds, different neural networks fire out of order, so your brain works out of sync. The effect is similar to a group of drummers all banging on their skins at the same time but not together or with any rhythm. We will talk much more about the concepts of coherence and incoherence in a later chapter, but for now it's enough to know that when your brain gets incoherent, you get incoherent. When your brain isn't working optimally, you're not working optimally.

For each outer-world person or thing or place you've experienced in your life that is a known, you have an emotion connected to it because emotions—which are energy in motion—are the chemical residue of experience. And if most of the time you're living by those addictive stress hormones, you might use your boss to reaffirm your addiction to judgment. You might use your coworkers to reaffirm your addiction to competition. You might use your friends to reaffirm your addiction to suffering. You might use your enemies to reaffirm your addiction to hatred, your parents to reaffirm your addiction to guilt, your Facebook feed to reaffirm your addiction to insecurity, the news to reaffirm your addiction to anger, your ex to reaffirm your addiction to resentment, and your relationship with money to reaffirm your addiction to lack.

This means your emotions—your energy—are comingled, even bonded, with every person, place, or thing you experience in your known, familiar reality. And that means there's no energy available for you to create a new job, a new relationship, a new financial situation, a new life, or even a newly healed body. Let me say it another way. If how you think and how you feel determines the frequency and information you are emitting in your energy field, which has a significant effect on your life, and if all your attention (and so all your energy) is tied up in your outer world of people, objects, things, places, and time, there is no energy left in your inner world of thoughts and feelings. Therefore, the stronger the emotion you are addicted to, the more you will place your attention on that person, object, place, or circumstance in your outer world—giving away most of your creative energy and causing you to feel and think equal to everything you know. It becomes difficult to think or feel in any new ways when you are addicted to your outer world. And it's possible that you can become addicted to all the people and things in your life that are causing all your problems in the first place. That's how you give your power away and mismanage your energy. If you review Figure 2.5, you'll find a few examples to illustrate how we create energetic bonds to all the elements in our outer world.

Take a look at Figure 2.6. On the left side of the diagram, you see two atoms bound by an invisible field of energy. They're sharing information. It's energy that is bonding them together. On the right side of the diagram, you see two people who are sharing an experience of resentment and who are also bonded by an invisible field of energy that keeps them connected energetically. In truth, they are sharing the same energy and so the same information.

SHARING ENERGY & INFORMATION

 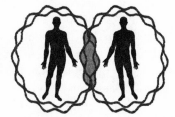

2 *Atoms Bonded to*
Make a Molecule

2 *People with the Same*
Emotions & the Same
Energy, Sharing the Same
Thoughts & Information
Bonded Together

Figure 2.6

Just like two atoms that bond together to form a molecule—which share energy and information—when two people share the same emotions and energy, and communicate the same thoughts and information, they become bonded together as well. In both cases, they are bound by an invisible field of energy that keeps them connected. If it takes energy to separate these two atoms, it is going to take energy and awareness to take our attention off the people and conditions in our life that we've given so much creative energy away to.

To separate the two atoms, it takes energy. By the same means, if your attention and energy are bound to the same people, places, and things in the outside, physical world, you can understand that it's going to take energy and effort to break those bonds when you're in meditation. This begs the question: How much of your creative energy is tied up in guilt, hatred, resentment, lack, or fear? The truth is that you could be using all that energy to re-create a new destiny.

To do that, you're going to have to get beyond all of those things in your outer world by taking your attention off them. That's why we use meditation as the model to change our internal state. This allows us to break from our associations to every body, every one, every thing, every where, and every time long enough to journey within. Once you overcome your emotional body and you take your attention off everything known to you in your outer world, you call your energy back to you, breaking the bonds with your past-present reality (which has been staying the same). You're going to have to make the transition from being somebody to being no body—which means you have to take your attention off your body, your pain, and your hunger. You're going to have to go from being someone to being no one (taking your attention off your identity as a partner, a parent, and an employee). You'll have to go from keeping your attention on some thing to placing your attention on no thing (forgetting all about your cell phone, your e-mails, and getting a cup of coffee) and from being somewhere to being no where (getting beyond any thoughts about the chair you're meditating in or where you'll be going later today) and from being in linear time to being in no time (with no distracting memories or thoughts about the future).

I'm not saying that your cell phone or your laptop or your car or your bank account is bad, but when you're overly attached to those things and they've captured your attention to such a degree that you can't get beyond thinking about them (because of the strong emotions you associate with them), those possessions *own you*. And then you can't create something new. The only way to do that is to learn to call all of that fractured energy back so you can overcome the emotions of survival that you have become addicted to and that keep all your energy bound to your past-present reality. Once you take your attention off all those exterior elements, you start to weaken your energetic and emotional bonds with those things and you finally begin to free up enough available energy to create a new future. That's going to require you to become aware of where you've been unconsciously placing your attention, and—like separating the two atoms—it's also going to take some energy to consciously break those bonds.

People come up to me all the time in workshops and tell me their computer hard drive crashed or someone stole their car or they lost their job and they don't have any more money. When they tell me they have lost people or things in their life, you know what I always say to them? "Great! Look how much available energy you have now to design a new destiny!" By the way, if you do this work well and manage to call your energy back to you, it will most likely be uncomfortable at first, even a little chaotic. Get ready, because certain areas of your life may fall apart. But don't worry. That's supposed to happen because you're breaking the energetic bonds between yourself and your same past reality. Anything that is no longer in a vibrational match between you and your future is going to fall away. Let it. Don't try to put your old life back together because you're going to be way too busy with the new destiny you're calling to yourself.

Here's a great example. A friend of mine who was vice president of a university showed up for a board meeting about three weeks after he started doing this meditation work. He was the backbone of that university. The students and faculty loved him. He walked into the board meeting and sat down—and they fired him. So he called me and said, "Hey, I don't know if this meditation process is working. The board just fired me. Aren't great things supposed to happen to me when I am doing the work?"

"Listen," I told him. "Don't you hold on to those emotions of survival, because then you'll be in your past. Instead, keep finding the present moment and creating from that place." Within two weeks he fell in love with a woman he later married. He also soon received an offer for an even better job as vice president of a much larger and better university, which he gratefully accepted.

A year later, he called me again to tell me that the college that fired him was now asking him to return as president. So you never know what the universe has in store for you as your old reality falls away and your new one begins to unfold. The only thing I can assure you of is this: The unknown has never let me down.

Calling Your Energy Back

If you're going to disconnect from the outer world, you have to learn how to change your brain waves. So let's talk about brain-wave frequencies for a moment. Most of the time that you are awake and conscious, you are in the beta range of brain-wave frequencies. Beta is measured in low-range, medium-range, and high-range frequencies. Low-range beta is a relaxed state when you don't perceive any threats from the outer world but you are still aware of your body in space and time. This is the state you are in when you are reading, paying attention to your daughter during a friendly conversation, or listening to a lecture. Mid-range beta is a slightly more aroused state, such as when you are in a group of people, introducing yourself to everyone for the first time, and you have to remember everyone's name. You're more vigilant, but you're not overly stressed or completely out of balance. Think of mid-range beta as good stress. High-range beta is the state you're in when you're jacked up on the hormones of stress. These are the brain waves you display when you exhibit any of the survival emotions, including anger, alarm, agitation, suffering, grief, anxiety, frustration, or even depression. High-range beta can be more than three times higher than low-range beta and twice as high as mid-range beta.

While you may spend most of your waking time in beta-frequency brain waves, you also dip into alpha-frequency brain waves throughout your day. You display alpha brain waves when you are relaxed, calm, creative, and even intuitive—when you're no longer thinking or analyzing and instead you're daydreaming or imagining, like a trance state. If beta brain waves indicate when you are placing the majority of your attention on your outer world, alpha brain waves indicate when you are placing more of your attention on your inner world.

Theta-frequency brain waves take over in that twilight stage when your mind is still awake but your body is drifting off to sleep. This frequency is also associated with deep states of meditation. Delta-frequency brain waves usually come during deep, restorative sleep. However, over the last four years my research team and I have recorded several students who can move into very deep delta brain waves during meditation. Their bodies are deeply asleep, and they are not dreaming, but their brain scans show that their brains are processing very high amplitudes of energy. As a result, they report having profound mystical experiences of oneness, feeling connected to everyone and everything in the universe. See Figure 2.7 to compare the different brain-wave states.

Gamma-frequency brain waves indicate what I call a superconscious state. This high-frequency energy occurs when the brain gets aroused from an internal event (one of the most common examples is during meditation when your eyes are closed and you are going within) instead of an event that happens outside the body. We'll talk more about gamma brain waves in later chapters.

BRAIN WAVES

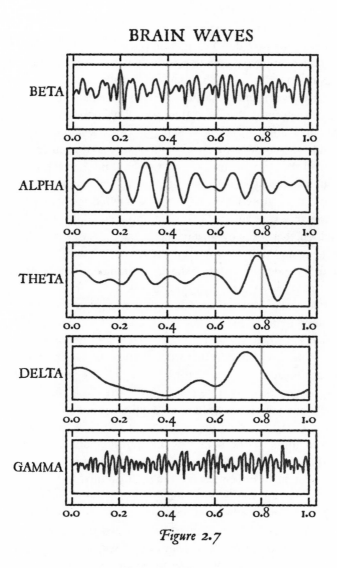

Figure 2.7

A comparison of different brain waves.

One of the biggest challenges people have when they meditate is switching out of high-range (and even mid-range) beta and slipping into alpha and then theta brain-wave frequencies. It's absolutely vital to do so, though, because when they slow down their brain waves to these other frequencies, they are no longer paying attention to the outer world and all the distractions they're so used to thinking about when they're under stress. And since they're not analyzing and strategizing, trying to prepare for the worst-case scenario in their future based on their fearful memories of the past, they have the opportunity to become present, to exist only in the now.

Wouldn't it be wonderful during a meditation to disconnect your association to all the elements in your outer environment, to get beyond your body, your fears, and your schedule and forget about your familiar past and your predictable future? If you do it right, you will even lose track of time. As you overcome your automatic thinking, your emotions, and your habits in meditation, that is exactly what happens: You get beyond your body, your environment, and time. You weaken the energetic bonds with your past-present reality and find yourself in the present moment. Only in the present moment can you call your energy back to you.

This does take some effort (although it will get easier with practice) because you're living by the hormones of stress most of the time. So let's look at what happens when you aren't in the present moment during meditation so you'll know how to handle that when it arises. Understanding this skill is important because if you can't get beyond your stresses, your problems, and your pain, you can't create a new future where those things don't exist.

So let's say you're sitting in your meditation and you start to have some stray thoughts. You're in the habit of thinking that way because you've been thinking the same way and putting your attention on the same people and things at the same time and place for years now. And you have been automatically embracing the same familiar feelings on a daily basis just to reaffirm the same personality that's connected to your same personal reality—repeatedly conditioning your body into the past. The only difference now is that because you're trying to meditate, your eyes are shut.

As you are sitting there with your eyes closed, you are not physically seeing your boss. But your body wants to feel that anger because every time you see her in your waking day—50 times a day, five days a week—you are in the habit of feeling bitterness or aggression. Similarly, when you get e-mails from her (which happens at least 10 times a day), you unconsciously have the same emotional reaction to her, so your body has grown accustomed to needing her to reaffirm your addiction to anger. It wants to feel the emotions it has become addicted to, and like an addict craving a drug, the body is craving the familiar chemicals. It wants to feel that familiar anger at your boss because you didn't get the promotion or it wants to feel judgment about your coworker who always wants you to cover for him. Then you start thinking about other colleagues who annoy you and other reasons to be upset with your boss. You're sitting there trying to meditate, but your body is throwing the kitchen sink at you. That's because it wants its chemical fix of familiar emotions that you normally feel throughout your waking day with your eyes open.

The instant you notice what's happening—that you are putting all of your attention on that emotion—you become aware that you're investing your energy into the past (because emotions are records of the past), so you stop and return to the present moment and you begin to disinvest your attention and energy out of the past. But then in a little while, you start to feel frustrated and angry and resentful again, and you realize what you are doing. You remember that your body is trying to feel those emotions in order to reaffirm its addiction to those chemicals, and you remember that those emotions drive your brain into high-range beta brain waves—and you stop. Every time you pause, settle your body down, and return to the present moment, you are telling your body that it is no longer the mind—*you* are the mind.

But then thoughts start drifting into your mind about the people you have to see and the places you have to go and the things you have to do later that day. You wonder if your boss has answered that e-mail yet, and you remember that you haven't returned your sister's phone call either. And today is trash day, so you remind yourself you need to put out the trash. And all of a sudden you become aware that by anticipating those future scenarios, you are investing your attention and your energy into the same known reality. So you stop, return to the present moment, and once more disinvest your energy out of that predictable, known future and make room for the unknown in your life.

Take a look at Figure 2.8. It shows that once you find yourself in that sweet spot of the generous present moment, your energy (represented by the arrows) no longer goes away from you to the past and future the way it did back in Figure 2.3. Now you are divesting your energy from that familiar past and predictable future. You are no longer firing and wiring the same circuits in the same way, and you are no longer regulating and signaling the same genes in the same way by feeling the same emotions. If you keep doing this process, you are continuously calling all that energy back to you by breaking the energetic bonds that keep you connected to your past-present reality. This happens because you are taking your attention and your energy off your outer world and placing it instead on your inner world, and you're building your own electromagnetic field surrounding your body. Now you have available energy that you can use to create something new.

TAKING YOUR ENERGY & POWER BACK

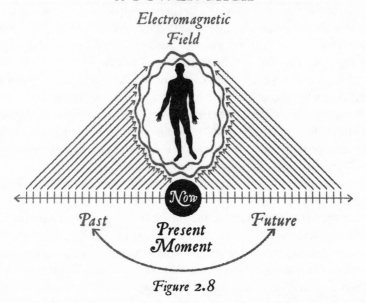

Figure 2.8

As you take your attention off your past-present reality or your predictable future reality, you are calling energy back to you and building your own electromagnetic field. Now you have available energy to heal yourself or to create a new experience in your life.

Not surprisingly, your attention eventually begins to wander again. As you continue to sit in meditation, your body becomes more annoyed and impatient because it wants to do something. After all, you've programmed it every day to get up and follow the same routine. It wants to quit meditating, open its eyes, and *see* someone. It wants to *hear* something on TV or talk to someone on the phone. It prefers to *taste* breakfast instead of sitting there doing nothing. It would like to *smell* coffee brewing, like it does every morning. And it would love to *feel* something like a hot shower before it starts the day.

The body wants to experience physical reality with its senses in order to embrace an emotion, but your goal is to create a reality from a world beyond your senses that's defined not by your *body* as the mind but by *you* as the mind. So as you become aware of the program, you keep settling your body down into the present moment. The body tries again to return to the familiar past because it wants to engage in a predictable future, but you keep settling it back down. Each time you overcome those automatic habits, your will becomes greater than your program. Every time you keep settling your body back to the present moment, like training a dog to sit, you are reconditioning your body to a new mind. Each time you become aware of your program and you labor for the present moment, you are stating that your will is greater than your program. And if you keep returning your attention (and therefore your energy) back to the present moment and you keep noticing when you are present and when you are not, sooner or later your body is going to surrender. It is this process of continuously returning to the present moment every time you become aware that you've lost it that begins to break the energetic bonds with your familiar known reality. And when you do return to the present moment, what you're actually doing is getting beyond your physical-world identity and unfolding into the quantum field (a concept I will explain in detail in the next chapter).

The hardest part of every war is the last battle. That means that when your body as the mind is raging, causing you to think that you cannot go any further, wanting you to stop and return to the world of the senses, you keep persevering. You truly step into the unknown—and sooner or later you will begin to break the emotional addiction within you. When you get beyond your guilt, your suffering, your fear, your frustration, your resentment, or your unworthiness, you are freeing your body from the chains of those habits and emotions that keep you anchored in the past—and as a result, you are liberating energy that is now coming back to you. As the body releases all of this stored emotional energy, it is no longer becoming the mind. You discover that right on the other side of your fear is courage, right on the other side of your lack is wholeness, and just beyond your doubt is knowing. When you step into the unknown and surrender your anger or hatred, you discover love and compassion. It's the same energy; it has just been stored in the body and now it's available for you to use to design a new destiny.

So when you learn to overcome yourself—or the memory of yourself and your life—you break the bonds you have with every thing, every person, every place, and every time that's keeping you connected to your past-present reality. And when you finally overcome your anger or your frustration, and you liberate energy that was trapped in the past, you call that energy back to you. As you liberate all of that creative energy that has been tied up in those survival emotions—within you and all around you—you are building your own personal energy field around your body.

In our advanced workshops, we've actually measured this effect of calling the energy back. We have experts who use very sensitive equipment called a gas discharge visualization (GDV) machine with a specially designed sensor (called a Sputnik antenna) developed by Konstantin Korotkov, Ph.D. It measures the ambient electromagnetic field in the workshop conference spaces to see how the energy changes as the workshop progresses. On the first full day of some of our advanced workshops, we sometimes see the energy in the room drop. That happens because once we start meditating and those students have to overcome themselves by breaking the energetic bonds with everyone and everything in their known reality, they are calling energy back to themselves. They're drawing energy from the greater field, and the field in the room can diminish as the participants begin to build their individual field of energy around their own bodies—and now they have available energy to use to design a new destiny. Of course, as our entire group gets beyond themselves the first day, they finally build their own light field, and as their energy keeps expanding each day, they begin to contribute to the energy in the room. As a result, we finally witness the energy in the room rise. To see what this sometimes looks like, find Graphics 1A and 1B in the color insert.

One way to increase your chances of a successful meditation is to give yourself enough time so you don't get distracted by trying to rush through the experience. When I meditate, for example, I allow for two hours. I don't have to take two hours every time, but I know myself well enough by now to realize that if I have only one hour, I'm going to tell myself there's not enough time. If I have two hours, on the other hand, I can relax, knowing I have plenty of time to find the present moment. Some days I find the sweet spot of the present moment pretty quickly, while on other days I have to work for an hour at bringing my brain and body back into the present.

I am a very busy person. Some days when I have just arrived home for three days between workshops or events, I wake up in the morning and immediately think of the three meetings I have planned that day with different staff members, mentally rehearsing what I have to talk about. Then I think about the e-mails I have to get done before I go to those meetings. Then I think about the flight I have to catch that afternoon. Then I make a mental note about the phone calls I have to make on the drive to the airport. You get the idea.

As that happens and I am thinking about the same people I have to see, the same places I have to go, the same things I have to do, all at the same time in my known familiar reality, I realize that I'm priming my brain and body to look like that future has already happened. I become conscious that my attention is in the known future, and I stop anticipating the known and turn back to the present moment. As I do that, I'm beginning to unfire and unwire those neural connections. Then I might get a little emotional and become impatient and a little frustrated thinking about something that happened yesterday. And since emotions are a record of the past and where I place my attention is where I place my energy, I become aware that I'm investing my energy in the past. Then the hormones of stress may get my brain aroused, and my body gets a bit fired up into high-range beta brain waves and I have to settle it back down into the present moment again. And as I do that I'm no longer firing and wiring the same circuits in my brain, and I'm disinvesting my energy out of the past.

And if I am aware of the same thoughts that are connected to those same familiar feelings, when I stop myself from feeling the same way, I am no longer conditioning my body into the past and I'm no longer signaling the same genes in the same ways. And if emotions are the end products of experiences in the environment, and if it's the environment that signals the gene, then when I stop feeling those same emotions, I am no longer selecting and instructing the same genes in the same ways. That not only affects the health of my body, but it also no longer primes my body to be in the same future, based on living in the past. So as I inhibit those familiar feelings, I am changing the genetic program of my body. And since the hormones of long-term stress down-regulate the expression of healthy genes and create disease, every time I am able to stop when I catch myself feeling any of those emotions that are related to stress, I am no longer conditioning my body to stay addicted to the emotions of stress.

THE SWEET SPOT OF THE
GENEROUS PRESENT MOMENT

No Familiar Past Now No Predictable Future

*The Generous
Present Moment*

Figure 2.9

When you are in the sweet spot of the generous present moment, your
familiar past and your predictable future no longer exist and now you
are ready to create new possibilities in your life.

If I do it properly—overcoming my familiar thoughts and emotions of my known past and future—then energetically, neurologically, biologically, chemically, hormonally, and genetically, that predictable future (as well as the familiar past I used to affirm it) no longer exists. If I'm no longer firing and no longer wiring those same old neural networks (by no longer thinking about those memories of the people or things at certain times and places), and I keep returning to the present moment, I am calling energy back to me. Take a look at Figure 2.9 and you can see how the familiar past and the predictable future no longer exist.

Now I'm in the sweet spot of the generous present moment, and I have available energy to create. I've built my own energy field surrounding my body. Every time I've labored—sometimes for hours—to get beyond myself and find that place called the eternal now, and I truly break through, I've always thought the same thing: *That was so worth it.*

Chapter 3

TUNING IN TO
NEW POTENTIALS
IN THE QUANTUM

Getting beyond our body, our environment, and time isn't easy—but it's worth it because once we disconnect from three-dimensional reality, we enter a whole other reality called the quantum, the realm of infinite possibility. Describing this reality is a bit challenging because it's unlike anything we are familiar with in the physical universe. The rules of Newtonian physics, the way we are used to thinking the world works, simply don't apply.

The quantum (or unified) field is an invisible field of energy and information—or you could say a field of intelligence or consciousness—that exists beyond space and time. Nothing physical or material exists there. It's beyond anything you can perceive with your senses. This unified field of energy and information is what governs all the laws of nature. Scientists have been working to quantify this process so we can more fully understand it, and they are discovering more and more all the time.

Based on my knowledge and experience, I believe there's a self-organizing intelligence that is energy, and it is observing all of the universes and galaxies into order. Sometimes people will say to me that this idea seems a bit unscientific. I always answer them with the same question: What happens after an explosion—order or disorder? Their

---

answer is always that disorder results. Then I ask: So why after the Big Bang, which was the biggest explosion ever, has so much order been created? Some intelligence must be organizing its energy and matter into form and unifying all the forces of nature to create such a masterpiece. That intelligence, that energy, is the quantum or unified field.

To give you some idea of what this field is like, imagine taking away all the people and bodies on Earth, all the animals and plants and physical objects—both natural and man-made—all the continents, the oceans, and even the earth itself. Imagine you could then take away all the planets and moons and stars in our solar system, including our sun. And then imagine taking away all the other solar systems in our galaxy, and then all the galaxies in the universe. There's no air, and there isn't even any light that you can see with your eyes. There's just absolute blackness, the void, the zero-point field. It's important to remember this because when you as a consciousness in the present moment unfold into the unified field, you will be in an infinite black space—void of anything physical.

Now imagine that not only do you not see anything here, but because you enter into this realm without a physical body, you also have no sight with which to see—nor do you have the capacity to hear, feel, smell, or taste. You have no senses here at all. The only way you can exist in the quantum is as an awareness. Or better said, the only way you can experience this realm is with your awareness—not your senses. And since consciousness is awareness, and awareness is paying attention and noticing, once you are beyond the world of the senses, when you pay attention to the energy of the quantum field, your consciousness is connecting to greater levels of frequency and information.

Yet as strange as this may sound, the quantum field is not empty. It's an infinite field filled with frequency or energy. And all frequency carries information. So think of the quantum field as being filled with infinite amounts of energy vibrating beyond the physical world of matter and beyond our senses—invisible waves of energy available for us to use in creation. What exactly can we create with all this energy swimming in an infinite sea of potentials? That's up to us because, in short, the quantum field is the state in which *all possibilities exist*. And as I just said, when we find ourselves in the quantum universe, we exist simply as *an awareness* or as *a consciousness*: specifically an awareness that is paying attention to or observing a field of infinite possibilities existing within an even greater consciousness and a greater level of energy.

As you enter this endless, vast space as an awareness, there are no bodies, no people, no objects, no places, and no time. Instead, infinite unknown possibilities exist as energy. So if you find yourself thinking about knowns in your life, you are back in the three-dimensional reality of space and time. But if you can stay in the blackness of the unknown for long enough, it will prepare you to create unknowns in your life. In the previous chapter, when I was instructing you to return to the present moment, I was referring to you stopping yourself from thinking about the predictable future or from remembering the familiar past and simply unfolding into this eternal vast space as an awareness—to no longer place your attention on anything or anyone material in this three-dimensional reality, like your body, the people in your life, the things you own, the places you go, and time itself. If you do that properly, you are nothing but awareness. That's how you get there.

Now let's back up a bit and look at how scientists came to discover the quantum universe, which happened when they began studying the subatomic world. They found that atoms, the building blocks of everything in the physical universe, are made up of a nucleus surrounded by a large field containing one or more electrons. This field is so large in comparison with the tiny electrons that it appears to be 99.999999999999 percent empty space. But as you just read, the space isn't actually empty; it's made up of a vast array of energetic frequencies that make up an invisible, interconnected field of information. So everything in our known universe, although it may appear to be solid, is actually 99.999999999999 percent energy or information.[1] In fact, most of the universe is made up of this "empty" space; matter is an infinitesimally small component in relation to the immense space of nothing physical.

Researchers soon discovered that the electrons that move around in that vast field behave in a completely unpredictable manner—they don't appear to be subject to the same laws that govern matter in our larger universe. They're here in one moment and then gone the next—and it's impossible to predict where and when the electrons will appear. That's because, as the researchers eventually discovered, the electrons exist simultaneously in an infinite number of possibilities or probabilities. It is only when an observer focuses his or her attention and looks for some "thing" material that the invisible field of energy and information collapses into a particle we know as the electron. That is called *collapsing the wave function*, or a *quantum event*. But as soon as the observer looks away, no longer observing the electron and taking his or her mind off the subatomic matter, it disappears back into energy. In other words, that particle of physical matter (the electron) can't exist until we observe it—give it our attention. And the moment we're no longer putting our attention on it, it turns back into energy (specifically an energetic frequency, which scientists call a wave) and into possibility. In this way, mind and matter are related in the quantum. (By the way, just as we, as a subjective consciousness, are observing the electron into form, there's an objective universal consciousness that is constantly observing all of us and our three-dimensional reality into order and form as well.)

So what that means for you is this: If you're viewing your life from the same level of mind every single day, anticipating a future based on your past, you are collapsing infinite fields of energy into the same patterns of information called your life. For example, if you wake up and you think, *Where's my pain?* your familiar pain soon appears because you expected it to be there.

Imagine what would happen instead if you were able to take your attention off the physical world and the environment. As you learned in the last chapter, when you take your attention off your body, you become no body— and you no longer have access to (or any use for) the senses. When you take your attention off the people in your life, you become no one—and so you no longer have an identity as a parent, a partner, a sibling, a friend, or even as a member of a profession, a religious group, a political party, or a nationality. You have no race, no gender, no sexual orientation, and no age. When you take your attention off objects and places in the physical environment, you are in no thing and no where. Finally, if you take your attention off linear time (which has a past and a future), you are in no time—you are in the present moment, in which all possibilities in the quantum field exist. Because you are no longer identifying with or connected to the physical world, you are no longer trying to affect matter with matter—you are beyond matter and beyond how you identity yourself as a body in space and time. In a very real sense, you are in the immense blackness of the unified field where nothing material exists. That's the direct effect of continuously laboring to get to the present moment that I described in the previous chapter.

The moment that happens, you unfold your attention and energy into an unknown field beyond matter where all possibilities exist—a field made up of nothing but invisible frequencies carrying information or consciousness. And just like the quantum scientists who took their attention off the electron only to find that it reverted to energy and possibility, if you were to take your attention off your life or get beyond the memory of your life, your life should turn into possibility. After all, if you focus on the known, you get the known. If you focus on the unknown, you create a possibility. The longer you can linger in that field of infinite possibilities as an awareness—aware that you are aware in this endless black space—without putting your attention on your body, on things, or on people, places, and time, the longer you invest your energy into the unknown, the more you are going to create a new experience or new possibilities in your life. It's the law.

Brain Changes

When you walk through the door to the quantum field, you can't enter as a some body. You have to enter as a no body—as only an awareness or a consciousness, a thought or a possibility, leaving behind everything else in the physical world and living only in the present moment. And as I said in the previous chapter, this process requires that you break your chemical addiction (at least temporarily) to the same emotions that used to drive your thoughts, and you stop feeling the same way so you can stop putting your attention on the three-dimensional world of matter (the particle) and instead put your attention on energy or possibility (the wave). Given all of that, you probably won't be surprised to learn that such an experience creates some pretty significant changes in your brain.

First, because you are perceiving yourself as being beyond the physical world, which means there's no outside danger to anticipate, your thinking brain—the neocortex, the seat of your conscious mind—slows down, becomes less aroused, and works in a more holistic fashion. Earlier, we talked about how living by the hormones of stress causes our brain waves to fire in a very disordered, incoherent pattern (which in turn means our bodies can't work efficiently) because we are trying to control and predict everything in our lives. We become excessively focused, shifting our attention from one person to another thing to some place at a certain time—activating the various neurological networks assigned to each one of these knowns.

Once we slip into the present moment and become aware of this infinite field of information where there is nothing physical—this eternal void—and once we are no longer analyzing or thinking about any body, any one, any thing, any place, or any time—we are no longer activating those different compartments of neural networks in our brain. And as we move our awareness from a narrow focus on matter (objects, people, places, our bodies, and time) in our external environment and instead open our focus and become aware of the vastness of this infinite blackness by putting our attention on nothing, on space, and on energy and

THE DIFFERENCE BETWEEN COHERENT & INCOHERENT BRAIN WAVES

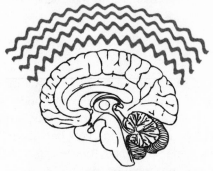

Coherent Brain Waves

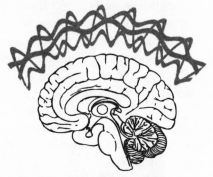

Incoherent Brain Waves

Figure 3.1

When we take our attention off the material world and begin to open our focus to the realm of the unknown and stay in the present moment, the brain works in a coherent manner. When your brain is coherent, it is working in a more holistic state and you will feel more whole.

When the brain is aroused due to the hormones of stress and we're narrowing our focus and shifting attention from people, objects, things, and places in our known outer world, the brain fires incoherently. When your brain is out of balance in this way, you will be more fragmented, unfocused, and living in more duality and separation.

information, our brain begins to change. The different compartments that were once subdivided now start to unify and move toward a coherent, whole-brain state. Different neural communities reach out and form bigger communities. They synchronize, organize, and integrate. And what *syncs in the brain begins to link in the brain.* Once your brain gets coherent, *you* get coherent. When it gets orderly, *you* get orderly, when it works well, *you* work well. In short, when it functions more holistically, you feel more whole. In other words, once you start connecting to the unified field as an awareness (or once you become more aware of it by paying attention to it), your biology becomes more whole and unified, since the unified field is by definition a unifying energy.

To more clearly see the difference between coherence and incoherence, take a look at Graphic 2 in the color insert as well as Figure 3.1. As you can see, when brain waves are coherent, they are in phase with one another; both their crests (their high points) and their troughs (their low points) match. Because coherent brain waves are more orderly, they are also more powerful—you could say they speak the same language, follow the same rhythm, dance to the same beat, and share the same frequency, so they find it easier to communicate. They're literally on the same wavelength. When brain waves are incoherent, on the other hand, the electrochemical messages or signals they are sending to different parts of the brain and body are mixed and erratic, so the body cannot then operate in a balanced, optimal state.

The second change our brains experience when we enter the quantum is that our brain waves move into a slower frequency—from beta brain waves to coherent alpha and theta brain waves. That's important because as we slow down our brain waves, our consciousness moves out of the thinking neocortex and into the midbrain (the limbic brain) and there, it connects with the autonomic nervous system—the body's subconscious operating system (See Figure 3.2). This is the part of the nervous system that is in charge of digesting food, secreting hormones, regulating body temperature, controlling blood sugar, keeping our heart beating, making antibodies that fight infections, repairing damaged cells, and myriad other functions of our bodies over which most scientists believe we have no conscious control. Basically, the autonomic nervous system keeps you alive. Its main job is to create order and homeostasis, which balances the brain and ultimately the body. The more we can linger in the present moment as no body, no one, no thing, no where, in no time, the more integrated and coherent our brain becomes. This is when the autonomic nervous system steps in and begins to heal the body—because our consciousness merges with its consciousness.

THE FLOW OF CONSCIOUSNESS
AS BRAIN WAVES CHANGE

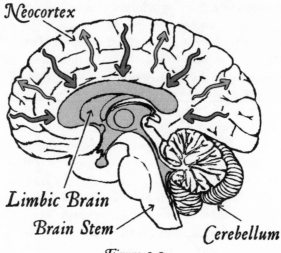

Figure 3.2

As you slow your brain waves down and become less aware of your body, your environment, and time, consciousness flows out of the neocortex and toward the limbic brain—the seat of your autonomic nervous system (represented by the dark arrows moving toward the middle of the brain).

At the same time, as these two systems intersect, the autonomic nervous system—whose job is to create balance—steps in and creates coherence in the neocortex, the seat of your thinking mind (represented by the lighter arrows moving out toward the edge of the brain).

In other words, when you are in the present moment, you get out of your own way. As you become pure consciousness, pure awareness, and change your brain waves from beta to alpha and even to theta, the autonomic nervous system—which knows how to heal your body much better than your conscious mind does—steps in and finally has an opportunity to clean house. That's what creates brain coherence. If you look at Graphics 3A–3C in the color insert, you'll see three different brain scans. Graphic 3A is a normal scan of someone in normal thinking beta brain waves. Graphic 3B was recorded while a student was performing an open focus, showing coherent synchronized alpha brain waves. Graphic 3C represents a deeper brain-wave state of coherent synchronized theta.

If in this state you are no longer reaffirming the known—your same life—and instead you keep investing your energy into the unknown (as you would invest money in a bank account), then you are able to create new, unknown possibilities in your life. Just as the material electron expands back to immaterial energy in the quantum field once scientists stop observing it, when you no longer observe your pain, your routine life, and your problems they will turn back into energy—into an infinite number of possibilities, into pure potential. Only once you are truly present in this potent place beyond this space and time—the place from where all things materially come—can you begin to create real change.

At a four-day advanced workshop in 2016 in Tacoma, Washington, we conducted a study to show how this actually works. We measured the brain waves of 117 workshop participants using electroencephalograms.[2] EEG measurements were taken before and after the workshop. We were looking to see if we could detect changes in two different measures of brain function. The first measure was how long it took the subjects to achieve a meditative state, defined by the ability to maintain an alpha brain-wave state for at least 15 seconds. We found that the participants were able to achieve meditative states 18 percent quicker by the end of the four-day workshop.

The second measure we looked at was the ratio between delta brain waves (associated with moving into deeper levels of the subconscious mind) and high-range beta brain waves (usually associated with high levels of stress). Anxious people usually have lots of high-range beta and a lower level of delta brain-wave frequencies. We were looking to see if meditation—specifically the successful practice of slipping into the quantum realm and becoming no body, no one, no thing, no where, in no time—might improve those values, and in fact it did. Participants lowered their high-range beta brain waves (indicating they were feeling less stress) by an average of 124 percent and increased their delta brain waves (indicating a greater feeling of oneness during meditation) by an average of 149 percent. The amount of high-range beta brain waves diminished relative to the amount of delta waves by 62 percent—and this all happened in only four days. Look at Figure 3.3 to see these results. You'll notice that some of the changes we measured were greater than 100 percent, indicating that these participants were able to make unusually significant improvements relatively quickly. That's pretty supernatural!

OUR TACOMA, WA, STUDY OF BRAIN CHANGES:

- *Speed of attaining stable alpha state* .... ↑ *18%*
- *Ratio of delta to beta brain waves* .... ↑ *62%*
- *High beta brain waves* .... ↓ *124%*
- *Delta brain waves* .... ↑ *149%*

Figure 3.3

This chart illustrates the changes of brain wave activity
in our advanced workshop in Tacoma, WA, in January 2016.

Changing Your Energy:
Combining a Clear Intention with Elevated Emotions

Once you're in the sweet spot of the generous present moment, where all possibilities exist in the quantum field, how do you turn one or more of those potentials, those immaterial possibilities, into reality in the three-dimensional world of matter? This requires two things: a clear intention and elevated emotion. Your clear intention is exactly what it sounds like—you have to get clear on what it is you want to create, getting as specific as possible, and describe it in detail. Let's say you want to go on a great vacation. Where is it you want to go? How do you want to get there? Who do you want to go with, or who do you want to meet when you're there? What sort of accommodations do you want to stay in? What do you want to do or see when you're there? What food do you want to eat? What do you want to drink? What kind of wardrobe will you pack? What will you buy to bring home? You get the point. Make it detailed—make it as real as you can because you are going to assign a letter as a symbol of possibility to all those conditions. As you read in the previous chapter, those thoughts, which make up your intention, are the *electrical* charge you are sending out into the unified field.

Now you have to combine that intention with an elevated emotion, such as love, gratitude, inspiration, joy, excitement, awe, or wonder, to name just a few examples. You have to tap into the feeling you anticipate you will have when you manifest your intent, and then feel the emotion *ahead of* the experience. The elevated emotion (which carries a higher energy) is the *magnetic* charge you are sending out into the field. And as you have read, when you combine the electric charge (your intention) with the magnetic charge (elevated emotion), you create an electromagnetic signature that is equal to your state of being.

Another way to describe these elevated emotions is to call them *heartfelt* emotions. Usually when we feel emotions like those I just mentioned, we notice that our heart begins to swell. That's because our energy is moving to that area, and as a result, we feel these wonderful elevated feelings that carry an intent to give, to care for, to nurture, to trust, to create, to connect, to feel safe, to serve, and to be thankful. Unlike the stress emotions (which we discussed in the previous chapter) that draw from the invisible field of energy and information that surrounds the body, these heartfelt emotions contribute to the body's energy field. In fact, the energy that is created when the heart opens makes the heart become more orderly and coherent, just like the brain, so it produces a measurable magnetic field.[3] It's this action that connects us to the unified field. And when we marry an intention (the electric charge) with that energy (the magnetic charge), we create a new electromagnetic field. Since energy is frequency and all frequency carries information, it is that elevated energy that carries your thought or intention.

Remember: Those potentials in the quantum field exist only as electromagnetic frequencies (frequencies with information) and you cannot perceive them with your senses as matter yet. It makes sense, then, that the new electromagnetic signal you broadcast would attract those electromagnetic frequencies in the field that are a vibrational match to it. In other words, when there's a vibrational match between your energy and any potential that already exists in the unified field, you begin to draw that new experience to you. *It* will find *you* as you become the vortex to your future. So in that way, you don't have to work to bring what you want to manifest to you and you don't have to go anywhere to get it (that's changing matter with matter). You have to become pure consciousness (no body, no one, no thing, no where, in no time) and change your energy—the electromagnetic signal you are broadcasting—and then you will draw that future experience right to you (changing energy into matter). You will literally tune in to the energy of a new future, and as you do so, the observer (the unified field) is observing you observe a new destiny, and it then endorses your creation. Take a glance at Figure 3.4.

ALL POSSIBILITIES IN THE QUANTUM FIELD EXIST IN THE PRESENT MOMENT AS ELECTROMAGNETIC POTENTIALS

No Familiar Past Now *No Predictable Future*

*The Generous
Present Moment*

Figure 3.4

Once we're in the present moment, there are infinite possibilities that exist in the quantum field as electromagnetic frequencies. As you combine a clear intention with elevated emotions, you are broadcasting a whole new electromagnetic signature into the field. When there's a vibrational match between your energy and the energy of that potential, the longer you're conscious of that energy, the more you will draw the experience to you.

Each letter represents a different potential: *R* is a new relationship. *J* is a new job. *P* is a problem being resolved in your life. *M* is a mystical experience. *G* is a genius mind. *H* is health. *A* is abundance. *O* is a new opportunity.

Before we go any further, I want to back up just a bit to emphasize how important elevated emotions are for this equation to work. After all, when you decide to observe a future in the quantum field that you want to manifest, if you're doing it as a victim or as someone who's suffering or feeling limited or unhappy, your energy is not going to be consistent with your intended creation and you won't be able to call that new future to yourself. That's the past. You may have a clear intention and therefore your mind may be in the future because you can imagine what you want, but if you feel any of those familiar limited emotions, your body still believes it's in the same limited past experiences.

As you learned in the previous chapter, emotion is energy in motion, and elevated emotions carry a higher frequency than survival emotions. So if you want to create change, you have to do it from a level of energy that's greater than guilt, greater than pain, greater than fear, greater than anger, greater than shame, and greater than unworthiness. In fact, any lower-vibrational energy that you are feeling cannot carry the thought of your future dream. It will carry only a level of consciousness equal to those limited emotions. Therefore, if you are going to perform something that's unlimited, you'd better feel unlimited. If you want to create freedom, you'd better feel free. And if you want to truly heal yourself, you'd better raise your energy to wholeness. The more elevated the emotion you feel, the greater the energy you broadcast and the more influence you will have on the material world of matter. And the greater your energy, the shorter the amount of time it takes for your manifestation to appear in your life.

In this process, you relax and allow a greater mind—the consciousness of the unified field—to organize an event that's right for you. You essentially get out of the way. When you are surprised by an unknown experience that seems like it came out of nowhere, that's because you created it in no where. Something appeared out of nothing because you created it in no thing. And it can happen in no time if you create it in the realm beyond linear time—that's the quantum field, where there is no time.

A French researcher named René Peoc'h, Ph.D., demonstrated the power of intention with newly hatched baby chicks.[4] When chicks hatch, they usually imprint on their mother, bonding with her and following her around. But if the mother isn't there when the chicks hatch, they'll imprint on the first moving object they encounter. For example, if a chick first sees a human, it will follow the human around in the same way.

For his study, Peoc'h built a special type of random event generator: a computerized robot that would turn randomly as it moved around an arena, going right 50 percent of the time and going left 50 percent of the time. As a control, he first recorded the robot's path in the arena with no chicks present. He found that over time, the robot covered most of the arena equally. Next, Peoc'h exposed newly hatched chicks to the robot. As expected, they imprinted on the robot as if it was their mother and followed it all over the arena. After the chicks had imprinted on the robot, he removed them from the arena and put them in a cage on one side, where they could see the robot but not move toward it.

THE PATH OF THE RANDOM
EVENT GENERATOR IN THE
EXPERIMENTS OF RENÉ PEOC'H

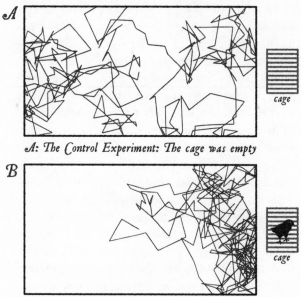

A: The Control Experiment: The cage was empty

*B: The Intention Experiment: The cage was filled with
the chicks that imprinted on the random event generator*

Figure 3.5

An illustration of the results of René Peoc'h's baby chick experiment. The box marked A represents the movement of the random event generator when the cage is empty. The box marked B shows the movement of the random event generator when the chicks were placed in the cage to the right of the arena. If the intentions of the chicks could influence the random event generator to move toward them a majority of the time, imagine what you can do in drawing your new future to you.

What happened next was astonishing—the intention of the baby chicks to be near to what they believed to be their mother (in this case, the robot) actually influenced the random movements of the robot. It no longer moved all over the arena but instead remained in the half of the arena closest to the chicks. (See Figure 3.5.) If the intentions of baby chicks can influence the movements of a computerized robot, just imagine what *you* can do in drawing your future to you.

In this place of the unified field, you're actually becoming aware of what already exists and you're bringing it to life with your attention and your intention. Here, you can be a genius. You can be abundant. You can be healthy. You can be wealthy. You can have a mystical experience. You can create a new job. You can resolve a problem in your life.

Remember: All these possibilities exist as electromagnetic potentials in the quantum field—you cannot experience them with your senses because they don't yet exist in this space and time. They exist only as frequency or energy carrying information that has to be tuned in to and observed into this space and time. And in order for you to do this properly, you are going to have to connect to that information and energy with your energy and intention.

Here's another way to look at it: If you're unified with the consciousness and the energy of every body, every one, every thing, every place, and every time within a vast unified field of potentials, then observing a potential in the quantum is just like becoming aware of your hand in the physical world—you're already connected to it; it already exists. Tuning in to the energy of your future and intentionally observing that potential in the quantum then causes infinite fields of energy to collapse into particles, called a quantum event, and that becomes an experience that can then manifest in your physical, three-dimensional world.

Then when you get up from your meditation, even though you're back in the three-dimensional world of matter, because you already experienced the elevated emotion you anticipated ahead of the experience, you have no choice but to get up feeling as if your intent has already manifested, or as if your prayer is already answered. You feel intimately connected to your new future, knowing it will show up in a way you can't predict (because if you can predict it, then it's a known). In effect, you get up as a new self—one who feels more like energy than matter.

But you must remain aware, because the moment you forget and start stressing about when it's going to happen or how it's going to happen, you'll return back to your old self—trying to predict the future based on the past. And then you'll start feeling the same old familiar emotions (with the same lower energy) that influence your same old thoughts, and you've just made the choice to stay trapped in the known. We could say that you'll disconnect from the energy of your future the moment you feel the familiar energy of the emotions of your past.

If you instead become successful at tuning in to this potential you have chosen over and over again and you get familiar with it, you will be able to tune in to it not only in meditation but also when you're in line at the bank. You'll be able to tune in to it when you're sitting in traffic. You can do it when you're shaving, when you're cooking, and when you're taking a walk. You can do it over and over again with your eyes open, just as you do when your eyes are closed in meditation. Just remember, every time you tune in to the energy of your future in the present moment, you are drawing your future to you.

And if you do it often enough, and you do it correctly, you'll change your biology from a past-present reality to a future-present reality. That is, you will change your brain neurologically from being a record of the past to becoming a map to the future. At the same time, as you teach your body emotionally what that future will feel like in the present moment, you'll recondition your body with this new elevated emotion. You'll be able to signal new genes in new ways, and you'll change your body to look like the future you chose with your clear intention has already happened. That means you begin to biologically wear your future.

Jace Goes Quantum

When my oldest son, Jace, finished graduate school, he went to work for a large company in Santa Barbara that made sophisticated cameras for the military. When he completed his contract, he moved to San Diego to work with a startup. After a while, though, he became disillusioned with the management and decided to leave the company and travel. He's a big-wave surfer, so he came up with an elaborate plan to go all over Indonesia, Australia, and New Zealand for seven months. He packed up his suitcase with the surfboards and off he went, and he had the time of his life. After six months, he called me from New Zealand and said, "Dad, listen, I have to start thinking about what I'm going to do when I get back to the real world. I want to create a new and better job than my previous ones, but I want to do it differently. I've learned a lot from taking time off."

"Okay," I responded. "There must be a potential in the quantum field that you can tune in to that's related to a new job for you. Take out a piece of paper and write the letter 'J' on it, and draw two squiggly lines around it to represent the electromagnetic field." (Hang on, because you're going to be doing something similar in the meditation at the end of this chapter.) Once he'd done that, I said, "That 'J' is a symbol that represents a possibility—your clear intention of the job you want. But now we have to get very clear on exactly what kind of job you want, so let's list what's important to you in this job. I want you to think about the conditions of what that letter 'J' for 'new job' means to you. Under that 'J,' I want you to write the word *intention* and list the specifics of what you want in your new job. You can write down anything you want except when or how it is going to happen."

"I want to be able to work from anywhere in the world," he told me, "and I want to make the same amount of money I was making at my old job—or more. I want to have independent contracts for six months to a year, and I have to *love* what I do."

"Good—anything else?" I asked.

"Yeah, I want to be my own boss and lead my own team," he said.

"Okay, now you have your clear intention," I told him. "Every time you think of this letter 'J,' can you associate the letter with the meaning you just gave it—all the specifics of what you want that you just listed?" He said he could do that.

Then I asked him to think about how he was going to feel when it happened. "Next to or below your sub-intentions that you listed to get clear on your new job," I told him, "I want you to write, 'Elevated Emotions—the Energy of My Future.' Now let's list them one by one. What are they?"

"Empowered, in love with life, free, and grateful," he told me, identifying the elevated emotions he would use to bring this job to him. All that was left was just making everything line up. Take a look at Figure 3.6 to see what Jace did.

"You have plenty of time on your hands right now. You are not doing much but surfing and relaxing on vacation," I told him. "So it should be easy for you to create your future. Will you commit to doing what it takes to broadcast a new signature into the field every day?" He agreed.

Then I reviewed with him the concept of finding the present moment and getting centered and raising his energy so that his energy could carry his intention for his future. "Just hold that symbol in your mind's eye while you radiate that energy into the space beyond your body in space," I instructed, "like tuning in to a radio station and picking up a frequency that carries information. The longer your awareness lingers in this energy or the longer you are conscious of the energy of your future, the more likely you will be to call the experience to you. So just tune in to the energy of your future every day. And remember, whatever you broadcast into the unified field is your experiment with destiny. When there is a vibrational match between your energy and the energy of this potential, it will find you. So, Jace, can you stay there?"

"Yeah," he replied.

CLEAR INTENTION + ELEVATED
EMOTIONS = A NEW ENERGY

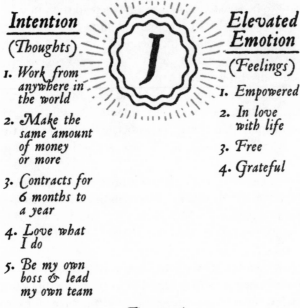

Intention

(*Thoughts*)

1. Work from anywhere in the world

2. Make the same amount of money or more

3. Contracts for 6 months to a year

4. Love what I do

5. Be my own boss & lead my own team

Elevated Emotion

(*Feelings*)

1. Empowered

2. In love with life

3. Free

4. Grateful

Figure 3.6

This is how my son Jace created his new job. *J* is a symbol that represents a potential new experience. On the left side, under *Intention*, he assigned specific conditions of the type of job he would like. On the right side, under *Elevated Emotion*, he assigned specific emotions he would feel when the experience happened. By combining these two elements, he changed his energy every day to draw his new job to him.

"And then, once you've been in that new state of being for some time, I want you to think about what you're going to do in your new job," I continued. "What choices will you make? What things will you do? What experiences await you and how will they feel? I want you to live in that future reality in the present moment. Simply remember your future from that new state of being." Just as people tend to obsess about the worst thing that could happen to them in their lives every day, I was instead asking my son to obsess about some of the greatest things that could happen when his new job found him. "Think about all the time you will have to surf, the traveling you can continue to do, the team of people you will work with, their strengths, and the money you can save for a new house and a new car," I encouraged him. "Have *fun* with those ideas each day." Just like the piano players and the muscle exercisers that you read about in the last chapter, Jace was about to prime his brain and body to look as if the future he wanted had already occurred.

"And since where you place your attention is where you place your energy," I continued, "I want you to invest your attention and your energy into that new future. And just as your body follows your mind to the shower every morning—to a known—if you keep doing this process, your body is going to follow your mind to an unknown." Jace agreed to do the meditation every day.

One month later he returned, and the moment he landed in Los Angeles, he texted me and asked, "Hey, Dad, I'm in the U.S. again. Can we talk?"

Uh-oh, I thought. *Here we go.* So I called him, and I asked how things were going.

"Great," Jace said. "But I kinda ran out of money. I don't know what I'm going to do."

Now the father in me wanted to say, "Don't worry, son. I'll spot you some money until you get back on your feet," but the teacher in me prevailed and responded, "That's so cool, because now you're really going to have to create. Now you're in the unknown. Let me know how it goes." And I hung up. I could feel his discomfort, but I know my son and I knew he would get focused and do the work.

Since he was really feeling the heat now, Jace had to seriously step up his game. He drove to Santa Barbara to see his college roommates, and a bunch of them went snowboarding for four days—just as they do together every year. When the four-day weekend was over, he stopped back in Santa Barbara before coming home, and he happened to walk into a surf shop. All of a sudden he saw the top surfboard fin designer in the world, who also just happened to be there.

They started talking, and before long the designer told Jace, "I'm looking for an engineer to design surfboard fins. We are going to revolutionize the industry together. I need him for six months to a year, and he can run his own show—do whatever he wants. All I care about is ending up with a high-quality product."

You know how this story ends. Jace got the job, with a one-year contract that he can renew at any time. He makes more money now than he did in his other job. He loves his new career because of his passion for surfing. Sometimes he texts me and says, "I can't believe they pay me to show up and do this." He's his own boss, he can work from wherever he wants to, and he gets to go surfing to try out all the fins. He's in love with life. He didn't have to send a résumé, he didn't have to make a phone call or write an e-mail, and he didn't have to go anywhere to interview or fill out an application. The experience *found him.*

When we become no body, no one, no thing, no where, in no time, we are taking our attention off all the distractions in our outer world that keep us from being present with the unified field of intelligence that is within us and all around us. We are turning inward and being present with a consciousness that is always present with us. The moment we line up with that omnipresent consciousness, as if we were looking directly in a mirror, it looks back at us. And it can finally reflect what we show it that we want. The longer we linger in this place of nothing material and invest our attention and energy into it, the closer we move to the unified field. And when we are at the altar of infinite potentials, when we change our energy, we change our lives.

As we move toward it and trust in the unknown—without returning our awareness to the material world of the senses in three-dimensional reality—we experience more oneness and wholeness within. That process begins to fulfill our lack, our separation, our duality, our disease, and our fractured personalities. Our biology becomes more whole as *we* become more whole.

After all, when we are whole, there simply is no lack. Nothing can be missing. At that point, we are simply observing what already exists in the quantum field of all possibilities or potentials and bringing it to life with our attention and our energy.

So now I have to ask you: What experience is out there in the quantum field waiting to find *you*?

Preparing to Tune In

This meditation requires a little advance preparation. First, I want you to think about a potential experience you want to have. Remember that just like the electron before it collapses into matter, the experience already exists as an energy or a frequency in the quantum field. This is the energy that you're about to tune in to. Some of our students have lowered their cholesterol levels just by tuning in to a potential. They've lowered their cancer markers. They've made tumors disappear. They've also created great new jobs, all-expenses-paid vacations, new healthy relationships, more money, profoundly mystical experiences, and even winning lottery tickets. Believe me, my team and I have seen it all. So go ahead, step into the unknown!

Once you have the new experience you want to create, assign a capital letter to it and then write that letter down on a piece of paper. Think of the letter as a symbol that represents that specific possibility in your life. Actually putting it on paper instead of only thinking about it is important because the act of writing it down solidifies that you want it. Then draw two squiggly circular lines around the letter to represent the electromagnetic field you need to generate around your body to match that potential in the quantum.

Now assign some meaning to that letter so you can get even clearer about your intention. Think of some specific refinements of what you want and list at least four of them. (The only thing I don't want you to consider including is any mention of a time frame.) For example, if your intention is a great job, your list might look like this:

- Making $50,000 a year more than I'm making now
- Managing my own team of awesome professionals
- Traveling all over the world on a generous expense account
- Having exceptional health benefits and great stock options
- Making a difference in the world

Now on that same piece of paper, write down the emotions you will feel when that imagined potential happens. You might write:

- Empowered
- Unlimited
- Grateful
- Free
- In awe
- In love with life
- Joyful
- Worthy

Whatever it is for you, write it down. And if you think you won't know how it's going to feel because you haven't experienced it yet, then try gratitude—that works really well. Gratitude is a powerful emotion to use for manifesting because normally we feel gratitude after we receive something. So the emotional signature of gratitude means it has already happened. When you are thankful or you feel appreciation, you are in the ultimate state to receive. When you embrace gratitude, your body as the unconscious mind will begin to believe it is in that future reality in the present moment.

These various emotions you just listed are the energy that is going to carry your intent. This is not an intellectual process—it's a visceral one. You have to really *feel* those emotions. You have to teach your body emotionally what that future is going to feel like before it happens—and you have to do that in the present moment.

Now you're ready for the meditation. You can purchase the *Tuning In to New Potentials* CD or MP3 download from **drjoedispenza.com** and follow along as I guide you, or you can choose to do the meditation on your own.

Tuning In to New Potentials Meditation

Start by resting your attention in different parts of your body as well as the space around those parts of your body. (You will learn more about doing this and why it's important in the next chapter, but for now, it's enough to know that focusing on the space around your body helps change your brain waves, moving you from an incoherent beta brain-wave pattern to a coherent alpha and theta brain-wave pattern). Become aware of the infinite, vast space way out behind your eyes in this eternal black space, the space in the center of your head, the space between the back of your throat and the back of your head, and then beyond your head in space. Then move to becoming aware of the space in the center of your throat, the space beyond your throat and around your neck, the space in the center of your chest, the space around your body, the space behind your navel, and finally the space around your hips in this endless black void. With each of these, take your time and feel it, become aware of it, and stay present with it.

Become aware of the vastness of space that the room you're in occupies in space, and then extend your awareness to the vastness of space beyond the room in space, and finally to the vastness of space that all of space occupies in space.

Now it's time to take your attention off your body, the environment, and time and to become no body, no one, no thing, no where, in no time, to become pure consciousness, to unfold as an awareness into this infinite black space and endless field where all possibilities exist. If you get distracted, simply return to the present moment (as we discussed in the previous chapter). Keep unfolding into this immaterial space by continuously reinvesting your attention into it.

Think about the potential that already exists in the quantum field that you want to tune in to by remembering your letter. Sense the energy of that future potential—within you and all around you—and tune in to your future. When you do this, you will be moving into a new state of being, broadcasting a whole new electromagnetic signature into the field. When there's a vibrational match between your energy and that potential, the new event is going to find you—you don't have to make anything happen. I want to be clear here. It might take more than a few meditations for your future opportunity to unfold. It could happen in a week, a month, or even longer. The key is to keep doing it until it occurs.

Once you are in a new state of being, broadcasting a new electromagnetic signature, now remember your future before it happens and begin to mentally rehearse what that future will be like by living in that future. Make it as real as possible, calling up those elevated emotions you listed so you can teach your body emotionally what that future feels like.

Surrender your creation to a greater mind, planting a seed in the infinite field of possibilities—and just let it go! Finally, bless your body with a new mind. Bless your life, bless your challenges, bless your soul, bless your past, and bless your future. Bless the divine in you, and open your heart and give thanks for a new life before it's made manifest.

Slowly bring your awareness back to the room and when you're ready, open your eyes. Get up from your meditation as though your future has already happened—and let the synchronicities and new possibilities *find you.*

Chapter 4

BLESSING OF THE
ENERGY CENTERS

We've been talking a lot about light and information or energy and consciousness. Now it's time to go a little deeper into those concepts to help explain how the next meditation works. As you already understand, everything in our known universe is made up of or emits either light and information or energy and consciousness—which are other ways of describing electromagnetic energy. In fact, these elements are so intimately combined that it's impossible to separate them. Look around you. Even if you don't see anything other than matter—objects, things, people, or places—there's also a sea of infinite invisible frequencies that are carrying encoded information. That means not only that your body is made up of light and information, of energy and consciousness, but also that you as a conscious being with a body are made of gravitationally organized light packed with information that is continuously sending and receiving various frequencies, all carrying different signals, just like a radio or a cell phone.

All frequency, of course, carries information. Think about radio waves for a moment. There are radio waves moving through the room you're sitting in right now. If you turned a radio on, you could tune it to a specific wavelength or signal, and then a little transducer in the radio would pick up that signal and turn it into sound that you could hear and understand as your favorite song, the news, or even a commercial. Just because you can't see the radio waves in the air doesn't mean they aren't there, carrying distinct information on a specific frequency all the time. If you change the frequency a small degree and tune in to another station, a different message will be carried on that wavelength.

Take a look at Figure 4.1A, which shows the entire light spectrum and demonstrates all the electromagnetic frequencies that we know of. The visible light spectrum—where we perceive the various array of colors present in this world we live in—makes up less than 1 percent of all the frequencies of light that exist. That means that the majority of frequencies are beyond our perception, and therefore most of our known reality in this universe cannot be experienced by our senses. So aside from our ability to perceive light being absorbed or reflected off objects and things, the truth is that we are able to perceive only a very small spectrum of reality. There's a lot of other information available to us besides what we can see with our physical eyes. Remember that when I refer to *light*, I am talking about *all* light, which includes the entire spectrum of electromagnetic frequencies—seen and unseen—and not just visible light.

THE LIGHT SPECTRUM OF ELECTROMAGNETIC FREQUENCIES

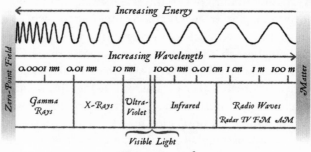

Figure 4.1A

This figure represents the entire spectrum of electromagnetic frequencies from the zero-point field slowing down in frequency all the way to matter. As energy increases (or as the frequency speeds up), the wavelengths decrease. As energy decreases (or as the frequency slows down), wavelengths increase. In the middle, labeled *visible light*, is the only spectrum of reality we perceive.

For example, even though we don't see x-rays, they still exist. We know this because we as human beings have the ability to create x-rays, and we can also measure them. In fact, an infinite number of frequencies exists within the spectrum of x-ray light. X-rays are a faster frequency than the visible light we see and therefore have more energy (because, again, the faster a frequency is, the higher its energy). Matter by itself is the densest of frequencies because it's the slowest and the most condensed form of light and information.

FREQUENCY & WAVELENGTH

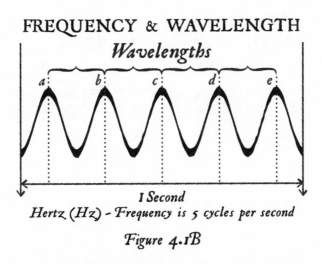

Wavelengths

I Second

Hertz (Hz) - Frequency is 5 cycles per second

Figure 4.1B

Here we see the relationship between frequency and wavelength. The number of cycles in a complete wave—represented between letters *a* and *b*, *b* and *c*, and so on—is one wavelength. The space between the two vertical arrows pointing down represents a time interval of one second. In this case, since there are five complete waves within the span of one second, we would say that the frequency is five cycles per second, or 5 Hz.

Take a look at Figure 4.1B. Move your eyes along the horizontal line running through the waves' hills and valleys, starting at the letter A and then moving to B and then to C. Each time you arrive at the next letter, you have just traveled a full cycle, what is referred to as a wavelength. So the distance between letters A and B is one wavelength. The frequency of a wave refers to the number of wavelengths or cycles produced in one second, which is measured in hertz (Hz). Therefore, the faster the frequency of a wave, the shorter the wavelength. The converse is also true— the slower the frequency, the longer the wavelength (Figure 4.1C). For example, light in the infrared frequency band has a slower frequency than light in the ultraviolet light frequency band, so the wavelengths for infrared light are longer, and the wavelengths for ultraviolet light are shorter. Here's another example, this time from within the visible light spectrum: The color red has a slower frequency (450 cycles/second) than the color blue (about 650 cycles/second). Therefore, the wavelength of red is longer than the wavelength of blue.

THE RELATIONSHIP BETWEEN FREQUENCY & WAVELENGTH

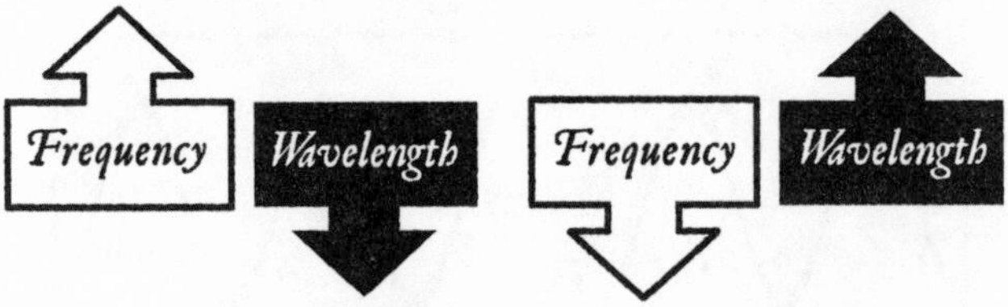

Figure 4.1C

As frequency increases, wavelengths get shorter.
As frequency decreases, wavelengths get longer.

Throughout history, people have made several different attempts to photograph and measure fields of light. One prominent example is Kirlian photography, discovered in 1939 by Russian electrician and amateur inventor Semyon Davidovitch Kirlian. With this technique, Kirlian was able to capture images of the electricomagnetic field that surrounds both living and nonliving objects. He found that by putting a sheet of photographic film on a metal plate, placing an object on top of the film, and applying a high-voltage current to the metal plate, an image of the electrical discharge between the object and the plate would show up on the film, appearing like a glowing silhouette of light around whatever was being photographed.

In one of Kirlian's many experiments, he reportedly photographed two seemingly identical leaves, one from a healthy plant and one from a diseased plant. The photograph of the leaf from the healthy plant showed a strong light field, while the other showed a much weaker glow, leading Kirlian to believe that his photographic technique might be a means of assessing health. While scientists today debate the usefulness of Kirlian photography as a diagnostic tool, research on the technique continues.

A more recent development along these lines comes from German bio-physicist Fritz-Albert Popp, Ph.D., who has spent more than three decades studying biophotons, tiny low-intensity light particles that are stored within and emitted by all living things. In 1996, Popp founded the International Institute of Biophysics (IIB), a network of research laboratories from more than a dozen countries around the world that study biophotons. Popp and his fellow IIB researchers believe that the information contained in these light particles, which are stored in DNA, communicates extremely effectively with the cells of the organism, thus playing a vital role in regulating the organism's function.[1] These biophotons can be detected by an extremely sensitive camera designed to measure their emissions: the stronger the emissions as well as the more intense and coherent the light field, the greater communication between cells and the healthier the organism.

In order to sustain life and health, our cells communicate with each other by exchanging vital information transmitted on different frequencies of light. Popp discovered that the reverse is also true: When a cell does not emit enough organized and coherent electromagnetic energy, that cell becomes unhealthy; it's not able to share information with other cells very well, and without that exchange, it doesn't have what it needs. So the mechanistic version of the inner workings of the cell that we learned in high school biology is dated. Charged molecules attracting and repelling each other are not responsible for the way cells work. Instead, the electromagnetic energy that the cell emits and receives is the life force that governs those molecules. That's a vitalistic view that supports the truth of who we are.

What all this means, in effect, is that we are quite literally beings of light, each radiating a very vital life force and expressing an actual light field around our bodies—the totality of each cell expressing and contributing to a vital field of light that carries a message. It would be safe to say, then, that the more we define reality with our senses and live our lives as materialists focusing primarily on the physical (and therefore the more we turn on the stress response), the more we may be missing out on valuable information. That's because the more we keep narrowing our focus on the matter, objects, things, people, and places in our outer world, the less able we are to sense those other frequencies that aren't visible to the naked eye. And if we're unaware of them, they do not exist to us.

As you have already read and, I hope, begun to experience yourself with the meditation in the previous chapter, it's possible for you to tune in to certain frequencies around you, just like you can tune a radio dial to 107.3. When you close your eyes and sit still and eliminate the external environment (the static that normally keeps you from sensing those other frequencies), you can train yourself to get a clear signal and receive information from it. When you do this repeatedly, you tune in to a new level of light and information that you can use to influence or affect matter. And when you do that, your body experiences syntropy (enhanced order) instead of entropy (disorder, physical breakdown, and chaos). Once you can quiet down your analytical, thinking mind and more readily tune in to this more orderly information, your body automatically responds by processing this new stream of consciousness and energy, thereby becoming more efficient, coherent, and healthy.

Convergent and Divergent Focus

At the beginning of the meditation in the last chapter, I asked you to rest your attention in different parts of your body as well as *in the space around* different parts of it. Now I want to dive deeper into why I ask you to do that in almost all my meditations. When you practice this, you sharpen your ability to master two different ways your brain can focus: using convergent focus and divergent focus.

Convergent focus is a single-minded or narrow focus on an object— anything having matter. That's the kind of focus you're displaying in my meditations when you rest your attention in a specific place in your body. It's the same kind of focus you use when you pay attention to objects in your environment. Typically, when you go to pick up a glass, call or text somebody, or tie your shoe, you use narrow focus. The majority of the time that you're in narrow focus, you're focusing on objects or things (matter) and people or places in the outer world—mostly things that have three dimensions.

Remember our previous discussion about living in survival mode with the hormones of stress continually pumping through our bodies, helping us stay at the ready to fight or flee? When we're in that state, we narrow our focus *even further* because paying very close attention to the external, physical world becomes very important. In effect, we become materialists, defining reality with our senses. The different compartments of the brain that normally work in community then begin to subdivide, no longer communicating effectively with each other—and no longer working together seamlessly in a state of coherence (orderliness). Now they're in an incoherent state, sending incoherent messages down the spinal cord to various parts of the body. We've seen this over and over again when we do brain scans to measure brain waves.

As I've said before, when your brain is incoherent, you are incoherent. And when your brain is not working right, you are not working right. It's as though instead of playing a beautiful symphony, your brain and body are producing a cacophony. And because of this unbalanced, incoherent state, you are left trying to control or force outcomes in your life. You try to predict a future that's based on the past, and you do that in part by paying more attention to your outer world of objects and things than to your inner world of thoughts and feelings. In other words, you stay in narrow, convergent focus—obsessively thinking about the same things over and over again. That's what stress does. It influences you to obsess about your problems so you can be prepared for the future worst-case scenario based on your past memories. Being prepared for the worst outcome gives you a better chance of survival because no matter what happens, you are prepared for it.

However, when you change your attention from using this narrow focus to adopting a more open and broad focus, as you will do in this meditation, you can become aware of the space and so the light and energy around your body in space. This is called a divergent focus. You go from focusing on *some thing* to focusing on *no thing*—on the wave (energy) instead of the particle (matter). Reality is both the particle *and* the wave; it's both matter *and* energy. So when you practice using narrow focus to rest your attention in different parts of the body—acknowledging the particle—and then you open your focus so that you sense the space around these parts of your body in space, acknowledging the wave, your brain changes into a more coherent, balanced state.

Entering the Subconscious Mind

In the 1970s, Les Fehmi, Ph.D., director of the Princeton Biofeedback Centre in Princeton, New Jersey, discovered how this shift in attention from narrow to open focus changes brain waves. Fehmi, a pioneer in attention and biofeedback, was trying to find a method for teaching people how to move their brain waves from beta (conscious thought) to alpha (relaxed and creative). The most effective way to make the shift, he discovered, was by directing people to become aware of space or nothingness—adopting what he called open focus.[2] The Buddhist tradition has been using this method of meditation for thousands of years. As you open your focus and sense information instead of matter, your brain waves slow down from beta to alpha. This makes sense because when you are sensing and feeling, you are not thinking.

As your thinking brain—the neocortex—slows down, you are able to get beyond the analytical mind (also called the critical mind), which separates the conscious mind from the subconscious mind (see Figure 4.2). Now you're able to move into the seat of your body's operating system—the autonomic nervous system, which you read about in the previous chapter—and now your brain can work in a more holistic fashion.

GETTING BEYOND THE ANALYTICAL MIND

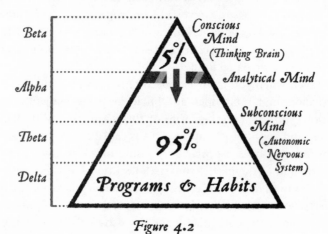

Figure 4.2

One of the main purposes of meditation is to move beyond the analytical mind. What separates the conscious mind from the subconscious mind *is* the analytical mind. As you slow your brain waves down, you move out of your conscious mind and thinking brain, past the analytical mind, into the operating system of the subconscious mind, where all those automatic programs and unconscious habits exist.

As you do the Blessing of the Energy Centers meditation I will teach you later on in this chapter, you'll place your attention in each of your body's energy centers (also referred to as *chakras*—meaning *wheels*—in ancient East Indian Vedic texts), and then you'll open your focus. Because where you place your attention is where you place your energy, as you place your attention in each center and your energy moves to it, each one of these individual centers begins to become activated.

It's no mystery that if you have a sexual fantasy in your mind and brain, for example, as energy moves into that center of your body it's going to become activated in a very specific way, and when it does, organs, tissues, chemicals, hormones, and nervous tissue are all going to respond. If you're hungry and you're thinking about what you're going to eat, it's no coincidence that your digestive juices turn on, you salivate, and your body prepares for the experience of eating dinner because energy is activating that area. If you're thinking about telling your boss off or arguing with your daughter, you secrete adrenaline ahead of the actual confrontation. In each of these cases, the thought you're thinking becomes the experience. I will explain this in more detail in the next section when we talk about the individual energy centers, but for now it's enough to know that this happens because each center produces its own chemical hormonal expression, which then activates the organs, tissues, and cells in each area.

So imagine what would begin to happen if you were able to slow your brain waves down in a meditation and get into the operating system of each of these energy centers by placing your attention in the space around each center, opening your focus. Each of these centers would then become more orderly and more coherent, which would signal neurons to create a new level of mind and activate the organs, tissues, and cells of that region, producing each center's own hormones and chemical messengers. And if you did this repeatedly, over time you would begin to effect real, physical change.

In the community of students who do this work, people have healed themselves of chronic bladder infections, prostate problems, impotence, diverticulitis, Crohn's disease, food allergies and sensitivities like celiac disease, ovarian tumors, elevated liver enzymes, acid reflux, heart palpitations, arrhythmias, asthma, lung conditions, back problems, thyroid conditions, throat cancer, neck pain, chronic migraine, headaches, brain tumors—and more. We've seen all kinds of improvements in people from doing this particular meditation, sometimes even after the very first time they do it. Those dramatic healings were possible because students were able to epigenetically change the expression of their DNA, switching some of their genes on and others off, changing how those genes express proteins in their physical bodies (as you learned in Chapter 2).

How Your Body's Energy Centers Work

We're about to take a closer look at each of the body's energy centers, but first I want to explain a bit more about how they work. Think of each of them as an individual center of information. Each has its own specific energy that carries a corresponding level of consciousness, its own emission of light expressing very specific information, or its own frequency carrying a certain message. Each also has its own individual glands, its own unique hormones, its own chemistry, and its own individual plexus of neurons. Think of these individual clusters of neurological networks as mini-brains. And if each one of those centers has its own individual brain, then each also has its own individual mind. (Take a look at Figure 4.3, which lists the location of each center as well as the anatomy and physiology that are associated with each.)

THE ENERGY CENTERS

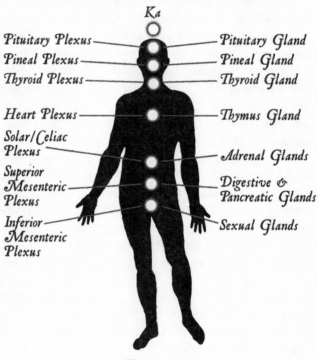

Figure 4.3

Each energy center of your body has its own biological makeup. They have their own glands, hormones, chemicals, and individual mini-brains (a plexus of neurons) and therefore their own mind.

As you learned in the second chapter, when consciousness activates neurologic tissue, it creates mind. Mind is the brain in action, so if each one of these energy centers has a plexus of neurons, then each has its own individual mind—or better said, each center has a mind of its own. What activates the mind is energy with a directive and intention, a conscious intent. When each of these centers becomes activated, it in turn activates hormones, tissues, chemicals, and cellular functions—and it emits energy.

For example, when your first center (the seat of your reproductive glands) is activated with energy, its mind has a very specific agenda and intention. When you as a conscious being have a thought or a fantasy—that's consciousness, by the way, acting on neurological tissue—the next thing you know, your body is physiologically changing and therefore so is your energy. Your body secretes chemicals and hormones from those corresponding glands to emotionally prepare you for intercourse. You have more energy in that center now, and it's releasing its own specific frequency carrying an intentional message.

That energy, carrying the conscious intention, is activating that reproductive center, and the mind in the brain is influencing the mind in the body at the level of its individual nerve plexus. This mind located in that specific area of the body, through this mini-brain, operates on the subconscious level through the autonomic nervous system. It's beyond your conscious control. We could say that the body is now following the mind as the mini-brain in that energy center activates the related glands, which in turn activate corresponding hormones that signal the appropriate chemicals to change the body's emotional state and physiology. And then you are emitting a very clear energy carrying a specific directive out of that center. We have all felt that kind of energy from a very sexual person. Once the energy is moving through that neurological tissue or plexus of neurons, it creates mind at that level, so when it's activated, that center has a mind of its own.

The second center also has its own mind. And when we activate its mini-brain and thus its mind, we trust our gut—and the same sequence of events happens in this center as we just saw in the first energy center, but with different corresponding neurocircuitry, hormones, chemicals, emotions, energy, and information. In fact, this area has been called *the second brain* because of the hundreds of millions of neurons and neural connections here (more than exist in either the spinal cord or in the peripheral nervous system). In fact, 95 percent of the feel-good hormone serotonin in your body is found not in your brain but in your bowels.[3]

So trusting our gut literally means trusting our instincts. It's almost as if our body and this center's brain can override our analytical, rational thinking brain and mind.

How about your heart center? What happens when you lead with your heart? Like the first two centers, this fourth center, located in the middle of the chest, has its own frequency, its own hormones, its own chemicals, its own emotions, and its own mini-brain that draws from a field of energy and information that surrounds it. And when you lead with your heart you tend to be more caring, kind, inspired, selfless, compassionate, giving, grateful, trusting, and patient. When this mini-brain gets that information, it sends instructions and messages to the organs and tissues that are located in that part of the body and you emit loving energy from this specific center of information.

Now let's look at each of these energy centers in more detail. Some of the centers will overlap a bit in function, but for the most part, if you know even just a little about the body, they are pretty self-explanatory. You can review Figure 4.3 again if you need to.

Getting Better Acquainted with the Energy Centers

The *first energy center* governs the region of your sex organs, including your perineum, your pelvic floor, the glands that are connected to your vagina or penis, your prostate if you're a man, your bladder, your lower bowel, and your anus. This energy center has to do with reproduction and procreation, elimination, sexuality, and sexual identity. The hormones estrogen and progesterone in women and testosterone in men are correlated with this center. This energy center is also associated with the inferior mesenteric nerve plexus.

A tremendous amount of creative energy exists in this first center. Think about the amount of energy you use to make life and create a baby. When this center is in balance, your creative energy flows easily and you are also grounded in your sexual identity.

The *second energy center* is behind and slightly below your navel. It governs the ovaries, uterus, colon, pancreas, and lower back. It has to do with consumption, digestion, elimination, and the breaking down of food into energy—including digestive enzymes and juices as well as the enzymes and hormones that balance your blood sugar levels. This center is also connected to the superior mesenteric nerve plexus.

This energy center is also related to social networks and structures, relationships, support systems, family, cultures, and interpersonal relationships. Think about it as the center for holding on or letting go—consuming or eliminating. When this center is in balance, you feel safe and secure both in your environment and in the world.

The *third energy center* is located in the pit of your gut. It governs the stomach, small intestine, spleen, liver, gall bladder, adrenal glands, and kidneys. The associated hormones include adrenaline and cortisol, the kidney hormones, and chemicals like renin and angiotensin, erythropoietin, and all the liver enzymes, as well as the stomach enzymes like pepsin, trypsin, chymotrypsin, and hydrochloric acid. This energy center is also related to the solar plexus, which is also called the celiac plexus.

This center is associated with our will, power, self-importance, control, drive, aggression, and dominance. It is the center of competitive action and of personal power, self-esteem, and directed intention. When the third center is in balance, you use your will and your drive to overcome your environment and the conditions in your life. Unlike the second center, this center becomes naturally activated when you perceive that your environment is not safe or is unpredictable, so you must protect and take care of your tribe and yourself. The third center is also active when you want something and you need to use your body to get it.

The *fourth energy center* is located in the space behind your breastbone. It governs the heart, lungs, and thymus gland (the body's main immunity gland, known as the "fountain of youth"). The hormones associated with this center include growth hormone and oxytocin as well as a cascade of 1,400 different chemicals that stimulate the immune system's health via the thymus gland (responsible for growth, repair, and regeneration of the body). The nerve plexus this center governs is the heart plexus.[4]

The first three centers are all about survival and reflect our animal nature or our humanity. But in this fourth energy center, we are moving from being self*ish* to being self*less*. This center is associated with the emotions of love and caring, nurturing, compassion, gratitude, thankfulness, appreciation, kindness, inspiration, selflessness, wholeness, and trust. It is where our divinity originates; it is the seat of the soul. When the fourth center is in balance, we care about others and we want to work in cooperation for the greatest good of the community. We feel a genuine love for life. We feel whole, and we are satisfied with who we are.

The *fifth energy center* is located in the center of your throat. It governs the thyroid, parathyroid, the salivary glands, and tissues of the neck.

The hormones associated with this center include the thyroid hormones T3 and T4 (thyroxine), the parathyroid chemicals that govern the body's metabolism, and circulating calcium levels. The nerve plexus this center governs is the thyroid plexus.

This center is associated with expressing the love you felt in the fourth center, as well as speaking your truth and personally empowering your reality through language and sound. When the fifth center is balanced, you voice your present truth, which includes expressing your love. You feel so pleased with yourself and with life that you just have to share your thoughts and feelings.

The *sixth energy center* is located in the space between the back of your throat and the back of your head (if that's too complicated to picture, just think of it as the center of your brain slightly toward the back of your head). It governs the pineal gland, which is a sacred gland. Some people call the pineal the third eye, but I call it the first eye. It's associated with the door to higher dimensions and shifting your perception so you can see beyond the veil or see reality in a nonlinear way.

When this center is opened, it's like a radio antenna you can use to tune in to higher frequencies beyond the five senses. This is where the alchemist in you awakens. I devote a whole chapter to the pineal gland later in the book, but for now, know that the pineal gland secretes hormones like serotonin and melatonin (as well as some other wonderful metabolites), which are responsible for your circadian rhythms of feeling awake in response to visible light during the day and sleepy in response to being in darkness at night. In fact, the pineal gland is sensitive to all electromagnetic frequencies besides visible light and can produce corresponding chemical derivatives of melatonin that change your view of reality. When this gland is in balance, your brain works in a clear manner. You are lucid, more conscious of both your inner world and your outer world, seeing and perceiving more each day.

The *seventh energy center* is located in the center of your head and includes the pituitary gland. This gland has been called the master gland because it governs and creates harmony in a downward cascade from this center of your brain to your pineal gland, your thyroid gland, your thymus gland, your adrenal glands, your pancreatic gland, and all the way to your sexual glands. This is the center of the body where you experience your greatest expression of divinity. This is where your divinity, your highest level of consciousness, originates. When this gland is in balance, you are in harmony with all things.

The *eighth energy center* is located about 16 inches (40 centimeters) above the head, so it is the only energy center that is not associated with an area of the physical body. The Egyptians called it the *Ka*. It represents your connection to the cosmos, to the universe, to the whole. When this center becomes activated, you feel worthy to receive—and that opens you up to insights, epiphanies, deep understandings, and creative downloads of frequency and information that come into your physical body and brain not from memories stored in your nervous system but from the cosmos, the universe, the unified field, or whatever you want to call that power that is greater than our individual selves. We access the data and memory of the quantum field through this center.

Evolving Our Energy

Now that I have described each of these energy centers in detail, let's take a more dynamic look at how they can work. Certainly, our bodies are designed to use energy in each of the centers as I have outlined. But what happens when we do more with our energy than just survive? What happens when instead of releasing all our energy outward (to procreate, to digest food, to run from danger, and so on), we begin to consistently evolve some of that energy upward from one center to the next, increasing its frequency as it ascends?

Here's what that would look like: We start out by channeling our creative energy from the first center. When we feel safe and secure enough to create, that creative energy evolves, ascending and flowing into the second center. When we have to master some limitation or overcome some condition in our environment, we are able to put the creative energy to good use, and then it will flow to the third center—the seat of our will and power.

When we successfully transcend the adversity in our life, which has challenged us to grow and overcome, we have the opportunity to feel more whole, more free, and more satisfied and we're then able to feel genuine love for self and others as the energy flows through and activates the fourth center. When that happens, we then want to express our present truth—what we've learned or the love or wholeness we feel—and that allows the energy to then move through and turn on our fifth center. After this, when the evolution of energy activates the sixth center, dormant areas of the brain open so that the veil of illusion is lifted and we perceive a broader spectrum of reality than we ever saw before. We then begin to feel enlightened, the body moves more into harmony and balance, and our external environment (including the natural world surrounding us) also moves into more harmony and balance as the energy ascends in activating the seventh center. Once we feel that enlightened energy, we begin to truly feel worthy and the energy can finally rise to activate the eighth center, where we receive the fruits of our efforts—visions, dreams, insights, manifestations, and knowingness that come not from anywhere within our minds and bodies as memories but from a greater power in and around us. This continuous flow of evolving energy from our first center to our eighth center is illustrated in Figure 4.4A.

THE FLOW OF CREATIVE ENERGY IN THE BODY

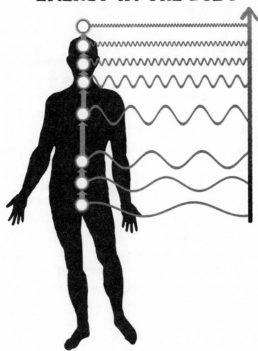

Figure 4.4A

As we evolve our creative energy, it can be channeled from the first center all the way up to the brain and beyond. Each energy center has its own individual frequency that carries its own individual intent.

That's the kind of personal evolution that happens when the energy flows consistently—the ideal. What all too often happens, however, is that the events of our lives and the way we react to them cause our energy to get stuck so that it doesn't flow in this magnificent pattern I just outlined. The places in your body where the energy gets stuck are the energy centers associated with the issues you're dealing with. Figure 4.4B depicts what happens when the energy gets stuck and can't flow to the higher centers.

HOW ENERGY GETS STUCK

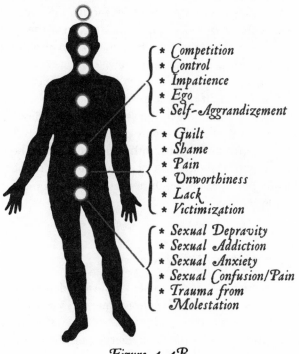

* *Competition*
* *Control*
* *Impatience*
* *Ego*
* *Self-Aggrandizement*

* *Guilt*
* *Shame*
* *Pain*
* *Unworthiness*
* *Lack*
* *Victimization*

* *Sexual Depravity*
* *Sexual Addiction*
* *Sexual Anxiety*
* *Sexual Confusion/Pain*
* *Trauma from Molestation*

Figure 4.4B

When energy becomes stuck in our body, it cannot flow to the higher centers. Since emotions are energy, these emotions get stuck in different centers and we cannot evolve.

If, for example, a person has been sexually abused or has been con-ditioned since childhood to think that sex is bad, their energy can stay stuck in the first center, the center associated with sexuality, and they may have problems accessing creativity. If, on the other hand, a person can access their creative energy but doesn't necessarily feel safe enough to use their creativity in the world (instead feeling victimized by their social and interpersonal relationships), or if they have been traumatized or betrayed by another person, they might hold on to that energy in their second center. Such a person would be likely to feel excessive amounts of guilt, shame, suffering, low self-esteem, or fear. Now, if a person can get their energy flowing up to the third center but they have ego issues and they feel self-important, self-absorbed, controlling, domineering, angry, overly competitive, and bitter, then their energy gets stuck in their third center and they may have control issues or motivation issues. If a person cannot open their heart and feel love and trust or if they are afraid to express love or how they truthfully feel, energy can also become frozen in the fourth and fifth centers, respectively.

While energy can get stuck in any of the energy centers, these first three centers are where it tends to get stuck most often. And when it's stuck, it can't evolve and flow in the seamless current described earlier, which switches on the higher energy centers where we're in love with life and want to give back. Getting that circuit flowing the way it was designed to do is the whole point of doing the Blessing of the Energy Centers meditation—we bless each of these centers so we can get stuck energy flowing again.

Drawing from Our Energy Field

As we discussed earlier, our bodies are surrounded by invisible fields of electromagnetic energy that are always carrying a conscious intention or directive. When we activate each of the body's seven energy centers, we could say that we are expressing energy out of these centers. Sim-ply put, when we as conscious beings activate a specific energy in each individual center, we stimulate the associated neurological plexuses to produce a level of mind that then activates the proper glands, tissues, hormones, and chemicals in each center. Once each unique center is turned on, the body emits energy carrying specific information or inten-tion from it.

However, if we keep living in survival and we are overly sexual, over-consuming, or overstressed by living our lives from the first three centers, we keep drawing from this invisible field of energy carrying information that surrounds the body, and we are consistently turning it into chemistry. The repetition of this process over time causes the field around the body to shrink. (See Figure 4.5.) As a result, we diminish our light and there is no energy that carries a conscious intention moving through these centers to create the correlated mind in each. Essentially, we've tapped our own energy field as a resource. That limited level of mind with its limited amount of energy in each center will send a limited signal to the surrounding cells, tissues, organs, and systems of the body. The result can produce a weakened signal and a lower frequency of energy carrying vital information to the body. Therefore, the lowering frequency of the signals creates disease. We could say that from an energetic level, all disease is a lowering of frequency and an incoherent message.

LIVING IN SURVIVAL

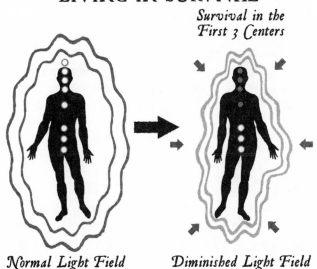

Survival in the
First 3 Centers

Normal Light Field   *Diminished Light Field*

Figure 4.5

The first three centers are energy consumers. When we overutilize these first three centers, we constantly draw from the invisible field of energy and turn it into chemistry. The field around our body begins to shrink.

Remember how I said that the lower three energy centers of the body are concerned with survival, so they represent our selfish nature? They're about using power, aggression, force, or competition so we can survive the conditions in our environment long enough to consume food to nourish ourselves and then procreate and keep the species going (as opposed to the upper five centers, which represent our selfless nature and are concerned with more altruistic thoughts and emotions). Nature has made these lower three centers very pleasurable so that we keep engaging the actions related to them and what they represent. Having sex (first center) and eating (second center) are quite enjoyable, as is connecting and communicating with others (also the second center). Personal power (third center) can be intoxicating, including the success of overcoming obstacles, getting what we want, competing against others and winning, surviving in a particular environment, and pushing ourselves to move our bodies around.

You can see, then, why some people may tend to overutilize one or more of their first three centers, and in so doing, consume more of the field of vital energy and information surrounding the body. For example, an overly sexual person draws extra energy from the field of energy surrounding their first center. A person trapped in shame or guilt who feels victimized, holds on to the emotions of the past, and constantly suffers is consuming excess energy from the energy field surrounding their second center and so holds on to energy in that center. An overly controlling or stressed person pulls additional energy from the field surrounding their third center. When our consciousness is not evolving, neither is our energy.

The Subatomic Level

All of this starts at the subatomic or quantum level—so let's discuss how that happens. Take a look at Figure 4.6. If you take two atoms each with its own nucleus and you put them together to form a molecule, the overlapping of the two circles where they bond is where they're sharing light and information. And because they're sharing information, they're sharing a similar energy that has a particular frequency. What's holding those two atoms together as a molecule is an invisible field of energy. Once these atoms join to form a molecule and exchange information, they will have different physical properties and characteristics, such as a different

FROM ENERGY TO MATTER

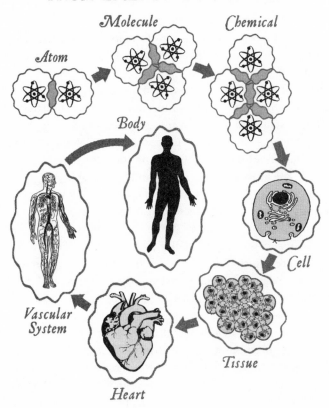

Figure 4.6

As atoms bond together and share energy and information, they form molecules. The molecule has an invisible field of light surrounding it made up of the energy and information that give it the physical properties to hold it together. As more atoms join that molecule, it becomes more complex and forms a chemical, also with an invisible field of light surrounding it that is the energy and information giving it the physical properties to hold it together.

As more atoms join the chemical, it becomes more complex and can form a cell. The cell is surrounded by its own specific invisible field of energy and information, giving it instructions to function. A group of cells that join together, in turn, become a tissue, with a field of energy and information that allows the cells to function in harmony. The tissues join together to become an organ, with a field of energy and information that allows the organ to function in a healthy manner.

The organs join together to become a system, again with a specific invisible field of light surrounding it, providing the physical properties for it to function as a whole. Finally, the systems join together to form a body. The body's surrounding field of light holds the energy and information providing it with the physical properties to hold it together and give it instructions for life.

density, a different boiling point, and a different atomic weight—to name a few—than when they were sitting side by side, separated. It's important to note that what is giving the molecule its specific properties as well as holding it into form and structure—into matter—is the invisible field of energy that is surrounding matter. Molecules could not bond without sharing information and energy.

If you add another atom, you form yet another different molecule that again has different physical properties and characteristics and a different atomic structure. And if you keep adding more and more atoms, you form a chemical, and there's an invisible field of energy around that chemical that's holding it together in physical form, giving life to that chemical. Those atomic forces are real and measurable.

If you take enough chemicals and you put them together, you're going to ultimately form a cell, and the cell also has an invisible field of energy surrounding it and giving life to the cell. The cell is actually feeding off different frequencies of light. It's not molecules and positive or negative charges that are instructing the cell to do what it does. According to the new field of biology called quantum information biology, it's the biophotons we discussed earlier and their patterns of light and frequency that the cell emits and receives that give the instructions. The healthier the cell, the more coherent the biophotons it emits. If you remember from what you've learned so far, coherence is an orderly expression of frequency. The exchange of information (via electromagnetic frequencies of light) between the cell and this field of energy surrounding it happens faster than the speed of light, which means it happens on the quantum level.[5]

To continue, if you put a group of cells together, you form a tissue, and that tissue has an invisible field of unifying coherent frequency and energy that causes all of those individual cells to work together in harmony, functioning as a community. If you take that tissue and further develop it into a more specialized function, you form an organ, and an organ also has an invisible field of electromagnetic energy. That organ literally receives information from this invisible energy field. In fact, the memory of the organ actually exists in the field.

The way this can affect transplant patients is fascinating. Probably the most famous example is the story of Claire Sylvia, who wrote a book called *A Change of Heart* about her experiences after receiving a heart and lung transplant in 1988.[6] All she knew at the time was that her new organs came from an 18-year-old male donor who had died in a motorcycle accident. After the transplant, the 47-year-old professional dancer and choreographer developed cravings for chicken nuggets, French fries, beer, green peppers, and Snickers bars, none of which were foods she had enjoyed before. Her personality also changed—she became more assertive, more confident. Her teenaged daughter even teased her about developing a man's gait. When Sylvia eventually tracked down the family of her donor, she discovered the foods she had craved after the transplant were indeed the young man's favorites. That vital information was stored in the light field of the organ.

The most dramatic story illustrating this involves an 8-year-old girl who, after receiving a heart transplant from a 10-year-old girl, began having vivid nightmares about being murdered.[7] The donor had indeed been murdered, and the perpetrator had not been caught. The patient's mother took her to a psychiatrist who was convinced that the girl was dreaming about events that had actually occurred. They contacted the police, who opened an investigation using the girl's detailed account of the murder, including information on the time and place of the crime, the weapon, the physical characteristics of the criminal, and the clothing the murderer was wearing. The killer was identified, arrested, and convicted.

So in these cases, that information in the energy field *surrounding* the transplanted organ changed the expression of the energy field of the individual once the person had a transplant—its different light and different information mixing with the transplant patient's preexisting field. The recipient can pick up on that information as memory in the field, and it influences their mind and their body. The energy, holding specific information, is influencing matter.

Then when you group organs together, you form a system—such as the musculoskeletal, cardiovascular, digestive, reproductive, endocrine, lymphatic, nervous, and immune systems, to name a few. These systems function by drawing information from the invisible field of energy and consciousness that surrounds them. And when you put all the systems together, you form a body that also has an invisible field of electromagnetic energy surrounding it, and that vital electromagnetic field of light is who we really are.

Now back to the hormones of stress. As I mentioned earlier, when you're in survival mode and you're drawing too much from this invisible field of energy to turn it into chemistry in your physical body—whether you're oversexed, overeating, overstressed, or all at once—this energetic field around your body diminishes. That means there's not enough energy or light surrounding the body to give the proper instructions to matter for homeostasis, growth, and repair. When that occurs, these individual centers no longer receive, process, or express energy, and they no longer produce a healthy neurological mind to send the necessary signals to the associated parts of the body where these centers innervate. Since that energy with a conscious intent moving through or activating neurological tissue creates mind, the energy centers diminish in the expression of the minds to regulate the cells, tissues, organs, and systems of the body because there's no energy moving through them. The body begins to function more like a piece of matter without the proper coherent energy of light and information. Those mini-brains become incoherent just as our brain becomes incoherent.

In addition, when the brain is incoherent and compartmentalized because of the hormones of stress, that incoherent brain then sends a very incoherent message—like static on a radio—down the central nervous system to each of the plexuses of neurons that have to do with communicating with the body. And when these mini-brains receive incoherent messages, then they send an incoherent message through the organs, tissues, and cells in each area in the body that's related to each one of these centers. This in turn affects the hormonal expression and nerve conductivity going to different organs and tissues and cells in the body, and this incoherence begins to create disease or imbalance. The result is that when these individual brains become incoherent, each corresponding area of the body becomes incoherent. And when they don't work well, we don't work well.

Increasing Energy

In the Blessing of the Energy Centers meditation, when you learn how to rest your attention in each of these centers and become aware of the space around them, you create coherence in each of these little brains in the same manner as you create coherence in the big brain between your ears. And as you acknowledge the particle (matter) by resting your attention in your perineum (for the first center), or in the space behind your belly button (for the second center), or in the pit of your gut (for the third center), or in the center of your chest (for the fourth center), and so on, you're anchoring your attention in that center. And where you place your attention is where you place your energy.

Then you'll move to placing your attention in—or opening your focus to—the space *around* each of those centers—tuning in to the energy beyond that center. And as you do this, it's vitally important that you move into a state of elevated emotion, such as love or gratitude or joy. As you know from previous chapters, this is important because the elevated emotion is energy, and the longer you can hold that open focus from a state of elevated emotion, the more you will build a very coherent field with a very high frequency around that center in your body.

Once you build that coherent field around a center, that center has a coherent energy with the right instructions to draw from. The atoms, molecules, and chemicals that form the cells that create the tissues that make up the organs and the systems of the body will be drawing from a new field of light and information and a more coherent energy carrying a more intentional message, giving new instructions to each center of the body. The body will then begin to respond to a new mind. As you surrender and move into the present moment, and you understand that where you place your attention is where you are placing your energy, you can build a new field of light and information and raise the frequency of the signal. And that intentional thought directs energy through each center to produce a new mind in that individual brain. As each center draws from a new field of frequency and information, the body moves back toward balance or homeostasis. And in this new state, you become more energy and less matter, more wave and less particle. The more elevated the emotion, the more energy you create and the more dramatic a shift can result.

If, on the other hand, you stay stuck in the survival emotions of worry, fear, anxiety, frustration, anger, distrust, and so on, you don't have this energy, this information, and this light around your body. As the frequency, light, and energy slow down and become more incoherent in each center, you become more matter and less energy until your body begins to become diseased. That's the point of doing this meditation: to speed up the frequency so it entrains the lower disorganized frequency back into coherence and orderliness, raising the frequency of matter or entraining matter to a new, more coherent mind.

But remember, you can't muscle this. You can't just will it or force it to happen. You can't do it by trying, you can't do it by hoping, and you can't do it by wishing, because you can't do it with your conscious mind. You have to get into your subconscious mind, because that's where the operating system is—the autonomic nervous system that functions and controls all these centers.

You have to get out of your beta brain-wave pattern, because beta keeps you in your conscious mind, separated from your subconscious or your autonomic nervous system that actually runs the show. The deeper you go in meditation—from beta brain waves to alpha brain waves and then even to theta brain waves (the half-awake, half-asleep state of deeper meditation)—the slower your frequency and the more access you have to the operating system. So in the Blessing of the Energy Centers meditation, your job is to slow your brain waves down and combine an elevated emotion with an intent to bless each energy center for the greatest good—loving them into life—and then surrender and allow your autonomic nervous system to take over, because it already knows how to do that without any help from your conscious mind. You're not thinking, you're not visualizing, and you're not analyzing. You're doing something that may at first seem much more difficult: You're planting a seed of information and letting go, allowing it to take the instructions and energy and use them to create more balance and order in your body.

We have actually measured how effectively our students can use this meditation to both increase the energy in each of their energy centers and achieve balance among the centers. To do this, we use the gas discharge visualization device that you read about in a previous chapter to take measurements of participants' energy fields both before and after they do the Blessing of the Energy Centers meditation. The GDV technology uses a specialized camera to take images of a subject's finger while a weak (and totally painless) electrical current is applied to the fingertip for less than a millisecond. The body responds to the current by discharging an electron cloud made up of photons. While the discharge is not visible to the naked eye, the GDV device's camera can capture it and translate it into a digital computer file. Then a software program called Bio-Well uses the data to create an image like the one you see in Graphic 4 in the color insert.

Graphics 4A–4D show how balanced (or imbalanced) the subject's energy centers are, both before and after meditation. The Bio-Well software uses the same GDV data to estimate the frequency of each energy center and compare it to the norm. Balanced energy centers would appear in perfect alignment, while imbalanced centers would make an off-center pattern. The size of the circle representing each energy center shows whether its energy is less than, equal to, or greater than average, and by how much. The left side of each example in Graphic 4 shows the measurements of the subject's energy centers taken before we started our workshop, while the right side shows the measurements taken a few days later.

Now look at Graphics 5A–5D. The left side of this figure shows the measurement of the energy field around each student's entire body before we started the event, while the right side shows the measurement of the field around the whole body afterward.

We have also used the GDV device to measure how this meditation (as well as any of the other meditations in this book) enhances the energy field surrounding the entire body. As you'll soon read in the instructions, at the beginning of the meditation I repeatedly ask you to place your attention not only on various parts of your body, but also on the space around those parts of your body—and then, at the end of the meditation, on the space around your entire body. As you have learned, where you place your attention is where you place your energy, so if you are putting your focus on this space, that's naturally where your energy is going to go. In doing this, you're using your attention, awareness, and energy to build and enhance the field of light and information surrounding your body. This in turn creates order and syntropy instead of disorder and entropy. Now you are more coherent energy and less matter—and you have your own enhanced field of light and information that you can draw from to create.

Blessing of the Energy Centers Meditation

This meditation has become one of the most popular meditations among our students and has created an impressive number of supernatural results. As I did in the previous chapter, I will give you some basic instructions so that if you choose to do the meditation on your own, you'll know how to proceed.

Begin by placing your attention in the first energy center, and then move to opening up your attention to the space *around* this center. Once you can sense this space around the energy center, bless that center for the greatest good, and then connect to elevated emotions—like love, gratitude, or joy—to raise the frequency of this center and also create a coherent field of energy.

Do this for each of the seven energy centers in the body, and when you come to the eighth center, a place about 16 inches above your head, bless this center with gratitude or appreciation or thankfulness, because gratitude is the ultimate state of receivership. This center will then begin to open the door to profound information from the quantum field.

Now open your focus and place your attention on the electromagnetic energy surrounding your entire body, building a new field of energy. As your body draws from a new field of electromagnetic energy, you become more light, more energy, and less matter—and you raise your body's frequency.

Remember: If you are going to create the unlimited, you have to feel unlimited. If you are going to heal in a magnificent way, you have to feel magnificent. Tap into elevated emotion and sustain it throughout the meditation.

Once you've blessed each of the energy centers, lie down for at least 15 minutes. Relax, surrender, and let your autonomic nervous system take the orders and integrate all of this information into your body.

Chapter 5

RECONDITIONING THE BODY TO A NEW MIND

In this chapter, we're going to discuss how to do a breathing technique we use before we start many of our meditations. I'm going to explain it in detail here because understanding how this works is vital to your ability to truly change your energy and free your body from the past. As you'll see, the proper use of the breath is one of the keys to becoming supernatural. To get all the benefits of this technique, your knowledge of *what* you will be doing and *why* you are doing it will serve as the foundation for the experience and so will make the *how* easier for you—not to mention making the technique more effective. Once you understand the physiology of how this particular breath works, you will be able to assign meaning to the activity, put more intention behind it, do it properly, and experience all of the benefits of using breath to pull the mind out of the body and then recondition your body to a new mind.

Before we start, I want to review the thinking-feeling loop we discussed in Chapter 2 because the concepts are central to the meditation in this chapter. As you will recall, thoughts cause biochemical reactions in your brain that release chemical signals, and those chemical signals make the body feel exactly the way you were just thinking. Those feelings then cause you to generate more thoughts that make you feel the same way you were just thinking. So your thoughts drive your feelings, and your feelings drive your thoughts, and eventually this loop hardwires your brain into the same patterns, which conditions your body into the past. And because emotions are a record of past experiences, if you can't think greater than how you feel, this thinking-feeling loop keeps you anchored to your past and creates a constant state of being. This is how the body becomes the mind—or in time, how your thoughts run you and your feelings own you.

So once your body becomes the mind of that emotion, your body is *literally in the past*. And since your body is your unconscious mind, it is so objective that it does not know the difference between the experience in your life that creates the emotion and the emotion you are creating by thought alone. Once you are caught in this thinking-feeling loop, the body believes it is living in the same past experience 24 hours a day, 7 days a week, 365 days a year. The body believes it's in the same past experience because to the body, *the emotion is literally the experience.*

Let's say you've had a few difficult experiences in your life that have branded you emotionally, and you've never got over the fear, bitterness, frustration, and resentment those experiences engendered. So every time you have an experience in your external environment that is similar in some way to what happened previously, the experience triggers you and you feel the same emotions that you did at the time of the first event. Once you feel the same emotion you felt 30 years ago when the event initially occurred, it's quite possible that you will behave in the same way you did at that time because those emotions are driving your conscious or unconscious thoughts and behaviors. Now those emotions have become so familiar to you that you believe that's who you are.

By the time you are in your mid-30s, if you keep thinking, acting, and feeling the same way without changing anything about yourself, the majority of who you are becomes a memorized set of automatic thoughts, reflexive emotional reactions, unconscious habits and behaviors, subconscious beliefs and perceptions, and routine familiar attitudes. In fact, 95 percent of who we are as adults is so habituated through repetition that the body has been programmed to be the mind, and the body, not the conscious mind, is running the show.[1] That means that only about 5 percent of who we are is conscious and the remaining 95 percent is a subconscious body-mind program. So in order to create something significantly different in our lives, we must find a way to pull the mind out of the body and change our state of being, which is exactly what the meditation I will teach you at the end of this chapter is designed to do.

How Energy Gets Stored in the Body

Now let's look at how the thinking-feeling loop works in relation to the body's energy centers—especially the first three, the survival centers, where it causes the most problems. That's because most people's thoughts and feelings activate those energy centers. As you'll remember from the previous chapter, each of the body's energy centers has its own individual energy, information, glands, hormones, chemistry, and neurocircuitry—and its own individual mini-brain or mind (or, really, each has a mind of its own). These mini-brains become programmed in the body to operate subconsciously through the autonomic nervous system. In this way, each center has its own energy and corresponding level of consciousness, and each is associated with specific emotions corresponding to that center.

So let's say you think a thought, such as *My boss is unfair.* Figure 5.1 depicts how thinking that thought turns on a neurological network in your brain. Then you have another thought, *I'm underpaid,* and you turn on a second neurological network. Then you think, *I'm overworked,* and now you're off to the races. Because mind is the brain in action, if you keep thinking more thoughts along the same lines and you activate enough networks of neurons firing in tandem—in a specific sequence, pattern, and combination—you produce a level of mind, which then creates an internal representation or an image of yourself in your brain's frontal lobe. That's where you can make your internal thoughts more real than your outer environment. In this case, you see yourself as an angry person. If you accept, believe, and surrender to that idea, that concept, or that image without any analysis, the neurotransmitters— chemical messengers that send information between neurons in your brain that produce that level of mind—begin to influence neuropeptides, which are chemical messengers created by the autonomic nervous system within the limbic brain. Think of neuropeptides as molecules of emotion. Those neuropeptides signal hormonal centers, in this case turning on the adrenal glands in the third energy center. As the adrenal glands release their hormones, you're feeling pretty ticked off. And you broadcast a specific energy signature through the third energy center that in effect carries the message, "Send me another reason to feel the way I'm already feeling—send me another reason to feel angry." As this center becomes activated, it produces a specific frequency that carries a particular message.

THE THINKING & FEELING
LOOP OF ANGER

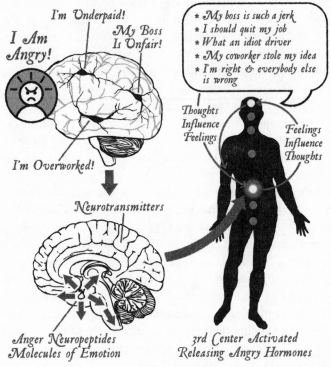

Figure 5.1

This graphic demonstrates how we store energy in the form of emotions in our third center as a result of getting caught in a specific thinking and feeling loop.

Your brain monitors your chemical state, and the moment you feel angry, it's going to think more corresponding thoughts equal to how you feel. *My boss is such a jerk! I should quit my job. What an idiot driver! My coworker stole my idea! I'm right and everyone else is wrong.* It fires and wires similar circuits in the same way over and over again, and if you turn on enough of those circuits, you keep producing that same level of mind. This reaffirms your identity with the same image in your forebrain. And then the limbic brain creates more of the same neuropeptides, which then signal the same hormones from your third energy center, and you start to feel even more angry and frustrated—which then influences you to think more of the same corresponding thoughts. The cycle can go on for decades, whether what you're thinking is justified or not, and then the redundancy of that cycle hardwires the brain into a certain pattern (in this case the pattern of anger) and repeatedly conditions the body emotionally into the past.

The body becomes the mind of anger, so the anger is no longer in the mind that's in your brain (the 5 percent of your thought that is conscious) but instead the emotion of anger becomes stored as energy in the body-mind, the 95 percent of your mind that is subconscious. Because it's subconscious, you're not aware that you're doing this, but that is exactly what is happening. So all that emotion, which was originally created from thought (because all thoughts have a corresponding energy), becomes stored as energy in the body, stuck in the third center, the solar plexus.

This stored energy produces a corresponding biological effect—in this case, it could be adrenal fatigue, digestive problems, kidney issues, or a weakened immune system—not to mention other psychological effects like a short temper, impatience, frustration, or intolerance. Over the years, you keep producing the same thoughts that keep signaling the same feelings and you continue hardwiring your brain into this very finite pattern—and in the same way you keep reconditioning the body to become the mind of anger. Thus an enormous amount of your creative energy is stored in the body's third energy center as anger, bitterness, frustration, intolerance, impatience, control, or hatred.

What if, instead of feeling angry, you start having thoughts that make you feel victimized or guilty? *Life is too hard! I'm a bad parent. I shouldn't have been so rude. Did I do something wrong?* If you take a look at Figure 5.2, you'll see that the same thing happens: Thinking those thoughts turns on a different network of neurons in your brain. If you fire and wire enough of those networks, you produce a different level of mind, and the brain creates the internal image of yourself that reaffirms your identity (in this case, as a guilty person). You start thinking, *God's going to punish me. Nobody loves me. I'm worthless.* Once you accept, believe, and surrender to these guilty thoughts without any analysis, the neurotransmitters activating neural networks in your brain influence a different blend of neuropeptides this time (neuropeptides that are equal to those thoughts about feeling guilty) and then those neuropeptides signal a different hormonal center—in this case, the second center. And over time, as you re-create the same loop of thinking and feeling and feeling and thinking, you're going to begin to store your energy in the body in the second center. This begins to produce a biological effect: Since you feel guilt in your gut, you may start to feel nauseated or sick, or you may experience pain in this area of your body—along with emotions like suffering, unhappiness, or even sadness.

THE THINKING & FEELING
LOOP OF GUILT

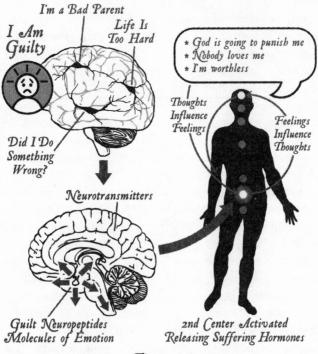

Figure 5.2

This graphic demonstrates how we store energy in the form of emotions in our second center as a result of getting caught in a different thinking and feeling loop.

If over time you keep feeling guilty, you think more guilty thoughts that fire and wire more neurons that signal more neuropeptides that cause the release of more hormones in the second center. As this happens, you continue to condition the body to become the mind of guilt and suffering, so you're storing more and more energy as emotion in the second center. You also continue to broadcast a specific energetic signature carrying specific information through the second energy center into your body's energy field.

So now let's say that you start having a totally different set of thoughts. What happens if you have sexual fantasies about someone? Now you're turning on a different network of neurons in your brain and you're producing a different level of mind. And just as before, if you get enough of those networks firing and wiring, you're going to get a different internal representation in the frontal lobe of your brain. And once the thought or image you are paying attention to becomes more real than your outer world, in that moment the thought literally becomes the experience and the end product of that experience is the corresponding feeling.

As a result, your body gets turned on. That center now is activated with a specific energy carrying a specific message or intent, which then turns on the individual plexus of neurons in that center to produce a specific mind, which then signals genes in the corresponding glands to make chemicals and hormones equal to those thoughts. Now you're convinced you're the stud or vixen of the universe. And if you accept, believe, and surrender to *that* thought or image of yourself without any analysis, then those neurotransmitters in the brain will begin to influence a different blend of neuropeptides in the limbic brain. They'll signal hormones in the first energy center, programming the autonomic nervous system to prepare that center to become activated. I think you're very familiar with the biological effects that happen next.

Those biological reactions will cause you to keep feeling a certain way, and you're going to think more corresponding thoughts equal to that feeling. And now you're storing energy in the first center, and you are broadcasting a vibrational signature carrying a specific message from that center into the energy field in your body. Your brain is monitoring how you're feeling, and you're going to generate even more corresponding thoughts—and the cycle continues. This is how the body responds to the mind and ultimately becomes the mind.

So now you understand how your thoughts condition your body to become the mind of whatever emotion you are experiencing and how, when that happens, you're storing more energy in the corresponding energy center for that emotion. The center where the majority of that energy gets stored is the one associated with the emotions you have been repeatedly experiencing.

If you are overly lustful, overly sexed, or overly preoccupied with wanting to be seen by others as sexually desirable, your energy is stuck in your first center. If you experience an overabundance of guilt, sadness, fear, depression, shame, unworthiness, low self-esteem, suffering, and pain, your energy will become stuck in your second center. And if you have problems with anger, aggression, frustration, control issues, judgment, or self-importance, your energy is stuck in your third center. (Hopefully by now you have done the Blessing of the Energy Centers meditation and have begun to experience how the energy in each of your centers is able to evolve from one center to the next, increasing its frequency as it moves up.)

In time, the body becomes the mind of that emotion, and once that energy as an emotion is stored (or more accurately, once it becomes trapped) in one or more of those lower energy centers, then the body is literally *in the past*. This means you no longer have energy available to create a new destiny. When that happens, your body becomes more matter and less energy because as you have read, the first three centers (which are based on survival emotions) shrink the vital field of energy surrounding your body.

To be clear, I am not saying that you shouldn't ever have sex, enjoy food, or even feel stressed. What I *am* saying is that when you are out of balance, it's because these first three centers are out of balance. And imagine if all three of these survival centers become overstimulated all at once—you can easily see how your body's energy would diminish over time. When that happens, there's not much available energy for growth, repair, healing, creation, or even just returning to balance.

By the same means, many people who feel out of balance may retreat from their lives and limit the amount of food they eat. By digesting less food, their body has more energy to balance itself. They may also abstain from sexual intercourse for a period of time to allow the body to restore itself. During their retreat, they will also remove themselves from the constant stimulation they normally receive from their environment, including their friends, kids, coworkers, appointments and schedules, job, computers, homes, and cell phones. This helps the body keep from reacting (consciously or unconsciously) to all those familiar elements in their outer world that they associate with thoughts and emotional memories from the past.

The breath technique I'm about to teach you gives you a way to liberate that trapped energy that's stored in the first three centers so it can be free to flow to the brain—from whence it came. And when you use the breath to liberate those emotions, that energy becomes available for higher purposes. You'll have more energy to heal yourself, create a different life, manifest more wealth, or have a mystical experience, to name just a few possibilities. Those emotions that are stored in the body as energy will be transmuted into a different type of energy carrying a different message through the elevated emotions of inspiration, freedom, unconditional love, and gratitude. It's the same energy; it's just locked up in the body. The breath is a way to pull the mind out of the body. You will be using your body as an instrument of consciousness to ascend your energy—turning those survival emotions into creative emotions. As you free your body from the chains of the past and liberate this energy, you have available energy to do the uncommon—to achieve the supernatural.

The Body as a Magnet

Think about a magnet as you look at Figure 5.3. Magnets, of course, have polarity. They each have a north pole and a south pole; one end has a positive charge and the other end has a negative charge. The polarity between the ends of a magnet is what causes the magnet to produce an electromagnetic field. The stronger the polarity between the two poles, the larger the electromagnetic field the magnet produces. You can't see that electromagnetic field, but it exists—and it can be measured.

ELECTROMAGNETIC FIELD
OF A MAGNET

Electromagnetic
Field
Figure 5.3

A magnet has a measurable invisible electromagnetic field surrounding it. The stronger the polarity between the north and south poles, the more current moves through the magnet and the bigger the electromagnetic field.

The strength of a magnet's electromagnetic field can even influence matter. If you were to take tiny metal shavings and lay them on a piece of paper, put another piece of paper over that first piece of paper, and then set a magnet on top of that second piece of paper, those metal shavings would organize themselves within the magnet's electromagnetic field. The electromagnetic field of the magnet is powerful enough to affect material reality—even though the frequency of this field exists beyond your senses. Figure 5.4 illustrates this.

HOW ENERGY INFLUENCES MATTER

Metal Shavings Organized by Electromagnetic Field

Figure 5.4

The electromagnetic field of a magnet will organize metal shavings placed under it into the patterns of its field.

The Earth is a magnet. And like any other magnet, it has a north pole and a south pole, as well as an electromagnetic field surrounding it. While this field itself is invisible, we're all familiar with one amazing way to see that it exists; the Earth's electromagnetic field deflects the sun's photons, and during a solar flare or a mass coronal ejection, that field deflects trillions of tons of photons hurled toward the Earth in a pulsating, colorful phenomenon known as the northern lights.

Your body is also a magnet. Ancient cultures (especially Asian cultures) have known this for thousands of years. Your north pole is your mind and brain, and your south pole is your body at the base of your spine. When you're living by the hormones of stress (the emotions of survival) or when you're overutilizing the other two survival energy centers, you are constantly drawing energy from this invisible field. The energy then no longer flows through the body, because the body, in survival mode, is pulling the energy from the field and storing it in the body—specifically in the first three energy centers. (This is what happens when the thinking/feeling loop we talked about earlier is activated.)

If this goes on long enough, the body won't have any electrical charge running through it at all, and without an electrical charge, it can't create the field of electromagnetic energy that normally surrounds it. When that happens, the body is no longer like a magnet. Now it's like a piece of ordinary metal—a magnet that's lost its charge. As you can see in Figure 5.5, the body then becomes more matter and less energy (or more particle and less wave).

THE BODY AS ENERGY
VS.
THE BODY AS MATTER

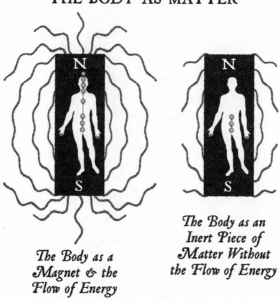

The Body as a Magnet & the Flow of Energy

The Body as an Inert Piece of Matter Without the Flow of Energy

Figure 5.5

When there is a flow of energy moving through the body, just as with a magnet, there is a measurable electromagnetic field surrounding the body. When we're living in survival and we're drawing from the invisible field of energy around the body, we diminish our body's electromagnetic field. In addition, when energy is stuck in the first three survival centers because we are caught in a thinking and feeling loop, then there's less current running through the body and there is less of an electromagnetic field.

Of course, if there were a way to get this energy that's stored in the first three centers moving again, the current would resume flowing and the body would re-create the electromagnetic field. The breath does just that—it gives us a way to pull the mind out of the body and to move all that stored energy from the first three centers up the spine to the brain, restoring the electromagnetic field surrounding the body. Once that happens, we can use that energy for things other than survival. Let's take a look at the way our physical bodies are constructed so we can understand what makes that possible.

THE BRAIN & THE SPINAL CORD INSIDE THE SKELETAL SYSTEM

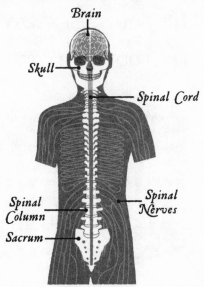

Figure 5.6

Your sacrum, your spinal column, and your skull are the bony structures that protect the most delicate system in your body: the central nervous system, which controls and coordinates all other systems.

Take a look at Figure 5.6. You have a bone at the base of your spine called your sacrum that looks like an upside down triangle with a plateau on the top. On top of that flat surface sits the spinal column, which extends all the way up to your skull. Inside that closed system is the central nervous system, which is made up of the brain and the spinal cord. The spinal cord is actually an extension of your brain. The skull and the spinal column protect this most delicate system.

The central nervous system is one of your body's most important systems because it controls and coordinates all the other systems in the body. Without the aid of the central nervous system, you couldn't digest your food, you couldn't void your bladder, you couldn't move your body, and your heart couldn't beat. You couldn't even blink your eyes without the nervous system. So you can think of the nervous system as the electrical wiring that runs the machine of your body.

Inside this closed system is cerebrospinal fluid that's filtered from the blood in the brain. This fluid bathes the brain and the spinal cord, and it's responsible for giving the central nervous system buoyancy. It acts as a cushion to protect the brain and spinal cord from trauma, and it flows in various rivers and paths that transport nutrients and chemicals to different parts of the nervous system all over the body. By its very nature, this fluid acts as a conduit to enhance electrical charges in the nervous system.

Now let's go back to your sacrum. Every time you inhale, that sacrum bone flexes back slightly, and every time you exhale it flexes forward just a little bit. This is an extremely subtle movement—too subtle for you to notice, even if you try. But it happens. And at the same time you inhale, the sutures of your skull (the joints between the individual plates of your skull, which fit together like pieces of a puzzle and give the skull a degree of flexibility) open up just slightly, and as you exhale, they close back up.[2] Again, this is extremely subtle. You can't feel it happening.

The movement of your sacrum back and forth as you slowly breathe in and out, along with the sutures of the skull opening and closing, propagates a wave within the fluid of this closed system, and it slowly pumps that cerebrospinal fluid up your spine all the way to the brain, passing through four chambers called cerebral aqueducts or ventricles. If you were to tag one molecule of cerebrospinal fluid and follow it from the base of your spine all the way up to your brain and then all the way back down to your sacrum, you'd see that it would take 12 hours to make a complete circuit.[3] So in essence, you flush your brain twice a day. Check out Figure 5.7 to see what that looks like.

THE MOVEMENT OF CEREBROSPINAL FLUID

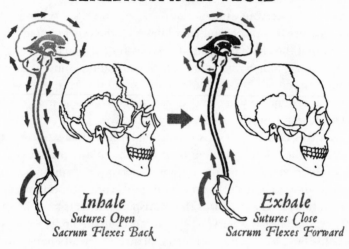

Inhale
Sutures Open
Sacrum Flexes Back

Exhale
Sutures Close
Sacrum Flexes Forward

Figure 5.7

As you inhale, your sacrum slightly flexes back and the sutures of your skull expand. As you exhale, your sacrum slightly flexes forward and the sutures close. It is this natural action of breathing that slowly propagates a wave to move cerebrospinal fluid up and down the spinal cord and throughout the brain.

So think about what would happen if you contracted the intrinsic muscles of your perineum (your pelvic floor, the same muscles you use for intercourse and elimination) and you locked them down, and then while they were locked down, you next contracted the muscles of your lower abdomen, locking those muscles down, and then you did the same with the muscles of your upper abdomen. If you kept squeezing and contracting those muscles in your first three energy centers by contracting your core muscles, that fluid in your central nervous system would move up, as illustrated in Figure 5.8. You'd be moving that cerebrospinal fluid in your central nervous system up your spine. Each time you tighten the muscles of those centers, the fluid would be forced upward.

Now imagine you then placed your attention on the top of your head. Where you place your attention is where you place your energy, so if you put your attention at the top of your head, that would become your target for moving energy. Now think about taking one slow, steady breath through your nose and at the same time, squeezing and holding the muscles of your perineum, then those of your lower abdomen, and then those of your upper abdomen—all while following your breath up your spine and through your chest, your throat, and your brain, and all the way to the top of your head. Imagine that when you get to the top of your head, you hold your breath as you keep squeezing. You'd be pulling that cerebrospinal fluid all the way up toward your brain.

CONTRACTING INTRINSIC MUSCLES TO MOVE CEREBROSPINAL FLUID UP TOWARD THE BRAIN

Using Core Muscles to Move Energy

Figure 5.8

As you contract the intrinsic muscles of your lower body and at the same time take in a slow steady breath through your nose, while placing your attention on the top of your head, you accelerate the movement of the cerebrospinal fluid toward your brain and you begin to run a current through your body and up the central axis of the spine.

That's significant because cerebrospinal fluid is made up of proteins and salts in solution, and the moment proteins and salts dissolve in solution, they become charged. If you take a charged molecule and accelerate it—as you would if you pulled that molecule up your spine—you create an inductance field. An inductance field is an invisible field of electromagnetic energy that moves in a circular motion in the direction the charged molecules are moving in. The more charged molecules you accelerate, the bigger and more powerful the inductance field. Take a look at Figure 5.9 to see what an inductance field looks like.

INDUCTANCE FIELD

By Moving Charged Molecules, an Inductance Field Is Created

Figure 5.9

Cerebrospinal fluid is made of charged molecules. As you accelerate charged molecules in one direction up the spine, you produce an inductance field that moves in the direction of the charged molecules.

MOVEMENT OF STORED ENERGY
FROM THE BODY TO THE BRAIN

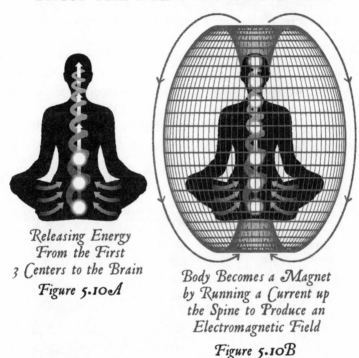

Releasing Energy
From the First
3 Centers to the Brain
Figure 5.10A

Body Becomes a Magnet
by Running a Current up
the Spine to Produce an
Electromagnetic Field
Figure 5.10B

As the inductance field is created by the acceleration of the cerebrospinal fluid up the spine, it will draw the stored energy in the first three centers back to the brain. Once there is a current flowing from the base of the spine all the way to the brain, the body becomes like a magnet and an electromagnetic torus field is created.

Think of the spinal cord as a fiber-optic cable that acts as a two-way highway simultaneously communicating information from the body to the brain and from the brain to the body. Every second, important information is relayed from your brain to your body (such as the desire to walk across the room or to scratch an itch). At the same instant, a lot of information from the body is carried up your spinal cord toward the brain (such as the knowledge of where your body is in space or the signal that you are hungry). Once you accelerate these charged molecules in one direction up the spine, the resulting inductance field will reverse the current of information flowing from the brain down through the body, and it will then draw energy from the lower three centers up the spine to the brain. Take a look at Figure 5.10A to see how that works. Now there's a current running through the body and the central nervous system—just like a magnet—and as a result, the same kind of electromagnetic field of energy that surrounds a magnet surrounds the body, as you can see in Figure 5.10B.

The field of electromagnetic energy you've created is a three-dimensional field, and as it moves, this energy creates a torsion field or a torus field. By the way, the shape of this electromagnetic field is a familiar pattern in the universe; this pattern shows up in the shape of an apple as well as in the shape of a black hole in a distant galaxy. (See Figure 5.11.)

THE TORUS FIELD

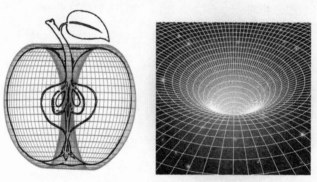

Apples & black holes in the shape of a torus

Figure 5.11

From apples to black holes, the shape of a torus is a
recurring pattern of creation in nature.

So now you understand that by doing this breathing technique, you're starting to stir up all this stored energy in a very big way. And if you do this technique correctly and you do it enough times, you are going to wake up a sleeping dragon.

Evolving the Energy to the Brain

Once this energy becomes activated, the sympathetic nervous system (a subsystem of your autonomic nervous system that arouses the brain and body in response to a threat in your outer environment) turns on, and energy begins to move up from the body's lower three energy centers to the brain. But instead of the body being aroused because of some external condition, you are turning on the sympathetic nervous system by passionately engaging the breath from within. As the sympathetic nervous system starts to merge with the parasympathetic nervous system (another subset of your autonomic nervous system that relaxes your brain and body, such as after a big meal), it is as if traveling energy from the lower centers is ejaculated into the brain. When this energy reaches the brain stem, a gate called the thalamic gate opens up and all that energy is permitted to enter the brain.

Once this energy that was initially stored in the body enters the brain, the brain produces gamma brain-wave patterns. (We've recorded many students producing gamma brain waves during this breathing technique.) Gamma brain waves—which I call superconsciousness—are notable not only because they produce the highest amounts of energy of all the brain waves, but also because that energy comes from within the body instead of being released in reaction to a stimulus in the environment, the outer world.

In contrast, the brain produces high-range beta brain waves when the body releases stress hormones, allowing you to be super alert to danger in your environment. In beta, the outer world seems more real than your inner world. While gamma waves create a similar type of arousal in the brain—which then causes a heightened sense of awareness, consciousness, attention, and energy related to more creative, transcendental, or mystical experiences—the difference is that in gamma, whatever is happening in your inner world becomes much more real to you than many experiences you've had in your outer world. Take a look at Figure 5.12 and review how similar beta and gamma brain waves are.

THE COMPARISON OF HIGH
BETA & GAMMA BRAIN WAVES

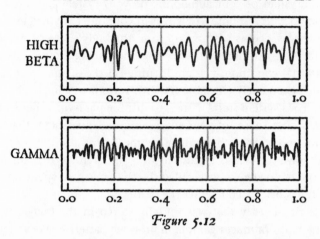

Figure 5.12

Through the release of the energy stored in the body's first three energy centers, the brain becomes aroused and moves into gamma brain waves. When this occurs, the brain may go into high-beta brain waves on the way to the gamma range. High-beta brain waves are typically produced by the arousal of the brain through stimulation from our outer environment, which causes us to put our attention on the cause.

Gamma brain waves are typically created by stimulation from our inner environment, which causes us to pay attention to whatever is going on in the inner world of our mind. This comparison shows how similar high-beta and gamma brain-wave patterns are, though gamma frequencies are faster.

Many of our students who do this breath technique produce significant high-beta brain waves on their way to the gamma range (the highest-frequency brain waves)—or they may simply stay in these very high-level beta states. We're finding that being in the highest levels of beta can also signal that the person is paying more attention to their inner world than to their outer world. In addition to seeing more energy in the brain after this breathing technique, we have also repeatedly observed more significant amounts of brain coherence.

Take a look at Graphics 6A and 6B in the color insert. You can see two students who have done the breath successfully. They have very high-frequency beta brain waves that transition to gamma brain waves. Notice the high amplitudes of their brain waves in gamma. The higher the amplitudes, the higher the energy in their brains. The students demonstrate

160 and 260 standard deviations above typical gamma brain waves. To give you a reference, 3 standard deviations above normal is usually considered high. In Graphic 6A(4) you can also witness much more brain coherence after the breath. The red patterns in the brain show extremely high amounts of brain coherence in every measured brain-wave state.

PRANA TUBE
The Tube of Light from the Movement of Energy Up & Down the Spinal Cord

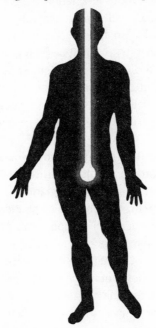

Figure 5.13

The prana tube is a tube of light or energy that represents the movement of life force up and down the spinal cord. The more energy moving along the spine, the stronger the field of the prana tube. The less energy moving along the spine, the weaker the prana and thus, the less life force delivered in the body.

As you do this powerful breathing technique, you are drawing the energy that's been stored in those lower three centers—the energy you use for orgasm and to make a baby, to digest a meal, to run from a predator—and instead of releasing it out into chemistry, you're going to draw it up your spine like you would draw fluid up a straw, and release it into your brain.

In fact, there's a tube of energy or light called the prana tube running along your spinal column (see Figure 5.13). *Prana* is the Sanskrit word for "life force." Yogis have known about this tube—which is not a physical structure but an energetic one—for thousands of years. This tube is considered etheric because of the electrical information in the spine that constantly moves through it. The more energy moves in the physical spinal cord, the more energy is created as light in this tube. And the more energy created in this tube, the more energy moves in the spine and the greater the expression of life. Sometimes when I teach this meditation, people will say to me, "I don't really feel my prana tube." Well, you don't really feel your left ear either until you put your attention on it, right? So when I ask you to contract your muscles and pull that energy up, you'll be pulling it up through the spine and creating a more powerful prana tube along your spinal cord.

It's important to add here that this is not a passive breath—it's an extremely active, passionate process. Moving this stored energy—energy that has been stored for years and years, maybe even decades—takes an act of intention and will. To evolve your limited survival emotions, as an alchemist turns base metals like lead into gold, you are taking self-limiting emotions like anger, frustration, guilt, suffering, grief, and fear and turning them into elevated emotions, such as love, gratitude, and joy. Other elevated emotions to consider tapping into include inspiration, excitement, enthusiasm, fascination, awe, wonder, appreciation, kindness, abundance, compassion, empowerment, nobility, honor, invincibility, uncompromising will, strength, and freedom—not to mention divinity itself, being moved by the spirit, trusting in the unknown or in the mystic or the healer within you.

Remember, evolving this energy takes a level of intensity that is greater than the body as the mind, greater than your addiction to any survival emotion. You must be inspired to become more energy than matter, using your body as an instrument of consciousness to ascend your energy. So don't let your body be your mind. Remember that you are liberating your stuck energy, turning guilt or suffering or anger or aggression into pure energy, and as the body liberates that energy, you're freeing yourself and you will feel overjoyed, in love with life, and inspired to be alive.

As you pull this energy up the spine in this meditation, you'll follow your breath all the way to the top of your head. When it gets there, I want you to hold your breath while you keep squeezing those muscles in your perineum and your abdomen. When you do that, you increase the pressure inside your spinal cord and spinal column. That pressure, called intrathecal pressure, is inside a closed system. It's the same pressure you exert when you take a breath and lift something heavy—you're pushing against your insides. But in this breath you'll be very specifically directing all that pressure, all that energy, and all that spinal fluid up your spine and into your brain.

HOW ENERGY FROM THE BODY ENTERS THE BRAIN THROUGH THE RETICULAR ACTIVATING SYSTEM

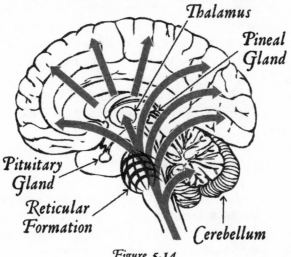

Figure 5.14

As the thalamic gate opens up, a lot of the creative energy that was stored in the body passes through the reticular activating system to each thalamus and the pineal gland. Then that energy is relayed to the neocortex, producing gamma brain waves.

When that pressurized fluid reaches the back of your brain stem, all of a sudden the lower-brain centers like the brain stem, cerebellum, and limbic brain open up to this energy through a cluster of nuclei called the reticular formation. That energy then passes through the thalamic gate up to the thalamus (the part of the brain that relays signals from the sensory receptors) located in the midbrain, which serves as a junction box. Next, all of that stored energy moves directly into your higher brain center, the neocortex. That's when gamma waves begin to occur. When the energy reaches the thalamus, it is also relayed to the pineal gland, and something amazing happens. That gland releases some very powerful elixirs, one of which anesthetizes the analytical mind and thinking brain.

See Figure 5.14, which shows the thalamus, the reticular formation, the thalamic gate, and the moment of energy hitting the higher brain centers.

We'll talk more about the pineal gland in a later chapter, but for right now, know that when that happens, it's like an orgasm in your head. This is a very powerful energy that has been called the movement of the kundalini. I personally don't like to use that word because it may conjure up opinions or beliefs from a limited understanding of this energy that may discourage some people from doing the breath, but I do want you to understand that this is the energy you are evoking with this breath.

If you look at Graphic 6B(4) in the color insert, you can see the area surrounding the pineal gland is quite active in the student producing gamma brain waves. Look at the blue arrows. The red area suggests the activation of energy in the pineal gland as well as a region of the limbic brain associated with strong emotions and formation of new memories. Graphic 6B(5) is a three-dimensional picture of the same student's brain. Once again, the pineal area shows a significant amount of energy coming from inside the brain.

Embracing Elevated Emotions

You've just read how the breathing exercise in this chapter pulls the mind out of the body as it liberates stored energy from the first three energy centers—the centers of survival. Once you do that, it's time to recondition the body to a new mind, the second part of the meditation, which involves attaining elevated emotional states.

I want to clarify here why embracing elevated emotions is so powerful. As you've learned from our discussion about genes in the second chapter, we now know that it's the environment that signals the gene, not the other way around. If an emotion is the end product of an experience in the environment, it is the emotion that turns gene expression on or off.

When you embrace these elevated emotions in this meditation, what you are actually doing is signaling your genes *ahead of the environment*. The body doesn't know the difference between an emotion created by an experience you are having in the outside environment and an experience you are creating internally by embracing this new, elevated emotion. So when you embrace that elevated emotion and think thoughts that are greater than the self-limiting ones that kept you stuck in the past, your body begins to prepare chemically for the future (because it thinks that future is happening now). In other words, if you do the meditation correctly enough times, the body responds as though the healing or any condition you are manifesting in your environment has already taken place.

These elevated emotions have a higher (and faster) frequency than more base emotions, like guilt, fear, jealousy, and anger. And since all frequency carries information, when we change the frequency, we change our energy. That new energy can then carry new information—a new consciousness or set of intentions or thoughts. The more elevated the emotion, the faster the frequency and the more you feel like energy instead of matter—and the more energy becomes available to create a more coherent energy field, shifting further away from disease and more toward health (or for that matter, toward signaling any gene). When your emotions are self-limiting, on the other hand, they have a lower frequency, and you feel more like matter instead of energy—and then it takes more time to create change in your life.

Here's an example: If at some point in your past you were shocked, betrayed, or traumatized by an event with a high emotional charge that has left you feeling pain or sadness or fear, chances are that experience has been branded into your biology in numerous ways. It's also possible that the genes that were activated by this experience might keep your body from healing. So in order for you to change your body into a new genetic expression, the inner emotion you create has to be greater than the emotion from that past outer experience. The energy of your empowerment or the amplitude of your inspiration must be greater than your pain or sadness. Now you are changing the inner environment of the body, which is the outer environment of the cell; the genes for health can be up-regulated while the genes for disease can be down-regulated. The more profound the emotion, the louder you're knocking on your genetic door and the more you're going to signal those genes to change the structure and function of your body. That's how it works.

We can actually prove this because in one of our 2017 advanced workshops in Tampa, we measured gene expression in a randomized selection of 30 workshop participants.[4] The results showed that our students were able to significantly change the expression of eight genes over the course of the four-day workshop by changing their internal states. There is only one possibility in 20 that the results were due to chance—that's the threshold of significance that statisticians usually use. The functions of these genes are far-ranging. They're involved in neurogenesis, the growth of new neurons in response to novel experiences and learning; protecting the body against various influences that tend to age cells; regulating cell repair, including the ability to move stem cells to those sites in the body where they are needed to repair damaged or aging tissue; building cellular structures, especially the cytoskeleton (the framework of rigid molecules that give our cells shape and form); eliminating free radicals, and so decreasing oxidative stress (associated with aging and many major health conditions); and helping our bodies identify and eliminate cancerous cells, thereby suppressing the growth of cancer tumors. Activating the genes for neurogenesis was particularly significant because most of the time our students were in meditation, they were so present in their inner world of imagination that their brains believed they were in the actual event. See Figure 5.15 below to learn what each of these genes does and why it is important for our health.

CHAC1	Regulates the oxidative balance in cells, helping reduce free radicals that cause oxidative stress (the most universal cause of aging). Helps neural cells form and grow optimally.
CTGF	Aids in healing wounds, developing bones, and regenerating cartilage and other connective tissue. Decreased expression is linked to cancer and autoimmune diseases like fibromyalgia.
TUFT1	Aids cell repair and healing, including regulating stem cells (the undifferentiated or "blank" cells that can turn into whatever type of tissue the body needs at the moment). Involved in the mineralization process of tooth enamel.
DIO2	Important for healthy placenta tissue and thyroid function (involved in the production of the T3 thyroid hormone). Helps regulate metabolism by reducing insulin resistance, thereby reducing occurrence of metabolic disease and possibly ameliorating cravings and addiction. Also helps regulate mood, especially depression.
C5orf66-AS1	Suppresses tumors, helping to identify and eliminate cancerous cells.
KRT24	Associated with healthy cell structure. Also suppresses certain types of cancer cells, including those found in colorectal cancer.
ALS2CL	Suppresses tumors, especially those contributing to squamous cell carcinoma, a type of skin cancer.
RND1	Helps cells organize the molecules that give them their rigid structure. Also aids neural cell growth and suppresses certain types of cancer cells (such as those found in throat and breast cancer).

Figure 5.15

These are the specific genes that were regulated in four days in our Advanced Workshop in Tampa, Florida, in 2017.

If our students have changed their gene expression by creating elevated emotions in just a few days, imagine what you can do if you practice this meditation for a few weeks. By using this breath technique to release the familiar emotions stored in the body from years of thinking and feeling the same way, and then by emotionally rehearsing new states every day, with practice these unlimited emotions will become the new normal for you. Your brain will think different thoughts equal to those elevated emotions. Finally, by embracing these unlimited emotions instead of the same limited ones, when you understand that you are signaling new genes and making new proteins that are responsible for the change in structure and function of your body, you can assign more meaning to what you are doing. That leads to a greater intention, which creates an even greater outcome.

It is a scientific fact that we use about 1.5 percent of our DNA. The rest is called junk DNA. There is a principle in biology called endowment that holds that nature never wastes anything that it is not going to use. In other words, if the junk DNA is there, there must be a reason—otherwise nature in its infinite wisdom would have evolved it away (because the universal law is *if you don't use it you lose it*). So think of your genes as a library of potentials. There are infinite combinations of gene variations that can be expressed in those latent genes. They are waiting for you to activate them. There are genes for an unlimited genius mind, for longevity, for immortality, for an uncompromising will, for the capacity to heal, for having mystical experiences, for regenerating tissues and organs, for activating the hormones of youth so you have greater energy and vitality, for photographic memory, and for doing the uncommon, just to name a few.

It's all equal to your imagination and creativity. As you signal any of those genes ahead of the environment, your body will express a greater potential by expressing new genes to make new proteins for a greater expression of life. So when I ask you to feel certain elevated emotions when you recondition the body to a new mind, know that as you embrace each emotion, you are knocking on your own genetic door. So I invite you to surrender to the process and fully engage in the experience.

Reconditioning the Body to a New Mind Meditation

Before we start the formal meditation, we are going to do some practice sessions. They build on several individual instructions so you can learn this step by step. Once you've mastered each individual step, we can put it all together. So let's start by sitting up straight in a chair and putting both feet flat on the floor, or sitting on the floor in the lotus (cross-legged) position with a pillow under your buttocks. Place your hands uncrossed in your lap. If you like, you can close your eyes.

When you're ready to begin, lift up your perineum, your pelvic floor—the same muscles that you use for intercourse and elimination. Do not hold your breath as you do this—breathe normally. Squeeze those muscles as tightly as you can and hold for five seconds; then let go and relax. Do it again and hold it for the same amount of time. Do it a third time, holding it for about five seconds, and then relax again. I want you to gain conscious control over these muscles because you are going to be using them in a different way.

Now contract the same muscles in the perineum and at the same time contract the muscles in your lower abdomen. Pull your lower abdomen up and in, locking down these first two centers. Hold for five seconds and then relax. Pull those same muscles up and in again and squeeze. Hold for five seconds again, and then relax. Repeat this once more. Remember to keep breathing as you do this—don't hold your breath.

Now, this next time, squeeze the muscles of your perineum, and at the same time squeeze the muscles of your lower abdomen while also contracting the muscles of your upper abdomen. You're tightening your entire core now—the first three centers. Hold all of those muscles for five seconds and relax. Do this again, pulling the muscles in a little more this time. Hold for five seconds and then relax. Now do it one more time, and as you squeeze and hold those muscles, see if you can squeeze them a little tighter and lift them a little higher. Hold for a while and then relax.

Since experience creates neurological networks in your brain, as you perform each step and build on the previous one, you are installing the neurological hardware in your brain in preparation for the experience. I am asking you to use the same muscles that you might have used for years, but now in a different way. This action will begin to milk these centers and liberate energy that's been stored in your body for a very long time.

Now we're going to change it up. Take your finger and place it on the top of your head, and work your fingernail right into the center of your scalp so you will remember where that point is once you take your finger away. Remember that where you place your attention is where you place your energy, so that point is your target. Put your hands back in your lap and *without contracting any muscles yet*, take one slow, steady breath through your nose. All I want you to do is follow your breath from your perineum, through your lower abdomen, through your upper abdomen, through the center of your chest, through your throat, through your brain, all the way to the top of your head where your finger was. When you get to the top of your head, hold your breath and keep your attention right on the top of your head and let your energy follow your awareness. Hold for about ten seconds and then relax.

Place your finger on the top of your head again, then take it away and make sure you can feel that point without your finger there. Rest your hands on your thighs. Now do one more breath without contracting any muscles. This time when you inhale through your nose, imagine you are pulling energy up that tube—like drawing fluid up a straw—all the way to the top of your head. When you get to the top of your head, hold your breath for about the same amount of time you did before, and let your energy follow your awareness—then relax.

Now it's time to start putting it all together. With this next breath, when you inhale through your nose, pull those muscles up and in at the exact same time. Start by locking the muscles of your perineum, engaging the muscles of your lower abdomen and simultaneously contracting the muscles in your upper abdomen. And as you squeeze the muscles in each center—with the intention of pulling all of that stored energy in the lower body into the brain—follow your breath through each of those three centers. As you continue to squeeze those muscles and lock those first three centers down, pull your breath up through your chest (the fourth center), then through your throat (the fifth center), then through your brain (the sixth center). Pull it all the way up to the top of your head, keep your attention there, and hold your breath as you keep squeezing your core muscles. Hold for about ten seconds and then relax as you exhale.

Repeat that breath at least two more times, tightening the muscles of your first three centers as you pull your breath up your spine through each energy center all the way to the top of your head. Then hold your breath for a time, and finally relax as you exhale.

Remember, as you do this, you're using your body as an instrument of consciousness and your full intent should be to pull the mind out of the body. You're liberating energy that has been locked in your lower three centers and moving it up to the higher centers where you can use it for healing your body or creating something new, instead of just for survival.

Practicing this many times so you are very familiar with these steps will be very useful before you begin several of the meditations in this book. Be patient with yourself; just like learning anything for the first time, you have to do this many times before you truly master it. In the beginning, it may feel awkward because you have to synchronize the actions of your body with the intention of your mind. Eventually, though, if you practice this technique enough, you will be able to coordinate all of these steps into one motion.

I am aware that there are many different breathing techniques, and you may well have had success with one or more of them in the past. Even so, I urge you to try this one, even if you already have some other favorite, because if you do something new, you can have a new experience. If you keep doing the same thing, you will keep creating the same experience. And if you do nothing, you get nothing. Yes, this technique takes some real effort, but once you become more skilled, you'll see it's worth the effort and then some.

You are now ready to begin the formal meditation. If you purchase my *Reconditioning the Body to a New Mind* CD or audio download from **drjoedispenza.com,** you'll find the recording includes a song I've specifically chosen to truly inspire you to raise your energy. As you listen, I want you to interpret the music as the movement of energy. If you do the meditation on your own, practice the breath while you listen to one inspiring song that's between four and seven minutes long. Then open your focus, putting your attention on different parts of your body as well as the space around those parts of the body. Next, unfold as pure consciousness into the unified field, staying in the generous present moment and becoming no body, no one, no thing, no where and in no time.

Now it's time to cultivate several elevated emotions one by one, emotionally rehearsing each. Remember: The more powerful your feelings, the more you are up-regulating your own genes. Bless your body, bless your life, bless your soul, bless your future as well as your past, bless the challenges in your life, and bless the intelligence within you that is giving you life. Finish by giving thanks for a new life before it has been made manifest.

Chapter 6

CASE STUDIES: LIVING EXAMPLES OF TRUTH

Over the years, I've found that stories serve a great purpose: to reinforce information in a practical manner. Hearing about someone else's experience makes it more real for us. Once we can relate to the challenges and triumphs a person has along their journey from one state of consciousness to another, we start to believe a similar experience can happen for us. Stories also make the ideas from the teachings become less philosophical and more personal.

The case studies that you are about to read concern real people who have applied the information you just learned in the previous chapters. They first understood the concepts as intellectual knowledge in their minds, then they applied it and experienced it in their bodies, and finally they turned it into wisdom in their souls. For these students to accomplish such supernatural changes, they ultimately had to master some aspect or limitation in themselves—and if they could do it, so can you.

Ginny Heals Her Chronic Back and Leg Pain

On December 9, 2013, Ginny was driving on the highway in Las Vegas when her car was hit from behind. Even though she slammed on the brakes, the impact catapulted her car into the car in front of her, resulting in a double impact. She immediately felt a burning sensation in her lower back as pain shot down her right leg. When the paramedics arrived, she described her pain as moderate, but over the next few days, the pain increased until it was constant and severe. Most of her pain was in her lower lumbar spine, caused by two herniated discs (L4 and L5). She also felt pain radiating all the way down her right leg to her foot.

Ginny saw a chiropractor three times a week, but the pain worsened. She then saw a pain management doctor who prescribed muscle relaxants, Neurontin (a nerve pain medication), and Mobic (a nonsteroidal anti-inflammatory drug). After nine months, the pain was still intense, so she had injections in her back. They didn't help.

As a result, Ginny had difficulty walking and found driving almost impossible. She also had trouble sleeping, managing to get only four or five hours a night. The constant pain in her lower back became worse when she was sitting, lifting something, or standing for long periods of time. Sometimes she could sit for only 20 minutes at a time. Because of all this, she spent most of her days in bed, where she was able to find a little relief when lying on her right side with her knees bent.

Ginny was unable to care for her two children, ages three and five, and she was also unable to work as much as she had before. She depended on her husband to drive her places since she could no longer drive herself. All of these factors created serious financial problems and emotional stress for the whole family. Ginny became depressed and angry at life. Although she had attended her first workshop with me before the accident and had been doing her meditations, after the accident she stopped meditating regularly because the pain got too severe and she said she couldn't sit or concentrate.

After two years, her doctor suggested lumbar surgery to repair the herniated discs. If that didn't work, he said, Ginny could consider additional surgery, including spinal fusion. She decided to go ahead with the initial surgery.

In the meantime, Ginny's husband convinced her to attend another one of my advanced seminars in Seattle, which started just one week before her surgery date. Staying seated for the flight was painful, but she made it. While Ginny enjoyed seeing her old friends and meeting new ones at the event, she also felt saddened and frustrated because she couldn't muster the same enthusiasm everyone else had. She just wanted to take some painkillers and go to bed. When she was leaving the first night's gathering, her good friend Jill, filled with compassion and hope, said with conviction, "Ginny, you will be healed tomorrow—right here!"

We started the next day at 6:00 A.M. Ginny decided to avoid taking any heavy medications so she could be present in the meditations and enjoy the experience. Unfortunately, her pain made it very difficult to focus during the first meditation and she wondered if the decision to attend had been a mistake.

During the second meditation after breakfast, though, things really shifted. Ginny decided to surrender and leave all her judgment behind. The meditation began as usual with the breathing exercise of pulling the mind out of the body, during which I told the participants to focus on two or three negative emotions or limited aspects of their personality. I asked them to move all that stored energy from the first three energy centers up from the base of their spine, all the way up to their brain—and eventually release it out of the top of their heads.

First, Ginny chose to work with her anger, which she believed had been a contributing factor in keeping her body in so much pain. During the meditation, she felt energy moving up her spine and then sensed an intense energy leaving her body through the back of her head. The second thing she picked to work with was her pain. As she worked with the breath to move much of the energy related to her pain from her body to her brain, she felt the same energy she had when she was working with anger, although this time she saw the energy become a bright color with purple overtones. Suddenly, she sensed the energy slow down and become less intense. The music changed, and the main part of the meditation began. Ginny was feeling completely relaxed. She had liberated that energy out of her body.

As usual, I guided the group to feel different parts of their bodies in space and to sense the space around their bodies. Then I guided them to the infinite black space that is the quantum field. I asked them to become no body, no one, no thing, no where, in no time and to become pure awareness—aware that they are aware in this endless vast space. At first, as I gave the instructions, Ginny had the distinct sense that she was floating. An intense sense of peace and unconditional love overtook her, and she lost track of time and space. She didn't feel her physical body at all, nor did she feel any pain. Yet she was fully present and could hear and follow all the instructions I was giving.

"I never experienced anything like that before," she told me later. "It was so profound that it's difficult to put into words. My senses were magnified, and I felt connected to everybody, everyone, everything, every place, and every time. I was part of the whole, and the whole was part of me. There was no separation."

Ginny got beyond her body, her environment, and time. Her consciousness had connected to the consciousness of the unified field (the place she described where there's only wholeness and there's no separation). She had found the sweet spot of the generous present moment, and her autonomic nervous system stepped in and did the healing for her.

In our advanced workshops, our students lie down after every meditation and surrender in order to allow the autonomic nervous system to take over and program their bodies. At the end of this meditation, when I asked everyone to come back to their new bodies, Ginny was surprised to discover that she felt absolutely no pain as she got up from the floor to stand—a process that she normally would have needed help with. She started walking without limping, her back straight.

We broke for lunch, but Ginny didn't feel like eating much or even talking a lot. She was still overwhelmed with the meditation experience. After two years of near-constant pain, it felt so freeing to be without it anymore. She started crying tears of joy and confusion simultaneously. She looked for two of her friends to share the good news, including Jill (who had been so sure the night before that Ginny would be healed). They encouraged Ginny to try movements that she hadn't been able to do when she was in pain—and she performed all of them without any pain at all. As the day continued, Ginny's pain stayed away, and she continued to feel connected to the unified field.

That evening, Ginny called her husband, who told her that somehow he just *knew* she'd be able to heal her pain at the workshop. She had a great dinner with her friends, and when she went to bed, she didn't take any of her pain medication or muscle relaxers. She slept through the night for the very first time in years, waking up filled with energy. The next day, I guided the group in a walking meditation (which you will read about and have a chance to try later). Ginny was able to walk straight and tall, with no pain or difficulty. Needless to say, she cancelled the surgery, and she has remained pain free.

Daniel Deals with Electromagnetic Hypersensitivity

About five years ago, Daniel was (as he put it) a "crazy, stressed-out, Israeli entrepreneur" in his mid-20s who pushed himself daily to work at "full power all the way" to build a successful business. Working 60-hour weeks was typical for him. One day, while he was raging and yelling at the top of his lungs at a client over the phone, he felt something pop in the right side of his head and he lost consciousness. When he woke, he wasn't sure what had happened or how long he had been out, but he had the worst headache of his life. He hoped resting would help it go away, but it didn't.

Mysteriously, his pain increased exponentially whenever he was near anything that emitted electromagnetic frequencies, including cell phones, laptops, video displays, microphones, cameras, Wi-Fi networks, and cell towers. If someone near him answered a cell phone, Daniel felt it. He'd never before experienced anything like this—in fact, he had previously worked in the computer field and never felt any ill effects from being around electronic equipment of any kind.

Daniel saw several different doctors and specialists, but none of them could find anything wrong with him. He went through an extensive battery of blood tests, brain scans, and physical examinations, but every one of the studies came back negative. Some of the doctors didn't believe him and even became condescending, rolling their eyes as if Daniel were making up his symptoms. Some wanted to give him antidepressants, but he wouldn't take them. They told him his pain was all in his head (which, of course, it was, but not in the way the doctors meant).

Then Daniel started seeing holistic doctors who suspected he had developed a rare condition called electromagnetic hypersensitivity (EHS). While the existence of EHS is still controversial in the medical community, the World Health Organization recognizes the condition.[1] The mechanism of EHS remains unknown, but when you consider that the brain is 78 percent water and that water containing minerals (such as those commonly found in the body, including calcium and magnesium) conducts electricity, you can see that for EHS-sensitive people, that natural electromagnetic charge might somehow become amplified around things that signal and emit electromagnetic radiation.

Like many others with EHS, Daniel also experienced chronic pain and fatigue in addition to his headaches. He'd sleep for 12 hours and still wake up exhausted. One of the holistic doctors suggested he take 40 nutritional supplements a day to combat the ill effects, but the supplements didn't help. He was still in near-constant agony. Before long, Daniel had to close his business. He went into debt and lost everything he had worked so hard to acquire. Finally, he declared bankruptcy and had to move in with his mother.

"I basically retreated from life," he told me. "I was a zombie because I couldn't think, I couldn't focus, I couldn't do anything. Nothing I did helped, and whenever I got anywhere near the real world, I got a really strong headache." In fact, Daniel told me that if he was ever near anything that emitted a signal, his headaches would be a thousand times worse—to the point that he would emotionally break down. Daniel spent most of his time curled up in a ball on his bed in his tiny room in his mother's house, crying from the pain. "I was wasting my life," he said, "watching all my friends get married, have children, get promoted, buy houses—everything." When he began to feel suicidal, his friends and family pushed him to try to find something that would help.

Because of the chronic fatigue, depression, and severe pain, Daniel had only about a half hour of energy each day, so he started to use that time to find something that might help his condition. Three years after his symptoms began, he read my book *You Are the Placebo*.

"Something clicked," he told me when I met him in a workshop I gave recently. "I knew this was the solution." So he started doing the Changing Beliefs and Perceptions meditation I talk about in that book. Very gradually, over time, Daniel felt a little less pain, so he kept doing the meditation. After a while, he discovered my Blessing of the Energy Centers meditation, and he started doing that.

"The very first time I did it," Daniel told me, "something happened that I didn't know how to explain." When he got to the sixth energy center, he said it was like a light show was going on in his head. He saw different areas of his brain that had been shut down suddenly start lighting up and communicating with each other. Then a huge beam of what he described as "loving light" shot out of the top of his head. His inward experience in that moment was more real than the memory of the past experience, which had created the pain in the first place.

From that point on, Daniel noticed a significant change. After meditating, he would have ten minutes without any pain at all. The pain-free periods kept getting longer and longer until a few months later, he was pain free. Then he got the idea that he should use the meditations to change his internal state while he was exposed to the electromagnetic fields that had been making him sick. So he started meditating in front of his cell phone and laptop. It was painful at first, but just as before, he'd eventually feel free of pain after meditating, and then those pain-free periods kept getting longer as time wore on.

Finally, Daniel was ready to take another big step. He hired a desk in a shared office space and decided to just sit there and meditate, surrounded by Wi-Fi, computers, microwaves, and all sorts of electromagnetic frequencies. Although the first few weeks were difficult, he found that it became easier as time wore on. After a while, he was meditating in that environment without pain for five hours a day. Eventually, his headaches just disappeared—and so did all his chronic pain and fatigue.

Today, Daniel considers himself 100 percent healed. He went back to work and got out of debt. Here's the kicker: Daniel works only about an hour to an hour and a half a day, and he's making way more money than he was when he was stressed out and trying to force his life into working the way he wanted it to. He's also truly enjoying life.

Jennifer, in Sickness and in Health

Five years ago, Jennifer's doctor diagnosed her with several new illnesses, in addition to the numerous other health issues she already suffered from. In total, her diagnoses included a few autoimmune disorders (lupus erythematosus and Sjögren's syndrome with sicca complex), some gastrointestinal disorders (celiac disease, salicylate intolerance, and lactose intolerance), chronic asthma, kidney disease, arthritis, and vertigo so acute it often resulted in vomiting.

Every day was a struggle. Even just brushing her teeth was difficult because she lacked enough strength to hold her arm up for very long. Her partner, Jim, often had to brush her hair for her. When Jim was away on business, which was often, Jennifer had to take a nap after work so she could have enough strength to cook dinner.

"The hardest thing was that I felt like a terrible mother because I couldn't do anything with my boys—and that broke my heart," she told me. "I would have to sleep most of the weekend just to be able to get up to go to work Monday morning. All the happy pictures I posted on Facebook during the weekend were captured in about one hour."

By this point, Jennifer weighed only 108 pounds and struggled to walk due to arthritis and severe swelling in her ankles and knees. She could no longer use her right hand to open containers or cut vegetables because of the pain and arthritis. At times she would lie in bed and hit her arms against her night table to stop the pain. Her body was in a constant state of acute inflammation, and even the specialists she saw said they couldn't do anything more for her and that she had to learn to live with all her conditions as best she could. Although she never admitted it to anyone, she feared she might only have a few years left to live. She may have been ready to give up, but Jim wasn't.

Every night Jim devoured books looking for alternative solutions, repeatedly encouraging Jennifer to keep going. Then Jim found *You Are the Placebo* and read about a woman with a similar condition who was able to heal herself. Jennifer and Jim agreed that she had to go to a workshop.

Two months later, in June 2014, Jennifer attended a weekend workshop in Sydney, Australia. She started to feel a bit better and registered for an advanced workshop in Mexico. Unfortunately, around the time she was scheduled to leave for the workshop, she developed an 8.5-millimeter kidney stone, and her doctor refused to let her fly. So she missed it, but she kept doing her meditations (getting up at 4:50 A.M. every day), and when I held the next advanced workshop in Australia the following year, both she and Jim attended.

"I remember the first night I could hardly make it up the stairs to our room, which was normal for me," she reported. "But by the end of the workshop, I was walking around like a healthy person and didn't have to use my asthma medication. The day before we left, Jim said that I was looking so well I should try some normal food. Apprehensive, I gave it a go—and no adverse effects! No pain, no asthma, no cramps, no headache—nothing! I think it was the best pizza I've ever had."

When she did her meditations, Jennifer really gave it her all. She repeatedly tuned in to the potential of health and felt an abundance of energy throughout her body that could carry her all day long. In the meditation, when I asked the students to live from that new state of being, she imagined her feet hitting the ground and heard her breath as she joyfully ran. By the end of her meditation, she was crying tears of joy. Eventually, Jennifer conditioned her body to forget what illness feels like, looks like, sounds like, and tastes like by raising her energy, changing her frequency, reconditioning her body to a new mind, and signaling new genes to repair her body.

"Now I eat normal food," she reports, "and I haven't used my asthma medication since June 2015. I can walk up to ten miles a day and lift forty-five pounds. I'm training, and my goal is to complete a half marathon, which I will soon do."

Felicia Overcomes Severe Eczema

Felicia had intermittently suffered from eczema and skin infections since she was three months old. The short-term relief provided by a strict diet and a regime of medications (creams, steroids, antihistamines, antifungals, antibiotics, and so on) never seemed to keep the condition at bay for long.

In 2016, as a 34-year-old medical doctor in the United Kingdom, Felicia found herself becoming increasingly frustrated by the limitations of her profession. After a decade of clinical practice where she'd seen more than 70,000 patients, she began to recognize a similar sense of frustration and disconnect emerging from her patients as well. While seeking more satisfying science-based solutions, she came across my work. Intrigued by possibility and hungry for alternative evidence-based ideas and solutions, Felicia signed up for a weekend workshop.

"The event was life changing," she says. "It gave me the tools to reevaluate and update my previous limited beliefs about myself, as well as what our bodies are truly capable of." The breathing technique was particularly intriguing to her. "I must confess," she says, "that I remained a little skeptical and held back, not allowing myself to truly surrender to the process."

During the months that followed, Felicia continued to meditate daily. Her skin improved and she successfully manifested a new relationship in her life. Feeling inspired, she sought new ways to pivot within her medical practice to adopt a more holistic approach. But to her great disappointment, all the United Kingdom medical indemnity bodies refused to insure any nonconventional approaches. Felicia felt trapped, and in December 2016, her eczema and skin infections returned.

Even so, she continued meditating and even signed up for an advanced workshop, creating her Mind Movie in preparation (a powerful tool for manifesting various things you want, which you will read about in a later chapter). She had very clear intentions for her future and included images of healthy skin, as well as a picture of a microphone on a stage with the affirmation "I inspire others by sharing truth fearlessly."

On the first day of the advanced workshop, we did the breathing technique to activate the pineal gland, and this time, Felicia decided not to hold back and to completely surrender to the process. "I noticed my breathing begin to hasten," she remembers. "An overwhelming energy started building in my throat. This intensified until my throat felt as if it was going to close up. Fearful, I pulled my body out of this position and returned back to my old state of being for the remainder of the meditation."

The following day, for the last meditation, Felicia was being fitted with the brain mapping equipment. She considered what an amazing opportunity it was to experience this new level of information. Feeling trapped in a profession that preaches limitation, she had the thought: *What if I could demonstrate to the skeptic, as well as to believers, how unlimited we all really are?* With this thought, she wanted to use this breath to connect to the unified field—with an elevated emotion of pure freedom and liberation—no matter what happened.

When the meditation began, she opened up to possibility and to the unknown. She quickly noticed that her breathing started to change and the overwhelming energy began to build in her throat. Each time the sensations intensified, instead of allowing them to overcome her as she had done the previous day, she stayed with the process. She returned her body to the present moment, ignoring the distraction, and placed all her energy and awareness on connecting to the field, to truth, and to love. Her body was persistently defiant, but after repeatedly overcoming her internal struggles, her body eventually surrendered.

"What I experienced on the other side was an exhilarating explosion of energy in my brain and an instantaneous connection with a loving consciousness within and all around me," she says. "It was an absolute knowing, a recognition of pure love, and with it came the most overwhelming emotion of joy that I've ever experienced in my entire life. It was like coming home. I just experienced this deep oneness. All the while I remained completely aware of all my external senses. I could hear the scientists behind me saying 'seizure.'" We had some new members on our team of neuroscientists, and they had never seen that kind of energy in the brain before.

As a medical doctor, Felicia might normally have been concerned at that somewhat alarming statement, but she understood that in that moment she was experiencing absolute truth and freedom for the very first time. For a few hours following her meditation, she felt somewhat dazed but physically lighter than before.

If you review the brain scans in Graphics 7A–7C, you can see Felicia's brain showing the classic changes that we witness when there is high energy in the brain. She starts in normal beta brain waves and then transitions into high-beta brain waves before she hits a high-energy gamma state. The energy in gamma brain waves is 190 standard deviations above normal. The area surrounding the pineal gland as well as the part of the brain that processes strong emotion is highly activated.

During the next few days, Felicia began to experience a sense of fearlessness and playfulness emerging from within her. She also experienced a string of synchronicities—including manifesting the scene from her Mind Movie where she was speaking into a microphone onstage. In fact, without knowing that scene had been in her Mind Movie, I pulled her onstage to share her experience. It was only once she returned home that she noticed her eczema was no longer bothering her.

"I looked at my skin, and all the rashes that had been there just a few days prior had completely resolved," she reported. (Look at Graphic 7D in the color insert. The first pictures were taken before the event. The second set of pictures was taken the next day, after the event. Her eczema is gone.)

To this day Felicia takes no further medication and her skin is clear. Her life continues to unfold in new, exciting, and surprising ways.

"I am so grateful for the realization that we are all unlimited," she told me. "Mark my words, if a once jaded, intensely analytical doctor can do it, absolutely anyone can."

Chapter 7

HEART INTELLIGENCE

Since our human ancestors first began etching their histories upon cave walls and stone tablets, like a thread through the needle of time, the heart has appeared as a symbol to represent health, wisdom, intuition, guidance, and higher intelligence. The ancient Egyptians, who referred to the heart as *ieb*, believed the heart, rather than the brain, was the center of life and the source of human wisdom. The Mesopotamians and the Greeks both thought of the heart as the center of the soul. The Greeks, however, considered it an independent source of heat within the body, while the Mesopotamians believed it was a fragment of the sun's heat. They even performed human sacrifices whereby they extracted a still-beating human heart to offer it to the Sun God. The Romans understood the heart to be the body's most life-giving vital organ.

In the 17th century, during the early years of the scientific revolution, French philosopher René Descartes argued that mind and body were two radically distinct substances. Through this mechanistic view of the universe, people began to view the heart as an extraordinary machine. The mechanism of the heart as a physical pump began to overshadow its nature as humanity's connection to an innate intelligence. Through scientific inquiry, the heart slowly ceased to be recognized as our connection to feelings, emotions, and our higher selves. It has only been through the new science of the last few decades that we've began to reconcile, understand, and recognize the true significance of the heart both as a source that generates electromagnetic fields and as our connection to the unified field.

We know that the heart, beyond its obvious role in sustaining life, is not simply a muscular pump that moves blood throughout our body but an organ capable of influencing feelings and emotions. The heart is a sensory organ that guides our decision-making ability as well as our understanding of ourselves and our place in the world. It's a symbol that transcends time, place, and culture. It's a commonly accepted premise that when we are connected to the heart's inner knowing, we can tap into its wisdom as a source of love and higher guidance.

You may well be wondering why it is that out of all the organs in the body (such as the spleen, liver, or kidneys), the heart is the only one to have intelligence. Since 2013, we've gone to great lengths to measure and quantify coherence and transformation, which are central to understanding the heart's role. Almost everyone recognizes that the elevated feelings of the heart connect us to the consciousness of love, compassion, gratitude, joy, unity, acceptance, and selflessness. These are feelings that fill us up and make us feel whole and connected, rather than the feelings of stress that divide communities and drain us of vital energy. The problem is that these elevated feelings of the heart often occur through chance—dependent upon something external in our environment—rather than as something we can produce for ourselves on demand.

Without a doubt, it's a challenge to maintain our mental and emotional equilibrium in today's fast paced, stress-filled, productivity-focused, hurry-up-and-finish culture, and the loss of this equilibrium can have serious ramifications for our health. For instance, at the turn of the 20th century, hardly anyone died of heart disease, while today it's the leading cause of death for both men and women. Each year in the United States alone, heart disease costs approximately $207 billion in health care services, medications, and lost productivity.[1] Stress is one of the main contributing factors to heart disease, and it's reaching an epidemic level. Fortunately, there's an antidote. What we've found in researching and studying the many facets of heart coherence is that we *can* in fact regulate our internal states, independent of the conditions in our external environment. Just like developing any skill, voluntarily creating heart coherence requires knowledge, application, and practice.

Integral to our understanding of the heart has been our partnership with the pioneering, groundbreaking work of the HeartMath Institute. HMI is a nonprofit research and education organization that works to better understand heart-brain coherence. Since 1991, HMI has researched and developed reliable, scientifically based tools to help people bridge the connection between their hearts and minds, as well as deepen their connection with the hearts of others. Their mission is to help people bring their physical, mental, and emotional systems into balanced alignment through the intuitive guidance of the heart.

The foundation of our partnership is built upon the shared belief that in order to create a new future, a person needs to marry a clear intention (coherent brain) with an elevated emotion (coherent heart). HMI's research has proven that by combining an intention or thought (which, as you have read, acts as the electrical charge) with a feeling or emotion (which you already understand acts as a magnetic charge), we can change our biological energy—and when we change our energy, we change our lives. It's the union of these two elements that produces measurable effects on matter, moving our biology away from living in the familiar past to living in the new future. At our workshops across the world, we teach our students to maintain and sustain these elevated states of being so they can cease living as victims of circumstance, swinging from one emotion to the next, and begin living as the creators of their reality. This is the process whereby we create a new state of being—or a new personality, which creates a new personal reality.

For the past several years, one of the goals of our partnership with HMI has been to teach our students to intentionally regulate and sustain something called heart coherence. Like the regular beating of a drum, heart coherence refers to the physiological function of the heart that causes it to beat in a consistent, rhythmic, orderly manner (the opposite, when it is not operating in an orderly manner, is heart incoherence). When we are in heart coherence, we can access the "heart's intelligence," which HMI defines as:

> The flow of awareness and insight that we experience once the mind and emotions are brought into balance and coherence through a self-initiated process. This form of intelligence is experienced as direct, intuitive knowing that manifests in thought and emotions that are beneficial for ourselves and others.[2]

As you'll discover in this chapter, the benefits of heart coherence are numerous, including lowering blood pressure, improving the nervous system and hormonal balance, and improving brain function. When you maintain and sustain elevated emotional states, independent of the conditions of your external environment, you can gain access to the kind of high-level intuition that fosters a better understanding of yourself and others, helps prevent stressful patterns in your life, increases mental clarity, and promotes better decision making.[3] In addition to HMI's research findings, our data strongly suggests that sustained heart-centered emotions promote healthier gene expression.[4]

Heart coherence begins with the steady, coherent drumbeat of the heart through cultivating, practicing, and sustaining elevated emotions; such emotions include gratitude, appreciation, thankfulness, inspiration, freedom, kindness, selflessness, compassion, love, and joy. The benefits of that coherent beat are felt throughout all systems of the body. Consciously or unconsciously, many of us practice feeling unhappy, angry, or fearful each day. So why not practice creating and maintaining joyful, loving, altruistic states instead? Wouldn't that eventually create a new internal order, resulting in overall health and happiness?

The Heart Bridge

As you read in the chapter on blessing the energy centers, the heart, located right behind the breastbone, is the body's fourth energy center. It is our bridge to greater levels of awareness and energy, as well as the center where our divinity begins. The heart is the intersection of our lower three energy centers (associated with our earthly body) and our upper three energy centers (associated with our higher self). It serves as our connection to the unified field and represents the union of duality or polarity. It is where separation, division, and polarized energy merge to become one—where opposites unify as the yin and the yang, good and bad, positive and negative, male and female, past and future.

When your heart becomes coherent, your nervous system responds by increasing the brain's energy, creativity, and intuition, which has a positive effect on virtually every organ in the body. Now the heart and the brain are working together, causing you to feel more whole, connected, and content—not only within your own body, but also with everything and everybody. When you are in a heart-centered state, the wholeness you feel consumes any feelings you may have of want and lack. From this creative state of wholeness and oneness, magic begins to happen in your life because you're no longer creating from duality or separation—you're no longer waiting for something outside of you to provide relief from the internal feelings of lack, emptiness, or separation. Instead, you are becoming more familiar with your new, ideal self and creating new experiences *of* yourself. If you keep activating your heart center properly enough times during the creative process each day, in time you will feel more like your future has already happened. How can you ever want or feel lack if you feel whole?

If the first three centers reflect our animal nature and are based on polarity, opposites, competition, need, and lack, the fourth center begins our journey to our divine nature. It is from within this heart center that we change our mind and energy from living in selfish states to living in selfless states, and then we feel less affected by separation or duality and are more prone to make choices for the greatest good of everyone.

All of us have felt the consciousness of the heart center at one time or another in our lives. This energy is related to being fulfilled and at peace with yourself and your surroundings. When we embrace the feelings related to the heart—feelings that lead us to give, nurture, serve, care, help, forgive, love, trust, and so on—we can't help but feel filled up, whole, and complete. I believe this to be our innate nature as human beings.

Homeostasis, Coherence, and Resilience

As you have now learned, the autonomic nervous system, the involuntary division of the nervous system, is divided into two subsystems: the sympathetic nervous system and the parasympathetic nervous system. As you know, the sympathetic nervous system when switched on regulates the body's unconscious actions and responses, such as increased breathing, elevated heart rate, excess perspiration, dilation of the pupils, and so on. Its primary function is to stimulate the fight-or-flight response when real or perceived danger is imminent. This system works to protect us in our outer environment. The parasympathetic nervous system complements the sympathetic nervous system in that it performs the exact opposite functions. Its role is to conserve energy, relax the body, and slow the high-energy functions of the sympathetic system. The parasympathetic system maintains protection in our inner environment. If you think of the ANS as an automobile, the parasympathetic system would be the brake and the sympathetic system the accelerator. Both branches of the ANS continuously relay communications between the heart and the brain; in fact, the heart and the brain have more nerve connections to each other than any other systems in the body.[5] These two systems, the sympathetic and parasympathetic, are always working to maintain a state of homeostasis (relative equilibrium between all systems) within the body.

When the body is in a state of homeostasis, we generally feel relaxed and safe within our current environment. From this state of homeostasis, where all the body's systems are working in harmony and minimal amounts of energy are wasted, we can intentionally affect the nervous system to create coherence. In order to feel these emotions of coherence, the neural connections between the heart and brain must be functioning optimally in a balanced and coordinated manner. When the heart is beating in such an orderly, coherent fashion, it brings the ANS into coherence, which in turn improves our brain functions by causing us to feel more creative, focused, rational, aware, and open to learning.

As you know, the opposite of coherence is incoherence. When the heart is beating incoherently, we feel out of balance, on edge, anxious, and unfocused. Because the body is operating in survival, we function more from an animalistic, primitive perspective than from the higher heart-centered emotions of our greater humanity and divinity. Incoherence is brought on by stress, which is the body and mind's response to disruptions and upsets in our external environment. If the parasympathetic nervous system functions best when we feel safe, then the sympathetic nervous system is activated mostly when we feel unsafe. The stress we experience when we feel unsafe is not necessarily about the event itself but the result of unmanaged emotional reactions to the event.

In a state of homeostasis, you can think of the body as a sophisticated, finely tuned machine, but when emotions such as resentment, anger, jealousy, impatience, and frustration persist, our internal equilibrium is thrown out of balance. If you think about a time recently when you felt stress, it probably felt somewhat like a fragmented rhythm. (As it turns out, this is exactly what the heart is doing—beating in a fragmented rhythm.) In a state of chronic stress, the body struggles to maintain homeostasis and we may begin to suffer from myriad stress-related symptoms. This constant stress draws from the invisible energy field around our body and depletes our vital life force, leaving little time or energy for repair and restoration. As a result of the body's reliance on the stress hormones, now we're caught in an addictive loop where incoherence and chaos start to feel normal, but at what cost?

The long-term effects of stress can be catastrophic. According to one Mayo Clinic study of people with heart disease, psychological stress was the strongest predictor of future cardiac events, including cardiac death, cardiac arrest, and heart attack.[6] Many people, because they live in states of chronic stress, don't even realize they are living under stress until an event such as a heart attack occurs. It makes sense, then, that if the heart is beating incoherently for extended periods of time, not working in balance and order, sooner or later it is going to fail.

Key to our ability to manage stress is what's known as resilience, which HMI defines as "the capacity to prepare for, recover from, and adapt in the face of stress, adversity, trauma, or challenge."[7] Resilience and the management of emotions are both integral to many important physiological processes involved in energy regulation, how fast the body bounces back after the stress response, and our ability to maintain health and homeostasis.

HRV: Communication between the Heart and Brain

We've been led to believe that the brain reigns over our biology. While this is partly true, the heart is an autorhythmic organ, which means the heartbeat is self-initiated from within the heart, not from the brain. For example, it's a known fact that in all kinds of species the heart can be removed from the body and placed in a salt solution called Ringer's solution, where it will continue to beat for extended periods of time—independent of any neurological connection to the brain. In a fetus, the heart begins beating before the brain is even formed (at about three weeks), while the electrical activity of its brain doesn't even begin until around the fifth or sixth week.[8] This demonstrates that the heart is capable of initiating communication with the central nervous system.

Another factor that makes the heart unique is that it contains nerves from both branches of the ANS, which means any and every change in both the parasympathetic and sympathetic nervous systems affects the way the heart works on a beat-to-beat basis. This is important because whether we are conscious of it or not, every emotion we experience influences our heart rhythm, which gets communicated directly through the central nervous system. In this way, the heart, the limbic brain, and the ANS have a very intimate relationship because balance or imbalance in one affects the other. (As a side note, the limbic brain—the seat of the autonomic nervous system—is also called the emotional brain, so when you change your emotions, you affect your autonomic functions.) Today, with about 75 percent accuracy, science can predict what someone is feeling just by looking at the beat-to-beat activity of the heart using heart rate variability analysis.[9]

HRV (heart rate variability) is a physiological phenomenon that measures environmental and psychological challenges as reflected by the variation of the heart's beat-to-beat intervals (thus the term *variability*). Among its uses, HRV can measure the flexibility of our heart and nervous system (which reflects our health and fitness), as well as how well we are balancing our mental and emotional lives.[10] By studying the heart's rhythms as measured by HRV, scientists can detect patterns that deepen our understanding of how humans process emotions and the effects of feelings and emotions on our well-being. In this way, continued HRV research offers us a unique window into the communication between the heart, brain, and emotions.[11]

Many studies show that having a moderate level of variability makes us better able to adapt to life's challenges.[12] But a low level of heart rate variability is a strong and independent predictor of future health problems, including all causes of mortality.[13] Low HRV is also associated with numerous medical conditions. When we are young, we have greater variability, but as we age, our variability decreases. HRV patterns are so consistent that when scientists look at an HRV reading, they can generally estimate the subject's age within approximately two years.

For many years, a steady heart rhythm was considered a sign of good health, but now we know that our heart rhythm changes with each and every heartbeat, even when we are sleeping. Over the years, HMI researchers have discovered information encoded within these beat-to-beat intervals by looking at the spaces *between* heartbeats in HRV readings rather than the spikes related to the beats themselves. This is somewhat similar to Morse code, where we understand communications by the intervals between transmissions.[14] In the case of our heart, the intervals between its beats are complex transmissions used to relay communications between the brain and body.

During the 1990s, researchers at HMI discovered that when people focused on their hearts and evoked elevated emotions such as appreciation, joy, gratitude, and compassion, those feelings could be observed as coherent patterns in the heart's rhythms. The opposite was true of stressful feelings, which caused the heart rhythms to be incoherent and to appear jagged and irregular. This discovery linked emotional states to HRV patterns (see Figure 7.1).[15] The researchers also observed that heart rate (beats per minute) and heart rhythm were two separate biological responses. For instance, a person could have a high heart rate and still maintain a state of coherence; therefore it was determined that the heart's rhythms can create coherent internal body states.

CHANGES IN ENERGY DURING AN ADVANCED WORKSHOP

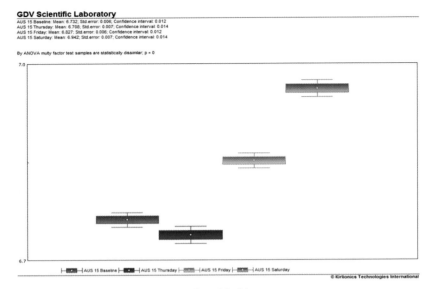

GDV Scientific Laboratory
AUS 15 Baseline: Mean: 6.732; Std.error: 0.006; Confidence interval: 0.012
AUS 15 Thursday: Mean: 6.708; Std.error: 0.007; Confidence interval: 0.014
AUS 15 Friday: Mean: 6.827; Std.error: 0.006; Confidence interval: 0.012
AUS 15 Saturday: Mean: 6.942; Std.error: 0.007; Confidence interval: 0.014

By ANOVA multy factor test samples are statistically dissimilar; p = 0

AUS 15 Baseline — AUS 15 Thursday — AUS 15 Friday — AUS 15 Saturday

© Kirlionics Technologies International

Graphic 1A

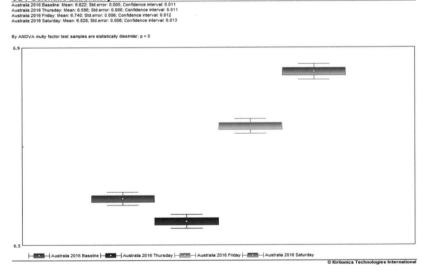

GDV Scientific Laboratory
Australia 2016 Baseline: Mean: 6.622; Std.error: 0.005; Confidence interval: 0.011
Australia 2016 Thursday: Mean: 6.586; Std.error: 0.006; Confidence interval: 0.011
Australia 2016 Friday: Mean: 6.740; Std.error: 0.006; Confidence interval: 0.012
Australia 2016 Saturday: Mean: 6.826; Std.error: 0.006; Confidence interval: 0.013

By ANOVA multy factor test samples are statistically dissimilar; p = 0

Australia 2016 Baseline — Australia 2016 Thursday — Australia 2016 Friday — Australia 2016 Saturday

© Kirlionics Technologies International

Graphic 1B

In some of our advanced workshops, when students break the energetic bonds with everyone and everything in their past-present reality, they draw from the ambient field to build their own individual electromagnetic field. When this occurs, the energy of the room can drop. Both figures demonstrate this phenomenon during two advanced workshops in Australia in 2015 and 2016. The red line is the baseline measurement on Wednesday—the day before the event starts, when no one is in the room. The blue line is Thursday—the first full day. You can see that the energy in the room decreased slightly. The green line is Friday—the second day. You can see how the energy of the room continues to rise as students break through on Friday. At this point, instead of drawing energy from the field, they are contributing energy to the field.

COHERENCE VS. INCOHERENCE

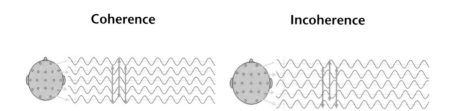

Coherence   **Incoherence**

Coherence

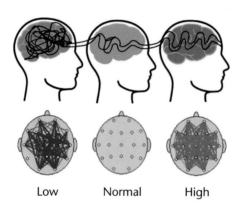

Low   Normal   High

Graphic 2

In the first image, both circles represent a top view of a person wearing an EEG brain cap. The head is facing forward, so the nose is pointing toward the top of the page and ears are on both sides. The tiny white circles represent different brain compartments, where we can measure brain waves in those specific areas. On the left, you can see how the arrows are all lined up in perfect order, showing the waves in phase. That's coherence. On the right, you can see that the waves of the brain are not in phase and the arrows do not line up with the peaks and valleys. That's incoherence.

Since I will be showing you different brain scans in the pages ahead, I want to familiarize you with how we measure coherence and incoherence. Look at the second set of images. If there is a lot of blue in the brain, it means there is low coherence (hypo-coherence) and different areas of the brain communicate less with each other. If there is a lot of red in the brain, it means that there is high coherence (hyper-coherence) and different areas communicate more with each other. If there is no blue and no red, it means normal or average coherence.

NORMAL BETA BRAIN WAVES

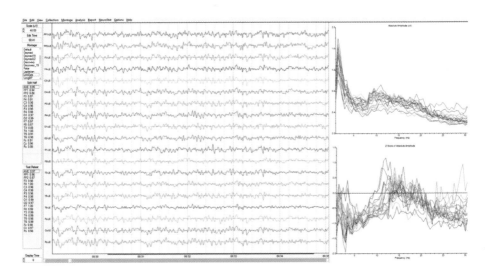

Graphic 3A

SYNCHRONIZED COHERENT ALPHA BRAIN WAVES

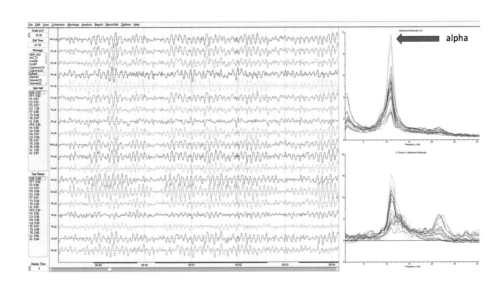

Graphic 3B

SYNCHRONIZED COHERENT THETA BRAIN WAVES

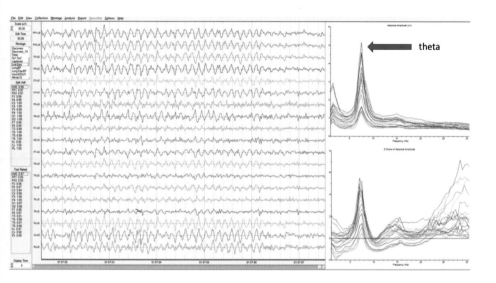

Graphic 3C

Look at each of the thin vertical blue lines on the strip charts in Graphics 3A, 3B, and 3C and follow them down to the bottom. You'll see how they represent one-second intervals. Each of the 19 horizontal wavy lines is related to different compartments of the brain being measured—the front, both sides, the top, and the back of the brain. If you count the number of cycles (from the top of one wave to the top of the next wave) between the two blue vertical lines, you will know the brain waves in each individual area of the brain. That's how we determine beta, alpha, theta, delta, or gamma brain waves. If you need to review the different frequencies of brain waves, review Figure 2.7.

When you go from a narrow focus to an open focus and you take your attention off matter (some thing) and place your attention on space or energy (no thing), your brain waves change from beta to alpha or to theta. Graphic 3A shows a normal thinking busy brain in beta brain waves. Graphic 3B shows a person who is in coherent global alpha brain waves. Notice how beautifully synchronized each part of the brain is when this person opens their focus. The blue arrow pointing to the peaks shows how the entire brain is coherent in 12-cycles-per-second alpha brain waves. Graphic 3C demonstrates a person in coherent theta brain waves. Once again, the blue arrow pointing to the top of the peaks demonstrates that the entire brain is synchronized in about 7 cycles per second, which is the theta range for brain waves.

CHANGES IN ENERGY FROM THE BLESSING OF THE ENERGY CENTERS MEDITATION

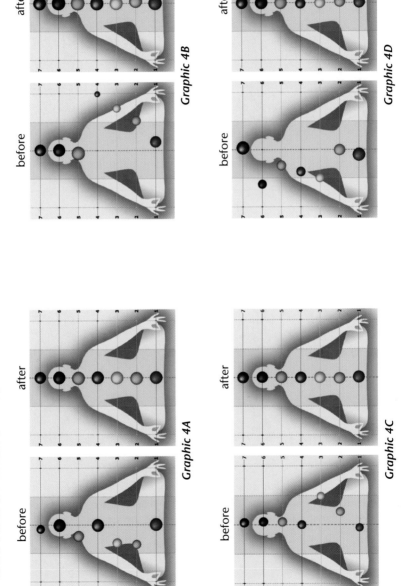

Graphic 4A

Graphic 4B

Graphic 4C

Graphic 4D

The images on the left show GDV measurements of students' energy centers before they started an advanced event. The images on the right side show the changes just a few days later after the Blessing of the Energy Centers meditation. Notice the difference in the size and the alignment of each center.

CHANGES IN OVERALL ENERGY
BEFORE AND AFTER AN ADVANCED WORKSHOP

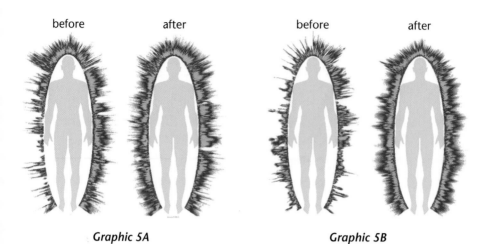

Graphic 5A

Graphic 5B

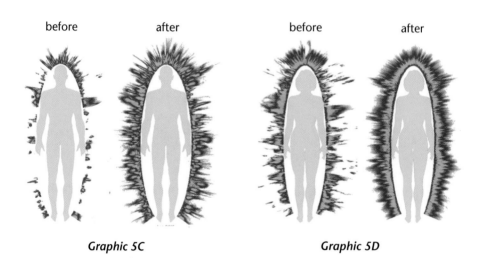

Graphic 5C

Graphic 5D

The images on the left demonstrate some GDV measurements of subjects' energy before they started an advanced workshop. The images on the right show the changes in their vital energy a few days after the workshop.

A STUDENT MOVING INTO
GAMMA BRAIN WAVES FROM THE BREATH

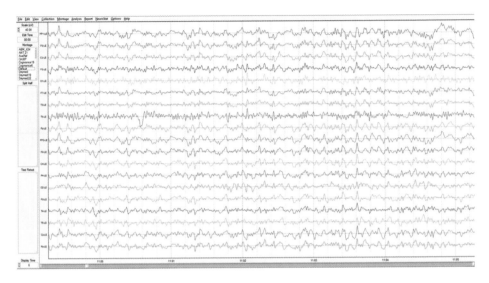

Graphic 6A(1)

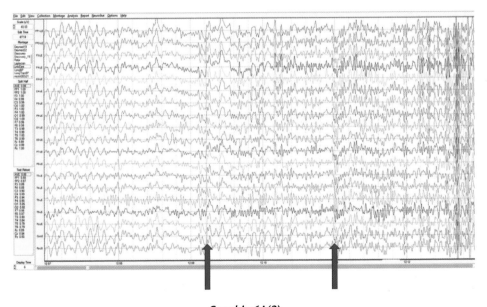

Graphic 6A(2)

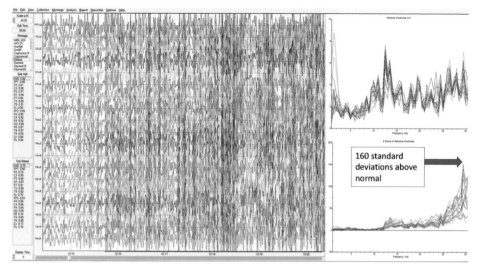

160 standard
deviations above
normal

Graphic 6A(3)

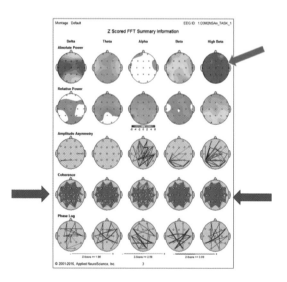

Graphic 6A(4)

Graphics 6A(1), 6A(2), and 6A(3) show a student transitioning to gamma brain waves as a result of the breath as he passes through high beta. His brain is very aroused with energy. You can see an obvious change in frequency in the brain when this occurs (shown by the blue arrows). The amount of energy in his brain is 160 standard deviations outside normal. Now look at Graphic 6A(4). When there is a lot of red in the brain, it means there is a lot of energy. When there is blue in the brain, it means there is very little energy. Therefore, the red arrow that points to the totally red circle means there is an enormous amount of energy in high beta brain state as it transitions to gamma. The software used here does not record gamma brain waves per se, but from viewing the other measurements in the charts above, we know that the amount of energy in the brain in the totally red circle reflects gamma as well as high beta. The blue arrows pointing to the row labeled Coherence show there is intense communication along with high energy in all measured brain frequencies.

ANOTHER STUDENT MOVING INTO
GAMMA BRAIN WAVES FROM THE BREATH

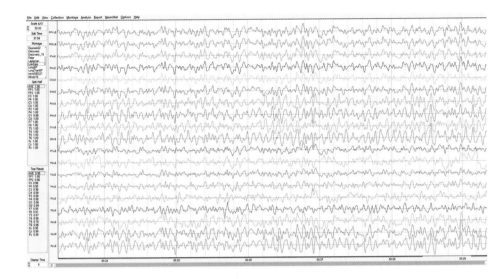

Graphic 6B(1)

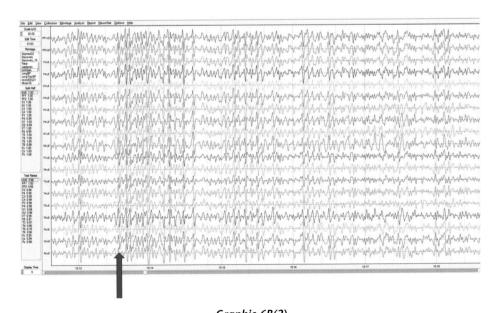

Graphic 6B(2)

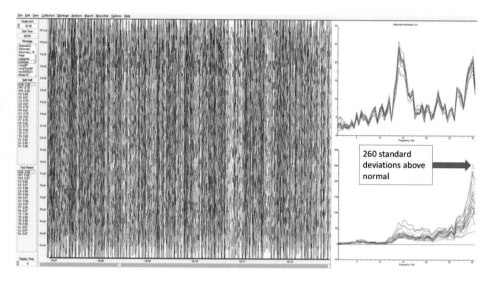

Graphic 6B(3)

You can see a similar transition in these graphics. The blue arrow at the bottom of the strip chart in Graphic 6B(2) shows the moment the brain is moving from high beta to gamma. Graphic 6B(3) shows that the energy in the brain is 260 standard deviations above normal. To put this in context, 99.7 percent of the population falls within 3 standard deviations above or below normal. Anything outside of 3 standard deviations is supernatural.

SCANS SHOWING THE AREA
SURROUNDING THE PINEAL GLAND ACTIVATED

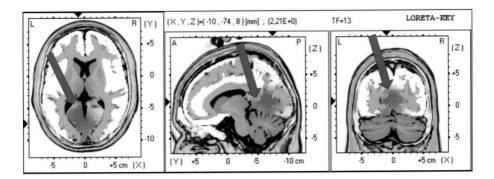

Graphic 6B(4)

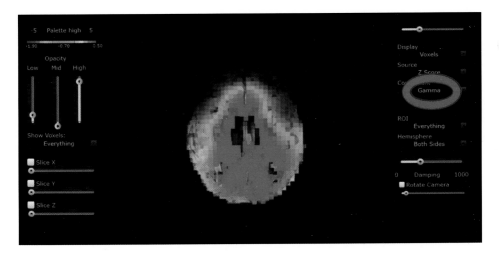

Graphic 6B(5)

The red area of the brain where the blue arrows are pointing in 6B(4) is the region that surrounds the pineal gland as well as a region called Brodmann area 30, which is associated with strong emotions and the formation of new memories. Our team sees this pattern in those areas of the brain repeatedly when students produce gamma brain waves. Graphic 6B(5) is a three-dimensional picture of the same student's brain from below, showing a significant amount of energy coming from inside the limbic brain.

FELICIA'S BRAIN SCANS

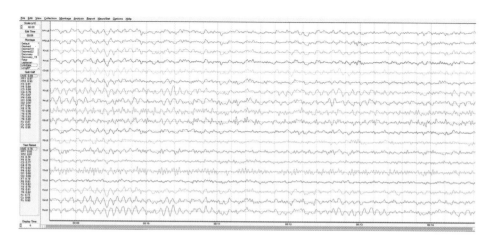

Graphic 7A(1)

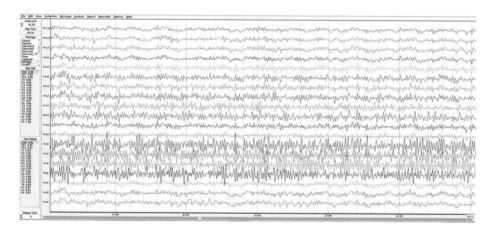

Graphic 7A(2)

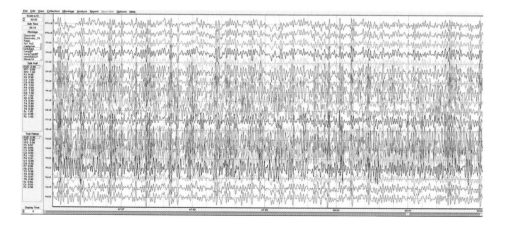

Graphic 7A(3)

FELICIA'S BRAIN SCANS

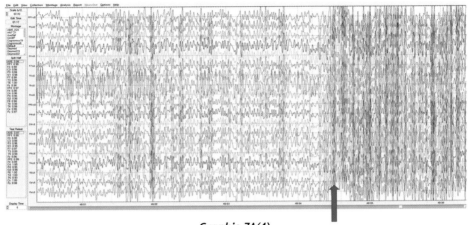

Graphic 7A(4)

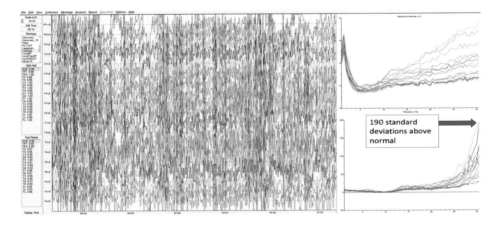

190 standard
deviations above
normal

Graphic 7A(5)

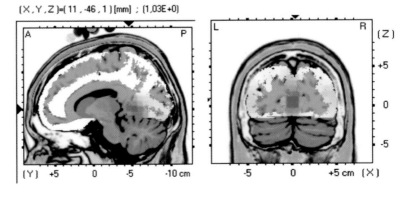

Graphic 7B

FELICIA'S CASE HISTORY, CONTINUED

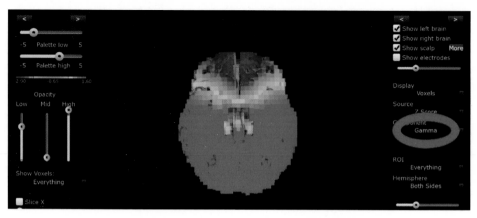

Graphic 7C

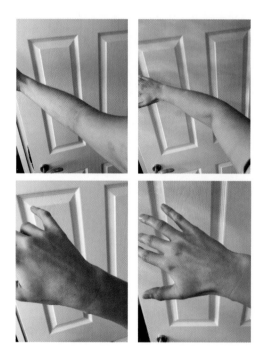

Graphic 7D

Graphics 7A(1) through 7A(5) show Felicia's brain transitioning from normal beta to high beta before she moves into a high-energy gamma state. (The blue arrow shows the transition.) The energy in gamma is 190 standard deviations above normal as she connects to the unified field. The area of the pineal gland as well as the part of the brain that processes strong emotion is highly activated, as seen in 7B. The image in 7C is the underside of the brain. The red region demonstrates that energy in gamma is coming from inside the limbic brain. Take a look at Graphic 7D to see the changes in Felicia's skin condition the following day after she received a biological upgrade from the unified field.

HEART COHERENCE AND BRAIN COHERENCE

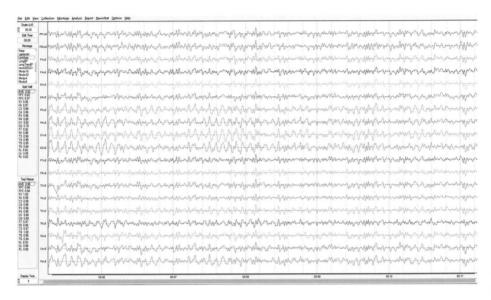

Graphic 8A

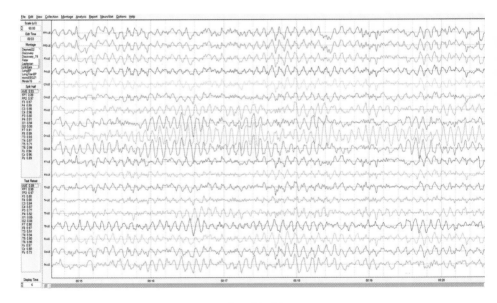

Graphic 8B

The first scan represents the measurement of a person's brain before she activates her heart center. The brain is in a dominant frequency of desynchronized beta brain waves, indicating a busy and distracted brain. The second scan measures the same brain about 10 seconds later as she moves into heart coherence. The entire brain goes into a coherent alpha brain wave state.

COHERENT ALPHA AND THETA
BRAIN WAVES FROM VIEWING THE KALEIDOSCOPE

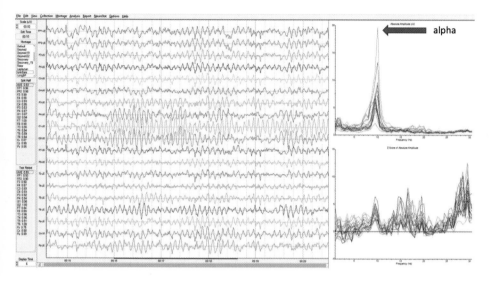

Graphic 9A(1)

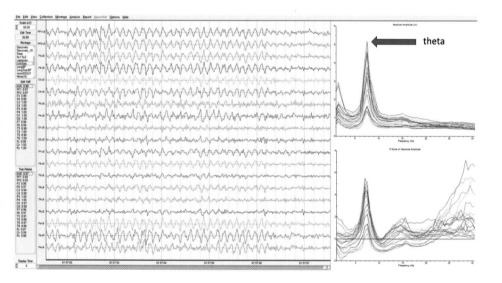

Graphic 9A(2)

Graphic 9A(1) shows a brain scan of a student who is in coherent alpha brain waves while watching the kaleidoscope. Graphic 9A(2) illustrates a person in coherent theta brain wave states viewing the kaleidoscope in trance. Graphic 9A(3) shows a three-dimensional image of the brain (nearly all in red) of another student, indicating almost the whole brain in a theta state. The red

CHANGES IN BRAIN ACTIVITY
WHILE VIEWING THE KALEIDOSCOPE

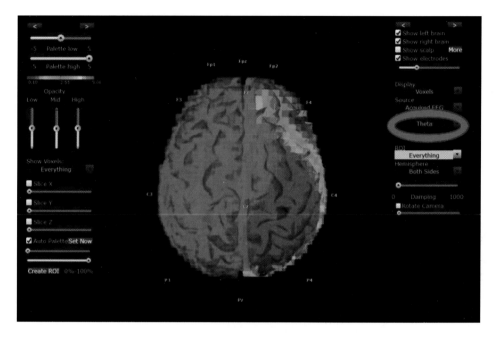

Graphic 9A(3)

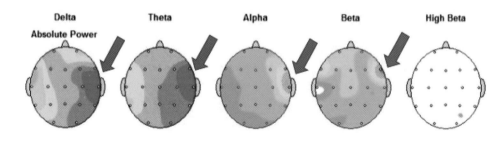

Graphic 9A(4)

oval on the right shows the brain is being measured in theta. Graphic 9A(4) shows the brain scan of a student at different brain wave frequencies watching the kaleidoscope. The red and orange areas marked with the blue arrows on the right of each brain show a strong amount of activity in delta, theta, alpha, and beta brain waves.

HIGH ENERGY IN THE BRAIN WHILE VIEWING THE MIND MOVIE

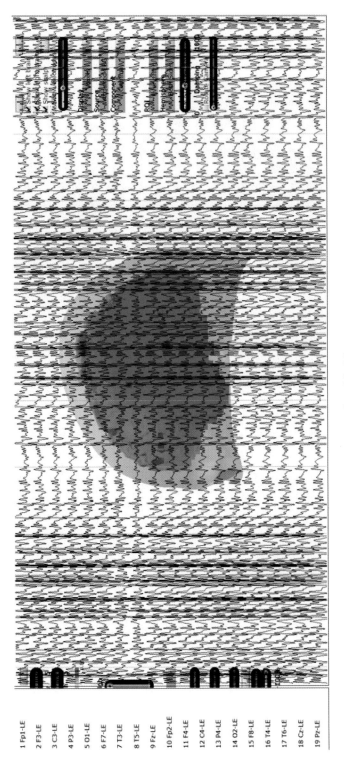

Graphic 10

This is a brain that is fully engaged in the Mind Movie experience. There is a significant amount of coherent high beta and gamma brain waves activating the entire brain.

BRAIN ACTIVITY WHILE
DIMENSIONALIZING A SCENE IN THE MIND MOVIE

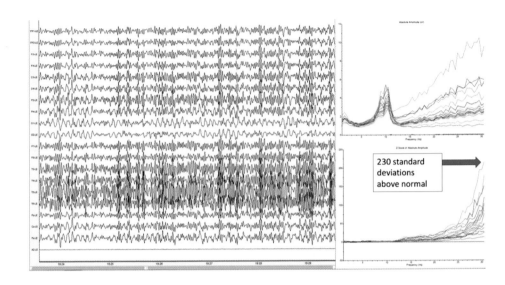

230 standard
deviations
above normal

Graphic 11A

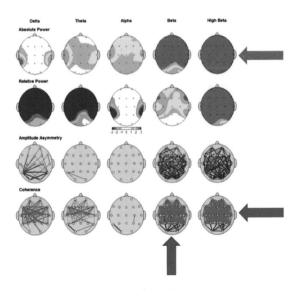

Graphic 11B

When this person dimensionalized a scene in her Mind Movie during a meditation, she reported that she had a full-on sensory experience without her physical senses. In Graphic 11A you can see her brain is in coherent high beta and gamma. The energy in her brain is about 230 standard deviations above normal. The red arrow in Graphic 11B shows there is quite a bit of energy in high beta as she moves into gamma. The blue arrows indicate that there is a lot of coherence in the brain as well. It is important to note that she cannot make her brain do this. The experience is happening to her.

BRAIN CHANGES BEFORE
AND AFTER A WALKING MEDITATION

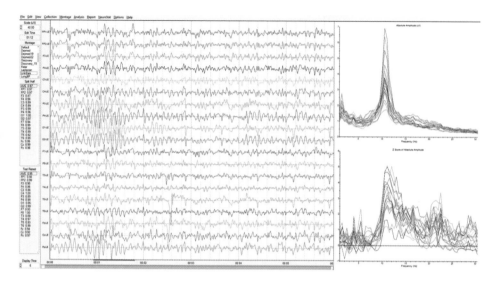

Graphic 12A

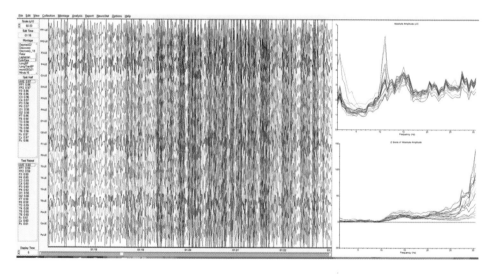

Graphic 12B

Graphic 12A shows a baseline measurement of a person with normal beta and alpha brain waves before his walking meditation. If you review his post-scan in Graphic 12B, an hour and twenty minutes later, you'll see he changed his brain to a high-energy gamma state.

STANDING WAVES OF INFORMATION

Graphic 13A

Fractal patterns in the form of complex geometric configurations are standing waves of frequency and information that can be de-scrambled by the brain into very powerful imagery. Although these images are two-dimensional, they give you an idea of how the patterns appear.

CORRELATION BETWEEN SOLAR
ACTIVITY AND HUMAN EVENTS

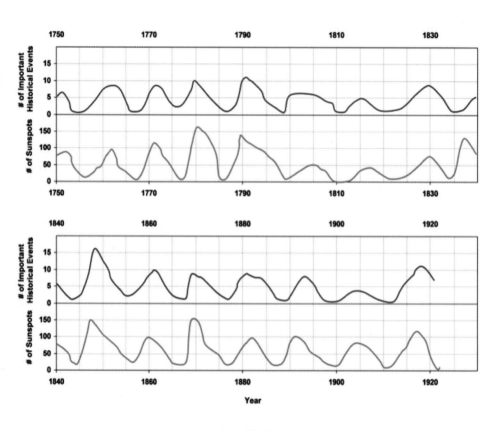

Graphic 14

For the years 1749 to 1926, Alexander Chizhevsky compared the annual number of important political and social events with increased solar activity. On the graph, the blue line illustrates sun flares and the red line relates to human excitability. Notice that every time there is high solar activity, there is a correlation with heightened human events.

Created from data provided in the translation of Alexander Chizhevsky's paper "Physical factors of the historical process."

COMPARING THE ENERGY OF THE ENTIRE DAY
WEDNESDAY, THURSDAY, FRIDAY, SATURDAY
TACOMA, WASHINGTON, 2016

Graphic 15A

COMPARING THE ENERGY OF THE ENTIRE DAY
WEDNESDAY, THURSDAY, FRIDAY, SATURDAY
CAREFREE, ARIZONA, 2015

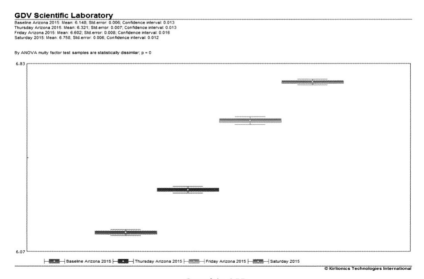

Graphic 15B

Graphics 15A and 15B demonstrate an increase in the collective energy of the room over 3 days in our advanced workshops. The first line, in red, is our baseline measurement and shows the room's energy before the start of the event on Wednesday. As you look at the red, blue, green, and brown lines (each color representing a different day), you'll see that each day the energy steadily increases.

COMPARING THE ENERGY IN THE MORNING
WEDNESDAY, THURSDAY, FRIDAY, SATURDAY
CANCUN, MEXICO, 2014

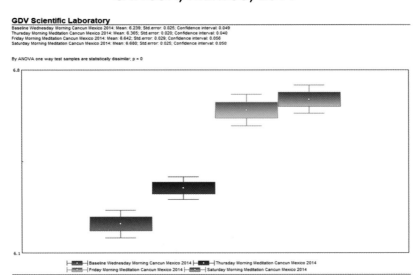

Graphic 15C

COMPARING THE ENERGY OF EACH MORNING MEDITATION
WEDNESDAY, THURSDAY, FRIDAY, SATURDAY, SUNDAY
MUNICH, GERMANY, 2015

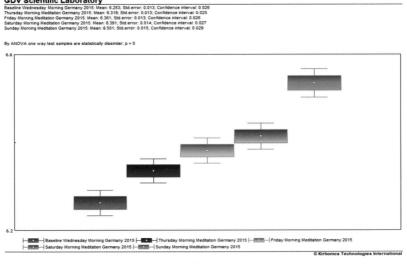

Graphic 15D

In Graphics 15C and 15D, the same color scale applies; however, these measurements reflect specific time intervals during each day's morning meditations. Graphic 15D has an extra green line because we measured the energy of the room during the 4 A.M. pineal gland meditation. As you can see, the energy was very high that morning.

HEART-RHYTHM PATTERNS

HRV INCOHERENCE
frustration, anxiety, worry, irritation

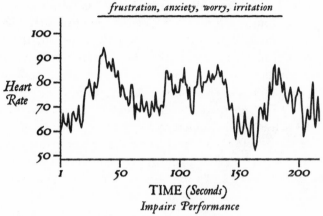

Impairs Performance

HRV COHERENCE
positive emotions, appreciation, love, courage

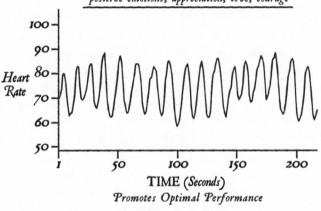

Promotes Optimal Performance

Figure 7.1

Compliments of the HeartMath Institute, the top HRV graph represents incoherent heart rhythms as a result of feeling emotions like resentment, impatience, and frustration. The bottom HRV graph represents coherent heart rhythms as a result of feeling emotions like gratitude, appreciation, and kindness.

When our HRV is in a heart-coherent pattern, it reflects increased synchronization and harmony within the two branches of the ANS, as well as in the activity occurring in our higher-level brain centers. So much of what we've learned from Western medicine has caused us to believe that we cannot control our body's autonomic nervous system (like heart rate and blood pressure) because such functions are beyond the domain of the conscious mind, not to mention the separation between the voluntary and involuntary nervous systems. We now know, however, that you don't have to be a yogi or a mystic to be able to master such skills. You just have to be supernatural, which can be learned. This is one reason why HMI teaches the importance of heart coherence not only to individuals, but also to the military, law enforcement, schools, athletes, and other high-functioning individuals—so people can maintain clarity, decision-making ability, and composure in high-stress situations.

The Benefits of Heart Coherence

When we choose to cultivate and experience elevated emotions and the coherent signal of those elevated emotions reaches the brain, if the amplitude of the signal is high enough, chemicals equal to those feelings and emotions are released into the body. We call this a feeling, and positive feelings like this make us feel lighter and freer—in other words, the energy of your whole state of being is elevated. If you are feeling an elevated sense of well-being in a safe environment, the energy of those feelings sets in motion a cascade of at least 1,400 biochemical changes in the body that promote growth and repair.[16] Instead of drawing from the invisible field of energy around your body to transform energy into chemistry, now you're adding to and expanding that field, resulting in a new expression of chemistry reflective of the change in energy. How? If the first three energy centers of the body are energy consumers when we are out of balance, the heart is an energy expander, and when you rest your attention in your heart to create and sustain elevated emotions, that coherent energy causes your heart to beat like a drum. It's that coherent, rhythmic beating that creates a measurable magnetic field around your heart, and thus your body. Just like the focused beat of a drum that produces a measurable sound wave, the stronger the coherent rhythm of the heart, the more expanded your field becomes.

When you are feeling hurt, anger, stress, jealousy, rage, competition, or frustration, on the other hand, the signal from the heart to the brain becomes incoherent, and this triggers the release of approximately 1,200 chemicals into the body equal to those feelings.[17] This chemical dump lasts approximately 90 seconds to two minutes. In the short term, these stressful feelings are not harmful; in fact, if they're resolved they improve your resilience. However, the long-term effects of unresolved survival emotions put the entire body into a state of incoherence, making you vulnerable to stress-related health challenges. These survival emotions draw from the field around your body, causing you to feel separate and materialistic because you are putting most of your focus and attention on matter, your body, the environment, time, and of course, the source of your problems.

Among HMI's most significant findings is that what we feel on a minute-to-minute, second-to-second basis influences the heart, and that our feelings and emotions are a key aspect of unlocking "heart intelligence." Because feelings and emotions are energies that emit powerful magnetic fields, the stronger the elevated feelings, the stronger the magnetic field. In fact, the heart produces the strongest magnetic field in the body—five thousand times greater in strength than the field produced by the brain.[18]

Place your finger on your wrist and feel your pulse. That pulse is a wave of energy called the blood pressure wave and it travels through your entire body, influencing everything, including brain function. Not only does the heart's magnetic pulse reverberate through every cell of the body, but it also produces a field around your body that can be measured up to 8 to 10 feet away using a sensitive detector called a magnetometer.[19] When you activate the heart by calling up elevated emotions, you are not only broadcasting that energy to every cell; you are also radiating those feelings out into space. This is where the heart moves beyond biology and into physics.

Using electroencephalograms, scientists at the HMI laboratory discovered that when the heart goes into coherence, the brain waves entrain with the heart's rhythm at a frequency of 0.10 Hz and also that the synchronization between heart and brain is increased when the subject is in a heart-coherent state. The coherent frequency of 0.10 Hz has been shown to be a state of optimum performance associated with increased access to our deeper intuition and internal guidance. Once the analytical mind is out of the way, the individual can move down the ladder of consciousness from alpha to theta to delta brain waves—the state in which restorative functions in the body take place. Coincidentally, we often see our students reporting profound or mystical experiences in deep delta around .09 to .10 Hz (.09 Hz is just a hundredth of a cycle per second off reported optimum coherence) while their hearts are in a very coherent state. However, the amplitude of energy produced by the heart increases the level of energy in the brain, in some cases more than 50 to 300 times the normal level or more.

Supporting evidence of heart-brain coherence was further demonstrated by a series of experiments performed by Gary Schwartz, Ph.D., and his colleagues at the University of Arizona. In their experiments, they found inexplicable communications between the heart and the brain that made no sense via neurological or other established communication pathways. This discovery established the fact that energetic interactions between the heart and the brain exist through electromagnetic fields.[20] Both examples point to the fact that when we focus our attention on our heart and emotions, the heart's beating acts as an amplifier. This increases the synchronization between our heart and brain and creates coherence not only in the physical organs, but also in the electromagnetic field surrounding our body.

Also noteworthy is that right behind the breastbone sits a small gland called the thymus, which has an intimate connection with the heart center. As one of the main organs of the immune system, the thymus serves a vital role in the promotion of T cells, which defend the body from pathogens such as bacteria and viruses. The thymus gland functions optimally up to the onset of puberty, but it begins to shrink as we get older because of natural decreases in the production of human growth hormone.

As with many vital organs, the thymus is also prone to the negative effects of long-term stress. When we're living in emergency mode for extended periods of time and diminish our vital energy field, all of our energy is directed outward to protect us from external threats, leaving little energy to protect us from internal threats. Eventually, this leads to dysfunction of the immune system. It makes sense, then, that as the heart center becomes activated with energy, by mobilizing the parasympathetic nervous system for growth and repair, the thymus gland should become more active as well, because now we're adding energy in that gland. Therefore, the thymus gland should also benefit from the practice of sustaining coherence within the body, aiding in the support of the overall vitality of our immune system and long-term health.

You learned earlier in this book that in my own independent studies, when our students were able to feel and sustain gratitude and other elevated emotions for a total of 15 to 20 minutes per day for four days, the energy of the emotions signaled the immune cell genes to make a protein called immunoglobulin A. The significant increase in IgA is a perfect example of one of the many positive cascading effects of heart coherence.

What all of this boils down to is that the quality of our heart's rhythm has consequences for our overall health. If the heart beats in harmonious rhythms, its efficiency reduces stress on other systems of the body, maximizes our energy, and creates states whereby we thrive mentally, emotionally, and physically. If there is disharmony in our heart rhythms, the opposite is true. This incoherence leaves us with less energy available for healing and for maintaining health and long-term building projects, creating unrest within our internal states and putting increased stress on the heart and other organs.[21] Heart attacks and heart disease, for example, occur when the body has been under stress for extended periods of time. When we intentionally choose elevated emotions, however, focusing less on disharmony and more on gratitude, our bodies respond positively and we enjoy improved health.

The next time you use an elevated emotion to tune in to your future and embrace those feelings before the event unfolds—and feel gratitude that the event has already occurred—just know that the worst thing that probably can happen to you is that you begin to heal.

The Effects of Chronic Stress

When we live in a constant state of stress, our heart center becomes incoherent and this stifles our ability to create. In response to chaotic heart rhythms, the brain becomes very *dis-integrated* and incoherent, and that incoherence is reflected in the two branches of the ANS. If the parasympathetic system is the brake and the sympathetic system is the accelerator, when they are working in opposition, your body is receiving a message akin to stepping on the gas while your foot is on the brake. It doesn't take a significant amount of automotive knowledge to understand the ramifications of these opposing forces—we wear out the brakes and put stress on the drivetrain, while the resistance wastes energy and reduces fuel efficiency. Eventually, this habituation of stress wears down the body so much that it eliminates our ability to repair and maintain health, depleting our vitality and resilience.

If resilience is based on efficient energy management, you may feel completely drained, out of sorts, and perhaps sick while under the influence of chronic stress. The more addicted we become to these states of stress, the less likely we are to open our hearts, go within, and consciously create heart coherence.

An experience I had at my home in a rural area of Washington State serves as a good example. One November evening I came home from work, parked my car as I always did, and began walking down the 40-yard path to my house. It was pitch black. About 30 yards from my front door, off to my right, I heard an ominous growl coming from behind some very large rocks. Immediately, I narrowed my focus on matter (some thing) and found myself thinking, *What could be lurking in the darkness?* I began searching in my mind and then my environment for knowns from my past memory bank in order to predict my future. *Could it be one of my dogs?* I wondered. I started calling out their names, but there was no response. As I took a few more steps, the growling became louder.

Without my having to think about mobilizing the energy in my body, the hair on the back of my neck stood up, my heart rate and respiratory rate increased, and my senses became heightened in preparation for fight or flight. I took out my cell phone and turned on the flashlight to narrow my focus on the possible threat, but I still couldn't see what was making the noise. From the darkness, the growling continued. I slowly backed up and finally fled to my barn, where my ranch hands were putting away the horses for the night. We grabbed our guns and flashlights and returned to the scene just in time to see a cougar and her cub scurrying away through the bushes.

You can probably gather from this story that a highly stressful situation like this is not the time to open your heart or trust in the unknown. It's not a time to take your attention off things in your outer material world to focus on a new possibility in your mind. It's a time to run, hide, or fight. But if you are perpetually hooked into the fight-or-flight state—even if there is no cougar in the bushes—you will be less likely to want to close your eyes and go within because you have to keep your attention on the perceived threat outside of you. No new information can enter your nervous system that is not equal to or relevant to the emotions you are experiencing, so you can't program your body for a new destiny. So it makes sense that the more you live addicted to the stress hormones in your normal life, the less likely you are to want to create, meditate, or open your heart and be vulnerable.

The "Heart-Brain"

In 1991, the pioneering work of J. Andrew Armour, M.D., Ph.D., showed that the heart literally has a mind of its own. With as many as 40,000 neurons, the heart has a nervous system that functions independently of the brain. The technical term coined for this system is the intrinsic cardiac nervous system, more commonly known as the "heart-brain."[22] This discovery was so monumental that it led to a new field of science called *neurocardiology*.

HEART COHERENCE AFFECTING BRAIN COHERENCE

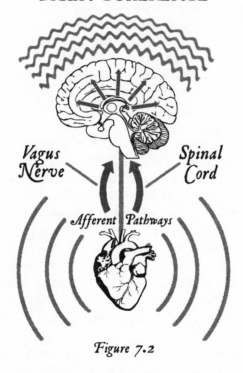

Figure 7.2

When the heart moves into coherence, it acts as an amplifier, sending coherent information through its afferent nervous pathways straight to the thalamus, which synchronizes the neocortex and the brain's survival centers.

The heart and the brain are connected by efferent (descending) and afferent (ascending) pathways; however, 90 percent of the connecting nerve fibers ascend from the heart up to the brain.[23] Armour uncovered that these direct, afferent neural pathways continuously send signals and information that interacts with and modifies activity in the brain's higher cognitive and emotional centers.[24] These signals from the heart to the brain connect through the vagus nerve and continue straight to the thalamus (which synchronizes cortical activity such as thinking, perceiving, and understanding language), then to the frontal lobes (responsible for motor functions and problem solving), and on to the brain's survival center, the amygdala (which signals emotional memory). The core cells of the amygdala even synchronize to the heart's beating.[25] (See Figure 7.2.) This means that if your heart center is open, it's keeping your brain's survival centers in check. It's possible, then, that the more heart centered you are, the less likely you will react to stressors in your life. The reverse is also true: the less energy you have in your heart center, the more likely you will be living in survival mode.

This tells us that our feelings and heart rhythms affect what emotional memories and responses transpire in us, so stress and anxiety can trigger brain-wave patterns to match an anxiety habit of the past. Conversely, just like a computer that matches patterns, elevated emotions of the heart can produce coherence in brain-wave patterns, so if you're summoning the feelings of your future by creating elevated states, your brain is beginning to lay the neural networks for those future emotions or that new destiny. Armour's discovery of the afferent neural pathways from the heart to the brain proves that the heart independently processes emotions, responds directly to the environment, and regulates its rhythms—without receiving information from the brain. That's because the heart and the ANS always work together. Also noteworthy is that the nerves facilitating this communication enable the heart to sense, remember, self-regulate, and make decisions about cardiac control independent of the nervous system.[26]

To put it simply, emotions and feelings originating in the heart play an important role in the way we think, process information, feel, and understand the world and our place in it.[27] Once the heart center is activated, it acts as an amplifier to jump-start the brain, enhance its activity, and create balance, order, and coherence throughout the body.

Living Heart Centered

As I said earlier, every thought you think produces correspond-ing chemistry equal to that thought, which in turn creates an emotion. Therefore, you are suggestible only to the thoughts equal to your emo-tional state. We now know that when our students are heart centered and feel more wholeness and oneness, they're less separate from their dreams. When they feel gratitude, abundance, freedom, or love, all of those emo-tions welcome corresponding thoughts. Those heart-centered emotions open the door to the subconscious mind so that you can program your autonomic nervous system equal to the thoughts of your new future. We also know that if they live in the feeling of fear or lack but try to think they're abundant, they can't produce a measurable effect, because change can only happen when thoughts are in alignment with the emotional state of the body. They can think positively all they want, but without a corre-sponding feeling or emotion equal to that thought, the message cannot be felt or understood throughout the rest of the body.

So you could repeat the affirmation *I am fearless* until you're blue in the face, but if it's *fear* you're actually feeling, the thought *I am fearless* never makes it past the brain stem, which means you're not signaling the body and ANS into a new, specific destiny. The feeling is what produces the emotional charge (energy) to stimulate your ANS into a different destiny. Without the feeling, a disconnect remains between your brain and body—between the thought of health and the feeling of health—and you can't embody that new state of being.

It's only when you change your energy that you can produce more consistent effects. If you sustain these elevated emotions on a daily basis, eventually your body, in its innate intelligence, begins to make relative genetic changes in the way I described earlier. That's because the body believes that the emotion you are embracing is coming from an experi-ence in your environment. So when you open your heart center, practice feeling an emotion before the experience occurs, and marry it with a clear intention, the body responds as if it's in the future experience. That heart-mind coherence then influences your body chemistry and energy in a series of ways.

If coherence between the heart and the brain can originate in the heart, and their synchronization results in optimal performance and health, then you should be taking time every day to focus on activating your heart center. By intentionally choosing to feel the elevated emotions of the heart rather than waiting for something outside of yourself to elicit those emotions, you become who you are truly meant to be—a heart-empowered individual. When you are living by the heart, you naturally choose love and innately demonstrate it through compassion and care for the well-being of yourself, others, and planet Earth. Through our partnership with HMI, our students have demonstrated that with practice, we can in fact produce, regulate, and sustain elevated feelings and emotions—independent of events in our external world.

In our workshops around the world, through the practice of regulating heart rhythms to sustain elevated emotions, we teach our students how to generate heart and brain coherence. We then measure their abilities using HRV monitors. During guided meditations, we ask our students to surrender to the feelings of gratitude, joy, and love, and we encourage daily practice outside of our formal instruction, because when one chooses to practice sitting in a state of coherence, it becomes a habit. I hope that with enough practice, our students can replace old mental scripts of feeling unworthy, fearful, or insecure with more elevated states of being and fall deeply in love with their lives. We've seen enough of them demonstrate that it is indeed possible to produce positive, measurable, tangible effects in their lives simply by shifting the paradigm of their thoughts and feelings. These dedicated individuals return to their homes, where the positive effects they've produced in their own lives ripple out to positively affect their families and communities, continuously expanding their vibrational influence of harmony and coherence throughout the world.

By repeatedly practicing the regulation of heightened emotional states, in time the constant feeling of elevated emotions creates a new emotional baseline. This baseline then begins to continuously influence a new set of thoughts equal to the heightened feelings. The summation of those novel thoughts creates a new level of mind, which then produces more corresponding emotions equal to those thoughts, further sustaining that baseline. When this feedback loop between the heart (body) and mind (brain) occurs, you are in an entirely new state of being—the consciousness of the unlimited mind and the energy of profound love and gratitude. The repetition of this process is what it means to recondition your body, rewire your brain, and reconfigure your biology equal to your new state of being. Now you are naturally, automatically, and regularly broadcasting a different electromagnetic signature of energy into the field. This is who you are, or who you have become.

Countless history books could be written through the lens of incoherent emotions. Whether the result is a Shakespearean tragedy, genocide, or a world war, survival emotions such as blame, hate, rage, competition, and retribution have resulted in an endless, unnecessary trail of pain, suffering, oppression, and death. The results have caused humans to live in opposition and conflict rather than in peace and harmony. This is a time in history when we can break that cycle. This is a pivotal moment in the story of humanity where ancient wisdom and modern science are intersecting to provide us with the technology and scientific understanding to learn not only how to more efficiently and effectively manage our emotions, but also what that means for our health, relationships, energy levels, and personal and collective evolution. It doesn't require moving mountains—only changing our internal state of being. This allows us to alter the way we act with one another, replacing stressful situations with positive experiences that give us energy, fill our spirit, and leave us with a sense of wholeness, connection, and unity. The brain may *think*, but when you turn your heart into an instrument of perception, it *knows*.

Examples from Our Workshops

To see an example of how heart coherence creates brain coherence, take a look at Graphics 8A and 8B in the color insert. The first image shows relatively low-normal beta brain-wave patterns before the person begins to create heart coherence. The second image shows a significant change once the person moves into sustained heart coherence just a few seconds later. That's because the heart acts as an amplifier to influence the brain to create very coherent synchronized alpha brain waves.

In Figures 7.3A and 7.3B you will see an HRV analysis from one of our students taken at an advanced workshop. She's having a pretty amazing day. The first chart, in Figure 7.3A, represents two meditations, one in the morning and one right before lunch, and each block represents five minutes of elapsed time. Where you see the first gray arrow on the top of the scan pointing down to the right is when she went into (and sustained) heart coherence. During our 7 A.M. meditation, she maintained this state for more than 50 minutes, until you see the second arrow pointing down to the left. At the bottom of the scan, where you see the second gray arrow pointing down to the right, is when she again went into heart coherence for 38 minutes during a meditation just before lunch, ending with the second gray arrow pointing down to the left. You can see she is developing the skill.

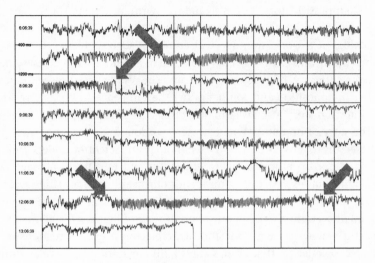

Figure 7.3A

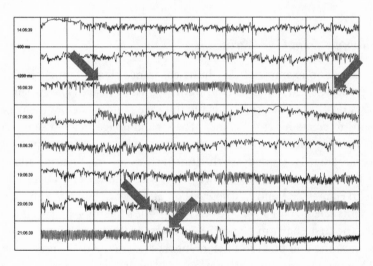

Figure 7.3B

Each set of gray arrows pointing inward in both figures represent a student going into heart coherence by sustaining an elevated emotional state. Every square block represents a five-minute time interval. From both Figures 7.3A and 7.3B, you can tell she's developing the skill to regulate her internal states.

In Figure 7.3B, at the bottom where the two arrows are pointing inward, the student spontaneously goes into heart coherence for over an hour. Her body is being conditioned to a new mind.

Now look at Figure 7.3B. In the next meditation later that afternoon, if you glance between the two gray arrows at the top of the figure, you can see that she goes into heart coherence again for almost 45 minutes. What makes this reading so fascinating, however, is what happens later that evening around 8 P.M. (see the second set of gray arrows pointing inward). Since there was no meditation taking place at the time, we asked her later what she had experienced. Her heart went into "super coherence" for more than hour while she was in her normal level of wakefulness.

She told us she'd been getting ready for bed when suddenly she felt an overwhelming feeling of love. It was so strong that she had to lie down and surrender to it. Her heart spontaneously went into heart coherence, and for an hour and 10 minutes while she lay on her bed, she fell deeply in love with her life. She sustained a change in her ANS. Where you see the last arrow is where she said she rolled over on her side and fell asleep. Not a bad way to end a day, wouldn't you agree?

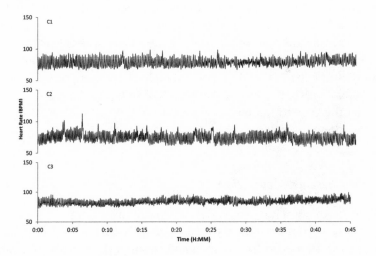

Figure 7.4

An example of three students sustaining heart-centered emotions for 45 minutes.

So ponder this: You know how easy it is to think a fearful or anxious thought about a future event that hasn't happened—and in your mind emotionally embrace this fictional outcome over and over? And you know how the more energy you feed the thought, the more you ruminate over other possible outcomes, and eventually those thoughts deliver you to a worst-case scenario? It's the emotions that are driving those thoughts. You've conditioned your body to be the mind in fear and anxiety. If this continues over a long period of time, your body may have a panic attack—an autonomic, spontaneous bodily function that your conscious mind can't control.

But what if instead of conditioning the body to the mind of fear and anxiety, you experienced sustained elevated emotions and conditioned your body to the mind of love and coherence? Instead of being afraid and dreading that a panic attack is going to happen again, you'd get excited and look forward to the prospect of having an autonomic *love attack*.

Figure 7.4 shows three more examples of students who are able to sustain heart coherence for extended periods of time. If you look closely, you'll see their hearts are all responding to a consistent state of elevated emotions for at least 45 minutes—that is, their bodies are responding to a new mind. I'd say that's pretty supernatural.

Figures 7.5A and 7.5B demonstrate two examples of people with very poor heart rate variability (noted with two sets of black arrows pointing upward) in the natural waking state. Take a look at the changes in heart rate variability when they practice heart coherence shown in the area between the gray arrows pointing inward. Even if it is only for 8 to 15 minutes, these students are changing their biology.

Heart Coherence Meditation

This meditation is based on the Heart Lock-In Technique developed by HMI. Close your eyes, allow your body to relax, and bring your attention to your heart. Start breathing in and out from the heart center, and continue to do this more slowly and deeply. When your mind wanders, keep returning your attention and awareness to your chest, your heart, and your breath.

Next, while you rest your attention in your fourth center, bring up some elevated emotions while continuing to breathe in and out of your heart center. Once you feel these heartfelt emotions in your chest area,

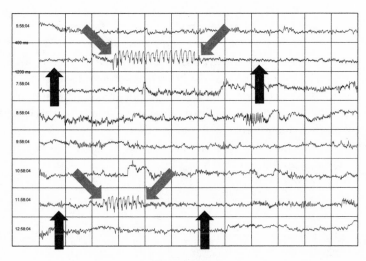

Figure 7.5A

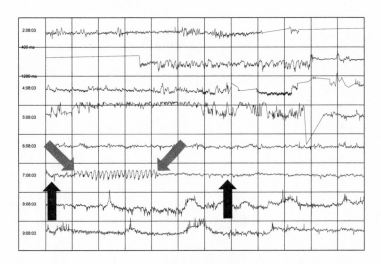

Figure 7.5B

In both figures, you can see two different students who have very little heart rate variability (demonstrated by the black arrows pointing upward). However, when it comes time to open their hearts, if you look between the two gray arrows, you will see a significant change. Even if it is just for 8 to 15 minutes, they are changing their physiology.

send that energy out beyond your body and marry it with your intention. Continue to broadcast that energy and intention all around you. Start with 10 minutes and try to extend the time you practice every day.

Eventually, when you come to know what it feels like in your body to experience these elevated emotions, you can practice throughout your day with your eyes open (you'll learn more about how to do this in Chapter 9, Walking Meditation). You might even set a reminder on your phone for four times a day, and when it goes off, take a minute or two to feel those elevated emotions.

Chapter 8

MIND MOVIES/
KALEIDOSCOPE

I had just finished a keynote lecture on a Saturday night in Orlando, Florida. The following morning, while packing my bags in preparation for my afternoon flight home, I turned on the television to catch up on the political situation in the United States. It was in the thick of the 2016 presidential election, and since I had been out of the country traveling and lecturing over the previous three weeks, I was curious about what had transpired during my time away. I quickly surfed through the channels to find a news station, set the remote down, and while halfway paying attention to the TV, continued packing. Suddenly, a commercial came on that caught all my attention, and in an instant I understood why we call television *programming*.

The commercial began with a nighttime exterior shot of a couple's home. As the camera zooms in on the house, the words "Night #14 with Shingles" appear on the screen. When the shot moves to the interior, tender yet foreboding music plays while an elderly man moans in pain at the foot of his bed. His concerned wife enters the room and asks him how he's doing. "It hurts," he replies. In the lower right corner in a tiny font almost the same color as the background are the words "Actor Portrayal."

The wife walks over with a look of despair and slowly lifts her husband's shirt, revealing huge, red-scabbed lesions covering more than half his lower back. The imagery is shocking, grotesque, and horrific, looking like nothing less than a large third-degree burn. In my 31 years of practice, I've examined hundreds of people with shingles and have never seen anything that looked so severe as the manufactured lesions in this commercial. I immediately knew it was designed to evoke a strong emotional response with the viewing audience—because it certainly did in me.

Once you see the rash on the man's back, the commercial achieves its goal of commanding your attention. Because the portrayal of the rash is so arresting, it changes the way you were feeling from only a few moments before your present state of watching it. The moment the commercial significantly changes your internal emotional state, it causes you to put more of your attention and awareness on the source of the disruption in your external environment. The stronger the emotion it causes (stimulus), the more you lean in and pay attention (response). This association of stimulus and response, or conditioning, is how long-term, or associative, memories are created.

This process of conditioning begins by pairing a symbol or an image with a change in an emotional state—a combination that opens the doorway between the conscious and subconscious mind. In the case of the shingles commercial, now that they have captured all your attention (and begun the programming process), you can't help but naturally wonder what they're about to say next. The commercial continues with a somber male narrator: "If you've ever had chicken pox, the shingles virus is already inside of you. As you get older, your immune system weakens and it loses its ability to keep the shingles virus in check." By using emotional branding, this is the first instance where the commercial raises ethical questions by telling the audience that the immune system weakens with age. Next, we see the man in the bathroom looking at himself in the mirror. He looks worried, broken, and defeated.

The scene changes to his wife talking on the phone in the kitchen. "I just can't stand seeing him like this," she says.

Next, we see the man doubled over on his bed, palm to forehead, wincing in pain. The narrator then makes a direct suggestion, reinforced by the same words appearing on the screen: "1 in 3 people will get shingles in their lifetime." The narrator continues while the same words remain on the screen. "The shingles rash can last up to 30 days."

The scene cuts to his wife pleading directly into the camera: "I just wish there was something I could do to help."

Again, we see the man in pain, and on the screen appear the words: "1 in 5 people with shingles will have long-term nerve pain." These words remain on the screen for the remaining narration, which says, "Some people with shingles will have long-term nerve pain, which can last a few months to a few years. Don't wait until someone you love develops shingles. Talk to your doctor or pharmacist about your risk."

Let's take a closer look at what this commercial is attempting to do. First, it puts you in an emotional state by changing how you feel. Once it captures your attention, you immediately become more open and suggestible to the information that follows. Now that you're more prone to accept, believe, and surrender to this information (without analyzing it), if you're feeling fearful, victimized, vulnerable, worried, shocked, weak, tired, or in pain, you're more susceptible to the information equal to those emotions. You might start wondering if the ailment could happen to you.

At various points during the commercial, certain "facts" appear written on the screen, allowing you to read along. This serves to reinforce the programming. Also, while the thinking brain is focused on reading the copy, the content of the narration slips behind the conscious mind and into the subconscious mind. Like an audio recorder, it records the entire script and creates an internal program.

Next, through a direct, literal suggestion, the narrator has instilled fear in you by personally suggesting you already have the shingles virus in your body and that because of the natural process of aging, your immune system is no longer strong enough to take care of the virus. This turns on your emotional brain (the seat of your autonomic nervous system), allowing it to become programmed. Once the suggestions make it to your autonomic nervous system, it takes the orders without question and gets busy making chemical changes in your body equal to the literal suggestions. In other words, your body is going to subconsciously and automatically be programmed to weaken your immune function. In conclusion, you're at risk and you'd better not wait until you contract it. The commercial's effect goes even a little further: if you've ever had chicken pox and after watching this you "think" your immune system is weak because of your age, you will decide you have an even greater need to prevent getting shingles, so you will be even more motivated to buy the drug.

If you happen to be a person who has shingles and you're watching this commercial, when you see that your condition is not as severe as the actor's shingles, you may find yourself thinking, *I should take the drug now so that it doesn't get any worse. I don't want to end up like him.* If you don't have shingles, at the commercial's end you may still be left quietly wondering, *Am I part of the two-thirds of the population that is safe? Or am I in the one-third of the population that will get the virus?* If you think, *I hope I'm not part of the one-third*, it means you believe there may be a chance that you're susceptible and vulnerable, leaving you unconsciously thinking that you already have it.

You know what I found most absurd about this commercial? They never even mention the drug, which means they don't have to reveal its side effects. Since the commercial had now piqued my curiosity, I stopped packing and looked on the Internet for another commercial by the same pharmaceutical company. I wanted to know what drug they were suggesting would alleviate the severity of the actor's exaggerated, manufactured lesions. After a quick search, I found several similar commercials with the same theme and wording but with slight variations. They all shared one thing in common, however; they were all designed to capture your attention.

In the next commercial I watched, a woman is wearing goggles and swimming in a lap pool. Everything is black and white. In a twist on the previous commercial, the narrator (speaking in an authoritative female British accent) *is* the shingles virus and the narration is coming from within the woman's head:

"Impressive, Linda. Age isn't slowing you down, but your immune system weakens as you get older, increasing the risk for me—the shingles virus. I've been lurking inside you since you had chicken pox. I could surface at any time as a painful blistering rash." The scene then abruptly cuts from black and white to color and a man lifts his shirt to reveal the worst shingles rash you've ever seen. Again, the grotesque, blistering lesion can't help but attract your attention. As quickly as the scene turns to color, it returns to the swimmer in black and white.

The commercial continues in a similar manner and formula as the previous one: First make an arresting statement or show a shocking image to change the viewer's emotional state, then cause them to be more suggestible to the information via the change in their emotional state, and finally use autosuggestion to make them wonder if they already have shingles. This ad also infers that even though you might be healthy, work out, and take care of yourself, you can still become a victim of the virus, further suggesting that no one is immune. Again, the words on the screen reinforce the message: "1 in 3 people get me in their lifetime. Linda, will it be you?" If you identify with the woman in any manner, the voice is talking directly to you.

The tone of the commercial then changes as a new male narrator begins speaking in a confident, lighthearted tone, devoid of worry or concern. In a similar British accent, the voice says, "And that's why Linda got me—Drug X." The scene remains in black and white except for the woman's bathing suit, her swim cap, and the name of the drug, which appears on the screen in a large, sophisticated font. Now the drug has been imprinted into your brain at yet another level. Once again, the ad has created an association between your health and safety and the drug that will protect you. The tagline comes on the screen as the narrator reads it aloud, stating that the drug helps "to boost your immune system against shingles. To help protect her against *you*, shingles."

At the end of the commercial, that narrator says, "Drug X is used to prevent shingles in adults fifty years and older. The drug is not to be used to treat shingles, and it does not help everyone." Here's the punch line: "You should not take the drug if you have a weakened immune system."

Whoa—*what?* Back up. Here's the irony: They just told you that as you age, your immune system weakens and you're at a greater risk for shingles. The drug is supposed to strengthen your immune system, *but* you shouldn't use it if you have a weakened immune system. Now comes the dilemma: If you still choose to take the drug, you believe the drug to be more powerful than your possibly weakened immune system. The programming worked.

What the clever, if not unethical, advertisers understand is that this message is confusing and disorienting to your conscious mind. At the same time, however, they are programming your subconscious mind with the idea that your immune system is weak, you probably already have the virus within you, and chances are high that you'll get shingles, even if you are healthy. In addition, you are told that without the medication, you are likely to suffer—even though there is no guarantee that the shingles will go away easily—and that it *still* might not work if your immune system is weak.

Finally come the side effects (which are not side effects, but direct effects): "A shingles-like rash, redness, pain, itching, swelling, hard lumps, warmth, bruising or swelling at the injection site, and headache. Talk to your doctor if you plan to be around newborns or people who are pregnant or have a weakened immune system because the vaccine has a weakened version of the chickenpox virus and you could infect them."

Wow! I started to wonder what planet I was living on. This type of programming makes you wonder if we really have free will or if we're all making choices based on what we have been conditioned to believe is the answer, whether that's a certain type of beer, shampoo or conditioner, the latest smartphone, or a pill that may or may not provide relief from the shingles virus you may or may not even have. Most of the time advertising appeals to lack and separation by reminding you to *want* what you don't have, *desire* what you need to fit into a social consciousness, or *satiate* a feeling of emptiness or loneliness. And of course, in this case, if you're sick or feeling like you're sick, the advertiser has the answer to your symptoms.

In one final search, I came across a similar commercial with the same theme—an actor dramatically suffering for 17 days, the shocking exposure of a huge lesion, and words on the screen to influence the viewer's thoughts while reinforcing the same content. Like the other commercials, this one explicitly informs the public that the drug is not used to treat shingles, but at the end of the commercial the handsome man smiles and declares, "I think I'm going to give it a try." Meanwhile, I'm left wondering why he would give it a try if he already has had shingles for 17 days, especially if the drug doesn't treat the condition. Now I'm really confused.

Years ago, I learned in my training that by definition, hypnosis is a disorientation of the inhibitory processes of the conscious mind, bypassing the analytical mind so that one becomes highly responsive to suggestions and information in the subconscious mind. As the conscious mind is busy and preoccupied trying to figure things out, the subconscious mind takes it all in without discretion. If you can disorient people with information (or in today's world, *disinformation*), shock, or confusion, you just opened the door to programming their subconscious mind.

In this chapter, we're going to learn how to do the opposite and positively reprogram the negative programming we've been conditioned to for most of our lives.

Three Minds in One Brain:
The Conscious, Subconscious, and Analytical Mind

By now, you know that when you change your brain waves from beta to alpha, you slow down your neocortex (the analytical, thinking brain). As your brain waves slow down, you leave the domain of the conscious mind and enter the realm of the subconscious mind. We could say, then, that if you are somewhat conscious and aware but not actively engaged in thought, your consciousness is moving out of the thinking neocortex and entering the midbrain, otherwise known as the subconscious, the home to the autonomic nervous system and the cerebellum.

If you've ever witnessed someone completely captivated by a television show, so much so that when you tried to speak to them they didn't hear you, it's possible that they were experiencing alpha brain-wave states—a state highly suggestible to information. Suggestibility is the ability to accept, believe, and surrender to information without analyzing it. In this state, the viewer is so engrossed, so focused on what they're watching, that they appear entranced and motionless. Nothing else exists to them except the object of their attention.

If the person doesn't analyze the information they are being exposed to, they are likely to accept, believe, and/or surrender to it because there is no analytical filter. It makes logical sense, then, that the more suggestible you are, the less analytical you are. The opposite is also true: The more analytical you are, the less suggestible you are to information; therefore, it is less likely that your brain will be in an alpha brain-wave or trance state. Take a look at Figure 8.1 to help you understand the relationship between suggestibility, the analytical mind, trance, and brain waves.

THE CONNECTION BETWEEN TRANCE, SUGGESTIBILITY, BRAIN WAVES & ANALYTICAL MIND

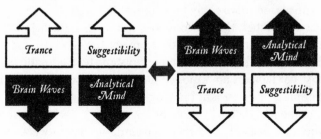

Figure 8.1

As your brain waves slow down and you get beyond your analytical mind, your brain moves into trance and you're more suggestible to information. The inverse is also true. As your brain waves speed up, you become more analytical, the brain moves out of trance, and you become less suggestible to information. Suggestibility is your ability to accept, believe, and surrender to information without analyzing it.

What the creators of the commercials I mentioned earlier fully understand is that the best way to program a person to take a desired action is to put them into an alpha brain-wave state so that the information presented is *not* analyzed. When the commercial is repeated, or a similar one with the same message is played over and over, sooner or later that program is going to enter the viewer's subconscious. The more we are exposed to the stimulus (in this case, the commercial), the more automatic the programmed response becomes. Eventually, when we've unconsciously memorized the stimulus and the response is automatic, the conscious mind no longer needs to think about or analyze the incoming information. Meanwhile, the subconscious mind maps the information, recording and storing it like a voice or video recording. Once it is mapped in your brain, each time you are exposed to the commercial, it continues to prime the same neural networks, further reinforcing the same program, thought, and belief. Now, not only can information influence your health, but it can also give you the solution to the problem the commercial is actually creating.

Other situations that increase suggestibility include shock, trauma, or a strong emotional reaction. For instance, when people are stunned or exposed to emotionally charged situations, it's common that the brain goes into an altered state. As the brain pauses because of a sensory overload, such as a motor vehicle accident, the person enters a suggestible state. In severe cases, the person surrenders to the shock, becomes frozen and numb, and their ability to think becomes impaired. Therefore, when someone is exposed to an aggressive rash and feels sickened by the images (combined with the right music and narration to create an ominous or foreboding mood), the door to the subconscious mind opens, making the person more easily programmable.

If you remember, the subconscious mind sits right below the conscious mind. The limbic brain is the home of the subconscious and the autonomic nervous system, which controls all the automatic biological functions that happen on a moment-to-moment basis. Once a thought is programmed, like a servant carrying out their master's orders, the ANS carries out the request of the thought.

If you are repeatedly told that your immune system weakens as you age, and that one out of three people who have had chicken pox in their life will get shingles, the emotionally charged experience allows the message to make it past your thinking, analytical mind. In response to this information, your ANS follows the orders and can begin to actually weaken your internal defense system.

For the advertisers to really get their money's worth in this commercial endeavor, it's best for them to repeatedly run the commercials late in the evening when we are most suggestible to programming. Why? Because melatonin levels rise in response to darkness, and melatonin causes our brain waves to slow down in preparation for sleeping and dreaming. Because our brain waves are moving from beta, to alpha, to theta, to delta in the evening, people are less analytical and their subconscious window opens. As daylight wakes us up in the morning and our brain begins producing serotonin, the reverse process occurs; our brain waves go from delta, to theta, to alpha (where, again, our subconscious is open to programming), and eventually to beta.

So if you're an advertiser and you know the majority of the public is not aware of the way subconscious programming works, why not create a series of late-night commercials with your desired messaging, accent it with just the right amount of fright and concern so as to capture the viewer's attention, and proceed to program their autonomic nervous system to get busy taking the orders just before they fall asleep?

A good rule of thumb: Don't watch anything on television or on the Internet or participate in any mode of entertainment that you don't want to experience—not only before bed, but ever.

Kaleidoscope Eyes: Entranced in Trance

For years, I've been thinking about how we're all constantly programmed into self-limited beliefs; that is, believing that we need something outside of us to change how we feel inside of us. This is, after all, what advertising is all about—the never-ending dependence on, and consumption of, external sources to make us feel happy or better. This belief, which reminds us of our separation from wholeness, is incessantly ingrained in us through the media, television shows, commercials, the news, video games, websites, and sometimes even music. It's a simple strategy, really: If you can suspend people in the feelings of lack, fear, anger, opposition, prejudice, pain, sadness, and anxiety, they remain dependent on someone or something outside of them to make those feelings go away. If you remain in a perpetual state of busyness, and are always preoccupied in survival emotions, you never actually have the opportunity to believe in yourself.

But what if it was possible to undo or reverse that programming so you had unlimited beliefs about yourself and your life? That's exactly what we've been doing for several years at our advanced workshops using two simple tools, including one that children have been playing with for ages—a kaleidoscope. The only difference is that we're applying it in a technologically advanced way to induce trance.

Up until this point, we've been moving into trance and alpha and theta brain-wave states with our eyes closed during meditation. But if we can create alpha and even theta brain-wave states with our eyes open, and intentionally expose ourselves to information relevant to our life's dreams and goals, we can reprogram ourselves into supernatural states rather than the unconscious states we experience daily. But why the kaleidoscope?

For many years now, my primary passion has been the mystical. Each time I have one of these profound and super-lucid experiences, they create lasting changes within me that deepen my understanding of myself and my connection to the mystery of life. Once you have a mystical experience and get your first glance behind the veil, you can never go back to business as usual, and with every subsequent mystical experience you have, you move closer to source, wholeness, oneness, and the indivisible unified field. The good news is that mystical experiences are no longer relegated to people like Teresa of Avila, Francis of Assisi, or a Buddhist monk who's been meditating for 40 years. Every person is capable of engaging, experiencing, and accessing the mystical.

When I'm having a mystical experience, it seems more real to me than anything I have ever known in my life, and I lose track of space and time. Often, just before I become entwined in it, I see in my mind (and sometimes in my outer world) circular, geometric patterns made of light and energy. They tend to look like mandalas, except they're not static; they're standing waves of interfering frequencies that appear as fractal patterns. The only way I can describe their properties is that they are alive, moving, changing, and ever evolving into more complex patterns within patterns.

These patterns look like what you see when you look into a kaleidoscope, but instead of being two-dimensional, they are three-dimensional. When I see and rest my attention on these divine geometric patterns, they change, and I know in a moment—as my brain takes that pattern of information and transduces it into vivid imagery—I am about to have a profound mystical experience. That's why my team and I wanted to create a kaleidoscope visual for my students—to hopefully induce those types of experiences. But we couldn't find any real footage of a kaleido-scope. At the time, all the fractal geometry media files on the Internet were computer generated, and I wanted to create a more realistic representation. After much searching, my team and I found a family that has been making kaleidoscopes for three generations, so we bought one of their best pieces.

Next, we rented a camera by RED, the leading manufacturer of the professional digital cinema cameras most often used in Hollywood films. We fitted the camera with a lens that attaches to the end of a fiber-optic filament, which we inserted inside the kaleidoscope. Once we placed the camera inside the kaleidoscope, we affixed a motor to the end that rotates so its internal crystals and oils would move in smooth, consistent transitions. For hours in a Seattle, Washington, studio we captured beautiful images and colors while filming against a black backdrop. The black represents the absence of anything physical (the place where we become no body, no one, no thing, no where, in no time). This is the infinite black space or void that you learned about in Chapter 3.

As we recorded all the footage over the course of several days, gravity caused the crystals and oil to fall and accelerate with every rotation, so a technician had to tediously account for every second, frame by frame, to ensure the transitions were smooth. If the transition was not fluid, it risked breaking the viewer's focus or trance state. It took months to refine our footage into the one-hour video that we use during our advanced workshops. Finally, we had talented composer Frank Pisciotti create the accompanying soundtrack. We wanted our students to be continuously mesmerized by the beautiful symmetry and changing geometric forms.

Mind Movies: The Motion Picture of Your Future

At our advanced workshops, every participant receives a fun and easy-to-use software program called Mind Movies to make a movie about their future self and their life. We use this in tandem with the kaleido-scope video. Depending on what the student wants to create in their life, the movie they make about their future exposes them to images and specific written suggestions and information designed to assist them in creating it—just like the shingles commercial helps you to read along. This could range from healing from a disease to strengthening their immune system, creating a new job, manifesting new opportunities, traveling the world, attracting abundance, finding a new life partner, having mystical experiences, and more. Its purpose is to remind them that they can accomplish their dreams, create the uncommon, and become supernatural. The goals of this personalized media presentation include:

1. Helping students get clear on the intention they want to create in their future;

2. Programing their conscious mind, as well as their unconscious mind, into that new future;

3. Changing their brain and body to biologically look like the future has already happened;

4. Repeatedly associating those pictures and images with music to create new neural networks in the brain and to emotionally recondition the body to a new mind. It's a way for them to remember their future.

The Mind Movie technology was founded by two business partners from Australia, Natalie and Glen Ledwell. They are not only the founders but also the poster children for its capabilities. Their journey began in 2007 when a friend showed them a movie he had created about his life. Later, he approached them with the idea of starting a business based on what would become Mind Movie software. Getting the business off the ground required them to create a website to distribute the software so they could instruct people from all around the world on how to make their own movies. Yet they already had four businesses and knew almost nothing about the Internet or e-commerce. Glen could barely turn on a computer and Natalie hadn't even heard of YouTube. They recognized, however, that Mind Movie had the potential to be a very powerful tool to help people build the belief that they could create real outcomes in their lives.

With that in mind, they decided to post a video about the power of Mind Movies on YouTube. At the end of the video, viewers were encouraged to visit their website, where they could learn how to build their own.

In early 2008, after receiving countless e-mails from customers telling them how Mind Movies had changed their lives, Natalie and Glen decided to go all in. They flew to the United States, attended an Internet marketing seminar, joined the Marketing Mastermind Group, and began planning Mind Movie's global launch. Yet when they arrived in the United States, they had nearly drained their bank account, leaving almost no money to pay for the remaining services required to launch the business. This meant learning, mastering, and implementing every-thing for the launch themselves. For months, they worked 12-hour days out of their office—otherwise known as their bedroom. In the process, they ventured so far outside their comfort zone that they no longer knew what a comfort zone was. Faced with daily technical, business, and per-sonal challenges, they had one secret weapon in their arsenal—their own Mind Movie.

In their Mind Movie, Natalie and Glen defined the number of cus-tomers they wanted to attract and who those customers would be. They described the respect of their industry peers and plotted out what they would do once their business was a success, such as the restaurants where they would eat and the family holidays they would take. Finally, they wanted to produce $1 million worth of sales (*Why not aim high?* they thought. Their marketing friends were doing million-dollar launches, albeit with $5,000 programs). They watched their Mind Movie multiple times a day to de-stress and remain focused and inspired, even though everything in their current reality seemed to be working against them. But they knew all their effort, risk, and dreams would culminate on the day of their global launch. The finish line was in sight—and then the unthinkable happened.

Scheduled for September 2008, their launch coincided with the global financial crisis. Financial institutions around the world were fac-ing cataclysmic losses, while families and individuals lost their savings, assets, and livelihoods in the worst downturn since the Great Depression. Meanwhile, Glen and Natalie were facing their own financial hardships. By launching the business, they'd racked up $120,000 in credit-card debt. If the business failed, they'd lose everything—their home, cars, and investments, in addition to being buried under an insurmountable debt.

On the morning of their launch, unbeknownst to them, their e-mail delivery system was down for scheduled maintenance, so none of their customers received confirmation e-mails for their purchase. By lunch-time, they had already received thousands of customer support e-mail complaints, in addition to challenges with their online bank (the bank wanted to freeze their account due to unusual activity). By evening, how-ever, they had experienced the most memorable day of their lives.

In the first hour on the first day, they had hit the $100,000 mark, and by day's end they'd grossed $288,000. In the end, Glen and Natalie ended up generating $700,000 based on a $97 program with no up-sells. But the story doesn't end there.

They were, of course, delighted with their achievement, but they faced one last monumental challenge. Because of the volatile and uncertain financial climate at the time, their bank froze their account so they couldn't access the money. This meant they couldn't pay commissions to their affiliates or the $120,000 they owed to creditors, or deliver profit sharing to the people who had helped them launch the business. Everything hinged on their funds being released. Finally, after six months of sticking to their vision and watching their Mind Movie, they gained access to their account, lifting the financial burden that had nearly sent them into bankruptcy. But here's where the story gets *really* good.

As the world was still reeling economically, the value of the U.S. dollar against the Australian dollar was still grossly different, so thanks to the exchange rate, when they transferred their money back to Australia, they ended up earning an extra $250,000. With that, as well as with the commissions they received in exchange for promoting partner affiliate programs, Glen and Natalie actually met their $1 million goal.

They credit a huge part of their success—which was the complete opposite of what everyone else in the world was experiencing—with the fact that they focused on their Mind Movie every single day.

While this is a great example of the potential of Mind Movies, and while the options to create your own Mind Movie are endless, the process is relatively the same. Students first pick their own song—one they will never tire of listening to. Next, they choose images and/or videos of either themselves or a future event and lay them out sequentially to tell a story of what their future looks like. Finally, we ask them to come up with specific words, phrases, or affirmations to add to the scenes, which they superimpose over the images. In the exact same way that TV commercials program people to be victims or to experience want and lack, Mind Movies can program students to be unlimited in a life they are capable of creating.

In our advanced workshops, our students watch the kaleidoscope video before they watch their Mind Movies because it helps them induce and sustain alpha- and theta-trance states with their eyes open, opening the doorway between the conscious and subconscious mind. Throughout their meditation while in an alpha or theta brain-wave states, they are more suggestible to their *own* reprogramming process. This is important because the more suggestible they are while using their Mind Movie, the less likely they are to become analytical and have constant internal thoughts such as *How's this going to happen?* or *This is impossible!* or *How am I going to afford that?* or *It didn't happen last time so why should it now?*

While the kaleidoscope induces students into trance to open the subconscious to programming, the Mind Movie *is* the new program. Mind Movies program our students' subconscious minds the same way that television commercials program us, but in more positive, unlimited, and constructive ways. When our brain's thoughts are silenced, the conscious mind is no longer analyzing incoming information. As a result, whatever information we are exposed to in this state encodes directly into the subconscious. Just like recording or videotaping something to be automatically played back later, we're recording a new program in the subconscious mind.

A great amount of research over the years has documented how the right and left hemispheres of the neocortex relate to one another. We now know that the right hemisphere processes spatial, nonlinear, abstract, and creative thinking, while the left hemisphere processes logical, rational, linear, methodical, and mathematical thinking. The latest research, however, also suggests the right hemisphere processes cognitive novelty and the left hemisphere processes cognitive routine.[1] This means that when we learn new things, the right hemisphere is more active, and when new learnings become routine, they're then stored in the left hemisphere.

The majority of people operate from the left hemisphere of their brain because they're hardwired into automatic habits and programs they've memorized. This is why language is stored in the left hemisphere—it's routine. You can think about the right hemisphere as the territory of the unknown and the left hemisphere as the territory of the known. It makes sense, then, that the right hemisphere would be romantic, creative, and nonlinear, while the left hemisphere would be methodical, logical, and structured. We've actually seen this dual processing occurring while watching our students' brain scans in real time.

Because the kaleidoscope's flow of geometric fractal patterns within patterns does not look like any one, any thing, any where, in any time, its patterns are designed to bypass the perceptual networks and associative centers in the brain that relate to known people, things, objects, places, and times. Its ancient geometrical patterns reflect repeating fractal patterns found all throughout nature; thus they activate lower-brain centers. It's for this reason you can't look into the kaleidoscope and see your Aunt Mary, a bicycle you owned in sixth grade, or the house where you grew up—because you're not activating or triggering the associative centers related to the memories primarily located in the left hemisphere of your brain. As you stop thinking and analyzing, and start moving into alpha or theta brain-wave patterns, more activity occurs in the right hemisphere. If the left hemisphere operates in the known, and the right hemisphere operates in the unknown, as activity increases in your right hemisphere, you are more open to creating something unknown and new.

Graphics 9A(1) and 9A(2) in the color insert show brain scans of two students who are in coherent alpha and theta states. In Graphic 9A(3), you'll see another student's entire brain in theta while viewing the kaleidoscope. Graphic 9A(4) shows the brain scan of a student watching the kaleidoscope; the right side of their brain is more activated while they engage in the novelty of the experience during a trance state.

When we play the kaleidoscope in our advanced workshops, we play it in a dark room so melatonin levels increase, thereby enhancing brain-wave changes. I ask students to relax and consciously slow down their breathing. As their respiration slows down, so do their brain waves, moving from beta to alpha. I then ask them to continuously relax into their body and to get ever more in touch with it. I want to get them into the state somewhere between half awake and half asleep, when they're most suggestible, further priming their brain to accept the programming of their Mind Movie.

Just as late-night infomercials influence people because the production of melatonin (in preparation for restorative sleep) causes their guard to drop, I want our students' melatonin levels to be elevated and their brain waves to be in alpha and theta so they are wide open to the information and the possibilities in their Mind Movie.

The Soundtrack of Your Future Life

Music has a way of calling up the memory of a specific time and place in our life. It's for this reason the entertainer Dick Clark said, "Music is the soundtrack of your life." The moment a magically nostalgic song starts playing, your brain begins recalling images of certain times and places, and those images connect you to the experience of different people and events. Neurologically speaking, the song acts as an external cue, causing a specific set of neural networks in your brain to fire. By association, you see images in your mind that have been frozen in time. We call this an associative memory.

If you take the memory of that song further and really feel it, get into it, and maybe even sing and dance along, you might notice that the corresponding emotions connected to your memories begin to move throughout your body. Whether the memory of that song relates to your first love, spring break your senior year of college, or what you felt before walking onto the field before the biggest game of your life, every one of those memories is strongly embedded with feelings and emotions. When you feel the emotion deeply enough, it connects you to the energy of your past, and the stronger the emotional response, the greater the memory. In the moment you feel and experience that memory, it brings your past to life, and in your mind you are instantly transported through time into the experience. Just as it did in the past, your body comes out of its resting state, causing you to feel the same emotions of your past and reproduce a level of mind equal to that past memory. For that moment, your entire state of being is in the past.

Long-term memories are stronger when the amplitude of the emotions associated with the event is high. Whether a long-term memory is positive or negative, however, has no bearing on how our mind processes the memory. For example, memories of traumas, betrayals, and shocking events carry equally powerful emotions, except they are negative rather than joyful. Once we remember and relive the pain, fear, anger, sadness, and intensity of the emotions connected to those traumatic memories, our internal chemical state changes. This causes us to pay more attention to whomever or whatever created the original emotions in our external environment.

So what if you could create a movie of your *future* and pair it with a song that motivates and inspires you so much that it pulls you out of your resting state, changes your state of being, and connects you to the energy of your *future memories*? If music is the soundtrack of your life, then just as certain songs transport you to the past, couldn't you bring your future to life in the same way?

This is where Mind Movies come in. By purposefully pairing very powerful and moving images of your future, adding words and phrases to reinforce the content, and combining them with elevated emotions and inspiring music, you create long-term memories that move your biology out of the past and into the future. In other words, the images elicit feelings that correlate to the experiences you want to have in your future. This could include images of homes you want to live in, vacations you want to take, a new career, the freedom of expression, a healed relationship or body, interdimensional experiences, and so on. These are just some of the infinite possibilities that exist in your future timeline. When you watch your Mind Movie, as you connect to the feelings and emotions of your future, the higher the emotions you feel, the more you pay attention to the images that created those emotions. Now you're creating long-term memories of your future—and you are bringing your future to life. The magical, interdimensional component of the future is your song, because it's the feelings associated with your song that change your energy equal to how you will feel when that future unfolds. This is why it's best to choose music that's inspirational, motivational, or aspirational.

Next, you add words of affirmation or knowing to the Mind Movie that remind you of who you are and what you believe about your future. You could even add a timeline if you want to. Some examples could include:

- The doors of dimension open to me so I may experience the mystical.

- My body is healing every day.

- My words are law.

- I feel loved deeply and daily.

- Wealth flows to me.

- All my needs are always met.

- My body becomes younger every day.

- The divine appears in my life every day.

- My life partner is my equal and teaches me by example.

- Synchronicities happen to me all of the time.

- I feel more whole every day.

- My immune system gets stronger each day.

- I lead with courage in my life.

- I am an unlimited genius.

- I am always aware of the power within me and all around me.

- I believe in myself.

- I embrace the unknown.

- When I call on Spirit it responds.

If you think of your favorite music video or a scene from your favorite musical, chances are you know all the words of the song as well as the images that correspond to every note, beat, melody, and harmony. Most likely, the power of that combination evokes a time and a place in your life that was inhabited by a particular set of people, feelings, emotions, and experiences. This is exactly what you're doing with your Mind Movies, except instead of remembering the past, you're creating memories of the future. If you heard your song enough times while observing the images of your future, isn't it possible that when you heard your song without viewing your Mind Movie, you'd be automatically transported into those images of a new future, just like you were transported back to your past? With practice, not only are you feeling the emotions that connect you to the memories of your future, but your biology is aligning to that future as well.

You already know why this happens: If your body is the unconscious mind, and it doesn't know the difference between the experience that creates the emotion and the emotion you create by thought alone, in the present moment your body begins to believe it is living in that future reality. Since the environment signals the gene, and emotions are the consequences of experiences in the environment, by embracing the emotions of the event before the actual experience, you begin to change your body to be biologically aligned to your future in the present moment. Since all genes make proteins and proteins are responsible for the structure and function of your body, your body begins to biologically change to look like your future is already happening.

Putting It All Together

What if you invited a group of people to retreat from their lives for four or five days, and in the process removed the constant stimulation in their external environment that reminded them of who they thought they were as a personality? If you separated them long enough from the people they know, the places they go, and the things they do every day at the exact same time, they would be reminded of who they really are: unlimited human beings. And if you spent the first day or two teaching them how to create more coherence in their hearts and brains—and they repeatedly practiced cultivating these states every day—it makes sense that sooner or later they would get better at opening their hearts and making their brains work more proficiently. In fact, they would be more focused on a vision of a new future without being distracted, and at the same time, they could more easily feel the emotions of that new future. As they created more coherence in their brains and hearts, they would create more coherence in their own energy fields, and this would create a clearer electromagnetic signature.

As they continuously worked on overcoming themselves, their bodies, their environment, and time—slowing down and changing their brain waves, unfolding into the unified field, and transcending this three-dimensional environment—it would become increasingly easier and more familiar for them to activate their heart center and create. After they practiced getting beyond their body, emotions, habits, pain, disease, identity, limited beliefs, analytical mind, and unconscious programs, by the time the practice of Mind Movies was introduced, they would be ready to absorb a greater degree of information equal to who they were becoming, which would increase their ability to connect with their future. This is how we use Mind Movies at our workshops.

You can think of a Mind Movie as a 21st-century version of a vision board (a tool used to clarify, focus on, and maintain specific life goals), except it's dynamic instead of static. When used with the kaleidoscope, the Mind Movie technology is a great tool to help you bring your future to life by repeatedly experiencing it. It's also is a great way to gain clarity on what you want to unfold in your life—and to remind yourself on a daily basis what that future holds for you. This is called intention.

Because Mind Movie technology is so versatile, it can be used across many applications and in a variety of settings. Not only can the technology be used to create relationships, wealth, health, careers, and other material items, it's also being used with children and teens to help them create a future vision so they feel they have some control over their lives. So many young people today are overwhelmed because of the frenetic pace, pressure, and demands of social media and modern society. Suicide is a leading cause of death for teens in the United States, so the founders of Mind Movie are using the technology in schools to help teens envision a brighter, more specific future for themselves.

Mind Movies are also used in corporate settings for team building and visioning. Entrepreneurs use the software to develop businesses, create mission statements, and strategize and create business plans. Imagine a team of motivated people not only reading and intellectualizing their mission statement, but also seeing it unfold in a dynamic, visual format—before it happens.

Integrative healing is another arena in which practitioners use this technology to help patients envision the healthiest version of themselves, assist them with their healing process, and keep them on task with a new lifestyle that must be maintained daily. This includes addiction treatment and recovery facilities helping patients become clear on the future they want to create in the next phase of their recovery. Mind Movies have also supported the generationally unemployed in finding new jobs or careers and living more future-oriented and productive lives, not only for themselves but also for their families.

As you can see, the applications for this technology are endless. No matter how it's applied, the power of Mind Movies resides in enabling people to construct a new reality by reminding themselves of the daily choices they must make, the new behaviors they must demonstrate, and the feelings they want to live by. Once you program these feelings and behaviors subconsciously, you can break your addiction to old habits, familiar lifestyles, and unconscious reactions. It's entirely up to you how creative you want to get when piecing together your future.

While anytime is a good time to watch your Mind Movie, I suggest watching it first thing in the morning and right before bed, because this is when you are most suggestible. If you watch it as soon as you wake up, you're starting your day off on a positive note by being mindful and focused on what you want to achieve for the day, as well as for your future. When you view it at night before you go to bed, your subconscious mind can contemplate it while you sleep, align your body and mind to your future, and come up with solutions that your autonomic nervous system can carry out while you sleep. Basically, you can use it anytime you need motivation or to make a different choice. They key is to make sure you're completely present when you watch it.

Since implementing Mind Movies, I've seen our students manifest new homes and heard stories of homes selling that had been on the market for years. I've seen vacations spontaneously appear and witnessed new relationships develop out of nowhere. I've listened to countless testimonials of abundance, freedom, new careers, new cars, healings of all kinds, relief from unbearable hardships, and of course, profound mystical experiences that have permanently altered the recipients. But it's not magic or sorcery. It's simply learning how to become a conscious creator—learning how to align to your own destiny.

Think of your Mind Movie as if you are turning on a radar device to track your future. Then, as you repeatedly visit the future in your heart and mind, all the thoughts, choices, actions, experiences, and emotions you experience between your present reality and your future reality become course corrections that deliver you to your target. The more you keep your future alive with your intention, attention, energy, and love, the more it starts to unfold as a new reality because you're remembering your future just as you remember your past. Your job, then, is to continuously fall in love with that vision of the future, keep your energy up, and not let the circumstances (environment), hardwired attitudes, familiar negative feelings, or unconscious habits derail you from your goals.

What makes this technology so profound is that we perceive reality based on pattern recognition—links between the neural networks in our brains and the objects, people, and places in our external environment. For example, when you see someone you recognize, the neural networks in your brain instantly recall memories and experiences with that person. By contrast, if someone is not wired in your brain, you probably won't recognize them. If your brain doesn't have the hardware (familiarity with the images, thoughts, and emotions from the Mind Movie) installed before your future unfolds—if you don't have the neural architecture wired into your brain—how will you recognize your new partner, your new job, your new house, or your new body? (Think of it like this: You can't open a Microsoft Word document on a Mac computer unless you already have the Microsoft Word software installed.) If you can't feel the emotions and create the energy of your future reality, you might not recognize or trust that future unknown experience when it finds you. That's because your energy and emotional state are not in alignment with that experience, so instead of feeling certainty or a knowing, you may feel fear or uncertainty.

So many of my advanced students have told me they are on their third, fourth, even fifth Mind Movie because everything in their previous ones has come true. I am always amazed and humbled to hear the stories of how their creations came to be. No matter how varied their manifestations are, they all share one thing: They trained the body to follow the mind toward an intentional future. This makes sense because if you have been putting in the time to study, memorize, and create the neural connections of your future, that is where you have been placing your attention. And as you know by now, where attention goes, energy flows.

Take a look at Graphic 10 in the color insert. This shows an example of a student's brain activity while he is watching his Mind Movie. There is an enormous amount of energy in his brain because he is fully involved in the experience.

Taking It One Step Further: Getting Dimensional

There's one final way we use the Mind Movie technology in our work. Once our students have neurologically mapped their entire presentation, I ask them to pick a scene from the Mind Movie and unfold into a particular space and time, experiencing that scene three-dimensionally in their mind during their meditation. If you notice, I never use the word *visualize* in my teachings. Visualization usually involves just seeing something in the mind's eye, so it appears as a flat or two-dimensional image. For example, if you visualize a picture of a car, you will create a *picture* of a car. Instead, I want you to experience everything in the scene using all five senses so it feels like a real-life, three-dimensional experience.

Many people who have been introduced to my work have wondered why I spend so much time on becoming aware of "the space" their body occupies in space, as well as opening their focus to the space around their body and the space that the room occupies in space. Aside from the coherent changes my cues produce in the brain, it's all training for this mindful activity of pairing our Mind Movie with the kaleidoscope during meditation.

When a student begins the dimensionalizing process, before they see anything in their mind, they are instructed to unfold as an awareness into the scene. When they start, I want the participant to become aware that they are in their scene only as a consciousness. This means they are not their body and they lack their senses. They begin as an awareness in the emptiness of space, as if they are incapable of seeing, hearing, feeling, tasting, or smelling anything.

Once they become aware that they are an awareness, I ask them to choose a scene from their Mind Movie. This causes their brain to naturally start adding sensory input, which begins to bring dimension to the scene in their mind. Next they are instructed to start sensing what's to their right, their left, above them, and below them. The act of sensing fills in this scene with three-dimensional structures, forms, and space. As they expand their awareness to what else is in the scene, their senses begin recruiting other senses, further filling in the scene with more forms, structures, curves, textures, scents, images, feelings, and space. Finally, when the scene comes to life in their mind, in the future space and time of that scene, they start inhabiting their body—not the body that is sitting there in the chair meditating, but the physical body of their future. They are asked to feel their arms, legs, torso, muscles, and so on until they can feel their entire body in that scene. Then they are ready to move about in that scene and experience that reality.

My theory is that when they simultaneously activate enough of the neural networks assigned to the objects, things, and people in a specific space and time, their possibility of having a full-on, holographic, IMAX-type experience increases. This is because as the student becomes present and unfolds into a fully dimensional scene, a large majority of the brain turns on, including the neural architecture that is allocated to both the sensory (feeling) and motor (moving) aspects of their body, as well as the proprioception (awareness of body position) of where they are in space. The next thing they know, they are having a real-life sensory experience of their future with their eyes closed, in the present moment.

Take a look at Graphic 11 in the color insert. It is the brain scan of a student who is experiencing a seemingly real Mind Movie scene in meditation. She has quite a bit of energy in her brain while she is dimensionalizing the scene. She described this moment as a full-on virtual sensory experience. Her subjective experience was quantified objectively in this scan.

Many of our students have reported that the experiences in their meditation were more real than any past external experience. Their senses were enhanced without external stimuli to excite their senses, yet all they were doing was sitting in their chair with their eyes closed. Many have reported that in their lucid experience, they smelled certain fragrances like colognes, the aroma of specific flowers like jasmine and gardenias, or the familiar scent of leather in their new car they were sitting in. I've also heard students report specific memories, like the stubble on their face from not shaving, the wind blowing through their hair, or the feeling that their body was filled with a powerful energy. Students have also given testimony to specific sounds they could clearly hear, such as distant church bells coming from a European church near where they were vacationing, or the bark of their dog when they were in their new home. Several students have also said that the colors they saw were incredibly clear and vivid, or they experienced amplified tastes like coconut, chocolate, and cinnamon. The combination of all of the different senses literally created a new experience for them.

It's our five senses that plug us into our external reality. Typically, when we have a new experience, everything we see, hear, smell, taste, and feel is sent to the brain through those five sensory pathways. Once all that sensory information makes it to the brain, clusters of neurons begin to organize into networks. The moment the neurons string into place, the limbic brain makes a chemical called an emotion. Because experience enriches the brain and creates an emotion that signals new genes in the body, in the rich sensory moment of a student's internal experience—without ever using their external senses—they're changing their brain and body to look like their future has already happened. Isn't that what experience does? I love to hear a person who has just come out of one of those experiences tell me, "You don't understand—I was there! I know it is going to happen because it already has and I already experienced it!" That's because the experience *has* already happened.

When we fully experience a reality in this field of consciousness and energy without a body, the energy of the new experience serves as the template for physical reality. The more energy you invest in your future, and the more you keep experiencing and emotionally embracing it before it happens, the more you leave an energetic imprint in that future reality. And your body should follow your mind to that unknown future, because that's where your energy is. As you continue to place your attention and energy on it, you fall more deeply in love with it, and because love bonds all things, you are bonding with that future and it is being drawn to you.

For more information about the Mind Movie or the kaleidoscope, please visit my website at **drjoedispenza.com/mindmovies** or **drjoedispenza.com/kaleidoscope**, respectively.

Kaleidoscope and Mind Movie Meditation

In our advanced workshops, we instruct our students to create a Mind Movie before they arrive at our event so they can integrate their Mind Movies with the kaleidoscope video during meditation. We begin by getting heart centered, which you learned in Chapter 7, locking into those elevated emotions for several minutes and radiating that energy beyond their bodies into space. Then we guide them in the following meditation.

Unfold into the present moment, and when you attain that state, open your eyes and stare into the kaleidoscope. Once in trance, switch to your Mind Movie. Spend maybe eight minutes with the kaleidoscope, then eight minutes watching your Mind Movie, and then repeat the cycle. When you've watched your Mind Movie enough that you can predict the next scene, you've mapped it neurologically. Over time, you'll associate different parts of the song you have chosen with the different images of your Mind Movie.

Finally, spend seven minutes watching the kaleidoscope while just listening to the music from your Mind Movie. As you gaze into the kaleidoscope in trance and hear your song, by association your brain automatically recalls different images from your Mind Movie. This causes you to further remember your future biologically—automatically and repeatedly firing and wiring neural networks. Now your brain is being programmed to look like the new future has already happened, while the emotions are signaling new genes to biologically change your body in preparation for your new future.

Watch the kaleidoscope in tandem with your Mind Movie every day for a month, or at least try to watch your Mind Movie twice daily—as soon as you wake up and right before you go to sleep. You might even want to keep a journal to record all the wonderfully unexpected adventures and serendipitous happenings that, as you look back, you will see as points on a map that led you to manifesting this future. Consider creating several Mind Movies—one for health and wellness, for example, and another for romance, relationships, and wealth.

Chapter 9

WALKING MEDITATION

Most spiritual traditions embrace four meditation postures, and at our advanced workshops we practice each of them. There's sitting, which hopefully you're in the process of mastering; there's standing and walking, which are combined in the meditations you'll learn in this chapter; and then there's lying down. While each type of meditation posture serves its own purpose, place, and time, each builds upon the other to help us maintain and regulate our internal states—no matter what is happening in our external environment.

But what could be the relevance of bridging the sitting meditation with the standing and walking meditation? Although practicing your meditation when you wake up is an ideal way to start your morning, if you can't maintain that energy and awareness throughout the course of your day, you're likely to fall right back into the unconscious programs that have been running your life for years.

For example, let's say you just finished your sitting meditation. When you open your eyes, you probably feel more alive, awake, clear, empowered, and ready to start your day. Perhaps your heart feels open, expanded, and connected, or perhaps you just overcame an aspect of yourself, shifted your energy, and emotionally embraced a new future. But more often than not, you may fall right back into your unconscious programs, and all the work you just did to create an elevated internal state dissolves into a never-ending to-do list: making lunches and sending your kids off to school, rushing to work, getting irate at the person who cut you off on the freeway, answering calls and returning e-mails, hustling to appointments, and so on. In other words, you're no longer in a creative state because you've just returned to the habitual programs and survival emotions of your past. When this occurs, you disconnect from the energy of your future and essentially leave the energy you created right where you were sitting in your meditation, as opposed to carrying it with you throughout the day. You've energetically returned to your past.

Since I too have been guilty of this, I started thinking about how our students could take this energy with them and embody it during the course of their day. That's why I created a meditation that includes standing and walking—so that when you become adept at raising your energy or frequency and marrying it with a clear vision, you now have a practice that enables you to maintain that elevated energy all day long so that over time this becomes your natural state of being. The purpose of this chapter is to help you do just that.

Walking into Your Future

You've already learned that throughout much of your day you are behaving unconsciously, unaware of what you're doing and why. For instance, you may not remember driving to work because you were lost in an argument you had a few days prior, or you may be focused on how you're going to respond to your significant other's angry text. Maybe you're simultaneously running three programs at once—texting, talking, and checking e-mails. You may not be aware of your nervous tics or their causes, your posture and how it's perceived as shy, or how your speech, facial expressions, and the energy you bring into a room affect your coworkers. These unconscious programs and behaviors occur because the body has become the mind, and it's the combination of these unconscious programs that makes up who you are. You know by now that when the body becomes the mind, you're no longer living in the present moment—and so you're no longer in a creative state, which means you're keeping your goals, dreams, and visions at arm's length.

By becoming aware of these unconscious behaviors and programs, however, you can work to actively broadcast a new electromagnetic signature that is in line with your future—and the more you broadcast that electromagnetic signature into the field, the sooner you will become it, and it will become you. When there's a vibrational match between your energy and that future potential that already exists in the quantum field, that future event is going to find you—or better yet, your body will be drawn to a new reality. You will become a magnet to a new destiny, which will manifest as an unknown, new experience.

For a moment, think of your future reality as if it already exists, vibrating as unmaterialized energy in the quantum field. Imagine your future as the vibration coming from a tuning fork that has just been struck. The sound it emits is a vibration traveling on a certain frequency. If you also exist as a tuning fork, as you change your energy to resonate within the same harmonic of that quantum possibility of your future, you connect with, and align to, that frequency. The longer you can maintain and tune your energy in to that frequency, the more you vibrate at the same harmonic of energy. Now you're connected to that future reality because you're operating at the same frequency or vibration. The closer frequencies come together in space and time, the more they influence each other until they entrain to one frequency. That's the moment when your future finds you. This is how you create new realities.

It stands to reason, then, that the instant your energy changes because you're feeling lower, survival emotions, there's dissonance and incoherence between you and your future reality. You are no longer resonating within the frequency of that possibility, and this causes you to become out of sync with the future you are trying to create. If you can't give up that reaction because the addiction to those emotions has a grip on you, you'll just wind up creating more of the same reality because your energy is vibrating equal to the reality you're reacting to.

In Chapter 3, you learned that all possibilities exist in the eternal now and that when you get beyond your identity as a body connected to people, objects, places, and time, you become pure consciousness. You become no body, no one, no thing, no where, in no time. It is in that elegant moment that you transcend the material realm of matter and enter the quantum field of information and energy. Now that you are beyond your associations to this physical reality, you are creating from the unified field; thus you are creating from a level of energy that is greater than matter. For the most part, our students have practiced this sitting down. The purpose of the standing and walking meditation is to make you more mindful of the present moment, to help you maintain and sustain elevated states throughout the day, to keep you more connected to that future with your eyes open, and to assist you in literally stepping into your new future.

When you begin practicing walking meditations, it's best to find a quiet place in nature so you're not easily distracted. The fewer people and less activity around you, the easier it is to stay focused. Eventually, when you get better at it, you can practice this in a shopping mall, while walking your dog, or somewhere else out in public.

In many ways, the standing and walking meditations are just like the seated ones. You begin by standing still, closing your eyes, and resting your attention in your heart, all the while slowing down your breath and breathing in and out of this center. When you feel heart centered, just as you do in your seated meditations, you begin cultivating elevated emotions that connect you to your future.

Once you feel fully grounded in these elevated emotions, for a few minutes open your focus and radiate that energy beyond your body until you feel it within you as well as all around you. Next, lay upon the energy of these elevated emotions the intent of what you want for your day or your future, whether it's to radiate a synchronicity, lead a noble life, make a difference in the world, create a new job or relationship, or something else. Now you are broadcasting a new electromagnetic signature into the field. The only difference is that instead of sitting with your eyes closed and radiating loving, elevated emotions, you're standing up with your eyes closed so that when you open your eyes and begin walking, you'll be able to embody that elevated energy.

As you continue to stand, eyes closed, with an open focus, you take your attention off of the outer world, and your brain waves slow down from beta to alpha states. This causes the thoughts, analysis, and chatter inside your head to quiet down, inducing a trance state and making you more suggestible. As you learned in the previous chapter, the longer you can remain in this trance state, the less resistance there is to new information entering your subconscious mind. When you're in an elevated emotional state that aligns you with your future, you will be more prone to accept, believe, and surrender to the intentional thoughts equal to those emotions. This means the thoughts, visions, pictures, and images your mind is creating can make it past the analytical mind and you can program the autonomic nervous system to create the biology of your new future.

Since you have created the energy of your new future while standing with your eyes closed, now it's time to open your eyes and begin walking. Don't look at anyone, and don't pay attention to objects or things, or anything else around you. Simply keep your focus open, transfix your gaze on the horizon, and remain in trance. The more you're in trance, the less likely you'll be to think in old, familiar ways. In the meantime, your mind will be connecting to the images of your new future rather than replaying programs of the past. Now you're ready to walk into your future as someone else.

Because you are walking as your future self, you now have to become aware of the way your current self has always *unconsciously* walked. It's time to alter your stride, your pace, your posture, your breathing, and your movements. You might smile instead of staring blankly. You may have to imagine what walking as a wealthy person feels like by modeling a wealthy person. You might adopt the posture of a courageous person you admire, walk within the elevated energy of your future healthy body, or walk as an open-hearted, loving, accepting person. Basically, you're consciously embodying the person you've always dreamed you could be, but walking as if your future self is imperative. For example, you might imagine that it's one or two years later and you already have all the things you want. The most important ingredient is for you to embody that future person *now*. If you already are that identity, you no longer need to wish you will become that person because it's already happened—you already embody the qualities of your future. You are simply thinking, acting, and feeling your future self.

As you begin to practice walking differently, and continue to practice day in and day out, you're going to get into the habit of walking like a wealthy person, thinking like a healthy person, standing like a confident person, and feeling like a free, unlimited, grateful person (gratitude means it already happened), instead of perhaps a beat-up, worn-down, stressed-out person. The more you practice, the more this new way of being will become a new habit, and these habits will become your new automatic patterns of thought, behaviors, and emotions. Once you start naturally feeling and embodying these elevated emotions, they will inhabit you, and you will actually become the person you want to be. Graphic 12 in the color insert shows a student who changes his brain in about an hour after doing a walking meditation.

Priming the Brain for Future Memories

The walking meditation is also about creating memories of things that haven't happened yet in linear time—in effect, remembering your future. When you produce elevated feelings with your eyes closed, radiate that energy beyond the field of your body, and then open your eyes and begin walking and leading with your heart (feeling those elevated emotions with your eyes open), the more you feel that emotion, the more you're going to pay attention to the pictures, images, and thoughts that are creating your feelings. This process naturally upgrades your neural circuitry by creating a new inward experience. Experience enriches the brain and creates memories. Now your brain is no longer living in the past; it's living in the future. The more you embody your elevated emotions correctly, the more your brain and body will look like the future experience has already happened. That means you're technically remembering your future.

Remaining in trance is important because as you align your body with your future *and* change your inner world, you're creating long-term memories. Since where you place your attention is where you place your energy, you may even want to flash scenes of your Mind Movie in your head while you're envisioning, embodying, and feeling your future. As you do this, those Mind Movie scenes will become the energetic and biological maps to your future. The act of feeling the emotions of your future (in the present moment) and combining these emotions with your intention does two things: It installs new circuits to make your brain an intentional map to the future and it also produces the emotional chemicals for that future event, which signals new genes in new ways, thus conditioning your body to prepare it for a new destiny.

Remember that this meditation is not about what you get in life; it's about who you become—or who you are in the process of becoming. If you are trying to "get" wealth, success, health, or a new relationship, you are still conditioned to thinking you are separate from some thing and you have to go *get* it. But the truth is that the more you become that person, the more reality will shape and mold equal to your new state of being. It's that process of consciously becoming that helps you maintain alignment to a different destiny. The more you practice the walking meditation and walk as your future self, the more you should be able to change your state of being with your eyes open, just as you did with your eyes closed. When you practice this enough times, you'll not only carry that energy with you throughout the day, but you'll embody it. This type of repetition will make you feel more mindful in your waking hours, and before you know it you'll start automatically behaving, thinking, and feeling differently. This is programming a new personality to a new personal reality.

Over time, who knows? You might find yourself naturally walking like a happy person; behaving like a courageous and compassionate leader; thinking like a noble, empowered genius; feeling like a worthy, abundant entrepreneur. In the middle of your day you might become aware of the fact that the pain in your body is gone because you're feeling so whole, unlimited, and in love with life. What you've done has made a habit out of being the person you want to be. This is because you installed the circuitry and signaled the latent gene to think, act, and feel in a new way. Biologically, you have become that person.

Becoming mindful and embodying your future self can occur many times throughout your day. Imagine that you're waiting for a friend who is running late, and instead of feeling frustrated and bothered, you're generating the energy of your future. When you're sitting in traffic, instead of getting impatient and angry, practice tuning in to the energy of your future with your eyes open. Imagine that when you're in line at the grocery store and judging a person for what they're buying, you redirect your thoughts to feeling incredibly grateful for your new life, walking as your future self. Imagine when you walk to your car in the parking lot or to your mailbox, you're naturally empowered by the thought of your new life. You'll then begin to accept, believe, and surrender to the thoughts equal to that emotional state, and as you surrender to those thoughts, your body will make the chemistry equal to that emotional state. This is how you begin to program your autonomic nervous system into a different destiny, and the more you practice it, the less likely you are to return to autopilot and miss the present moment.

The Walking Meditation

Begin by finding a quiet space in nature. Disconnect from your external environment and anchor yourself in the present moment by closing your eyes. Acknowledge your heart center, where the soul and heart intersect with the unified field, and bring elevated emotions such as gratitude, joy, inspiration, compassion, love, and so on to this center. If you are going to believe in your new future with all of your heart, it had better be open and activated.

Rest your attention on the heart, allowing your breath to flow in and out of this center—ever more slowly, more deeply, and more relaxed—for about two minutes. Return to creating elevated emotions within your heart for two to three minutes. Radiate that energy into the space surrounding your body in space and stay present with that energy. Tune in to the energy of your future.

After a few minutes, hold a clear intention in your mind's eye. You might pick a representative symbol that connects you to the energy of your future, the way you learned in Chapter 3. Change your state of being with the feelings of these elevated emotions, and focus on broadcasting that new electromagnetic signature into the field. Remain in this state for two to three minutes.

Next, open your eyes, and without looking at anything or anyone, open your focus and keep your awareness on the space around your body in space while maintaining a trance state. Begin walking with your eyes open while you stay entranced. With each step you take, embody that new energy—that new frequency of whatever you're creating in your future. As you take this energy with you during your waking, daily life, walking as your new self, you are activating the same neurological networks and producing the same level of mind as when you meditate with your eyes closed.

Next remember your future. Let the images come, feeling them and embodying them. Own them. Become them. Continue to walk for about ten minutes, and then stop to recalibrate. Once again, close your eyes and raise your energy. Stay present with this energy for about five to ten minutes. For the next ten minutes, with your eyes open in trance, walk again with intent and purpose as your future self. With each step you take, embodying this new energy, you move closer to your destiny and it moves closer to you.

Do this cycle two times. When you finish the second round, stop and stand still one last time, really focusing on how you feel with your fourth energy center open. You can use this opportunity to affirm who you are based on how you feel. For example, if you're feeling unlimited, you can literally acknowledge, "I am unlimited." Next, place your hand over your beautiful heart, and be willing to feel valuable and worthy enough to receive what you have created. Raise your energy to its zenith and feel gratitude, appreciation, and thankfulness.

Now acknowledge the divine within you—the energy that powers you and gives rise to all of life. Give thanks for a new life before it's made manifest. Acknowledging the power within you, ask that your life be filled with unexpected wonder, synchronicities, and coincidences that create a joy for existence. Radiate your love while loving your new life into existence.

Chapter 10

CASE STUDIES:
MAKING IT REAL

In the case studies that follow, you'll be introduced to people just like you who took time out of their busy lives to create a new future. Every day they defined themselves by a vision of this future instead of by the memories of their past. You could say they were more in love with their future than they were with their past. The act of doing the work daily and turning the practices in the last three chapters into a skill led them to become more supernatural. Pay attention to how simple they made it.

Tim Gets the Key to His Future

At an advanced workshop in Seattle, which typically coincides with Halloween, we ask our students to dress up as their future selves on the first night. Tim dressed up as a supernatural swami. He'd always wanted to be a swami, subscribed to the lifestyle, and at a young age had left his hometown in Connecticut to study in an ashram. At the start of the event, participants also received a gift from our company—a key to symbolize unlocking the potential of each participant's future self.

Tim had attended several advanced-level workshops in the past. The first time he made a Mind Movie, he inserted a picture of gold and silver coins in one of his scenes. For years, he had been trying to surrender the emotion of fear, but at a certain point he realized that behind the fear was unworthiness; so for Tim, the coins were a symbol of worthiness.

"Everybody wants wealth," he told me. "But because I was on the spiritual path, into yoga and everything else that goes with it, I had the mentality that I had to be poor and embrace poverty to truly walk the talk. So instead of the gold and silver coins merely representing wealth, they represented being worthy to receive."

For Tim's Seattle Mind Movie, he added more images to evolve his vision. As another symbol for worthiness, Tim used a Chinese character that meant "wealth," but because he never desired money, below the symbol he placed the word *affluence*. He preferred affluence because when he looked up the word's definition, he found that its Latin root meant "to flow toward." *Wouldn't it be great,* he thought, *if everything I wanted flowed toward me?*

Although Tim is very analytical, after continuously watching his Mind Movie in tandem with the kaleidoscope, he found he could quickly bypass the analytical mind and get into the subconscious mind, the operating system, to program his future.

During the workshop, when it came time to dimensionalize a scene in his Mind Movie, he had a profound experience. He started to feel joy and then a wildly enthusiastic love for life, almost like a burning sensation in his heart. He said he felt as if he could set the world on fire. Then, during the meditation, I told the students it was time to open up and receive, and that's when Tim says energy began to enter his body.

"I don't know where it came from," he told me. "But it was like someone had turned on a spigot. I shot straight up. The energy came in through the top of my head and then moved out through my hands. My palms were face down, yet without conscious control, the energy caused them to lift and turn over. I lost track of time and space and had no idea where I was, but for the rest of the meditation I was in an ecstatic, exalted state. I knew somehow that everything was going to be different and that I was no longer the same person."

When the energy downloaded into Tim, he believed it was carrying a message of worthiness, because he was never the same afterward.

"I am convinced that the new information that came into my body rewrote my DNA, erasing the old self, because that part of my personality is now gone," he says. When Tim got home to Phoenix, where he owned and operated a futon shop, he returned to business as usual on Monday morning. On Thursday, a woman who had purchased a futon from him several years earlier came into his shop. Since the day she purchased the futon, they had formed a friendship and every few weeks she would stop by to chat. She was now retired and came into the shop to tell Tim she had just finished making out her will. She wanted Tim to be her executor. Tim felt honored, and he thanked her.

"Here it is," she said, placing it on the counter along with a key. "Read it."

Tim began scanning the document to discover that not only was he the executor, but she was also bequeathing him $110,000 worth of gold and silver coins. The key she placed on the counter was the key to her safe-deposit box, where she kept the coins (which, of course, matched the picture in Tim's Mind Movie). In an instant, Tim remembered the similar "key to his future" he had received at the advanced workshop in Seattle. Now that's being worth it!

Sarah Can't Touch the Ground

On Labor Day 2016, Sarah severely injured her back attempting to prevent a five-ton boat from crashing into a dock. For seven weeks, she was in agony as she endured physical therapy, took a cocktail of medications, and made countless visits to the chiropractor. After nothing else helped, her doctors scheduled Sarah for surgery. But first, she decided to attend an advanced workshop in Cancun.

Because of how much pain Sarah was in, her son suggested she bring a wheelchair. She decided not to, and when she arrived at the hotel she collapsed on the floor in pain. Later, when she got into the pool on a float, she had severe spasms when she attempted to get out.

Sarah was not new to my work, so she came to Cancun with her meditation cushion and her Mind Movie. In her Mind Movie, she was healthy, strong, and able to run again. She could play basketball with her son and lacrosse with her daughter. Every time Sarah saw herself in the scene performing aerial yoga, she embraced the joy she knew she would feel if she could actually do it, and when she heard the song from her Mind Movie, her energy rose.

During the first few days, when she was tightening her core muscles and drawing energy up her spine with the breathing technique, she felt her sciatic nerve pulsating. It was as if a warm electric current was traveling up the nerve. At the same time, she had the intention that the energy was a healing light ascending her spinal column.

On the third day, she started her morning by searching the Internet until she found an image of a woman doing aerial yoga. She carried that image in her mind all day. That afternoon, our students were working with the kaleidoscope and their Mind Movies. After they unfolded into the quantum field, I then asked them to dimensionalize a scene from their Mind Movie. When the meditation was finished, I instructed them to lie down on the floor—but as Sarah told me later, she couldn't find the floor. She kept reaching lower and lower, searching for it, but it was no longer there. The next thing she knew, she was in another dimension having a full-on IMAX-like sensory experience—but without her senses. She was living a future scene of her Mind Movie. Enough circuits in her brain had turned on to make her internal experience as real as any external experience she had ever had. She was not visualizing this scene—she was *in* it, living it.

"I realized I was in another reality, a different time and space—I was in my future," she explained. "And I was actually performing aerial yoga. I was hanging upside down and the floor wasn't there. I kept reaching for it, but I was just swinging upside down from this beautiful red silk scarf. I felt freedom from my pain. I was swinging freely in space." Eventually she did lie down, with tears of joy flowing down her cheeks. When she came out of that meditation, all of her pain was gone.

"I knew I was healed," she said. "I was in awe of the power of my mind and I felt tremendous gratitude. I continue to manifest things from my Mind Movie—in fact, my Mind Movie can't even keep up with my life."

Terry Walks into a New Future

In September 2016, while practicing her walking meditation along Australia's beautiful Sunshine Coast, Terry had a profound experience. Toward the end of her meditation, when she stopped for the final part, she was feeling connected, uplifted, and expansive. As she followed my instructions, she opened herself up to the field with the intention of being worthy of her future life. With no warning, she felt an electric charge enter her body through the crown of her head, where it continued to flow down into her heart. As the energy coursed through the rest of her body, surging through her thighs and down into her feet, her legs began shaking uncontrollably.

"The only way I can describe it is that there was an intense shaking from the inside," she told me, "but it was a voltage of energy that my body had never experienced. I thought I was going to fall over. It was at that point I lost all conscious control over my lower body." She burst into uncontrollable tears, and with that release, her mind and body also began to let go. Time appeared to stand still. Terry understood that her body was surrendering a lifetime of past unresolved emotions. As the surge of electricity continued to move through her, she felt huge amounts of dense, dark matter falling away from her body.

"I believe this matter was trauma, not only from my lifetime, but also past lifetimes," she remembered. "It included the trauma of my father nearly dying from a suicide attempt when I was eight, which has cast a shadow over my life by preventing me from allowing myself to receive unconditional love." She felt all her limiting beliefs—many of which she had acquired through deep emotional conditioning and the unconscious beliefs of others—simply dissolve.

"Everything that was not in alignment with who I really am just fell away," Terry said. "I experienced true liberation, something my soul has been yearning for for a very long time. I knew in that moment that my soul had guided me to that very beach, at that very moment, with all these people, to do this important work."

She fell to her knees, an overwhelming amount of love flowing through her. Kneeling in the sand, humbled by this power, she saw that every choice she had made up to that point was necessary for her to arrive at this poignant moment. In that instant, she observed who she had been for the last year, consistently choosing to do the meditations every day, all the while falling in love with herself. She knew that her future self in that moment was calling her past self to have this experience of profound love.

When Terry came back to the three-dimensional reality of her senses, she felt an overwhelming sense of peace and oneness with everything around her. She reported a deep reconnection to her physical, mental, emotional, and spiritual self, and said she felt more like "herself" then she had in a very long time.

"This experience reminded me that I am, as we all are, an aspect of divine energy," she said, "and that I *am* worthy of receiving it."

Chapter 11

SPACE-TIME
AND TIME-SPACE

We live in a three-dimensional universe (*uni-* meaning "one") where everything that exists is made up of people, objects, places, and time. For the most part, it is a dimension of particles and matter. Through our senses we experience these things as form, structure, mass, and density. If I placed an ice cube, your cell phone, or an apple pie in front of you, for example, you could not experience any of these objects without your senses; it's your senses that give rise to your *experience* of physical reality.

While the ice cube, cell phone, and apple pie all have height, width, and depth, they only exist to you because you can see, hear, taste, smell, and feel them. If you lost your five senses or they were simultaneously eliminated, you would be incapable of experiencing these physical objects because you would have no *awareness* of them; they would literally not exist to you because in this three-dimensional reality you can't experience them without your senses—or can you?

According to astrophysics, in this realm of three dimensions—the known universe (let's call it space-time reality)—there's an infinite amount of space. Take a moment to ponder that concept. From the small perch where we sit staring out into the universe when we look up at the night sky, we see only a sliver of the universe. It appears to us as infinite, and yet infinite is even bigger than that. In other words, in the realm of space-time, *space is eternal*—it has no end and goes on forever. But what about time?

The way you and I typically experience time is by moving our bodies through space. For example, it might take you five minutes to set this book down, walk to the kitchen, pour a glass of water, and return. This occurs because a thought that originated in your mind created a vision of what you were going to do in the kitchen, you acted on that thought, and consequently you experienced time by moving from one point to another through space.

Before you walked to the kitchen and as you were sitting in your chair, when you became conscious of the kitchen in relation to where you were sitting, you experienced a separation of two points of consciousness: where you sat and the kitchen. To close the gap between those two points of consciousness, you moved your body through *space*, and that took *time*. It makes sense, then, that the greater the space or distance between two points, the greater the time it takes to get from one point to the other. Conversely, the faster the speed at which you travel between these two points, the shorter the amount of time it takes.

This measurement of the time it takes an object to move through space is the foundation for Newtonian physics (or classical mechanics). In the Newtonian world, if we know certain properties about an object, such as its force, acceleration, direction, speed, and the distance it will travel, we can make time-based predictions; therefore, Newtonian physics is based on knowns and predictable outcomes. We can say, then, that when there's a separation between two points of consciousness, as you move from one point of consciousness to another point of consciousness, you are *collapsing space*. As a result of collapsing space, *you experience time*. Take a look at Figure 11.1 to further understand the relationship between space and time in our three-dimensional world.

Here's another example: If I am writing this book and I want to finish this chapter, it's going to take time. I may not have to move my body very much through space, but I still experience time. Why? Because where I presently am in the process of writing this chapter represents one point in consciousness, and finishing the chapter represents another. The completion of this chapter represents a future moment separate from the present moment. The space between—the closing of the gap between these two points in consciousness—is the experience of time. If you look at Figure 11.1 again, it will help you gain a better understanding about time.

To achieve my desired goal of arriving at the end of the chapter, I repeatedly have to do "something." This requires me to use my senses to interact with and move through my environment with a coordinated set of behaviors—and again, this takes time. If I cease writing and do something else, such as watch a movie, it's going to take more time for me to reach my intended result; therefore, to achieve my goal of completing this chapter I must consistently align my actions to match my intentions.

THE RELATIONSHIP BETWEEN SPACE & TIME IN THE 3-D WORLD

In this realm space is eternal

Point of   **Time**   *Point of*
Consciousness   *Consciousness*

As We Move Through Space, We Experience Time

Figure 11.1

As we move through space from one point of consciousness to another point of consciousness, we experience time. When we collapse space in our 3-D world, time is created.

In this material world of three dimensions, because we use our senses to navigate space, we place most of our attention on physical things such as people, objects, and places. They all are made of matter and they are localized (meaning they occupy a position in space and time). These all represent points of consciousness from which we experience separation. For instance, when you observe your best friend sitting across the table from you or look at your car parked in the driveway, you notice the space between you and your friend or the car. As a result, you feel separate from them. You are here and your friend or the car is there. In addition, if you have dreams and goals, then where you are in the present moment and where your dreams exist as a reality in your future also creates the experience of separation. It's safe to say, then, that:

1. In order for us to navigate this three-dimensional reality we need our senses.

2. The more we use our senses to define reality, the more we experience separation.

3. Because most of this three-dimensional reality is sensory based, space and time create the experience of separation from every one, every thing, every place, and every body, in every time.

4. All things material occupy one position in space and time. That's called locality in physics.

In this chapter, we are going to explore and contrast two models of reality: space-time and time-space. Space-time is the physical Newtonian world based on knowns, predictable outcomes, matter, and the three-dimensional universe in which we live (which is made up of infinite *space*). Time-space is the nonphysical quantum world—an inverse reality based on unknowns, endless possibilities, energy, and the multidimensional multiverse where we also live (which consists of infinite *time*).

I'm going to challenge your understanding and perception of the nature of reality, because if you're going to experience the mystery of self as a dimensional being, you're going to need a road map to get there.

Stress and the Consequences of Living in a Perpetual State of Survival

Because we use our senses to observe and determine physical reality, we identify as a body living in space and time, yet separate from everything in our environment. Over time, this interaction creates the experience of our identity. Throughout our lives, via the different interactions we have at certain times and places with people, things, and objects, our identity evolves into a personality. The quality of these interactions with our external environment creates lasting memories and these memories shape who we become. We call this process *experience*, and it is life's experiences that shape who we are. And as you know, the majority of people's personality is based on past experiences.

As you learned in Chapter 8, to our brains, the material objects, things, people, and places that we perceive daily occur to us as patterns, and the recognition of these patterns is called memory. If the self is created from memories of past experiences, then memories are based on knowns; therefore, most of our three-dimensional world is based on knowns. This is where most us focus our attention. When you align everything material in your external world with the memories of your past experiences, you recognize them as familiar. You're matching a physical reality with a set of neurological networks in your brain. This is called pattern recognition and it's the process whereby most people perceive reality through a lens of the past.

We could say, then, that we're materialists not only living in this dimension, but also enslaved to and limited by it—because we've defined ourselves as a body, living in an environment, at certain times, and our *focus* is more on matter and less on energy. From a quantum perspective, we're keeping our attention on the physical particle (matter) instead of the immaterial wave of possibilities (energy). This is how we become immersed in this three-dimensional reality.

When stress is thrown into the equation, our body begins to draw from the invisible electromagnetic field of energy around us to produce chemistry. The greater the frequency, intensity, and duration of the stress, the more energy our body consumes. The very nature of these chemicals endorses our senses, causing us to pay attention to matter and knowns. As this vital field of energy around our body shrinks, we *feel* more like matter and less like energy. In fact, when our frequency slows down, our bodies become more dense as we run out of energy.

As we've discussed, this is fine for the short term when danger, crisis, or a predator is lurking around the corner—in fact, the fight-or-flight response has been a cornerstone of our evolution. In this state, stress chemicals heighten our senses, narrowing our focus to whatever matter in our environment represents potential danger. When this happens, our neocortex—the part of our brain involved in sensory perception, motor commands, spatial reasoning, and language—fires and becomes aroused. For survival purposes, this narrows our focus on our body and the external threat, causing us to become preoccupied by the time between the moment of the perceived threat and the moment we reach physical safety—both of which are points of consciousness. The more we experience stress, the more we feel separation.

As you read in Chapter 2, the long-term effect of living in survival mode is that we begin to thrive on—and become addicted to—these stress chemicals. The more addicted we are to them, the more we believe we are our bodies that are local—that is, that are living in a particular place in space and occupying a particular position in linear time. The result is a manic, frenetic state where we continuously shift our attention from one person, to one problem, to one thing, to one place in our environment. The evolutionary trait that once protected us now works against us, and we live on constant high alert, obsessing about time. Because we view our external environment as unsafe, all of our attention is on our environment.

As our outer world now appears more real than our inner world, we're addicted to someone or something in our external environment, and the longer we live in this state, the more our brain moves into high-beta brain waves. And as you know by now, prolonged high-beta brain waves cause us to feel pain, anxiety, worry, fear, anger, frustration, judgment, impatience, aggression, and competition. As a result, our brain waves become incoherent—and so do we.

When the emotions of survival have a hold on us, we need the conditions in our external world (our problems with different people, financial hardships, fear of terrorism, disdain for our job) to reaffirm our addiction to those emotions. These emotional addictions cause us to become preoccupied by whatever we think might be causing the upset in our environment—whether it be "some one" or "some thing"—and as a result the survival gene switches on. Now we're living in a self-fulfilling prophecy.

If you understand that where you place your attention is where you place your energy, you know that the stronger the emotional reaction associated with the cause, the more you will consistently place all your attention on a person, thing, or problem in your external world. When you do this, you are giving quite a bit of your power away to some one or some thing. Now all your attention and energy is anchored in this three-dimensional realm of the material and your emotional state is causing you to continuously reaffirm your present reality. You can become emotionally attached to the reality you really want to change. This mismanagement of your energy keeps you enslaved to the world of the knowns, trying to predict the future based on the past; what's more, when you're in the survival state, the unknown or the unpredictable is a scary place. So for you to truly make changes in your life, you would have to step into the unknown—and if you don't, nothing ever really changes.

The Newtonian 3-D Space-Time Reality: Living as a Some Body with Some Thing, Some Where, in Some Time

If feelings and emotions are a record of the past, and those feelings are driving your hardwired thoughts and behaviors, you'll keep repeating your past and therefore become predictable. Now you're firmly ensconced in the Newtonian world because Newtonian physics is based on predictable outcomes. The more you live in stress, the more you are simply matter trying to affect matter—matter trying to fight, force, manipulate, predict, control, and compete for outcomes. As a result, everything you want to change, manifest, or influence is going to take a lot of time, because in this space-time reality you have to move your physical body through space to create the outcomes you want.

The more you are living in survival and using your senses to define reality, the more you experience separation from a new future. Between where you are presently, as one point of consciousness, and where you want to be, as another point of consciousness, lies a very long distance, not to mention that your constant obsession on how it's going to happen is based on how you *think* and *predict* it should happen. But if you're predicting, your thinking is based on knowns, so there's no room for an unknown or new possibility in your life.

If you are trying to buy a house, for example, you need to save for a down payment, look for a house, get a loan, go through the application process, beat out other buyers, and then spend 30 years dragging your body back and forth to work (through space) trying to pay it off. These two points in consciousness—having the idea to buy the house and having the house with the mortgage paid off—are going to take time to intersect. In a similar way, if you want a new relationship, you might go online, set up a profile, scroll through countless other profiles, make a list of people to reach out to, contact each one, and eventually go on many dates in the hopes of finding someone intriguing. If you want a new job, you might take the time to create a résumé, search for open positions, and go on interviews.

What these processes have in common is they require *time*, which you experience as linear. You may get what you want but the more you live in survival, the more time it's going to take because you're *matter* trying to influence *matter*, and there is a distinct separation in space and time between where you are and where you want to be.

We can agree, then, that in this three-dimensional reality, within your experience of time, there's a definite past, present, and future. Since you live in linear time, you also experience a separation from time because the past, present, and future appear as separate moments in time; you are *here* and your future is *there*. Figure 11.2 graphically represents how the past, present, and future all exist as distinct, discontinuous moments.

LINEAR TIME WITH A PAST, PRESENT, & FUTURE

Past   Present   Future

Time as Separate Moments

Figure 11.2

In our 3-D reality, the past, present, and future exist as linear, distinct, separate moments in time.

As I said earlier, thanks to Newtonian physics we've unraveled the natural laws of force, acceleration, and matter, allowing us to predict outcomes. If we know the general direction, velocity, and rotation of an object traveling through space, for the most part we can predict where it's going to end up and how long it will take. This is why we can travel from New York to Los Angeles by plane, predict how long it's going to take to get there, and know where the plane will land.

Within the understanding of Newtonian physics and this three-dimensional world we live in, many of us spend most of our lives focusing our attention outward on trying to become a some one, have some body, own some things, go some where, and experience some thing in some time. When we don't have the things we want, we experience lack, and lack and separation cause us to live in a state of *duality* and *polarity*. It's natural for us to want what we don't have; in fact, this is how we create things. When we experience separation from our future desires, we think and dream of what we want and then set about performing a series of actions in linear time to get them.

If we're always under financial stress, for example, we want money; if we have a disease, we want health; if we feel lonely, we want a relationship or companionship. Because of this experience of duality and separation, we are driven to create, and this is how we naturally evolve and grow toward our dreams. But if we are *matter* focused on *matter* trying to influence *matter*, to get money, health, love, and so on, as we've established, it's going to take quite a bit of time and energy.

When we finally attain what we were seeking, the *emotion* we feel from the fruition of our creation (or the meeting of those two points of consciousness) satiates the sense of lack we formerly experienced. When the new job comes, we feel secure; when the new relationship manifests, we feel love and joy; as we heal, we feel more whole. If we are living in this state, we are waiting for "some thing" or "some one" outside of us to change how we feel internally. Once we feel relief from the experience of lack, because we are embracing the emotion correlated with the manifestation of the external event, we pay close attention to whomever or whatever caused the relief. This cause and effect forms a new memory, and to some degree, we evolve.

When something in our world doesn't happen, or seems to be taking a long time to happen, we experience *more lack* because we feel even *more separate* from what we're trying to create. Now our own emotional state of lack, frustration, impatience, and separation is keeping our dreams at a distance, further increasing the time it will take for our desired outcome to occur.

From Some Body to No Body, from Some One to No One, from Some Thing to No Thing, from Some Where to No Where, and from Some Time to No Time

If Newtonian laws are an *outward* expression of the physical material laws of space-time—a dimension where there's more space than time—we could say in a sense that quantum laws are the inverse. The quantum is an *inward* expression of the laws of nature: an invisible field of information and energy that unifies everything material. This immaterial field organizes, connects, and governs *all* the laws of nature. It is a dimension where there's more time than space; in other words, it's a dimension where *time is eternal.*

As you learned in Chapters 2 and 3, when we take our attention off people and things at certain places in our external world—no longer placing our attention on our body and ceasing to think about time and schedules—we become no body, no one, no thing, no where, and in no time. We do this through a process of disconnecting from our body, our identity, our gender, our disease, our name, our problems, our personal relationships, our pain, our past, and so on. This is what it means to get beyond the self: to go from the consciousness of some body to no body, from the consciousness of some one to no one, from the consciousness of some thing to no thing, from the consciousness of some where to no where, and from the consciousness of being in some time to being in no time (see Figure 11.3).

MOVING FROM THE WORLD OF THE SENSES TO WORLDS BEYOND THE SENSES

Stepping Into the Quantum

Material 3-D Reality of Newtonian World	*The Door to the Quantum as Pure Consciousness*
Consciousness of:	*Consciousness of:*
Some Body	*No Body*
Some One	*No One*
Some Thing	*No Thing*
Some Where	*No Where*
Some Time	*No Time*

Figure 11.3

When we take our attention off our body, our environment, and time, we get beyond the "self"—*living as a physical body, being someone as an identity, owning some things, living in some place at some time*—and we become no body, no one, no thing, no where, and in no time. Now we are moving our consciousness and awareness away from the material world of Newtonian physics and toward the immaterial world of the unified field.

And take a glance at Figure 11.4.

GETTING BEYOND THE SELF
When we get beyond ourselves, we move from:

A narrow focus	**to**	*An open focus*
Attention is on objects, things, people, & places (Particle)	**to**	*Attention is on space, energy, frequency, & information (Wave)*
Material (Matter)	**to**	*Immaterial (Antimatter)*
3-D Newtonian world	**to**	*5-D Quantum world*
Predictable	**to**	*Unpredictable*
Space-Time (a realm of eternal space)	**to**	*Time-Space (a realm of eternal time)*
State of separation, duality, polarity, & locality	**to**	*State of unity, oneness, wholeness, & nonlocality*
The known	**to**	*The unknown*
Limited Possibilities	**to**	*Unlimited Possibilities*
The universe	**to**	*The multiverse*
Domain of the senses	**to**	*Domain beyond the senses*

Figure 11.4

The distinction between the two worlds of matter and energy.

As we move from a narrow focus to an open focus and begin to surrender all aspects of self, we move away from the external world of people, things, places, schedules, to-do lists, and so on and turn our attention to the inner world of energy, vibration, frequency, and consciousness. Our research shows that when we take our attention off objects and matter, and instead open our focus to energy and information, different parts of the brain work together in harmony. The result of this unification of the brain is that we feel more whole.

When we do this properly, our heart begins to open, beat more rhythmically, and thus become more coherent. As the heart moves into coherence, so too does our brain, and because our identity is out of the way—meaning we've gotten beyond our body, a particular place in our known environment, and time—the act of eliminating those things causes us to move to alpha and theta brain-wave patterns and we connect with the autonomic nervous system. As the ANS becomes activated, its job is to restore order and balance, causing coherence and wholeness in our heart, brain, body, and energy field. This coherence is then reflected in all aspects of our biology.

It is in this state where we begin to connect to the quantum (or unified) field.

From the Illusion of Separation to the Reality of Oneness

If Newtonian physics explains the physical laws of nature and the universe on a grand scale—the gravitational force of the sun upon planets, the speed with which the apple falls from the tree, and so on—the quantum world deals with the fundamental nature of things at their smallest scale, such as atomic and subatomic particles. Newtonian laws are physical constants of nature, so the Newtonian world is an objective world of measurability and predictable outcomes.

Quantum laws, however, deal with the unpredictable and the unseen— the world of energy, waves, frequency, information, consciousness, and all spectrums of light. Governing this world is an unseen constant—a single field of information called the unified field. We can think of the Newtonian world as dealing with the objective—where mind and matter are separate—and of the quantum world as dealing with the subjective, where mind and matter are unified by energy, or better yet, where mind and matter are so connected that it's impossible to separate the two. In the quantum or unified field, there's no separation between two points of consciousness. It is the domain of oneness, or unity consciousness.

Whereas in our three-dimensional reality *space* is infinite, in the quantum world *time* is infinite. If time is infinite and eternal, it's no longer linear—meaning there is no separation of past or future. With no past or future, everything is happening right *now*, in this eternal present moment. Because *time* is infinite in this time-space reality, as we move through time we experience space (or spaces).

In the material world of things, when we move through space we experience time—yet in the immaterial quantum world of energy and frequency, the opposite is true:

- In the world of space-time, as we increase or decrease the *speed* with which we go from point A to point B, the time it takes to get there changes.

- In the world of time-space, as we become aware of an increase or decrease in the speed of the *frequency* or *vibration* of energy, we can go from one space to another space or from one dimension to another dimension.

When we collapse space, we experience time in the material reality. When we collapse time, we experience spaces or dimensions in the immaterial reality. Each of those individual frequencies is carrying information, or a level of consciousness, that we experience as different realities, as we become aware of them. In Figure 11.5, you can see that as you move through time you experience different dimensions in the eternal present moment.

THE RELATIONSHIP BETWEEN TIME & SPACE IN THE 5D WORLD

In this realm time is eternal

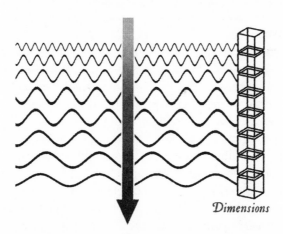

Dimensions

As we move through time (the eternal now, where all possibilities exist) we experience different spaces or dimensions

Figure 11.5

In the world of the quantum, where time is eternal, everything is happening in the eternal present moment. As you move through time, you experience other space(s), other dimensions, other planes, other realities, and infinite possibilities. Like standing between two mirrors and looking both ways at yourself into infinite dimensions, the boxes represent an infinite number of possible yous, all living in the present moment.

In space-time, you experience the environment with your body, your senses, and time. Time appears linear because you are separate from objects, things, people, and places—as well as the past and the future. In time-space, however, you experience this realm with your awareness— as a consciousness, *not* as a body with senses. This realm exists beyond your senses. You access this domain when you are totally in the present moment so there is no past or future, just one long now. Since your awareness is beyond the realm of matter, because you have taken all your attention off matter, you can become aware of different frequencies all carrying information, and these frequencies allow you to have access to different unknown dimensions.

So if you are in a realm above the senses and unfolding as consciousness into the energy of the unified field, you can experience many possible dimensional realities. (I know that this is a big bite to take in all at once, so hang in there. If you are confused, it means you're about to learn something new.)

When I say that as you move through time you experience space or spaces, I mean all *possible* dimensions and *possible* realities. We could say, then, that in this time-space reality, all possible spaces or dimensions exist in infinite time. This is the unified field: the realm of possibility, unknowns, and new potential realities, all of which exist in endless time—which is every time.

Let's think of it another way. Everybody I know is always saying that they want or need more time to get more things accomplished. If you had more time, you could create more experiences, do more things, and therefore get more things done. This would mean more possibilities could happen and you could live more of life.

So now imagine that there was an infinite amount of time (because the past and the future no longer exist, so time is standing still) and you had all the time you needed. Wouldn't you agree that you could have endless possible experiences and therefore could live many lives? We could say, then, that an infinite number of experiences would be available to you *equal* to your imagination. To say it yet another way:

- If time is eternal, then more spaces can exist in that infinite time;

- If we keep elongating or making more time, it makes sense that we can fit more spaces in time;

- If there is infinite time, then there are infinite spaces we can fit in time—which are endless possibilities, potential realities, dimensions, and experiences.

In the quantum field, there is no separation of past or future because everything that *is* exists in the eternal now, or the eternal present moment. If everything that *is* exists unified or connected in the quantum field, then its infinite frequencies contain information about every body, every one, every thing, every where, and every time. As your consciousness begins to merge with the consciousness and energy of the unified field, you will go from the consciousness of some body to the consciousness of no body to the consciousness of every body; from the consciousness of some one to the consciousness of no one to the consciousness of every one; from the consciousness of some thing to the consciousness of no thing to the consciousness of every thing; from the consciousness of some where to the consciousness of no where, to the consciousness of every where; and from the consciousness of being in some time to the consciousness of being in no time to the consciousness of being in every time. (Take a look at Figure 11.6.)

LOSING YOURSELF IN NOTHING
TO BECOME EVERYTHING

Material 3-D Reality of Newtonian World	*The Door to the Quantum as Pure Consciousness*	*Immaterial 5-D Reality of the Unified Field*
Consciousness of:	*Consciousness of:*	*Consciousness of:*
Some Body	*No Body*	*Every Body*
Some One	*No One*	*Every One*
Some Thing	*No Thing*	*Every Thing*
Some Where	*No Where*	*Every Where*
Some Time	*No Time*	*Every Time*

Figure 11.6

As your consciousness merges with the consciousness of the unified field, and you unfold deeper into it, you will become the consciousness of every body, every one, every thing, every where, in every time. In this realm, there is no separation between two points of consciousness, which means there is only Oneness.

The Atom: Fact and Fiction

To help you understand how the quantum field is constructed, you first need to revisit the possibilities that exist in the atom. When we reduce matter to its smallest unit of measurement, we get the atom, and the atom vibrates at a very high frequency. If we could peel back the atom like an orange, we'd find a nucleus and subatomic particles such as protons, neutrons, and electrons, but for the most part we'd find that it's 99.999999999999 percent empty space, or energy, as you read earlier.

Take a look at Figure 11.7. On the left we see the classical model of the atom that we were taught in grade school, but this is in fact an outdated model. In actuality, electrons don't move in fixed rotations around the nucleus like planets orbiting the sun. Instead, as you see on the right, the space around the nucleus is more like an invisible field, or a cloud of information—and as we know, all information is made up of light, frequency, and energy. To get an understanding of just how small these subatomic particles are, if the nucleus of an atom were increased to the size of a Volkswagen Beetle, the size of the electron would be equal to the size of a pea. Meanwhile, the space where the electron could exist would be 85,000 square miles—that's twice the size of Cuba. That's a lot of empty space for the electron to exist in.

THE CLASSICAL MODEL OF AN ATOM
VS.
THE QUANTUM MODEL OF AN ATOM

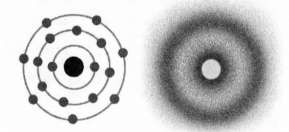

Figure 11.7

The classical model of the atom, with electrons rotating around the central nucleus in an orbit, is outdated. Electrons exist as waves of probability in an invisible cloud of energy surrounding the nucleus. Therefore, the atom is mostly immaterial energy and very little matter.

According to Heisenberg's uncertainty principle, we never know where the electron is going to appear in the electron cloud, yet from *nothing* comes *something*. This is why quantum physics is so exciting and unpredictable: The electron is not always physical matter; rather, it exists as the energy or as the probability of a wave. It is only through the *act of observation* by an *observer* that it appears. Once an observer (mind) comes along and looks for it, the act of observation (directed energy) causes all that potential energy to collapse into an electron (matter); thus it manifests from a realm of infinite possibilities (an unknown) to a known. It becomes local in space and time. When the observer is no longer observing it, the electron turns back into possibility—that's the wave function. In other words, it turns back into energy, returning to the unknown and to its own agenda. When it turns back to energy and possibility, it becomes nonlocal. In the realm of the quantum, mind and matter are indivisible. Therefore, if Newtonian physics is the world of the predictable, the quantum is the world of the unpredictable.

When we close our eyes in meditation and open our focus to infinite space, this is exactly what we are doing. We are putting more of our attention on energy, space, information, and possibility rather than on matter. We are becoming less aware of the material realm and more aware of the immaterial realm. We are investing our energy into the unpredictable and unknown and disinvesting our attention and energy from the predictable and the known. Each time we do this we develop a deeper understanding of what the unified field is.

Before we go any further, let's briefly review what we just learned. Take a moment to review Figure 11.8. The three-dimensional Newtonian world is made up of objects, people, places, matter, particles, and time (basically most of the nouns or everything we know in our external world), and in this world there's more space than time. As a body, we use our senses to define this infinite space we live in—a universe of form, structure, dimension, and density. This is the realm of the known and predictable.

SPACE-TIME THE REALM OF INFINITE SPACE NEWTONIAN WORLD	THE NEXUS OF THE QUANTUM THE BRIDGE
• *3 Dimensional Universe* • *Height, width, depth* • *Density, form, structure* • *Matter, particles: bodies, people, things, places, time* • *Time is linear– past–present–future* • *Senses create separation, duality, polarity, locality* • *Locality–bodies, people, things occupying space & time* • *The known–predictable* • *The Consciousness of:* SOME BODY SOME ONE SOME THING SOME WHERE SOME TIME	*The Consciousness of:* NO BODY NO ONE NO THING NO WHERE NO TIME SPEED OF LIGHT

Figure 11.8

A summary of space-time in our 3-D Newtonian world and the bridge that allows us to enter as consciousness into the realm of time-space in our 5-D quantum world.

TIME-SPACE THE REALM OF ETERNAL TIME QUANTUM WORLD	INFINITE UNKNOWN POSSIBILITIES
• *5 Dimensional Multiverse* • *Nonlocality, formless, structureless* • *Antimatter, waves: energy & consciousness, frequency & information, vibration & thought* • *Time is infinte, eternal & nonlinear* • *Everything is happening in the eternal now* • *No senses create wholeness, oneness, unity, connectedness, possibilities* • *The unknown-unpredictable* • *The Consciousness of:* EVERY BODY EVERY ONE, EVERY THING EVERY WHERE EVERY TIME	*The Consciousness of:* ANY BODY ANY ONE ANY THING ANY WHERE ANY TIME

Figure 11.9

A summary of the time-space 5-D reality of the quantum world.

Because we experience the material universe with our senses, our senses provide us with information that occurs as patterns in our brain, which we recognize as structures, and it is through this process that things in our external environment become knowns. It is also through this process that we become a some body, a some one, with some things, in some place, and in some time. Finally, because we experience the universe with our senses, we experience separation; therefore, this is a realm of duality and polarity.

Now review Figure 11.9. If the Newtonian world is a material world defined by the senses, in the quantum world the opposite is true. This is an *immaterial* world defined by *non-sense*; in other words, there's nothing sensory-based here, and there is no matter. Whereas the Newtonian world is based on predictable knowns such as matter, particles, people, places, things, objects, and time, this is an unpredictable dimension made up of light, frequency, information, vibration, energy, and consciousness.

If our three-dimensional world is a dimension of matter where there's more space than time, the quantum world is a dimension of *antimatter*— a place where there's more time than space. Because there is more time than space, all possibilities exist in the eternal present moment. Whereas the three-dimensional world is our universe, meaning one reality, the quantum world is a multiverse, meaning many realities. If the space-time reality is based on separation, then the immaterial quantum world, or unified field, is based on oneness, connectedness, wholeness, and unity (nonlocality).

In order for us to go from our known space-time (three-dimensional) universe, a universe made up of matter where we experience duality and polarity, to the unknown time-space (five-dimensional) multiverse—a place where there is no matter, but instead light, information, frequency, vibration, energy, and consciousness—we have to cross a bridge. That bridge is the speed of light. When we become pure consciousness and become no body, no one, no thing, no where in no time we are crossing that threshold from matter to energy.

When Einstein introduced the equation $E=mc^2$ in his theory of special relativity, for the first time in the history of science he demonstrated from a mathematical standpoint that energy and matter are related. What converts matter to energy is the speed of light—which means anything material traveling faster than the speed of light leaves our three-dimensional reality and turns into immaterial energy. In other words, in the three-dimensional world the speed of light is the threshold for matter—or anything physical—to retain its form. No "thing" can travel faster than the speed of light, not even information. Anything traveling from one point to another that is traveling slower than the speed of light is going to take time. Therefore, the fourth dimension is time. Time is the nexus that connects the three-dimensional world to the fifth-dimensional world and beyond. Once something is traveling faster than the speed of light, there is no time or no separation between two points of consciousness because every "thing" material becomes energy. This is how you go from three dimensions to five dimensions, from a universe to the multiverse, from this dimension to all dimensions.

Let me give you an example to help simplify this complex idea. French physicist Alain Aspect performed a famous quantum physics experiment in the early 1980s called the Bell test experiments.[1] In the study, scientists entangled two photons, causing them to bond together. They then shot the two photons in opposite directions, creating distance and space between them. When they influenced one photon to disappear, the other photon vanished at exactly the same time. This experiment was a cornerstone study in the breakthrough of quantum physics because it proved that Einstein's theory of relativity wasn't completely correct.

What it showed was that there is a unifying field of information existing beyond three-dimensional space and time that connects all matter. If the two particles of light were not connected by some invisible field of energy, it would have taken time for information to travel from one local point in space to the other local point in space. According to Einstein's theory, if one particle disappeared, the other particle should disappear a moment later—unless they were occupying the same space at the same time. Even if the second photon was affected a millisecond later, because they were separated by space, time would have played a factor in relaying the information. This would have reaffirmed that the ceiling of this physical reality is the speed of light and everything material that exists here is separate.

Because the two particles vanished at exactly the same time, it proved that all matter—bodies, people, things, objects, places—and even time are connected by frequency and information in a realm beyond three-dimensional reality and time. Every "thing" beyond the material is unified in a state of oneness. The information was communicated between those two photons nonlocally. Since there is no separation between two points of consciousness in the five-dimensional reality, there is no linear time. There is only all time(s).

Mystical quantum physicist David Bohm called the realm of the quantum the implicate order where everything is connected. He called the explicit order the material realm of separation.[2] If you look at Figures 11.8 and 11.9 again, it will help you get your mind around both worlds.

When you take your attention off being some body, some one, some thing, some where, in some time, and you become no body, no one, no thing, no where in no time, you are becoming pure consciousness. Your consciousness merges with the unified field—which is made only of consciousness and energy—where you connect to the self-organizing consciousness of every body, every one, every thing, every where in every time. Thus, as you surrender as an awareness (without your senses) into this field of oneness where there is no separation, and you keep going deeper into the void or blackness, because nothing physical exists there, you as a consciousness become less separate from the consciousness of the unified field. If you can keep becoming more conscious and aware of it and keep paying attention to it, you are investing your energy in it and your attention directly at it. Thus, as you keep moving toward it, you will feel less separation and more wholeness.

Finally, since only the eternal present moment exists in the unified field, because there is no linear time (only all time), the consciousness and energy of the unified field that is observing all matter into form is always in the present eternal moment. Therefore, in order for you to connect and unify with it, you will have to be completely in the present moment as well. If you review Figure 11.10, it shows how you can collapse your own separation and individual consciousness to experience the oneness and wholeness of the unified field.

One last point about the speed of light. In this realm of the material world, visible light is a frequency based on polarity (electrons, positrons, photons, and so on). If you look ahead a bit at Figure 11.11, according to scale, approximately one-third of the way up from the slowest frequency is where the division of light takes place. Above this wave or frequency is where matter goes from form to energy and singularity, and below this frequency are division and polarity. When the division of light takes place, photons, electrons, and positrons come into being because the visible light field holds the information template of matter as organized frequency in patterns of light. This division of light is where the Big Bang occurred—where singularity became duality and polarity, and where the universe eventually appeared as organized information and matter. That's why this void is eternal blackness: There is no visible light.[3]

THE JOURNEY TO ONENESS

As we collapse 2 points of consciousness, we experience less separation & more oneness & wholeness. When our consciousness merges with the consciousness of the unified field (as we move closer to it), we experience no time & no space.

MATERIAL REALITY - *Attention Outward*

Some Body
Some One
Some Thing
Some Where
Some Time

*Omnipresent Observer,
Source Energy,
Unified Field*

BECOMING CONSCIOUSNESS - *Attention in the Moment*

No Body
No One
No Thing
No Where
No Time

We Are Present With It

ONENESS CONSCIOUSNESS - *No Space & No Time to All Space(s) & All Time(s)*

Every Body
Every One
Every Thing
Every Where
Every Time

As we move closer to It, we become It!

Figure 11.10

The more we live with our attention on the outer world, living as a some body, being some one, owning some thing, living some where, in some time in our 3-D reality, the more we experience separation and lack. As we move our attention away from the outer world and toward the inner world, into the present moment, our consciousness aligns with its consciousness; now we are present with it. As we surrender deeper into the unified field as a consciousness, we experience less separation or lack and more oneness and wholeness. If there is no separation between two points of consciousness, then there is no space and no time—but all time(s) and all space(s). Therefore, the more whole we feel and the less lack we experience, the more we feel like our future has already happened. Now we are no longer creating from duality but from oneness.

Because matter vibrates at such a slow frequency, to enter the time-space dimension or the unified field, you can't enter as a body or matter, so you must become no body. You can't take your identity so you're going to have to become no one. You can't take things so you must become no thing. You can't be some where so you're going to have to get to no where. Finally, if you're living by a familiar past or predictable future where time appears linear, to get to the place of time-space you're going to have to experience no time. How do you do this? You keep placing your attention on the unified field—not with your senses but with your awareness. As you change your consciousness, you raise your energy. The more you become aware of this invisible field, the more you're moving further away from the separation of matter and closer to oneness.

Now you're in the quantum, or the unified field. This is the realm of information that connects every body, every one, every thing, every where, and every time.

The Unified Field: Becoming Every Body, Every One, Every Thing, Every Where, in Every Time

Matter is very dense, and because of its density it vibrates at the slowest frequency in the universe. In Figure 11.11, you see that as you raise matter's frequency by speeding it up faster and faster, matter as we know it dematerializes into energy. At some point just beyond the visible light spectrum—above the realm of duality and polarity—any information about matter converts to more unified energy. As you can see, the higher the frequency, the more orderly and coherent that energy becomes. At this level of frequency and energy, duality and polarity unify to become one. We call this love, or wholeness, because there is no longer any division or separation. It is where positive and negative join; where male and female unite; where the past and future merge; where good and bad no longer exist; where right and wrong no longer apply; where opposites become one.

As you continue up this scale away from matter and separation, you continue to experience greater and greater degrees of wholeness, order, and love. The orderliness of this more coherent energy is carrying information and that information is more and more love. If you continued speeding matter up even faster, eventually it would be vibrating so fast as a frequency that it would exist as a straight line. Infinite frequencies exist in that line, which means infinite possibilities exist there as well. This is the zero-point field, or the point of singularity of the quantum—an omnipresent, ubiquitous field of information that exists as energy and frequency that is observing all of reality into order from a single point.

FROM THOUGHT TO ENERGY
TO MATTER

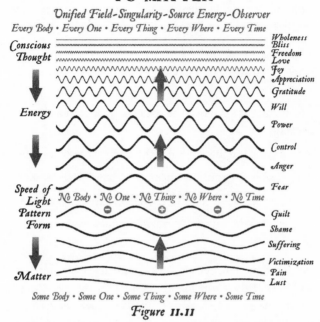

Figure II.11

Everything starts from a conscious thought. As conscious thought slows down in frequency, it slows down in energy until ultimately it takes on form and becomes matter.

At the frequency of the speed of light, the pattern of all matter is reflected as a template to become structure. It is at the speed of light that energy divides into polarity or duality and electrons and positrons, etc., are created. Above the speed of light, there are greater degrees of order that are reflected as greater degrees of wholeness.

As we journey in consciousness from matter and get beyond ourselves, turning our attention inward toward the unified field, once we cross the plane of visible light, we become no body, no one, no thing, no where, in no time. It is in this realm that we experience as an awareness of other dimensions, other realities, and other possibilities. Since frequency carries information and there are infinite frequencies in the quantum, we can experience other planes that exist there.

If you look at the arrows moving from matter toward the unified field—the top straight line—representing all possibilities, you will see that you must journey through the lower frequencies between matter and light, which are different levels of thoughts and emotions. Look at the different levels of consciousness that you have to pass through to arrive at oneness and you will understand why most never make the journey.

We could call this the mind of God, unity consciousness, source energy, or whatever nomenclature you want to use to define the self-organizing principle of the universe. This is the place where all potentials or possibility exists as a thought—the ultimate source of a loving intelligence and an intelligent love that is observing all of this physical reality into form. Therefore:

- The greater the frequency we experience, the greater the energy;

- The greater the energy, the greater the information we have access to;

- The greater the information, the greater the consciousness;

- The greater the consciousness, the greater the awareness;

- The greater the awareness, the greater the mind;

- The greater the mind, the greater ability we have to affect matter.

In the hierarchy of universal laws, quantum laws trump Newtonian (or classical) laws. This is why Einstein said, "The field is the sole governing agency of the particle," for the quantum field governs, organizes, and unifies all the laws of nature and is always directing energy into order by patterning light into form. On our own planet, we need only look at nature to see how Fibonacci's sequence, otherwise known as the golden ratio (a recurring mathematical formula found throughout nature that brings about order and coherence) brings order to matter. It's the zero-point field made of possibilities or thought (because thoughts are possibilities) that is slowing its frequency down, creating order and form.

The unified field is a self-organizing intelligence that is always observing the material world into order and form. The more you can surrender to it, move closer to it, and become one with it, the less separation and lack you feel and thus the more wholeness and oneness you experience. When you as an awareness unfold into this infinite realm of possibilities, you begin to feel connected to the consciousness of every one, every body, every where, every thing, in every time—including your future dreams. Since consciousness is awareness and awareness is paying attention, the first step to experiencing the unified field is to become aware of it, because if you're not aware of it, it doesn't exist. Thus, the more you pay attention to this field, the more you will become aware of it.

There is a caveat, however. As we've seen, the only way you can enter the realm of pure consciousness is to become pure consciousness; in other words, the only way to enter this kingdom of thought is as a thought. This means you have to get *beyond* your senses by taking your awareness off matter and particles, and instead place it on energy or the wave. If you can unfold as an awareness into this unseen, immaterial realm of infinite blackness and become aware that you are an awareness in the presence of a greater awareness, your consciousness will merge with a greater consciousness.

If you can do this, if you can get out of the way and linger as a consciousness or awareness in this field, if you can keep surrendering to this intelligent love—the same innate intelligence that's creating the universe and giving you life—it's going to consume you. This loving intelligence is both personal and universal, within you and all around you, and when it consumes you it's going to create and restore order and balance in your biology because its very nature is to organize matter in a more coherent way. Now you are moving through the eye of the needle, and on the other side of the eye there is no longer the separation of two points of consciousness. There is one consciousness—or oneness. This is where all possibilities exist.

Because you are entering the domain of consciousness, thought, information, energy, and frequency, the bridge that gets you from space-time to time-space is going from being some body, some one, some thing, in some place, in some time, to being no body, no one, no thing, no where, in no time. This is the nexus—the threshold to the unified or quantum field (go back and review Figures 11.8 and 11.9).

In this realm of infinite unknown possibilities, unlimited new potentials and experiences await you—not the same old familiar ones that you've experienced time and time again. After all, isn't that what the unknown is? An unknown is just a possibility that exists to you as a new thought. When you are in this realm of pure thought as a thought, the only thing limiting you is your imagination. But when in this realm of thought, if you find yourself thinking again about some one, some thing, some body, some where, in some *known* time, your awareness (and thus your energy) is back in the known reality of three-dimensional space and time—back to the realm of separation.

Since every thought you think has a frequency, the moment you start thinking about the pain in your body, or the advancement of your disease, or the problems at work, or the issues you have with your mother, or the things you must do within a certain amount of time, you are back in this space and time. Your awareness is back in the realm of the material world, and your thoughts are producing the same frequency equal to matter and particles (review Figure 11.10). Your energy is back to vibrating at the same level of the known physical world of three-dimensional reality, so you exert less of an effect on your personal reality. You are back to vibrating as matter, and we know how that goes.

As your frequency moves further and further into density, you are moving further and further away from the unified field; as a result, you feel separate from it. In this scenario, if your dreams exist as thoughts in the unified field, it's going to take a lot of time for your dreams to come true.

If you are thinking about some body, some one, some thing, at some place, in some time, you are not getting beyond your identity, which has been shaped by the totality of your past experiences. You are literally still in the same memories, habitual thoughts, and conditioned emotions that you've associated with all the familiar people and things at certain times and places in your known reality—which means your attention and energy are bound to your past-present personal reality. You're thinking equal to your identity, so your life is going to stay the same. You're the same personality trying to create a new personal reality.

When I say you have to get beyond yourself, it means to forget about your *self*—take your attention off your personality and your past-personal reality. It makes sense, then, that to heal your body, you're going to have to get beyond your body. To create something new in your life, you're going to have to forget about your same old life. To change some problem in your external environment, you're going to have to get beyond your memory and the corresponding emotions related to that problem. And if you want to create a new, unexpected event in your future timeline, you'll have to stop unconsciously anticipating the same predictable future based on your familiar memories of the past. You are going to have to move to a greater level of consciousness than the consciousness that created any of those realities.

In the unified field there is no where to go because you are every where; there is no thing you can want because you are so whole and complete that you feel like you have every thing; you can't judge any one because you are every one; and it's no longer necessary to become any body because you are every body. And why would you be worried that there is never enough time if you exist in a domain where there's infinite time?

The more whole you feel the less lack you experience, and therefore the less you want. How can you want, or live in lack, when you feel whole? If there is less lack, there is less of the need to create from duality, polarity, and separation. How can you want when you're whole? When you create from wholeness, you feel like you already have it. There is no longer wanting, trying, wishing, forcing, predicting, fighting, or hoping—after all, hope is a beggar. When you create from a state of wholeness, there are only knowing and observing. This is the key to manifesting reality: being connected, not separate.

If time in your three-dimensional world is created by the illusion of space between two objects or two points of consciousness, then the more *one* you are with the unified field, the less separation there is between you and everything material. When your consciousness merges or becomes more connected to the unified field—to the realm of wholeness and unity—there is no longer separation between two points of consciousness. This wholeness is then reflected in your biology, chemistry, circuitry, hormones, genes, heart, and brain, thus restoring balance to your entire system. A greater frequency or energy is now moving through your autonomic nervous system—a system that continuously gives you life and whose agenda it is to create balance and order. This energy is carrying a message of wholeness, and as a result you become more *holy*. The greater the frequency you experience, the shorter amount of time it takes to unfold in this three-dimensional space-time reality.

As we learned earlier in this chapter, when you diminish the space between two points of consciousness, you collapse time. When this illusion of separation no longer exists, you perceive less space between you (an identity, living in a body, in a physical environment, in linear time) and people, objects, things, places, matter, and even your dreams. Therefore, the closer you move to the unified field, the more connected you feel you are to every one and every thing.

You as a consciousness are in the realm of oneness, and because there is no separation, time is eternal. And remember: When there is infinite time, there are infinite spaces, possible dimensions, and realities to be experienced. Wherever you "think" you are, or whoever you "think" you are, you are. In fact, there is nothing to try to create because it already exists as a thought in the realm of all thoughts. All you have to do is to become aware of it and observe it into being by experiencing it.

BECOMING UNLIMITED POSSIBILITIES

Material 3-D Reality of Newtonian World	*The Door to the Quantum as Pure Consciousness*	*Immaterial 5-D Reality of the Unified Field*	*Realm of Unlimited Possibilities*
Consciousness of:	*Consciousness of:*	*Consciousness of:*	*Consciousness of:*
Some Body	No Body	Every Body	Any Body
Some One	No One	Every One	Any One
Some Thing	No Thing	Every Thing	Any Thing
Some Where	No Where	Every Where	Any Where
Some Time	No Time	Every Time	Any Time

Figure 11.12

Once we become the consciousness of every one, every body, every thing, every where, in every time . . . from a theoretical standpoint, we can create any *body*, become any *one*, have any *thing*, live any *where*, and be in any *time*.

Take a peek at Figure 11.12 to follow along. As you do this and move your attention from being some body, to being no body, to becoming every body, you can create any body. As you move from living as some one, to becoming no one, to being every one, you can become any one. As you can take your attention off some thing, move into the realm of no thing, you merge with every thing, thus you can have any thing. As you move your awareness from some where, to no where, you will be every where, and you can live any where. And finally, when you shift your consciousness from some time, to no time, to become every time, you can be in any time.

Now that's becoming supernatural.

In the work I do around the world, I have labored for many years teaching our students how to get beyond themselves. I now know the first step in this process is for them to master their body, get beyond the conditions in their external environment, and transcend time. When they accomplish that, they find themselves on the precipice of experiencing the unified field. Once they arrive at this nexus, however, they must be taught that there is even more to experience.

If learning means making new synaptic connections, the more you learn about something the more you can appreciate it, become aware of it, and experience it because now you can engage it with a new set of neural networks. It is in the act of learning that you further change or enrich your experience, after all—if you haven't learned anything new, your experience will probably stay the same since you're perceiving reality with the same neural circuitry as before. Knowledge is the harbinger that evolves your experience.

For example, I love red wine and I lead several wine tours a year in different parts of the world. Many people who come to these weeklong events initially tell me that they "know" nothing about wine. How I translate this statement is that they probably never learned anything about, or have had limited exposure to, the fermented grape. The truth of the matter is that because they have limited knowledge and experience from their past, they have very limited neural hardware installed to perceive any real taste or nuance. We could say, then, that they just don't know what to look for to truly enjoy the experience.

But what if they learn how winemakers produce wine and understand its history, the type of grapes they use, and why they are used? Then they learn about how the wine is stored in oak barrels, for how long, and why. This would familiarize them with the whole process and reasoning as to what makes a particular wine so enjoyable.

That's the process, but now think of that great wine in the bottle. If they are not aware of the plum flavor, the notes of black cherry and currants, its hints of vanilla and leather, the smell of its floral perfumes, its percentage of tannins, and whether it was aged in oak barrels or stainless steel drums, and for how long, then they don't know what to look for and they are not going to be able to fully experience it. Only in the moment when they know what to look for and what to become aware of does it exist. We could say, then, that their awareness changes their experience.

I know this to be true because in just one week those same people who initially said they didn't like red wine or knew nothing about it walk away with a whole new experience of interacting with it. After many full days of learning and discovering what to look for—repeatedly staying present and focusing all their awareness on specific flavors and aromas, day after day experiencing all types of wines and deciding what they like and don't like, continuously paying attention and therefore firing, wiring, and assembling new neural connections—those folks get very specific about what type of wine they like. In one week, they gain a whole new level of appreciation, awareness, and understanding. Again, the experience changed them. The same is true when it comes to the unified field. If you are not aware of it, then it doesn't exist for you, yet the more you know about it and the more aware you are of what to look for, the more you can pay attention to it with your awareness and experience it more deeply. And it should change you.

Starting at birth, you're trained to keep your attention on matter and not on energy. You are conditioned into believing you need your senses to experience reality; in other words, if you don't see, hear, feel, smell, touch, or taste something, it doesn't exist. Because of this, the majority of people place most of their attention on matter, objects, and the particle, while taking very little time to put their attention on energy, information, and the wave. For instance, you are not aware of your big toe on your left foot until you put your attention on it. It has always existed for you but you were unaware of it. The moment you put your awareness on it, however, it comes into being. The same is true for the unified field. The more you become aware of it, the more it will exist in your reality. By focusing solely on matter, people exclude possibility from their life. That's what the wave is—an energy of possibility. The more you pay attention to it, the more possibilities should show up in your life.

Because wherever you place your attention is where you place your energy, the moment you become aware of the unified field, your attention upon it causes it to expand. For example, when you place your attention and awareness on your pain, it expands, because you experience more of it. If you keep attending to your pain and experiencing more and more of it, it becomes a part of your life. The same thing also happens with the unified field; when you place your attention on it and become more aware of it, it expands. And just as I said about pain, when you experience more of it, it exists as a part of your life.

Simply by placing your attention on the unified field—as you become aware of it, notice it, experience it, feel it, interact with it, and stay present with it moment after moment—it shows up and unfolds in your reality on a daily basis. How does it show up and unfold? As unknowns: serendipities, synchronicities, opportunities, coincidences, luck, being in the right place at the right time, and moments filled with awe.

In my best description from experience, this unified field is a divine, loving intelligence and an intelligent love that is within and around you, so each time you focus your attention on it, you are becoming aware of the presence of the divine within and all around you. As you place your attention on it, the divine should appear more in your life. Since consciousness is awareness and awareness is paying attention, when you are aware of it and pay attention to it, you begin to merge with it. Your experience of it will literally cause you to *become it*, and as you unfold deeper and deeper into this unified field, there's more and more for you to explore and experience.

If you look at Figure 11.11 again, as you move closer and closer to that straight line that represents Source energy or oneness, it makes sense that the only way you can move closer to it is by keeping your attention on it and becoming more conscious of it. If you do this correctly, as you journey away from duality or separation and toward unity and oneness, since feelings are the end product of experience, you should *feel* more and more levels of love, unity, and wholeness. Once you feel and experience more of this intelligent love, three things happen in your life.

The first thing that happens is that as you place your attention and awareness on the unified field, as you move closer to Source and deeper into it, you experience more of it. That journey carves a neurological path from your thinking brain straight to your autonomic nervous system. Now each time you venture deeper into it, as you slow your brain waves down, you're building a neurological highway with more lanes, and that neuro-pathway becomes thicker because you are using it more. Over time, this enables you to more easily merge with the field.

The second thing that happens is that because experience enriches the brain, each time you interact with this unified field and experience it, your brain changes. This is what experience does; it enriches and refines brain circuitry. Now you are installing the hardware in your brain to be more aware of this field the next time you merge with it. Likewise, since experience produces an emotion, as you *feel* the unified field you begin to embody it; thus you embody more of the divine.

According to the quantum model of reality, since all disease is a lowering and incoherency of frequency, the moment the body experiences this new coherent elevated frequency, the energy from that event raises the body's vibration into coherence and order. Numerous times in our advanced workshops around the world, when our students' bodies have been upgraded by a new frequency and new information, we've witnessed instantaneous changes in their health.

Since the autonomic nervous system's agenda is to create balance and health, the instant we get out of its way, stop analyzing, cease thinking, and fully surrender, this intelligence steps in and creates order. But this time it's carrying a newer, more self-organizing message with a greater frequency from the unified field. That very same coherent energy raises the frequency of matter. It's like changing the frequency of a static-filled radio station to one that is carrying a clear frequency and signal. The body is receiving a more coherent signal.

When this happens you will feel intense love, a profound joy for existence, a heightened sense of freedom, indescribable bliss, an awe for life, elevated levels of gratitude, and a humbled sense of true empowerment. In that moment, the energy from the unified field—in the form of emotion—is reconditioning your body to a new consciousness and a new mind. In a heartbeat, the elevated emotions signal new genes in new ways, changing your body and moving it out of your biological past.

The third thing that happens as you move closer toward the unified field is that you begin to hear or experience knowledge and information differently. That's because you've changed your brain's circuits and are no longer the same person. You will meet truth on a whole new level, and things that you thought you knew will seem like a brand-new encounter. Your inner experience has changed your perception of what is happening in your outer world. In other words, you've awakened.

Once you have an experience, a feeling, or a better understanding of the unified field—once it changes your brain's circuitry—it allows you to experience and perceive reality in new ways. In fact, you will see a spectrum of life that your brain did not have the circuitry to perceive before. The next time your brain fires those networks, you already have the hardware to experience even *more* of the reality. You are now perceiving more of a reality that has always existed; you merely lacked the circuits to perceive it previously.

If on a consistent basis you can make this journey all the way to Source (see Figure 11.11 again) and connect with it, the moment you truly interact with it, you will begin to behave more like it. Its nature becomes your nature, and now more intelligent love is being expressed through you. What are its innate qualities? You will become more patient, forgiving, present, conscious, aware, willful, giving, selfless, loving, and mindful, to name but a few of them. You realize that which you have been seeking is seeking you. You become it, and it becomes you.

The discipline, then, is to:

- Allow your consciousness to merge with a greater consciousness;

- Surrender deeper into intelligent love;

- Trust in the unknown;

- Continuously surrender some aspect of the limited self to join the greater self;

- Lose yourself in nothing to become everything;

- Relax into an infinite deep sea of coherent energy;

- Keep unfolding deeper and deeper into oneness;

- Continuously let go of control;

- Feel greater and greater degrees of wholeness, and finally;

- As a consciousness, moment by moment become aware, pay attention to, experience, be present with, and feel more and more of this unified field all around you—without returning your awareness back to three-dimensional reality.

If you do this properly, you won't be using any of your senses because you're beyond your senses. You'll simply be awareness.

Space-Time, Time-Space Meditation

Begin by resting your awareness on your heart, and once you are locked in on the space your heart occupies in space, become aware of your breathing. Allow it to flow in and out of your heart, all the while deepening and relaxing your breath. Keeping your attention on your heart, call up an elevated emotion and sustain this feeling for a period of time while paying attention to your breathing. Radiate that energy beyond your body in space.

Next, using any song that inspires you (like the one you used for the meditation in Chapter 5), do that meditation to pull the mind out of the body. Take all the energy stored in your body as survival emotions and liberate it into elevated emotions, using a level of intensity that is greater than the body as the mind.

For the next 10 to 15 minutes, listen to one or two songs (without lyrics) that will induce trance. Now become pure consciousness, becoming no one, no body, no thing, no where, in no time, unfolding as an awareness into the unified field.

Now it's time to become connected to the consciousness of every one, every body, every thing, every where, in every time, unifying with a greater consciousness in the unified field. All you have to do is become aware of this field, pay attention to it, stay present with it, and feel it moment by moment. You will begin to feel more wholeness and oneness, which will be reflected in your biology because your body is experiencing more coherent energy moving through it and you are building your energy field. Maintain this state for about 10 to 20 minutes, surrendering deeper and deeper into it. When you're done, bring your awareness back to a new body, to a new environment, and to a whole new time.

Chapter 12

THE PINEAL GLAND

As you now know, when we as a consciousness move beyond the world of the senses in this three-dimensional reality, we can tap into frequencies that carry specific information beyond the vibration of matter and the speed of light. When this happens, the brain processes extremely high amplitudes of energy. Time and time again, we've measured and observed this phenomenon in our advanced students' brain scans. You've also learned that when there is an increase in energy in the brain, there will always be an increase in consciousness and awareness—and vice versa. In fact, it's very difficult to determine whether it is the energy or the level of consciousness that causes these extreme measurements. But I don't think we can separate the two because you cannot have a change in energy without a change in consciousness, or a change in frequency without a change in information.

As you connect to deeper levels of the unified field, the brain is activated by a greater energy that carries specific information in the form of thoughts and imagery. The brain then literally tracks and records this profound inner event, and to the person having the experience, whatever is happening in their mind seems more real than any past external event. In that moment, the increased energy in the form of a profoundly powerful emotion captures all the mind's attention. This is the instant the brain and body receive a biological upgrade.

If someone can sit in a chair with their eyes closed during meditation and have a significantly heightened sensory experience without
their senses, it begs the question *What is happening in the brain to explain
this supernatural effect?* To the person having the experience, despite the
fact that they are sitting still, it seems more real than any other experience (determined by their senses) that they've ever had. This begs more
inquiry: *How can we have a fully amplified sensory experience without our
senses? What are the specific functions of the brain and body that translate
interactions with the quantum field into profound inner experiences?*

In other words, if we can interface with a more coherent field of
information, which then creates such stimulating inner events, there
must be a neurological, chemical, and biological explanation for such
supernatural occurrences. What are the unique systems, organs, glands,
tissues, chemicals, neurotransmitters, and cells involved that could give
rise to such intensely profound experiences? Could there be physiological components that are just sitting dormant, waiting to be activated?

Four states of consciousness will help provide a framework for the
information in this chapter. The first is wakefulness, which of course is
when we are aware and conscious. Next is sleep, where we are unconscious and the body is restoring and repairing. Then comes dreaming,
which is an altered state of consciousness when the body is catatonic
but our minds are engaged in inner visual imagery and symbolism.
And finally there are transcendental moments of consciousness that are
beyond our understanding of reality. These transcendent events seem to
change us and the way we look at the world forever. I want to give you
my best understanding about the biology, chemistry, and neuroscience
of those transcendental experiences. Let's start with the molecule melatonin, which is responsible for all of this.

Melatonin: The Dreaming Neurotransmitter

When you wake up in the morning and return to the world of the
senses, the moment your eye perceives light through your iris, receptors
in the optic nerve send a signal to a part of your brain called the supra-
chiasmatic nucleus. It then sends a signal to the pineal gland, which
responds by making serotonin, the daytime neurotransmitter.

As you will recall, neurotransmitters are chemical messengers that
transmit and communicate information between nerve cells. The neurotransmitter serotonin tells your body it's time to wake up and start your

day. As you integrate information between all your senses in order to create meaning between your inner and outer world, serotonin stimulates your brain waves from delta to theta to alpha to beta, causing you to once again realize you're in a physical body in space and time. Thus, when your brain is firing in beta brain waves, you put much of your attention on your outer environment, your body, and time. That's normal.

As night falls and it gets dark, a similar but inverse process occurs. The inhibition of light sends a signal along the same route back to the pineal gland, but now the pineal gland transmutes serotonin into melatonin, the nighttime neurotransmitter. This production and release of melatonin slows down your brain waves from beta to alpha, making you sleepy, tired, and less likely to want to think or analyze. As your brain waves slow down to alpha, you become more interested in returning your attention to your inner world rather than your outer world. Eventually, as your body falls asleep and goes into a catatonic state, your brain waves move from alpha to theta to delta, thus inducing periods of dreaming as well as deep, restorative sleep.

By living within the rhythm of our external environment, within this diurnal pattern of wakefulness and sleep (based on where we live in the world), our brain becomes automatically entrained to the daily production of these chemicals at very specific times in the morning and evening. This is called the circadian rhythm. Most of us know that when we move out of this natural rhythm we become out of sorts, such as when we travel to another part of the world where the sun rises and sets several hours ahead of our normal time zone. This is jet lag, and we need some time to recalibrate. When the body gets out of its natural circadian rhythm, it will usually take a few days to readjust to the new environment's rhythm of sunrise and sunset. This is all chemistry produced from our interaction with our external three-dimensional world—from our eyes' reaction to the sun and the frequency of visible light.

Melatonin induces rapid eye movement (REM) sleep, a phase of the circadian rhythm that causes dreaming. As the thoughts and chatter in our head diminish, giving way to sleep and eventually the dreaming state, the brain begins to internally see and perceive in images, pictures, and symbols. But before we get into why melatonin is so important, let's take a closer look at the molecular structure of this dreaming neurotransmitter.

The process of creating melatonin starts with the essential amino acid L-tryptophan, the raw material responsible for making serotonin and melatonin. To be converted into melatonin, it must pass through a series of chemical changes known as methylation. Methylation is the process of taking a single carbon and three hydrogens (known as a methyl group) and applying it to countless critical functions throughout our body such as thinking, repairing DNA, turning genes on and off, fighting infections, and so on. In this case, it's part of the production of melatonin.

In Figure 12.1, we see methylation in action. Because this methyl group is made up of very stable chemicals, the basic structure of the five- and six-sided rings stay the same during this series of chemical reactions. However, as different groups of molecules attach to those rings, they change the properties and characteristics of the molecule.

Beginning with L-tryptophan, the pineal gland transmutes it into 5-hydroxytryptophan (5-HTP), which then becomes serotonin. Serotonin is a more stable molecule than 5-HTP, can sustain itself in the brain, and has a more useful function, as we'll soon see. Through another chemical reaction, the pineal gland converts serotonin into N-acetylserotonin and then an additional reaction turns it into melatonin. And all of this happens in the pineal gland. In a 24-hour cycle, the production of melatonin is highest between the hours of 1 A.M. and 4 A.M. This is important to remember.

THE METHYLATION PROCESS OF SEROTONIN & MELATONIN

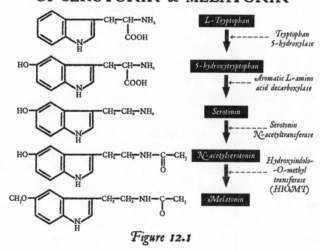

Figure 12.1

The methylation process of the amino acid L-tryptophan
into serotonin and melatonin.

We now know there's an inverse relationship between our adrenal hormones and melatonin. As adrenal cortisol levels go up, melatonin levels go down. This is the reason why we can't sleep when we're under stress. In antiquity, this served as a biological safety mechanism. For instance, if you were chased by a predator a few times on the way to the watering hole, and then you spotted more large beasts in your territory, your body, in its innate intelligence, would want to prevent you from becoming prey yourself. In such cases, sleep and restoration become less important than surviving. More aptly put—staying alive by remaining awake through the night is more valuable than sleeping and risking death.

When the body is trying to rest in this vigilant state, it never gets the restorative sleep it needs because the survival chemicals, like cortisol, have switched on the survival genes. If the perceived stressor is not a saber-toothed tiger, but instead your strained relationship with your ex-spouse, whom you must interact with daily, that chronic stress keeps the survival system activated. Now this safety valve is no longer adaptive but maladaptive. This type of chronic stress alters typical levels of melatonin (and even serotonin), knocking the body out of homeostasis.

But if you lower the levels of cortisol, melatonin levels will increase. In other words, when you break the stress response by overcoming the emotional addiction to those chemicals, your body can go back to long-term building projects instead of constantly dealing with the perceived emergency. Take a look at Figure 12.2 to review the relationship between melatonin and cortisol.

THE INVERSE RELATIONSHIP BETWEEN ADRENAL HORMONES & MELATONIN

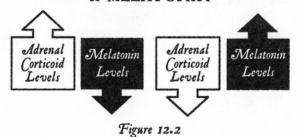

Figure 12.2

As stress hormones go up, melatonin levels go down.
As stress hormones go down, melatonin levels go up.

SCIENTIFIC FACTS
ABOUT MELATONIN

- *Stops the excess secretion of cortisol in response to stress*
- *Improves carbohydrate metabolism*
- *Lowers triglyceride levels*
- *Inhibits atherosclerosis (hardening of the arteries)*
- *Heightens the immune response (cellular and metabolic)*
- *Decreases the development of certain tumors*
- *Increases life span in laboratory rats by 25 percent*
- *Activates a neuroprotective role in the brain*
- *Increases REM sleep (dream sleep)*
- *Stimulates free radical scavenging (anti-aging, antioxidant)*
- *Promotes DNA repair and replication*

Figure 12.3

A chart showing some of the benefits of melatonin.

Melatonin has many other interesting applications. For example, it's been proven to improve carbohydrate metabolism. This is important because when certain people respond to stress, the body takes carbohydrates and stores them as fat—and fat is nothing more than stored energy. This is a result of primitive genes signaling the body to store energy in case there's a famine. Melatonin has also been known to help with depression. It's even been proven to increase levels of DHEA, the anti-aging hormone. For more facts about the importance of melatonin, the dreaming neurotransmitter, see Figure 12.3.[1]

Now let's deepen your understanding of all the information you've been studying in this book up until this point.

Activating the Pineal Gland

For years, I spent enormous amounts of time studying the pineal gland and seeking researchers who did extensive measurements of its metabolites and tissue. My interest was in tying together my findings with some ancient mysteries. One abstract in particular piqued my interest:

The pineal gland is a neuroendocrine transducer secreting melatonin responsible for physiological circadian rhythm control. A new form of bio-mineralization has been studied in the human pineal gland and consists of small crystals that are less than 20 microns in length. These crystals are responsible for electromechanical, biological transduction mechanism in the pineal gland due to the structure and piezoelectric properties.[2]

That's a lot of words to digest, but let's break it down into two meaningful points. The key words here (in reverse order) are *piezoelectric properties* and *transducer*.

The piezoelectric effect occurs when you apply pressure to certain materials and that mechanical stress is changed into an electrical charge. To put it in simple terms, the pineal gland contains calcite crystals made of calcium, carbon, and oxygen, and because of their structure, they express this effect. Like an antenna, the pineal gland has the capacity to become electrically activated and generate electromagnetic fields that can tune in to information. That's point number one. In addition, in the same way an antenna pulsates a rhythm or frequency to match the frequency of an incoming signal, the pineal gland receives information carried on invisible electromagnetic fields. Since all frequency carries information, once the antenna connects to the exact signal of the electromagnetic field, there must be a way to convert and descramble that signal into a meaningful message. That's exactly what a transducer does—and that's the second point.

A transducer is anything that receives a signal in the form of one type of energy and converts it into a signal in another form. Take a moment to look around you. The space you are sitting in is filled with TV, radio, and Wi-Fi waves that are all different frequency ranges of invisible electromagnetic energy. (You can't see any of them with your eyes, but they're still there.) For example, the antenna that picks up a range of frequencies carrying a signal to your TV is transduced into a picture on your TV screen. When you tune in to an FM station, you are tuning your antenna to a specific electromagnetic frequency. The information carried in that frequency range is then transduced into a coherent signal, which is the music you hear with your ears.

The study I quoted says the pineal gland is a neuroendocrine transducer, capable of receiving and converting signals within the brain. When the pineal gland acts as a transducer, it can pick up frequencies above our three-dimensional space-time, sensory-based reality. Once the pineal gland is activated, it can tune in to higher dimensions of this space and time—which we learned in the previous chapter is the realm of time-space. And like a TV, it can then turn the information carried on those frequencies into vivid imagery and surreal, lucid, transcendental experiences in our mind, including profoundly heightened multisensory visions beyond our vocabulary. This is a bit like experiencing a multidimensional IMAX movie.

At this point, you may be wondering, *Since this little gland exists inside my skull, how am I going to exert mechanical stress on the crystals in it, create a piezoelectric effect, and activate the pineal gland so it becomes like an antenna? And how will that antenna pick up frequencies and information beyond matter and light so that it can transduce those electromagnetic signatures into meaningful imagery, like a transcendental experience beyond this three-dimensional reality?*

For the pineal gland to become activated, four important things must happen. I will address three of them now, and then I will give you the fourth step when it's time to learn the meditation.

1. The Piezoelectric Effect

Critical to creating the piezoelectric effect in the pineal gland are the calcite crystals mentioned above and shown in Figure 12.4. Remember, these are very tiny crystals, approximately 1 to 20 microns in length. To put this in context, their size can range anywhere from one-hundredth to one-quarter the width of a human hair. For the most part they are octahedron, hexahedron, and rhombohedron in shape.

As we already learned in Chapter 5, the purpose of the breathing technique we do before many meditations is to pull the mind out of the body by liberating potential energy (stored as emotions) in the lower three energy centers. As we inhale and contract those intrinsic muscles, follow our breath from the perineum all the way up our spine to the top of our head, and then hold our breath and squeeze those muscles more, we're increasing intrathecal pressure. As I mentioned earlier in the book, this is the internal pressure created when you push up against your insides—for example, when you hold your breath and lift something heavy.

The word *piezoelectric* is derived from the Greek words *piezein*, which means "to squeeze or press," and *piezo*, which means to "push." So it's no coincidence that I ask you to hold your breath and squeeze those intrinsic muscles. When you do this, you are pushing cerebrospinal fluid up against the pineal gland, exerting mechanical stress on it. This mechanical stress translates into an electrical charge, and it's this exact action that compresses the stacked crystals in the pineal gland and creates a piezoelectric effect: The crystals of the pineal gland generate an electric charge in response to the stress you're applying.

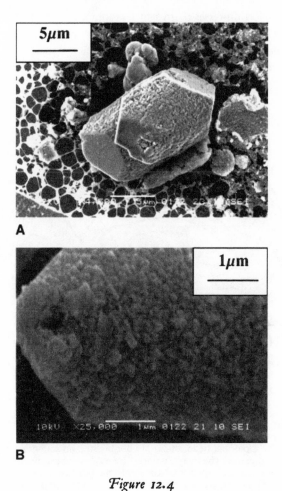

Figure 12.4

A picture of a calcite crystal found in the pineal gland.

One of the unique characteristics of the piezoelectric effect is that it's reversible, meaning that the materials exhibiting the direct piezoelectric effect (the crystals) also exhibit a converse piezoelectric effect. Once the crystals in the gland are compressed and are creating an electrical charge, the electromagnetic field that is emanating from the pineal gland causes the crystals in it to stretch as the field increases. When the crystals generating the electromagnetic field reach their limit and can stretch no further, they contract and the electromagnetic field reverses direction and moves inward toward the pineal gland. When the electromagnetic field reaches the pineal gland crystals, it compresses them again, producing yet another electromagnetic field. This cycle of expanding and reversing the field perpetuates a pulsating electromagnetic field.

VENTRICLES OF THE BRAIN

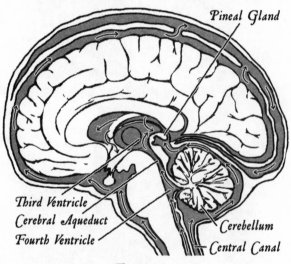

Figure 12.5

When we inhale through our nose, and at the same time squeeze our intrinsic muscles, we accelerate the cerebrospinal fluid into the brain. As we follow the movement of energy to the top of our head, then hold our breath and squeeze, we are increasing intrathecal pressure. The increased pressure moves the cerebrospinal fluid from the fourth ventricle through a small canal into the third ventricle (arrows). At the same time, fluid traveling around the cerebellum (arrows) compresses the crystals of the pineal gland. The mechanical stress that is applied produces an electrical charge in the pineal gland, creating a piezoelectric effect.

It's no wonder, then, that I ask you to hold your breath, squeeze, and contract those muscles—and it's no surprise that I insist you repeat this process over and over. As you keep doing the breath and holding and squeezing again and again, with every cycle of breathing you are activating the piezoelectric properties of the pineal gland. The more you do this, the more you speed up the cycles per second of the expansion and contraction of this electromagnetic field, making the pulses get faster and faster. Now the pineal gland becomes a pulsating antenna, capable of picking up subtler and subtler, faster electromagnetic frequencies.

Take a close look at Figure 12.5. We talked about the movement of cerebrospinal fluid during the breath in Chapter 5, but let's build on the teaching. As the fluid enters the brain, it moves up through the central canal, through the space between the spinal column and the spinal cord. From this juncture, it flows in two directions. First, the fluid moves into the fourth ventricle, followed by the third ventricle. As the fluid travels from the fourth to the third ventricle, it passes through a narrow path or channel, and nestled right at the back of the third ventricle rests what looks like a tiny pinecone (that's what *pineal* means). This is the pineal gland, and it's about the size of a large grain of rice. Second, the cerebrospinal fluid also flows around the back of the cerebellum to the other side of the pineal gland—surrounding the entire gland with pressurized fluid.

By increasing the intrathecal pressure, you funnel a greater volume of fluid into the chamber of the third ventricle as well as from the space around the cerebellum. So when you hold your breath and squeeze, this extra volume of fluid exerts pressure from both directions up against the crystals, causing them to compress and create the piezoelectric effect. This is the first event that must take place to activate the pineal gland.

2. The Pineal Gland Releases Its Metabolites

Cerebrospinal fluid moves through a closed system called the ventricular system (review Figure 12.5). The ventricular system facilitates the movement of this fluid from the base of the spine, up through the spinal column, through the four chambers of the brain (called aqueducts or ventricles), and back down to the sacrum (the base of the spine). When you inhale and follow your breath to the top of your head and then hold your breath and squeeze up and in, you are accelerating the cerebrospinal fluid.

On the surface of the pineal gland are tiny hairs called *cilia*, Latin for "eyelashes" (see Figure 12.6). The action of the accelerated fluid moving faster than normal through the chambers of the ventricular system tickles the tiny hairs, which overstimulates the pineal gland. Because the pineal gland is shaped like a phallus, the stimulation produced by the acceleration of fluid moving past it, combined with the electrical activation created by an increase in intrathecal pressure in a closed system, causes the gland to ejaculate some very profound, upgraded metabolites of melatonin into the brain. You're now one step closer to activating the pineal gland and having a transcendental experience.

CILIA AT THE END
OF THE PINEAL GLAND

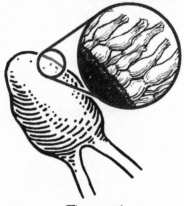

Figure 12.6

The tiny cilia of the pineal gland become stimulated as the cerebrospinal fluid accelerates through the ventricular system.

3. Energy Is Delivered Directly to the Brain

Much like sending a rocket ship into space, overcoming gravity to get it off the ground is the part that requires the most energy, so to move that energy from our lower centers demands a great deal of intensity and effort. The breath becomes our passionate intention to free ourselves from the self-limiting emotions of our past. The spinal column becomes the delivery mechanism for this energy, and the top of the head becomes the target.

As you know by now, every time you perform the breath, you send charged particles up the spinal column. As these particles increase in velocity and acceleration, they create what's known as an inductance field (see Figure 12.7). This inductance field reverses the flow of two-way information that typically facilitates communication from the brain to the body and the body to the brain. Much like a vacuum, the inductance field draws the energy from those lower centers—energy involved with orgasm, consumption, digestion, fight-or-flight stress, and control—and delivers it directly to the brain stem in a spiraling motion. As the energy travels up through each vertebra, it passes the nerves that run from the spinal cord to different parts of the body, and some of that energy is then transferred through the peripheral nerves that affect the tissues and organs of the body. The current that runs along these nerve channels activates the body's meridian system, resulting in all the other systems of the body getting more energy.[3]

THE ACTIVATION OF THE PERIPHERAL NERVOUS SYSTEM AS ENERGY MOVES UP THE SPINE

Figure 12.7

As energy is released from the body to the brain, it passes by each spinal nerve exiting between each vertebra. The excitation of this system further switches on the peripheral nerves, which then transfer more energy to different tissues and organs in the body. As a result, more energy is delivered throughout the body.

Once the energy reaches the brain stem, it must pass through the reticular formation. It's the job of the reticular formation to constantly edit information going from the brain to the body as well as from the body to the brain. This formation is part of a system called the reticular activating system (RAS), which is responsible for levels of wakefulness. For instance, when you wake up from a deep sleep because you hear a sound in your house, it's the RAS that alerts you and arouses you. That's its rudimentary function. However, as the sympathetic nervous system is activated and merges with the parasympathetic nervous system, instead of depleting the body's stored energy, it releases that energy back to the brain. Once this energy reaches the brain stem, the thalamic gate opens like a door and energy moves through the reticular formation to the thalamus, where it relays information to the neocortex. Now the reticular formation is open and you experience greater levels of awareness. In a sense, you become more conscious and awakened. (Think of the thalamus as a big train station with tracks leading to the higher centers of the brain.) That's how the brain goes into gamma brain-wave patterns.

THE TWO THALAMI IN THE MIDBRAIN & THE PINEAL GLAND SITTING IN THE MIDDLE FACING THE BACK OF THE BRAIN

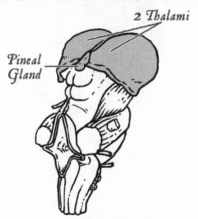

Figure 12.8

Right between each thalamus located in the midbrain sits the tiny pinecone-shaped pineal gland, facing the back of the brain.

As a side note, there are two individual thalami in the midbrain (one on each side), which feed each hemisphere in the neocortex. The pineal gland sits right between them facing the back of the brain (see Figure 12.8). When the energy reaches each thalamic junction (remember the thalamus is like a relay station to all other parts of the brain), these thalami send a message directly to the pineal gland to secrete its metabolites into the brain. The effect is that the thinking neocortex becomes aroused and goes into higher brain-wave patterns, like gamma. The nature of those chemical derivatives of melatonin relaxes the body and at the same time awakens the mind.

If you remember, when you're in beta brain waves, your sympathetic nervous system is aroused for an emergency in your outer world and utilizes energy to survive. The difference with gamma brain waves is that instead of losing vital energy, you're liberating and creating more energy in your body. You're not in any emergency or survival state when this occurs; you're in bliss, and your sympathetic nervous system is switching on to arouse you to pay more attention to whatever is happening within your mind.

In Chapter 5 I said that when energy moves from the body to the brain, a torus field is created around the body. As you run a current up your spinal column by accelerating the movement of cerebrospinal fluid, your body becomes like a magnet and you create an electromagnetic field around it. A torus field represents a dynamic flow of energy. At the same time the torus field is moving up, out, and around your body, when the pineal gland becomes activated, a reverse torus field of electromagnetic energy is drawing energy *into* your body through the top of your head. Since all frequency carries information, now your pineal gland is receiving information from beyond the visible light field and from beyond your senses (see Figure 12.9).

When these three happenings occur in tandem, it's going to feel like you're having an orgasm in your head. You've now created an antenna in your brain, and this antenna is picking up information from realms beyond matter and beyond space and time. Information is no longer coming from your senses or your eyes' interaction with your environment. Instead, you're getting information from the quantum field moving to another eye—your third eye—from the pineal gland in the back of your brain.

THE REVERSE TORUS

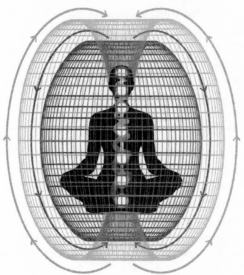

*Energy moves from the unified field
into the body*
Figure 12.9

As energy from the lower three centers is activated during the breath
and moves up the spine to the brain, a torus field of electromagnetic energy is
created around the body. When the pineal gland becomes activated, a reverse torus
field of electromagnetic energy moving in the opposite direction draws energy
through the top of the head into the body from the unified field. Since energy is
frequency and frequency carries information, the pineal gland transduces
that information into vivid imagery.

When Melatonin Gets an Upgrade, Magic Happens

When your pineal gland (or the third eye) is awakened, because it is
picking up higher frequencies, these higher energies alter the chemistry
of melatonin; the higher the frequency, the greater the alteration. It's this
translation of information into chemistry that primes you for those transcendental, mystical moments. Now you're opening the door to higher
dimensions of space and time. This is why I like to call the pineal gland
an *alchemist*—because it transmutes melatonin into some very profound,
radical neurotransmitters.

THE PRODUCTION OF OTHER METABOLITES FROM MELATONIN

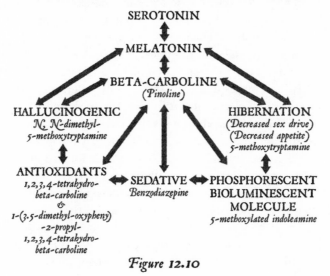

Figure 12.10

Check out the different metabolites of melatonin that are created when the pineal gland connects to frequencies faster than normal visible light and the mystical molecule gets a biological upgrade.

Take a look at Figure 12.10. As higher frequencies and higher states of consciousness interact with the pineal gland, one of the first things to happen is that these frequencies transmute melatonin into chemicals called benzodiazepines. Benzodiazepines are a class of drugs, from which Valium is created, that anesthetize the analytical mind, so all of a sudden the thinking brain relaxes and stops analyzing. According to functional brain scans, benzodiazepines suppress neural activity in the amygdala, the brain's survival center. This limits chemicals that cause you to feel fear, anger, agitation, aggression, sadness, or pain.[4] Now your body feels calm and relaxed, but your mind is awakened.

Another chemical created from melatonin produces a class of very powerful antioxidants called pinolines (see Figure 12.10). Pinolines are important because they attack free radicals, which harm your cells and cause aging. These antioxidants are anti-cancer, anti-aging, anti–heart disease, anti-stroke, anti-neurodegenerative, anti-inflammatory, and anti-microbial. That's a perfect formula to upgrade melatonin's normal role as an antioxidant to the role of a supercharged antioxidant that further restores and heals the body to a greater degree than the melatonin molecule normally does. (See the powerful antioxidants listed in Figure 12.10 that are all produced from metabolites of melatonin.)

If you take that molecule and tweak it again into a cousin of melatonin, you find the same chemical that makes animals hibernate. When melatonin (which makes us sleepy and dreamy) alters just slightly into this more powerful molecule, it carries a message to extend rest and repair even further. This message also causes the body's metabolism to slow, in some cases for months. It makes sense, then, that when mammals hibernate, they break the typical habits of their habitat; for example, they lose their sex drive, their appetite, their interest in or need to move about in their environment, and their connection to social networks. They hide to protect themselves and to feel safe, and during this time of going within, their body goes into stasis. The same might be true for us as these values elevate. Because the body is no longer the mind, we temporarily lose our interest in the outer world; and because we have no biological drives and aren't distracted with bodily needs, we're able to move more fully into the present moment and go deeply within. If you're going to dream the dream of the future, wouldn't it be a good idea to get your body out of the way?

If you take that molecule and advance it yet again, you produce the same chemical found in electric eels—a phosphorescent, bioluminescent chemical that amplifies energy in the nervous system. You can refer to Figure 12.10 again. This chemical can be powerful enough to cause a significant shock. I have a strong hunch this is the rare chemical that influences the brain to process those increased amplitudes of energy that we've repeatedly measured in our students. Just imagine an electric eel that literally lights up with energy when it gets stimulated. That's what happens in the brain when it gets activated. But the energy and information that are created do not come from an experience in our environment that we perceive through our senses, but instead from *within* the brain, caused by an upgrade in frequency. When we see those high-energy levels in the brain, we know that the person is having a profound, subjective experience that can be measured objectively.

Think about that for a moment. Via sensory input from our environment through our eyes, the pineal gland makes serotonin and melatonin. This visible light coming from the sun causes us to move into harmony with our environment, which we call the circadian rhythm. As a result of this process, serotonin and melatonin carry information equal to the frequency coming from the physical world. Because we perceive visible light through our senses, those molecules are inherent to humans; thus they are equivalent to the realm of our three-dimensional reality.

Remember, as Einstein said, that the ceiling of this material world is the speed of light. But what happens as the brain processes an increase in frequency and information from a realm *beyond* the senses and beyond the speed of light? Is it possible that information and energy coming from the unified field change the chemistry of melatonin to become another chemical counterpart in the brain? And could our brain translate those frequencies into a message? If energy is the epiphenomenon of matter, it makes sense that the information coming from a frequency *faster* than visible light would be able to alter the molecular structure of melatonin into profound elixirs within our brain. The pineal gland is responsible for translating that information into a chemical variation of melatonin; therefore, that molecule carries a different message equal to that frequency. That new frequency is now influencing an enhanced superchemical. That's no longer natural—that's supernatural. Melatonin gets an upgrade.

Not only does this phosphorescent, bioluminescent chemical increase the energy in the brain, but it enhances the imagery the mind internally perceives so that everything looks as though it's made of vivid, surreal, luminescent light. As a result, people have reported experiencing colors they've never seen before because they exist outside their known experience of the visible light spectrum. These colors appear as profound, otherworldly glowing lights in a Technicolor, lucid, opalescent world of suspended beauty. Everything appears as if it's emitting beautiful light made of vivid, radiant energy that you can feel. This world of golden, shimmering, bright halos within and around everything appears more illuminated than your sensory-based reality. And of course, it will be difficult to take your attention off all its beauty. Because all of your attention is on this experience, it will seem as though you are actually there, totally present, in this other world or dimension.

Take a look at Figure 12.10 again. Alter melatonin one more time and you produce the chemical dimethyltryptamine (DMT), one of the most powerful hallucinogenic substances known to man. This is the same chemical found in ayahuasca, a traditional spiritual plant medicine used in ceremonies by the indigenous people of the Amazon. DMT's primary active ingredient is said to create spiritual visions and profound insights into the mystery of the self. When ayahuasca or other plant chemicals containing this molecule are ingested, the body receives only DMT, but when the pineal gland is activated, it receives the whole blend of aforementioned chemicals—and this causes some very profound inner experiences. Some of these experiences have been reported to create profound time dilation (time appears infinite), time travel, journeys to paranormal realms, visions of complex geometric patterns, encounters with spiritual beings, and other mystical interdimensional realities. Many of our students during the pineal gland meditation report amazing encounters beyond their known physical world.

When these chemicals are released in the brain, the mind has experiences that appear more real than anything that person has ever encountered in their sensory-based reality. This new dimension is difficult to articulate with language. The novel experience that results will occur as a complete unknown, and if you surrender to it, it's always worth it.

Tuning In to Higher Dimensions: The Pineal Gland as a Transducer

Depending on the translation you're using, in Matthew 6:22 Jesus said, "If thine eye be single, thy whole body shall be full of light." I believe he was talking about activating the pineal gland, because this allows us to experience a broader spectrum of reality. Many of our students can attest to the fact that when their pineal gland becomes activated—when they fully connect with the unified field—their whole body becomes filled with energy and light. Beginning from the cosmic field, energy from beyond their senses enters through the top of their head and travels down throughout their whole body. When this occurs, they experience downloadable information beyond their memory base or the predictable knowns of their daily lives—and it all begins with the chemical alteration of melatonin in the pineal gland.

In all of my research about the pineal gland, I've evolved my own understanding of it into the following definition: *The pineal gland is a crystalline superconductor that sends, as well as receives, information through the transduction of energetic vibrational signals (frequency beyond the senses, also known as the quantum field) and translates it into biological tissue (the brain and the mind) in the form of meaningful imagery, the same way as an antenna translates different channels onto a TV screen.*

When the pineal gland is activated, because you now have this tiny antenna in your brain, the higher the frequency it picks up, the more energy it exerts toward altering and transmuting the chemistry of melatonin. As a result of this change in chemistry, you're going to get a very different experience from what melatonin normally produces. Perhaps a better way to say it is that you're going to get a clearer picture. Think of it this way: The higher the frequency, the more your experience will feel like you've gone from the picture of a 1960s television screen to a 360-degree IMAX 3-D experience, complete with surround sound. Melatonin, the dreaming neurotransmitter, evolves into a more powerfully lucid neurotransmitter to make our dreams more real.

Throughout this process, the pineal gland has a co-conspirator called the pituitary gland. The pituitary gland looks like a pear and sits behind the bridge of the upper nose, right in the middle of the brain. The front (anterior) part of it is responsible for making most of the chemicals that influence the glands and hormones associated with each of our energy centers. Once the pineal gland is activated and it releases certain upgraded metabolites[5] the back (posterior) of the pituitary gland awakens, causing it to produce two important chemicals—oxytocin and vasopressin.[6]

The first chemical, oxytocin, is known to produce elevated emotions that cause your heart to swell with love and joy (it's been referred to as the chemical of emotional connection or the bonding hormone). When oxytocin levels are elevated above normal, most people experience intense feelings of love, forgiveness, compassion, joy, wholeness, and empathy—not an inner state you'd probably be willing to trade for something outside of you. (These states are, after all, the beginning of unconditional love.)

When oxytocin levels go up beyond a certain level, research shows that it's difficult to hold a grudge. In a study conducted by scientists at the University of Zurich, 49 participants played a variation of what is known as the Trust Game 12 consecutive times. In this game, an investor with a certain amount of money must decide either to keep it or to share some of it with another player called the trustee. Whatever sum the investor shares with the trustee is automatically tripled. The trustee is then faced with a decision: keep all the money, leaving the investor with nothing, or share the tripled sum with the investor, who is obviously hoping to make a profit. Basically, the *either/or* decision comes down to betrayal. While a selfish act is a win for the trustee, it leaves the investor at a loss.

But what if oxytocin is introduced into the equation? In the study, the researchers gave some players a squirt of oxytocin in their nose before the game, giving the others a squirt of placebo. The researchers then took fMRI (functional magnetic resonance imaging) scans of the investors' brains as they made their decisions regarding the amount to invest and whether or not to trust.

After the first six rounds, the investors were given feedback on their investments and were notified that their trust had been betrayed about half of the time. The participants who received the placebo before playing the game felt angry and betrayed, so they invested much less in the closing six rounds. The participants who received a squirt of oxytocin, however, invested the same amount as they had in the first rounds, despite having been betrayed. The fMRI scans showed the key areas of the brain affected were the amygdala (associated with fear, anxiety, stress, and aggression) and the dorsal striatum (which guides future behaviors based on positive feedback). Participants who received the oxytocin had much lower activity in the amygdala, equating to less anger and fear of being betrayed again, as well as less fear of financial loss. They also had much lower activity in the dorsal striatum, meaning they no longer needed to rely on positive results to make future decisions.[7]

As this study demonstrates, the moment the posterior pituitary releases its chemicals and oxytocin levels go up, this shuts down the survival centers in the brain's amygdala, meaning it cools off the circuits for fear, sadness, pain, anxiety, aggression, and anger. Then the only thing we feel is a love for life. We've measured the levels of oxytocin in our students before and after our workshops. At the conclusion of the event, some of them had elevated their levels significantly. When we interviewed those students, many of them kept saying, "I'm just so in love with my life and everyone in it. I never want this feeling to go away. I want to remember this feeling forever. This is who I really am."

The other chemical the pituitary gland makes as the pineal gland is activated is called vasopressin, or antidiuretic hormone. As vasopressin levels go up, the body naturally retains fluids, causing the body to become more water-based. This is important because if you're going to process a greater frequency, you need water to act as a conduit to better handle the higher frequency in the body, and to then translate that frequency into your cells. The moment vasopressin goes up, it creates a more stable thyroid gland—which affects the thymus and the heart, which affects the adrenals, which affects the pancreas, which produces a chain cascade of positive effects all the way down to the sexual organs.[8]

When we tune in to these higher frequencies, we have access to a different kind of light—a frequency faster than visible light—and all of a sudden we are activating a greater intelligence within us. Now, because the pineal gland is activated, we can pick up higher frequencies, which in turn produces a change in chemistry. The higher the frequency we pick up, the more it alters our chemistry—which means the more visual, hallucinogenic, and higher-energy experiences we have. The crystals in our pineal gland, acting like a cosmic antenna, are the doorway to these higher vibrational realms of light and information. This is how we have internal experiences that are more real than our external ones.

These pineal metabolite chemicals your body produces fit into the same receptor sites as serotonin and melatonin, but they carry a very different chemical message from a realm *beyond* sensory-based material reality. As a result, the brain is now primed for a mystical experience, opening the door to other dimensions and moving the individual from a space-time reality to a time-space reality. Since all frequency carries a message and that message is a change in chemistry, once the pineal gland gets activated and you start experiencing and processing these higher frequencies, energies, and elevated levels of consciousness, they often present themselves as complex, changing geometric patterns usually perceived in the mind's eye. This is good—this is information.

When you have these mystical experiences, because your nervous system is so coherent, it's able to tune in to these super coherent messages. In the darkness of the void, the pineal gland becomes the vortex for these very organized patterns and packets of information, and as you place your attention on them, just like a kaleidoscope they constantly change and evolve. The same way a TV picks up frequencies and turns them into pictures on the screen, the pineal gland chemically transduces higher frequencies into vivid, surreal images.

In Graphic 13 in the color insert, you can see some of these geometric patterns, which are called divine (or sacred) geometry. Such patterns have been around for thousands of years. In Chapter 8, I mentioned that these patterns appear to look like ancient mandalas. They're energy and information in the form of frequency, and if you can surrender to them, your brain (via the pineal gland) will transduce those forms, messages, and information into very vivid pictures, imagery, or lucid experiences. The best thing to do when you see or experience these patterns is to surrender to them and not try to make anything happen.

These patterns and forms usually do not appear as two-dimensional or static; instead, they are alive, have depth, and comprise mathematical and very coherent fractal patterns, never ending and infinitely complex. Another way to see this is through the concept of *cymatics*. Derived from the Greek word for "wave," cymatics are a phenomenon based on vibration or frequency. Here's a way to picture them: Imagine if you took the cover off of an old speaker box and laid it flat. If you filled that speaker with fluid, shined a light on it, and began playing classical music up through it, the frequency and vibration of the music would eventually create coherent standing waves. These waves would interfere with each other and eventually create geometric patterns within patterns within patterns. As with a kaleidoscope, you would see these evolving geometric arrangements becoming more highly organized. The difference between the images in the kaleidoscope and cymatics is that the images in the kaleidoscope appear two-dimensional. Geometric patterns such as cymatics, however, appear to be alive and are three-dimensional or even multidimensional. In addition to water, the vibrational effects of cymatics are translatable to sand and air; in other words, these three mediums pick up vibration and frequency and turn them into coherent geometric patterns. (If you search, you can find several videos showing this on YouTube.)

When your pineal gland picks up information, it's picking up these same types of waves in the environment around you. These coherent, highly organized standing waves that exist beyond the visible light spectrum are constantly being consolidated into packets of information and transduced into images by your pineal gland. They are just patterns of information that are intersecting in a very coherent way, and when you put your awareness on them, they change and evolve to become increasingly more fractal, intricate, beautiful, and divine. It's all information, and just like a transducer, your pineal gland takes that information and descrambles it into imagery. This is one of the reasons I decided to use the kaleidoscope as a tool in our advanced events, to train students' brains to be disarmed when they experience this mode of complex imagery, as well as to more easily recognize—and open up to—receiving this type of information. Additionally, as the kaleidoscope causes the brain to move into alpha or theta brain waves and you become more suggestible, you can see how gazing into it in a state of trance primes your subconscious mind for a mystical experience.

Once your pineal gland picks up the imagery, fasten your seatbelt because things are going to get exciting. You might come out of your body and travel down a tunnel of light, or your entire body might become filled with light. You might even feel like you've become the entire universe, and when looking down at your body, even find yourself wondering how you're going to get back into it.

When you start having these very profound, unknown experiences, you have one of two choices: You can contract in fear because it's the unknown, or you can surrender and trust—*because* it's the unknown. The more you surrender and trust, the deeper and more profound your experiences become, and because the experience is so profound, you're not going to want to rouse yourself back to wakefulness, thereby changing your brain waves back to beta. Instead, this is the time to surrender, relax, and go even deeper into this transcendental state of consciousness. In this moment, you are not sleeping, you are not awake, you are not dreaming—you are transcendent of this reality. If your brain chemistry is right, your body will be totally and completely sedated. This is what we are training for: to experience greater levels of wholeness, oneness, love, and higher consciousness.

But there's more . . .

Alteration in Chemistry Creates a New Reality

Imagine if in this moment all your senses were increased by 25 percent. If that were the case, everything you were seeing, hearing, tasting, smelling, and feeling would cause you to become more aware of everything around you. If awareness and consciousness are the same, then as your consciousness is heightened, the energy your brain is receiving would also be increased (because you can't have a change in consciousness without a change in energy, or vice versa). As your brain connects to a different frequency that is processing a new stream of consciousness, it is literally turning on, and because your senses feel amplified, you've produced an elevated level of awareness. The higher the energy or frequency, the greater the alteration in your chemistry, and the greater the alteration in your chemistry, the more lucid your experience will be. So when you're in this transcendental state, you feel more awake and more aware than you are in your day-to-day reality. As your awareness amplifies, you would feel as if you were truly in that transcendental reality.

If you're picking up information from beyond your senses, information that is not originating from visible light or the sun, then it makes sense that it's called the "third eye." Because you had such a profound internal experience, and since new experiences assemble new neural networks, that experience enriches the circuitry in your brain. As your body processes these higher energies, that energy alters your chemistry, and if the end result of an experience is an emotion, then this experience creates elevated feelings and emotions. When it's activated, you are seeing with a different eye, with inner vision.

If the accumulation of feelings equals an emotion, and emotion is energy, then we know that when you experience survival emotions, because they are a lowering of frequency, you feel more like the density of matter and chemistry. But as you experience these higher states of consciousness, because they vibrate at a higher frequency you will begin to feel less like matter or chemistry and more like energy. That's why I call this energy in the form of feelings elevated emotions.

If the environment signals the genes in a cell, and experiences from the environment create emotions—*and emotions are the chemical feedback from the experience in the environment*—then if nothing ever changes in the external environment, nothing changes in the internal environment of the body (which is still the outer environment of the cell). For example, when you live by the same self-limiting emotions for years, your body never biologically changes because it doesn't know the difference between the emotion coming from the outer environment and the emotion coming from your inner environment. Instead, the body believes it is living in the same environmental conditions because the same emotions are producing the same chemical signals. Just as the body lives in an external environment in which nothing is changing, the cell too lives in a chemical environment in which nothing is changing.

But when you start having these internal experiences of heightened awareness and expanded consciousness—experiences that are more real and sensory than any in the past—the moment you feel that new heightened emotion or ecstatic energy, you've altered your internal state, and as a result you're going to pay more attention to the images of the reality created within you. And if you have a new experience that is so real it captures all the brain's attention, that new experience (or awakening) embosses the event neurologically in your brain. That new emotion now creates a long-term memory and those new emotions signal new genes, but this time the experience that's creating the long-term memory is not coming from your outer environment; it's coming from your inner environment—which is still the outer environment of the cell.

Because the event is so powerful that you cannot *not* be aware, therefore:

- The higher the energy, the higher the consciousness;
- The higher the consciousness, the greater the awareness;
- The greater the awareness, the broader experience of reality you have.

As we know, all perception is based on how the brain is wired from our experiences in the past. We don't perceive things in our reality the way they are; we perceive reality the way *we* are. If you just had an internal experience in which you saw profound mystical beings; witnessed a glow, a halo, or light around everything; felt the wholeness, oneness, and interconnectedness of everything and everyone; or experienced a completely different time and space, when you open your eyes after the experience, your spectrum of reality in your waking state will be broadened. That's because the inner experience changed your brain and now you're neurologically wired to perceive a greater expression of reality. This is how you begin to change who you are from the inside out. This is how you alter your experience of the three-dimensional world of matter.

Evolution, on both an individual and a species level, is a slow process. You have experiences, you get hurt, you learn your lesson, you grow a little bit. Then you have some more pain, you get the next lesson, you move on to the next challenge, you succeed and achieve goals, you set more goals, you grow again, and the cycle continues. It's a slow process because you're not receiving much new information from your outer environment.

But once you have these unknown internal experiences that are more real than anything in your external world, you can never again see reality in the same manner because the experience changes you so profoundly. Another way to say it is that you receive an upgrade or a software update. If all of the reality you perceive is based on your experiences, and you've just had an interdimensional experience, your brain is now going to be able to perceive what has always existed but you have never before had the brain circuitry to perceive.

If you continuously have these expansive experiences, you'll continuously experience a broader and broader spectrum of reality. This lifts the veil of illusion, and when that veil is lifted you can see reality as it truly is—vibrating, shining, connected, and shimmering in luminescent light—and energy is driving the whole process. You're now tuning in to a greater spectrum of information where all of a sudden everything looks and feels different than it did when you saw it simply as matter—and your relationship changes. This is how the mystics and masters made their way: by tuning in to their inner world and thus broadening their perception of the nature of reality in their outer world. Imagine who you could become if you stopped living by the hallmarks of the lower three energy centers, including survival, fear, pain, separation, anger, and competition, and instead lived from the heart and operated out of love, oneness, and connection to all things, both seen and unseen.

By having enough interdimensional experiences from information beyond the senses, the mystics and masters no longer saw equal to the genes they were born with. They no longer processed things the way the brain they'd been given at birth had been wired—the way the human brain has been imprinted for thousands of years. Instead, because of their interaction with the field, they created the awareness, the circuitry, and the mind to perceive a different reality—one that's always been there.

These mythic and magical properties of the pineal gland, the brain's alchemist, are certainly not new information, although it seems modern science is just now catching up to what ancient civilizations have always known.

Figure 12.11

This crop circle found in Roundway, UK, on July 23, 2011, shows the chemical structure of melatonin . . . maybe someone is trying to tell us something.

Melatonin, Mathematics, Ancient Symbols, and the Pineal Gland

On July 23, 2011, a crop circle that looks very much like the chemical structure of melatonin appeared in the English countryside in Roundway near Devizes, Wiltshire. (See Figure 12.11.) Is the crop circle an elaborate hoax? Or is somebody somewhere in another dimension trying to tell us something? As you read this section, you can decide for yourself whether such things happen by coincidence or intelligent design.

The brain has two hemispheres, and if you divided them in half by slicing the brain down the middle, you would perform what is known as a sagittal cut. When looking at the sagittal cut in Figure 12.12, pay particular attention to the location and collective formation of the pineal gland, thalamus, hypothalamus, pituitary gland, and corpus callosum. Does that formation remind you of anything? Meant to signify protection, power, and good health, it's the ancient Egyptian symbol called the Eye of Horus. Is it possible that there was an ancient teaching about the autonomic nervous system, the reticular activating system, the thalamic gate, and the pineal gland? The Egyptians must have known the significance of the autonomic nervous system and realized that activating the pineal gland meant they could enter the otherworld, or other dimensions.[9]

THE EYE OF HORUS, THE LIMBIC BRAIN & THE PINEAL GLAND

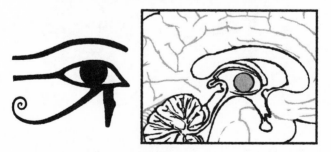

Figure 12.12

If you slice the brain down the middle, you can view the limbic brain.
Take a look and you'll notice a striking resemblance to the Eye of Horus.

In the Egyptian system of measurement, the Eye of Horus also represented a fractional quantification system to measure parts of the whole. In modern mathematics, we call this the Fibonacci constant, or Fibonacci's sequence. As I mentioned earlier in the book, this is a mathematical formula that shows up everywhere in nature, displayed in patterns you can see in sunflowers, seashells, pineapples, pinecones, eggs, and even the structure of our Milky Way galaxy. Also known as the golden spiral, the golden mean, or the golden ratio, the Fibonacci constant is characterized by the fact that every number after the first two is the sum of the preceding two.

If you superimposed this formula over the brain and began dividing squares while adding another square and another square, you'd get a fractal pattern, a never-ending pattern that repeats itself at every scale. Starting at the pineal gland, this formula outlines the exact structure of the brain (see Figure 12.13). Are you beginning to think there might be something special going on with the pineal gland?

FIBONACCI'S CONSTANT

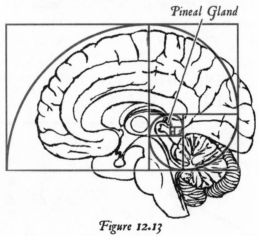

Pineal Gland

Figure 12.13

If you follow the golden ratio, Fibonacci's constant, along the circumference of the brain, the spiral will end at the exact point of the pineal gland.

In Greek mythology, Hermes was a messenger of the gods who could move in and out of earthly and divine realms. He was considered a god of transitions and dimensions, as well as a guide to the afterlife. His main symbol was the caduceus, which consists of two snakes wrapped around a rod, the top of which unfolds into wings or birds. (See Figure 12.14.) The caduceus, which Hermes used as a staff, is often considered a symbol of health. Do you think those snakes moving up the staff represent the movement of energy up the spine from the body to the brain, and the wings the liberation of the self when the energy arrives at the pineal gland to signify enlightenment? The crown represents our highest potential and our greatest expression of the divine when we activate our pineal gland (represented by the pinecone). The crowning of the Self is the conquering of the self. This is why I chose this image for the cover of this book.

THE CADUCEUS: THE ALCHEMY OF THE SELF

Figure 12.14

Tuning In to Higher Dimensions of Time and Space Meditation

Since melatonin levels are at their height between 1 A.M. and 4 A.M., that's the best time to do this meditation. Start by activating your heart center for one song. Then bless your energy centers, starting with the lowest one, as you learned in the Blessing of the Energy Centers meditation in Chapter 4. Bless this energy center by resting your attention first in the space of that energy center, and then in the space around it. Do this for the first and then for the second energy center, and then focus your attention on the first *and* second center at the same time. Continue this process with each energy center, creating a bigger field by connecting each new energy center to the prior centers. Eventually you'll align all eight centers and the energy around your entire body simultaneously. This should take about 45 minutes. Then lie down for 20 minutes and let your autonomic nervous system take the orders to balance the body.

Now sit up and do the breath, bringing that energy all the way up to the top of your head. Hold it and squeeze, compressing the crystals of the pineal gland, thus activating it and creating an electromagnetic field. That field is going to stretch as far as it can go and then it's going to reverse and compress those crystals. As you increase the frequency, you're going to pick up higher and higher vibrational realms, and then your brain is going to take that information and turn it into imagery. One last point about this breath: I want to emphasize that it is not necessary to take a fast, deep breath and then squeeze your intrinsic muscles and then hold your breath to the point that you turn purple. Instead, I want you to take a very slow, long, steady breath, coordinating the breath with the contraction of your intrinsic muscles equally as you inhale and slowly follow that breath all the way to the top of your head.

This is the fourth way you can activate the pineal gland. When you're done with the breath, rest your attention between the back of your throat and the back of your head in space—you are locating that gland, and by placing your attention there, you are placing your energy there. Keep your attention there for about 5 to 10 minutes. As a thought, an awareness, and consciousness, get really tiny and move into the chamber of the pineal gland and sense the space of that room, in the center of this organ, in space. Linger there for about 5 to 10 minutes. Then sense the frequency and space beyond the boundaries of the gland. Radiate the energy beyond that room into the big black space. Direct that energy to carry the intention that this gland release its sacred metabolites for the mystical experience. Broadcast that information into the space beyond your head, in space.

Now open up, tune in to the energy beyond your head in that vast, eternal black space, and just receive. The longer you're conscious of this energy, and the more you can receive that frequency, the more you are altering and upgrading melatonin to its radical metabolites. Don't expect anything to happen, don't try to anticipate—just keep receiving. Finally, lie down again, and let the autonomic nervous system take over. Enjoy the scenery!

Chapter 13

PROJECT COHERENCE: MAKING A BETTER WORLD

We are living in a time of extremes, and these extremes are both a reflection of an old consciousness that can no longer survive and a future consciousness in which planet Earth herself, and all of us on Earth, are transforming. This old consciousness is driven by survival emotions like hatred, violence, prejudice, anger, fear, suffering, competition, and pain—emotions that serve to seduce us into believing we are separate from one another. The illusion of separation taxes and divides individuals, communities, societies, countries, and Mother Nature herself. The mindlessness, carelessness, greed, and disrespect of human activity is threatening life as we know it. By pure logic and reason, this type of consciousness cannot sustain itself for much longer.

Because everything is moving toward extreme polarities, undeniably many of the current systems—whether political, economic, religious, cultural, educational, medical, or environmental—are being pulled apart as antiquated paradigms collapse. We can see this most prominently in journalism, where no one knows what to believe anymore. Some of these changes reflect people's choices, while others reflect increasing levels of personal awareness. One thing is apparent, however; in this age of information, everything that is not in alignment with the evolution of this new consciousness is coming to the surface.

If you aren't aware that there is an increase in frequency and energy occurring at this time—an increase in anxiety, tension, and passion— then you might not be paying attention to your own state of being and mankind's interconnectedness to this energy. In addition to the upheavals in our highly charged political, social, economic, and personal environments, many people also feel as if time is speeding up—or that more momentous happenings are occurring in a shorter amount of time. Depending on your outlook, this could be either an exciting time of awakening or an anxiety-inducing moment in history. Regardless, the old must fall away or break down so that something more functional can emerge in its place. This is how people, species, consciousness, and even the planet itself evolve.

This excitement in energy both within humans and nature begs several questions: Could greater influences be at play that are affecting mankind's correlation to violence, war, crime, and terrorism—and conversely, peace, unity, coherence, and love? And is there a reason why all of this is happening at this particular time?

The History of Peace-Gathering Projects

To date, the power of temporary peace-gathering projects has been exhibited and thoroughly field tested in more than 50 demonstration projects and 23 peer-reviewed scientific studies scrutinized by independent scholars around the world.[1] The results have consistently demonstrated a positive effect in the immediate reduction of crime, warfare, and terrorism by an average of greater than 70 percent.[2] Think about that for a moment. When a group of people come together with the specific intention or collective consciousness to change some "thing" or to produce an outcome, if they create it with the energy and emotions of peace, unity, or oneness—without physically doing anything—that unified community can produce changes 70 percent of the time. To quantify the results of these studies, scientists use a measurement called lead-lag analysis.

The purpose of lead-lag analysis is to uncover correlations between people and incidents. For example, if you looked at the lead-lag analysis of a chain-smoker, it would show that the more a person smokes, the greater chance they will have of developing lung cancer. In relation to peace-gathering projects, the studies have found that the greater the number of meditators or peace gatherers (combined with the amount of time they meditate), the greater influence the gathering has upon decreasing incidences of crime and violence in society.

A powerful example is the Lebanon peace project, which brought together a group of meditators in Jerusalem in August and September of 1983 to demonstrate the "radiating influence of peace." Although the number of meditators fluctuated over time, it was often large enough to achieve the *super radiance effect* for both Israel and nearby Lebanon. This effect happens when a group of specially trained meditators come together at the same time on a daily basis to create and radiate a positive effect on society. The results of the two-month study showed that on days when there was a high participation of meditators, a 76 percent reduction of war deaths occurred. Other effects included reduced crime and fires, decreased traffic accidents, less terrorism, and increases in economic growth. The results were then replicated in seven consecutive experiments over a two-year period during the peak of the Lebanon war.[3] All of this was achieved simply by combining people's intention for peace and coherence with the elevated emotions of love and compassion. This clearly demonstrates that the more unified the consciousness of a group of people within a specific elevated energy is, the more it can change the consciousness and the energy of others in a nonlocal way.

In what's considered one of the top three peace-gathering studies in the Western hemisphere, a RAND Corporation think tank assembled a group of nearly 8,000 (and sometimes more) trained meditators to focus on world peace and coherence during three periods ranging from 8 to 11 days each, from 1983 to 1985. The results showed that during this time, worldwide terrorism was reduced by 72 percent.[4] Can you imagine the results and positive effects, as well as the speed with which they would occur, if this type of meditation and mindfulness was a part of the education curriculum?

In still another study, this time in India from 1987 to 1990, 7,000 people gathered to focus on world peace. During that three-year period, the world witnessed remarkable transformations toward world peace: The Cold War ended, the Berlin Wall came down, the Iran-Iraq war came to an end, South Africa began to move toward abolishing apartheid, and terrorist attacks subsided. What surprised everyone was the swiftness with which these global changes occurred, all in a relatively peaceful manner.[5]

In 1993, from June 7 to July 30, approximately 2,500 meditators gathered in Washington, D.C., in a highly controlled experiment to focus on peace and coherent energy. For the first five months of the year, violent crime had been steadily on the rise, yet soon after the study began, a significant statistical reduction in violence (as measured by FBI Uniform Crime Reports), crime, and stress in Washington, D.C., began to occur.[6] These results point to the fact that a relatively small group of people united in love and purpose can have a statistically significant effect on a diverse population.

On September 11, 2001, due to the immediacy of global media, human beings all over the planet felt horror, shock, fear, terror, and grief as planes crashed into New York City's World Trade Center, the Pentagon in Washington, D.C., and a field near Shanksville, Pennsylvania. In an instant, the world's collective consciousness tuned in to this event. Powerful emotional outpourings around the globe occurred as people bonded, formed communities, and took care of one another.

During the unfolding of events on 9/11, scientists at Princeton University's Global Consciousness Project were collecting data via the Internet from more than 40 devices around the world. As data poured in to a central server in Princeton, New Jersey, the scientists witnessed dramatic changes in the patterns in their random event generator. (Think of a random event generator as a computerized coin toss. It's measuring heads or tails, or ones and zeros, so according to statistics it should produce nearly 50/50 results.) The dramatic changes in patterns right after the event caused the scientists to determine that the collective emotional response of people's outpouring was enough that it could actually be measured in the Earth's magnetic field.[7]

What all of these studies ultimately point to is that there's significant evidence that group meditations of the right size with skilled meditators who change their emotions and energy can influence and create nonlocal, measurable effects on peace and global coherence. If these peace-gathering projects are a force for coherence throughout a society, are there antithetical forces that could be working against humans to produce incoherence?

The Earth's Relationship to Solar Cycles

As the Earth rotates daily on its axis, every morning the sun brings light to the darkness, warmth and comfort to the chill of night, photosynthesis to plants, and security to humans. It's for this reason that as far back as 14,000 B.C.E., adoration of the sun has been sketched onto stone tablets and cave walls. Countless mythologies (including civilizations in ancient Egypt and Mesopotamia, the Mayans and the Aztecs, and the Australian Aborigines, to name just a few) have extolled the sun as worthy of worship, as well as a source of enlightenment, illumination, and wisdom. No matter the location, most cultures have recognized the sun as the prime controller of all life on Earth because without it, life here could not exist.

For the most part humans are electromagnetic beings (entities that constantly send and receive messages via vibrational energies) whose bodies are made up of gravitationally organized light and information. (In fact, everything material in this three-dimensional world is gravitationally organized light and information.) Just as we are individual electromagnetic beings, we are but a small link in the chain of an electromagnetic world, the individual parts of which cannot be separated from the whole.

On a grand scale, it is impossible to deny the interconnectivity between the sun's energy, the Earth's energy, and the energy of all living species. On a micro level, all you have to do is look at the life cycle of a fruit or vegetable to understand this interdependence. The vegetable or fruit begins as a seed, and when environmental conditions such as water, temperature, nutrient-rich soil, and photosynthesis conspire, these conditions enable the seed to germinate. Eventually the blossom of the seed becomes an integral part of an ecosystem, as well as a source of sustenance and nourishment for various forms of life. This complex chain and delicate balance of events all begins with the Earth's uniquely situated location in our solar system. Known as the circumstellar habitable zone, this is a range of orbital distance around a star (our sun) in which a planet can support liquid water.

While the sun may be almost 93 million miles away, when it becomes active it has significant consequences to life on Earth because the Earth and the sun are related by electromagnetic fields. The purpose of the Earth's electromagnetic field (see Figure 13.1) is to protect it from the harmful effects of solar radiation and sunspots, cosmic rays, and other forms of space weather. Although not totally understood, sunspots are relatively dark, cool areas of the sun caused by interactions within the sun's magnetic field; they can be up to 32,000 miles in diameter. You can think of sunspots as a cap on a seltzer bottle; if you shake the bottle and then remove the cap, it's going to produce a large release of photons (light) and other forms of high-frequency radiation.[8]

THE EARTH'S
ELECTROMAGNETIC FIELD

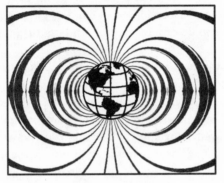

Figure 13.1

The Earth's electromagnetic field.

If it were not for the protection and insulation of Earth's electromagnetic fields, life as we know it could not exist, for we would be constantly bombarded by a steady stream of deadly particles. For example, when there are solar flares, the Earth's electromagnetic field protects the planet by deflecting trillions of tons of photonic emissions called mass coronal ejections. Mass coronal ejections are huge explosions of plasma and magnetic fields from the sun's corona that can extend millions of miles into space. Their effects tend to reach the Earth an average of 24 to 36 hours after they occur.

These ejections compress the Earth's field, heating the Earth's iron core. As this core becomes altered, it changes the planet's electromagnetic field. These ejections are a part of solar cycles that occur approximately every 11 years—and they have the potential to disturb all living organisms on the Earth.

The recording of solar cycles began in 1755, but in 1915 an 18-year-old Russian boy named Alexander Chizhevsky took mankind's understanding of the sun and its relation to the Earth to the next level when he spent his summer observing our sun. During that summer he began hypothesizing that periods of solar activity might have effects on the organic world. A year later he entered World War I, and when not fighting for Russia, he again cast his observations toward the sun. He noticed in particular that battles tended to wax or wane depending on the strength of solar flares (see Graphic 14 in the color insert).[9] Chizhevsky later compiled the histories of 72 countries from 1749 to 1926, comparing the annual number of important political and social events (such as the start of wars, revolutions, outbreaks of diseases, and violence) with increased solar activity, demonstrating a correlation between the sun's activity and human excitability. Equally interesting, solar activity has also been associated with great human flourishing, including innovations in architecture, science, the arts, and social change.[10]

Every place where you see the red line spiking in the graphic represents an active solar flare or sunspot that occurred between the years 1750 and 1922. The blue lines represent historically important events that took place within the same period. Chizhevsky eventually determined that 80 percent of these countries' most significant events occurred during solar events and geomagnetic activity.[11] The solar release of energy—which is always carrying information—seems to be in almost perfect coherence with the activities, the energy, and the consciousness of our planet. It just so happens that at the time of this writing, in 2017, we are in the midst of a very active solar cycle.

In the past decade, much has been said about how this solar energy is affecting the planet and all of life that inhabits it. In 2012, doomsayers thought the end of the Mayan calendar, which correlates to the December solstice, meant the end of the world was at hand. Today astrologers talk about the Age of Aquarius (an astrological age is a period consisting of approximately 2,150 years that corresponds to the average time it takes for the vernal equinox to move from one constellation of the zodiac into the next) and how it will usher in a new awareness for humanity. Astronomers and cosmologists talk about galactic alignment, a rare astronomical event occurring every 12,960 years that brings the sun into alignment with the center of the Milky Way galaxy.

Regardless of what you believe, all of these occurrences point to solar cycles that increase the energy coming toward the Earth from the sun. Since we are electromagnetic beings, connected to the Earth through electromagnetic fields and shielded from the sun by electromagnetic fields, this increase in energy from the sun is going to change both the energy of the Earth and our personal energy. This means that this new energy has the potential to influence human beings in either positive or negative ways, depending on our individual energy. For example, if you are feeling separation, living by survival emotions and enslaved to the hormones and chemicals of stress, your brain and heart are going to fire incoherently. This will cause your energy and awareness to become divided and out of balance, and the increase in energy from the sun is going to enhance that state of being. Therefore, if you are living in incoherence, that incoherence is going to become amplified.

By the same means, if you are living in the coherent alignment of head and heart, working daily in your meditations to connect to the unified field and to overcome your limited beliefs and attitudes, you are going to be propelled even further into the truth and understanding of who you are and what your purpose is.

The bottom line is that we are in the midst of an initiation, and it is going to take a tremendous amount of will, awareness, and consciousness to stay focused so as not to succumb to these excitable energies. If we can maintain our focus, then instead of being victims of the uncertainty, we can transmute this energy into greater degrees of orderliness, coherence, and even peace, both personally and globally. In the simplest terms, this energy is going to endorse who you are being—that is, how you are thinking and feeling.

The Schumann Resonance

In 1952, German physicist and professor W. O. Schumann hypothesized there were measurable electromagnetic waves in the atmosphere in the cavity (or space) between the Earth's surface and the ionosphere. According to NASA, the ionosphere is an abundant layer of electrons, ionized atoms, and molecules that stretches from approximately 30 miles above the surface of the Earth to the edge of space, about 600 miles up. This dynamic region grows and shrinks (and further divides into sub-regions) based on solar conditions, and it's a critical link in the chain of sun-Earth interactions.[12] It's this "celestial power station" that makes radio communications possible.

In 1954, Schumann and H. L. König confirmed Schumann's hypothesis by detecting resonances at a main frequency of 7.83 Hz; thus the "Schumann resonance" was established by measuring global electromagnetic resonances generated and excited by lightning discharges in the ionosphere. You can think of this frequency as a tuning fork for life. In other words, it acts as a background frequency influencing the biological circuitry of the mammalian brain (the subconscious brain below the neocortex, which is also the home of the autonomic nervous system). The Schumann frequency affects our bodies' balance, health, and very nature as mammals. In fact, the absence of the Schumann resonance can cause serious mental and physical health issues in the human body.

This was demonstrated through research by German scientist Rutger Wever from the Max Planck Institute for Behavioral Physiology in Erling-Andechs, Germany. In the study, he took young, healthy student volunteers for four weeks at a time and placed them in hermetically sealed underground bunkers that screened out the Schumann frequency. Throughout the four weeks, the students' circadian rhythms changed, causing them to suffer emotional distress and migraine headaches. When Wever introduced the Schumann frequency back into the bunkers, after only a brief exposure to 7.83 Hz, the volunteers' health returned to normal.[13]

As far back as we know, the Earth's electromagnetic field has been protecting and supporting all living things with this natural frequency pulsation of 7.83 Hz. You can think of the Schumann resonance as the Earth's heartbeat. The ancient Indian rishis referred to this as OM, or the incarnation of pure sound. Whether by coincidence or not, 7.83 Hz also happens to be a very powerful frequency used with brain-wave entrainment, as it is associated with low levels of alpha and the upper range of theta brain-wave states. It is this range of brain waves that allows us to get beyond the analytical mind and into the subconscious. Thus this frequency has also been associated with high levels of suggestibility, meditation, increased human growth hormone levels, and increased cerebral blood-flow levels.[14] It appears, then, that the Earth's frequency and the brain's frequency have very similar resonances and that our nervous system can be influenced by the Earth's electromagnetic field. Perhaps this is why getting out of the city and into nature often provides such a calming effect.

The Concept of Emergence

In 1996, researchers at the HeartMath Institute discovered that when an individual's heart is in a state of coherence or harmonious rhythm, it radiates a more coherent electromagnetic signal into the environment—and that this signal can be detected by the nervous systems of other people, as well as animals. In fact, as you know by now, the heart generates the strongest magnetic field in the body and it can be measured several feet away.[15] This provides a credible explanation for the fact that when someone walks into a room, you can feel or sense that individual's mood or emotional state, independent of their body language.[16] From a purely scientific standpoint, we can then ask, if this phenomenon works on an individual level, can it work on a global level?

In 2008, more than a decade later, the HeartMath Institute launched the Global Coherence Initiative (GCI), a science-based, international effort that seeks to help activate the heart of humanity to promote peace, harmony, and a shift in global consciousness. GCI is based on the beliefs that:

1. Human health, thoughts, behaviors, and emotions are influenced by solar geomagnetic (the Earth's magnetic field) activity;

2. The Earth's magnetic field is a carrier of biologically relevant information that connects all living systems;

3. All human beings influence the Earth's electromagnetic field of vital information;

4. Collective human consciousness where large numbers of people are intentionally focused on heart-centered states creates or affects the global information field. Therefore, elevated emotions of care, love, and peace can generate a more coherent field environment that can benefit others and help offset the current planetary discord and incoherence.[17]

Because human heart rhythm and brain frequencies (as well as cardiovascular and autonomic nervous systems) overlap with the Earth's resonance field, GCI scientists suggest we are part of a biological feedback loop in which we not only receive relevant biological information from the field, but we also feed information into this field.[18] In other words, human thoughts (consciousness) and emotions (energy) interact with and encode this information into the Earth's magnetic field, and this information is then distributed on carrier waves (the signal on which the information is impressed or carried) around the globe.

To further their research and test this hypothesis, using state-of-the-art sensors located in various locations around the globe, the HeartMath Institute created the Global Coherence Monitoring System (GCMS) to observe changes in the Earth's magnetic field. Designed to measure global coherence, the GCMS uses a system of highly sensitive magnetometers to continuously measure magnetic signals that occur in the same range as human physiological frequencies, including our brain and cardiovascular systems. They also continuously monitor activity caused by solar storms, flares, and solar-wind speed activity resulting from solar storms, disruptions of the Schumann resonances, and potentially the signatures of major global events that have a strong emotional component.[19]

Why are they doing this and what does it point to? If you can intentionally create a coherent electromagnetic field around your body, and you are related or connected to someone in your life who is also intentionally creating an electromagnetic field around their body, the waves of this shared field would begin to synchronize in a nonlocal way. As the waves from both individuals synchronize, they generate bigger waves and stronger magnetic fields around you, connecting you to the Earth's electromagnetic field with an increased field of influence.

If we could create a community of people scattered all over the world, with each individual intentionally raising the energy of their own personal field toward greater peace, isn't it possible that this community could begin to produce a global effect within the Earth's electromagnetic field? This intentional community could then create coherence where there is incoherence, and order where there has been disorder.

The evidence from peace-gathering studies suggests that our thoughts and feelings do in fact have a measurable effect on every living system. You may have heard of this as the concept of emergence—envision the synchronicity of a school of fish or a flock of birds flying in unison, where all creatures appear to be operating from one mind, connected by an invisible field of energy in a nonlocal way. What is unique about this phenomenon is that it is not a top-down phenomenon, meaning there is no leader. Instead, it is a bottom-up phenomenon, meaning everyone is leading because they are acting as one mind. When a global community comes together in the name of peace, love, and coherence, according to emergence we should be able to produce an effect in the Earth's electromagnetic field, as well as in each other's fields. Just imagine, then, what it would be like if we were all behaving, living, thriving, and operating as one. If we understood we were of one mind—one organism connected and united through consciousness—we would understand that to hurt another, or affect another in any way, is to do the same to ourselves. This new paradigm in thinking would be the largest evolutionary leap our species has ever made, causing the need for warring, fighting, competing, fearing, and suffering to become an antiquated concept. But how could this possibility become a reality?

Coherence versus Incoherence

In order for us to create some type of effect in the Earth's field (which in turn can influence another individual's field), as you might guess, we have to activate two significant centers in the human body—the heart and the brain. As we learned in Chapter 4, while the brain is of course the center of consciousness and awareness, the heart—the center of oneness, wholeness, and our connection to the unified field—has its own brain. When people can regulate their internal states of care, kindness, peace, love, gratitude, thankfulness, and appreciation, as their hearts become more coherent and balanced, they send a very strong signal to the brain, causing the brain to become more coherent and balanced. This is because the heart and the brain are in continuous communication with each other.

By the same means, once someone moves beyond the association to their body, their environment, and time and takes their attention off matter and objects, they become no body, no one, no thing, no where, in no time. As you well understand by now, when they get beyond themselves and put their awareness on the immaterial world of energy, they connect to the unified field, the place where there's no longer separation between any body, any one, any thing, and any where, in any time. This causes them to unify with the consciousness of every body, every one, every thing, and every where in every time. As a consciousness, they have now entered the quantum field of energy and information, the place where consciousness and energy can influence the material world in nonlocal ways.

The side effect of this process is that it creates more coherence in the brain and in our energy so our biology becomes more whole. In our research, we've found that when the brain becomes more coherent, it affects the autonomic nervous system and the heart. The heart, our connection to the unified field, then acts like a catalyst to amplify the process of coherence back into the brain. Because the heart sends more information to the brain than the brain sends to the heart, the more coherence you can achieve through the elevated emotions of the heart, the more the brain and the heart synchronize. This synchronization produces measurable effects not only within the body, but also within the electromagnetic field surrounding the body—and the bigger the field we produce around our body, the more we can affect others in a nonlocal way. How do we know this? Because we've seen this over and over in our students' HRV measurements.

Evidence of the influence of the heart's electromagnetic field upon the field of another's heart can also be seen in a HeartMath study in which 40 participants were divided into groups of four around 10 card tables. While the heart rhythms of all four participants at the table were being measured, only three people were trained to raise their emotions through HeartMath techniques. When the three trained participants raised their energy and sent positive feelings to the untrained participant, that person also went into higher states of coherence. The authors of the study concluded that "evidence of heart-to-heart synchronization across subjects was found which lends credence to the possibility of heart-to-heart biocommunications."[20]

Key to the process of coherence is getting beyond the analytical mind. (We know this because we've measured it enough times in the brain scans of our students. Their participation has also demonstrated that with enough practice, coherence can be achieved in a relatively short amount of time.) When the thinking brain is quieted, it moves into alpha or theta brain-wave states, and this opens the doorway between the conscious and subconscious mind. The autonomic nervous system then becomes more receptive to information. By raising our energy through the feelings of elevated emotions, we become less matter and more energy, less particle and more wave. The bigger the field we can create with these energies—as energy, awareness, and consciousness—the more we can influence others in a nonlocal way.

The greater energy you can create through the elevated emotions of the heart, the more you're going to connect with the unified field, which means you're going to experience more wholeness, connection, and oneness. But you can't experience that connection when you're incoherent, feeling separate, or living by the hormones of stress. When the chemicals released during stress arouse the brain, we feel disconnected from the unified field and we tend to make less evolved choices. We know without a doubt that the emotions of competition, fear, anger, unworthiness, guilt, and shame keep us separate from one another because they produce slower and lower frequencies than elevated emotions like love, gratitude, care, and kindness, which produce faster and higher frequencies. We also know that the faster the frequency, the more energy is present. This prompted us to ask several questions:

- What if we assembled a community of several hundred people in one room, had them open their hearts and generate elevated energetic states, and then asked them to send the intention for the greatest good of a select group of people gathered in the same room?

- What would happen if the electromagnetic field around each person's body merged with the field of the person sitting next to them?

- Could those elevated emotional states then begin to produce a change in energy in the room?

- Is it possible that everybody experiencing elevated emotions and energy could begin to create coherence within a community?

Building a Collective Coherent Field

Since early 2013, we've partnered with our friends at the HeartMath Institute to further our research. Since we began measuring our students' physiological states, we've scanned thousands of brains and hearts, resulting in a significant amount of information. We have been overwhelmed and mystified by some of the data we've collected when common people start doing the uncommon.

Over the course of this journey, in collaboration with HeartMath, we've witnessed amazing measurements in our students. We've taken equally amazing measurements of the collective energy in the rooms where our students have gathered—measurements that show consistent, daily increases in energy—using a sophisticated sensor from Russia called Sputnik (mentioned briefly in Chapter 2).

Since elevated emotions, related to the activity of the autonomic nervous system, produce electromagnetic fields, increasing those emotions results in changes in blood microcirculation, perspiration, and other functions of the body. Because Sputnik is so sensitive, it can quantify environmental fluctuations by measuring barometric shifts, relative humidity, air temperature, electromagnetic fields, and more.[21]

Take a look at Graphics 15A and 15B in the color insert. In these measurements from our workshops, you can see a trend that demonstrates an increase in the collective energy of the room. The first line in red is our baseline measurement and shows the room's energy before the start of the event. As you look at the red, blue, green, and finally the brown lines (each color representing a different day), you can see that each day the energy steadily increases. In Graphics 15C and 15D, the same color scale applies; however, these measurements reflect specific time intervals during each day's morning meditations. This means our students are getting better at raising the energy of the room by creating more unified coherence.

The Sputnik readings demonstrate that the collective energy created by our students from the first day of the workshop to the final day consistently makes incremental increases. Within that trend, we've found that most groups are extremely focused and the energy rises every day. About one-quarter of the time, the energy stays relatively the same for the first day or two, but in the following days, the energy increases significantly. We believe this is because during the first day or two, the group is working on overcoming themselves by breaking the energetic emotional bonds that keep them connected to their past-present reality. So during this time, they are drawing from the unified field to build their own personal electromagnetic fields. This siphoning from the field tends to cause the collective energy in the room to drop. But once those individual fields become greater, more enhanced, and coherent, they entrain to one another, which is when we tend to see dramatic increases in the energy of the room.

Figure 13.2 shows that when two coherent waves come together, they create a bigger wave. This is called constructive interference. The bigger the wave, the higher the amplitude of energy. As a result of our students' more coherent waves coming together during our workshops, the energy of the group field increases, and then there's more energy to heal and to create or access greater levels of mind, which can sometimes lead to mystical experiences.

CONSTRUCTIVE INTERFERENCE

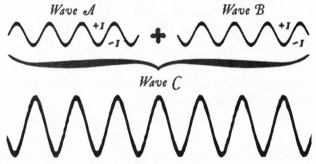

Wave A   *Wave B*

Wave C

The higher the amplitude, the higher the energy

Figure 13.2

Constructive interference is when two coherent waves come together to create a bigger wave. Amplitude is the measurement of the height of a wave. The higher the amplitude, the higher the energy. If a community of people are all gathered and are creating coherent electromagnetic fields, when their energies interfere, it makes sense that the energy of the room will increase.

My team and I have been consistently humbled by our students' profound healings, their ability to increase and regulate elevated states, and their reports of mystical experiences or acute insights into their lives as a result of learning how to regulate their brain waves, open their hearts, and go into coherence. Some of these occurrences could be labeled as miracles, but we believe it's just a part of the process of becoming supernatural. This led us to wonder if our students could affect the nervous systems of others, and if so, what the implications of that would be. These questions would spark the birth of Project Coherence.

Project Coherence

In collaboration with the HeartMath Institute, we performed numerous experiments whereby we took a small, random sampling of about 50 to 75 people at our advanced workshops, attached HRV monitors to their chests, and placed them in the front row of the room for three meditations over the course of 24 hours. Since HRV not only provides insight into the coherence of the heart, but also gives us information about the brain and emotions, we wanted to measure subjects' HRV for a full 24 hours.

To start the meditation, everyone in the room placed their attention on their heart center and began breathing through this center slowly and deeply, as you learned to do in Chapter 7. Next, they cultivated and sustained an elevated emotion for two to three minutes, broadening their hearts' electromagnetic fields and moving from a state of selfishness to a state of selflessness. Then we had the collective of 550 to 1,500 students broadcast the energy of their elevated emotions beyond their body into the space of the entire room. Next, we had them lay the intentional thought in that frequency for the greatest good of the students sitting in the front of the room wearing the HRV monitors—that their lives be enriched, their bodies be healed, and mystical experiences find them.

Our goal was to measure the collective energy in the room and its potential nonlocal effect on the people wearing the HRV monitors. Could those elevated levels of energy and frequency in the form of love, gratitude, wholeness, and joy cause another person's heart to go into coherence—even if they were on the other side of the room? Our results confirmed our hypothesis. Not only did the broadcast energy produce a coherent effect on the people wearing the HRV monitors, but each of their hearts went into coherence at the exact same time, in the exact same meditation, on the exact same day—and this was not a one-time occurrence. We repeatedly found consistent results across our events. What does this mean?

Our data supports the HeartMath Global Coherence Initiative's belief that an invisible field exists upon which information is communicated. This field links and influences all living systems, as well as our collective human consciousness. Because of this field, information is communicated nonlocally between people at a subconscious level through the autonomic nervous system.[22] In other words, we are bound and connected by an invisible field of energy, and this energy field can affect everyone's behaviors, emotional states, and conscious and unconscious thoughts.

Because all frequency carries information, the magnetic fields produced in the hearts of the student body acted as carrier waves for this information. If at our workshops we can produce nonlocal effects on others, shouldn't our elevated, heart-centered emotions be able to produce nonlocal effects on our children, partners, coworkers, or anyone we have a relationship or share a connection with?

If you look at Figure 13.3, you notice 17 people going into heart coherence at the exact same time, on the exact same day, during the exact same meditation. All of these students who went into heart coherence were being entrained by the energy of others. The students sending the energy embraced the intention for the greatest good of those people wearing the heart rate monitors. The results show that when we get out of our own way, we can become one mind and nonlocally connect to one another. Through that connection, we can influence the autonomic nervous system of others so they will feel more balanced, coherent, and whole. Imagine what could happen if you had thousands of people all doing the same for the entire world.

Shortly after these global meditation events, our students began sending us e-mails asking that since we showed that we could indeed create a measurable change in the energy of a room where 550 to 1,500 people were gathered, could we then produce the same effect on a global scale? So it was our students who requested we organize global meditations, giving birth to Project Coherence. We broadcast our first Project Coherence over Facebook in November 2015, with more than 6,000 people from all over the world joining together online to collectively create a more loving and peaceful world. In our second meditation, more than 36,000 online viewers participated, and in our third global meditation, more than 43,000 joined forces. It is our intention to continue to host these Project Coherence events, each time creating a stronger radiating influence of peace and love over the planet. In time, we hope to measure these effects.

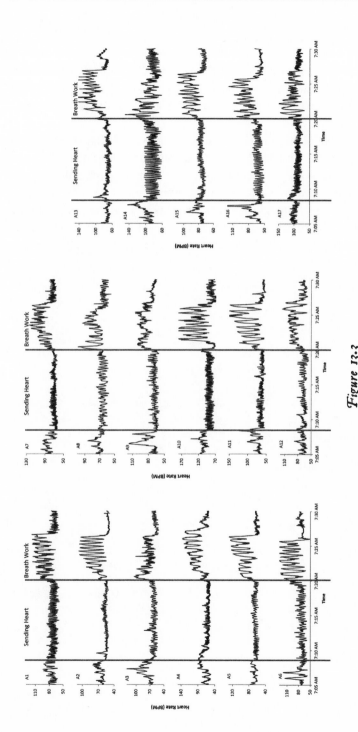

Figure 13.3

Figure 13.3. This is a graph showing 17 people going into heart coherence at the exact same time, on the exact same day, during the exact same meditation. The area between the vertical lines shows everyone going into heart coherence.

Project Coherence Meditation

Start by acknowledging your heart center. With focus and awareness, lock into that center, open your focus, and begin to become aware of the space it occupies in space, as well as the space around the space your heart occupies in space.

Then move as a thought and an awareness into the center of the Earth and radiate your light beyond the Earth in space. All I want you to do is raise your frequency and hold on to that emotion. Still as a consciousness and awareness, slowly move away from the Earth, and then take the Earth as a thought and place it in your heart. As you hold the entire planet in your heart, raise the frequency of the Earth as a thought, and broadcast that energy beyond your body in space. Radiate your love into the Earth.

Chapter 14

CASE STUDIES: IT COULD HAPPEN TO YOU

In this final set of supernatural case studies, please note that none of the people you will read about here tried to make anything happen. They simply had an intention and at the same time surrendered the outcome to something greater. When they hit that moment—whether it was a healing or a mystical experience—their personality wasn't creating the experience. Something greater came through them and did it for them. They connected to the unified field, and it was their interaction with this intelligence that moved them in some way. As you know by now after everything you have read in this book, that intelligence also lives within *you*.

Divine, Can You Hear Me?

In 2014, Stacy began experiencing severe headaches. For 25 years, she had worked in health care, as both a registered nurse and an acupuncturist. She had always maintained a healthy lifestyle and rarely took medications, so the sudden appearance of headaches so excruciating they nearly caused her to black out was alarming. After a year of exploring countless alternative therapies, she finally went to a doctor who ordered a CAT scan.

The diagnosis was a meningioma, a benign tumor that wraps around certain nerve tissue in the spinal nerves. Stacy's was sitting on or near her eighth cranial nerve, which began obstructing her acoustic nerve and creating significant changes in her neurological functions. The acoustic nerve has two branches—one for hearing and the other for balance—so in addition to unrelenting pain and loss of hearing, she was dizzy and nauseated. As the lesion grew, it also began pushing against another cranial nerve that ran along her face and continued down into her shoulder, resulting in a diagnosis of pitcher's shoulder. Soon, she also experienced pain in her eye.

According to her physician, the only solution was a craniotomy, which basically entailed drilling a large hole in the back of her head to remove the tumor. Stacy did not want to pursue this path, so she continued exploring other healing modalities. By the time she attended her first weekend workshop in Seattle in 2015, she estimated she had lost 70 percent of her hearing in her left ear. In the fall of 2016, she attended her first advanced workshop in Cancun, where she felt herself surrender at a whole new level. Then, in the winter of 2017, she attended another advanced workshop in Tampa.

On Thursday, she had a very intense earache that became much worse the next day. She said the sensation she felt was that her ear was closing up. By the end of that day, after the Blessing of the Energy Centers meditation, her earache curiously ended. Then on Sunday morning during the pineal gland meditation, Stacy lost track of time and space.

"I almost felt like I was going to fall off my chair," she said. "In that moment, this amazing flash of light consumed the left side of my head. Imagine if you put a thousand diamonds together and shined a light on them—that wouldn't even begin to touch this light. Then—*boom!*" Her body shot upright and a bluish-white light, like nothing she had ever seen or experienced, entered her ear.

"It was the most divine, loving feeling that I've ever had," she reported. "I felt like the hand of God was caressing me with grace. It was so powerful and amazing that I struggle to put it into words, but every time I think of it, I still cry."

First, her sinuses cleared, then the whole left side of her head cleared, and then her left shoulder relaxed and let go. Finally, for the first time in three years, she could hear out of her left ear.

"I just sat there in awe, laughing and crying as tears flowed down my face," she said. "Music was playing and I could hear it crystal clear. It was as if I could hear the celestial sound of angels singing above the song. I knew what I was hearing was beyond the normal auditory range. The energy continued to move through the back of the left side of my head, which for years had felt like cement."

When I instructed everyone to lie down, relax, and let the autonomic nervous system take the orders, the energy continued to move through Stacy's whole body, down her arms, and into her hands. She began to shake uncontrollably.

"It was as if I could feel every synapse and muscle in my body firing—in my toes, my legs, my head, and my neck and chest. My heart center felt wide open. I just remember thinking, *Whatever this is, I'm taking the ride.*" She completely surrendered to the unknown and once again, she lost track of time and space.

When that portion of the meditation ended, she found herself sitting in her chair, with the energy slowing and quieting down. Her thinking brain began to kick in. Even though she could hear, she began to doubt what had just occurred; perhaps her ear was not totally healed, perhaps the tumor was still present, or perhaps she wasn't even worthy of healing. No sooner did she have that thought than the energy and light appeared in front of her. But this energy was different.

"It was red like the heart and blue like energy, and it was three-dimensional," she remembered. "It was about two feet in front of me and was almost slithering like a snake. All this was happening with my eyes closed. It was multidimensional, beautiful, crazy, gorgeous, fractal, and it came right up to my face. It was almost as if this energy wanted to say, 'You have doubts? We'll show *you*!' Then it shot into my heart, my chest opened up, I sat back on the chair, and my arms fell wide open. I knew it was the energy of everything—the energy of chi, of Spirit, of the divine, of the universe.

"Life is different now," she told me. "For one, my hearing is at a hundred percent. But it's more than that. It's hard to put into words, but I know that no matter what, I'm going to be okay. Life will never be the same because I know underneath everything, it's Spirit who is looking to be heard and healed."

Janet Hears "You Are Mine"

While Janet occasionally meditated, it was never a regular habit—yet one afternoon 25 years ago during a meditation, she had what she calls a spontaneous experience. With her eyes closed, she was suddenly in the presence of an incredibly bright light, yet the light had a softness that didn't hurt her eyes. She described it as the purest, most intense, perfect love she had ever experienced. For the next 25 years, she prayed, meditated, and did everything else she could to try to re-create that transcendental experience.

In the spring of 2015, Janet attended an advanced workshop in Carefree, Arizona. She was in a state of deep depression and exhaustion, unable to see any solutions to the problems in her life, yet she was determined to have a healing or breakthrough. Above all else, she was excited to be with more than 500 people united in the belief that they were greater than their physical bodies.

For the duration of the workshop, Janet went after the mystical with a level of intensity that was greater than her depression. During the pineal gland meditation, she was sitting in the lotus position and resting her loving intention in the space of her pineal gland. All of a sudden the gland activated and a brilliant white light coming from inside her head illuminated her pineal gland. It was the same light she had experienced 25 years earlier.

"The light came into the space of my pineal gland and illuminated all of the crystals in the little cave of that tiny gland," she later explained. "The light continued to illuminate my entire being down to the cellular level. My spine then straightened, my head went back, and I just embraced it—I just let it all happen. I was simultaneously in ecstasy, bliss, gratitude, and love."

Next an inverted triangle of light came down from above her, through the top of her head. She knew this triangle was the presence of a loving intelligence. The point of the inverted triangle joined the peak of her pineal gland, forming a double-geometric shape. The intense frequency of coherent light was carrying a message for Janet. The light kept saying to Janet over and over, "You are mine. You are mine," which she took to mean, "I love you more than anything else in the world."

"Please enter and take charge of my life," Janet responded, and as she surrendered to it, she started to experience a download of information coming through the top of her head in the form of the brilliant light. The light was threaded with strands that looked like luminous cobalt-blue pearls. The light moved slowly and descended through her entire body. This energy was the result of a reverse torus field (the field that moves in the opposite direction of the upward field created during the breath), and it was energy from the unified field—from beyond the visible light spectrum and beyond our senses. The inner experience was so real that it rewired her brain and sent a new emotional energetic signal to her body, and in an instant her past was washed away. The download of the frequency of coherence and wholeness gave her body a biological upgrade. By the time she left the workshop, her depression and her exhaustion were completely gone. "This ecstatic experience," she insisted, "has changed my life forever."

Connected beyond Time and Space by Love

During a Project Coherence meditation broadcast from Lake Garda, Italy, participants from all over the world joined us in the belief that we are more than just matter, bodies, and particles and that consciousness influences matter and the world. During the meditation, Sasha was in New Jersey visualizing bringing the Earth into her heart.

"When we went to the heart, I felt all of these shoots and leaves growing from my heart center and through my body," she told me. "There were branches, leaves, and blossoms coming out my arms, fingers, and ears, as well as white blossoms all over my face. I had literally become the surface of the Earth garden."

As soon as the meditation was over, Sasha looked down at her phone and saw that her best friend, Heather, had sent her a picture from Ireland. While we had been doing the meditation, Heather had been walking through a garden. She happened to look down and saw moss growing on a rock in the shape of a heart. Heather took a picture of the moss with her phone and sent it to Sasha with a note that said, "Saw this and had the overwhelming feeling of your presence. Love you."

Donna Helps Souls Cross Over

When Donna attended her first weekend workshop in 2014 in Long Beach, California, she never would have called herself a meditator—she'd only meditated a handful of times before. A technical writer, she had a very analytical mind. But that's the beauty of this work: When you have no expectations, you are often more open to wherever the experience takes you. So she was totally taken by surprise when at some point during one of her meditations that weekend, she slipped out of her everyday consciousness and found herself surrounded by hundreds of interdimensional beings.

"They weren't angry or malevolent," she told me, "but it was very clear to me that they wanted something from me. Some of them were fairly young—like 12 or 13. I knew immediately they were the people my fiancé had killed."

Donna was engaged to a former United States Army Ranger, and during his service in Iraq, he'd been a sniper. When Donna returned home from the workshop and told her fiancé about her experience, he confirmed that some of the people he killed to protect his fellow soldiers were quite young.

While she found the connection curious and fascinating, she didn't know what to do with the information, but there was no question in her mind that the experience was real because it was beyond anything she could have simply conjured.

Two years later, Donna was at an advanced workshop in Carefree, Arizona. After completing the first meditation, she turned to a friend sitting next to her and said in a daze, without even being aware of what she was saying, "There are beings in this room, and they are here to help us."

Early Sunday morning, for the pineal gland meditation, Donna was slated to have her brain scanned. Once again, at some point during the meditation, Donna found herself suddenly in the company of the same interdimensional beings who had surrounded her during her first workshop two years earlier. But this time they were standing in a line off to her right.

"Again, I felt like they wanted something from me, but I didn't know what it was," she said. "Then, in my mind's eye, as though I was looking through a virtual-reality headset, I saw another line forming on my left. There were two types of beings in this line. One type looked human-like, but they were very large and had a shimmering golden look, and the other type seemed to have a blue hue to them."

She innately knew that if she took the people who were killed by her fiancé in the war, who were lined up on the right, and gave them to the beings on the left, the people on the right would receive what they needed. Because the people who had been killed by sniper fire had died so suddenly, without any warning, some were confused about whether they were alive or dead. Some weren't sure where to go or what to do, while others were trying to stay in this dimension because they were attached to their loved ones and couldn't move on. They were stuck in between matter and light, yet somehow they recognized that Donna was the bridge, or the facilitator, who could help them cross over. And it was all happening in a very real, very lucid experience.

"To say I handed them over to the other beings is not quite right," she explained, "but it was something like me passing them over. It's really beyond language, but when they passed to the other side, it seemed like they passed through the other beings. And then I could see them running across a field of waist-high red mist. I could feel all the freedom, joy, and happiness they were experiencing as they ran across this field."

Again, as if looking through a virtual-reality headset, Donna turned to the right in her mind's eye and saw a winding dirt road filled with people stretching far into the distance. She sensed they were from Bosnia and Serbia, which she couldn't quite make sense of.

"It felt almost as if the word got out. I didn't have the sense that they were unaware they were dead. It was more like they were stuck in limbo—they didn't know how to get to the other side." This was the longest meditation of the workshop, perhaps two to three hours, but to Donna, it seemed like it was ten minutes.

Donna attended another advanced workshop in Cancun in the fall of 2016. This time, when I asked the students to surrender their consciousness to merge with the consciousness of the unified field, Donna had the experience of becoming the universe. She went from the consciousness of some body, some thing, some one, some where, in some time, to the consciousness of no body, no thing, no one, no where, in no time, to the consciousness of every body, every thing, every one, every where, in every time. In the instant her consciousness connected with the unified field—the field of information that governs the laws and forces of the universe—she *became* the universe. She was in bliss.

"Since that experience, my life has become magical and I'm experiencing a new energy and vitality like never before," she reported later. "I keep having one powerful experience after another, and I can never go back to the way my life was before starting to practice this work."

Jerry Returns from the Brink of Death

On August 14, 2015, Jerry was putting a project together on his back deck. As he was reading the directions, he felt a sudden sharp pain right below his sternum. He thought perhaps it was gas, so he took some medication, but it didn't go away. Instead, he lay down to rest and it got worse.

By the time he tried to get up, he started losing his ability to stand and thought he might pass out. As the pain became more intense and his breathing grew shorter, he called an ambulance. With all his might, he dragged himself about 15 feet outside to the driveway so the paramedics wouldn't have to kick in his door. Kneeling on the driveway, he collapsed waiting for the emergency medical technicians. When they arrived, they assumed he was having a heart attack and immediately began to follow that protocol.

"You guys don't understand. I'm having a really hard time breathing," he told them. "We have to get to the hospital right away." Jerry knew what he was talking about. He'd worked for 34 years as a medical technician in the very emergency room where they were about to take him.

Jerry knew everyone in the ER, and once he arrived, doctors, nurses, technicians, and specialists began frantically running lab work on him. When a doctor who was also Jerry's friend told Jerry that red flags had come up in every test administered, Jerry knew things were not looking good. One test in particular was particularly alarming; his levels of protease, amylase, and lipase (enzymes produced by the pancreas) were 4,000 to 5,000 units per liter, way above the norm of about 100 to 200. They put Jerry in the intensive care unit.

"The pain soon worsened, and none of the drugs they were giving me worked," Jerry said. "They told me that a duct to my gallbladder had been blocked and it was causing trouble in my pancreas. Worst of all, fluid started to develop in my lungs. I was now down by 80 percent breathing capacity in both lungs. That's when the doctors put me on a ventilator, and I knew things were bad." The doctor then asked his team to "turn on the TV to Boston," allowing the doctor to have an immediate teleconference with other doctors in a larger hospital in the nearest big city.

"In all the time I'd worked at the hospital, I'd only seen the TV to Boston come on a few times for the most serious of traumas or for people who were dying," Jerry said. "It means they have no idea what is happening. When a doctor you have trusted for years tells you they don't know what's going on . . . well, that's when my stress hormones started to kick into high gear." While all of this was happening, the medical staff told Jerry's wife that if there was any end-of-life paperwork she needed to get in order, now would be the time to go home and get it. She left sobbing.

Jerry soon realized he needed to start taking care of himself. He knew that if he allowed the stress hormones to start taking over, he was not going to win.

"I went from being a guy who hadn't been sick in years, who did yoga all the time and ate well, to all of a sudden being in the ICU. I kept telling myself, *I can't go down this road. I can't give in to the fear*—so I didn't." Since he'd recently read my book *You Are the Placebo*, he started thinking, *I gotta change these thought patterns. I can't allow these thoughts to make more cortisol to get into the body and start doing more damage to what's left of me.*

The doctors eventually found out that Jerry had a large mass blocking a duct in his pancreas. The mass was not letting the mucus drain, so everything in the gland was backing up and spilling over into his bloodstream.

"My doctors stayed with me for three days straight," he says. "They put an oxygen mask on me because I couldn't breathe. I had IVs on both sides, and meanwhile, I kept thinking, *Watch your thoughts, relax, put something into the quantum field that's going to help you and not hurt you, because you're already knocking on the door. I'm gonna be okay. This too shall pass. I'm gonna be all right.*" Whenever he was conscious, Jerry placed his energy on overcoming himself, changing his state of being, and creating a different outcome—constantly tuning in to a different potential in the unified field. Fortunately, he had a private room, giving him plenty of opportunity to do his meditations whenever he wanted to.

Jerry spent a week in the ICU, and by the end of that time when he moved to a progressive care unit, the oxygen mask was gone and Jerry was walking around. Even so, he could not eat or drink anything for nine weeks. (If he ate anything, or even had water, his pancreas would release acid into his body, eventually killing him.) The only nourishment he received was through an IV.

When Jerry was admitted to the hospital, he weighed 145 pounds. When he was discharged, he weighed 119. When he finally went home (still with an IV pole), he continued to do the work. As October drew near, the mass was still present. His doctors suggested he see a specialist in Boston to undergo surgery. Because Jerry was a medical professional, two days before the surgery he suggested his medical team take some more tests and scans so the doctors would have the most up-to-date information.

"I know all the x-ray technicians and yet when they told me I no longer had a mass, I didn't believe them. I called in the radiologists and the doctors. They just kept saying, 'Jerry, we're looking at your film right now. We're telling you, there's nothing there. I'm calling the guys in Boston to tell them there will be no surgery.'"

Jerry later realized that by constantly raising his energy, moving into a feeling of health, and changing the thoughts and belief that he was sick to the thoughts and belief he was going to be fine, the higher frequency caused him to heal.

"I wasn't going to allow myself to think, *Woe is me. This is gonna be bad.* I kept working on this every day, for as much of the day as I could. I put the right message, intention, and energy out into the quantum field to heal myself—and eventually, I did."

AFTERWORD
Being Peace

What I hope you take away from this book is that it's not enough to change your state of being only when you meditate. It's not sufficient to just think and feel peace with your eyes closed, and then open them and carry on throughout the day in limited, unconscious states of mind and body. In many of the peace-gathering projects and studies mentioned in Chapter 13, when the experiments concluded, very often the reduced violence and crime returned to their former baseline levels. This means that we actually have to demonstrate peace, which requires us to get our bodies involved, and that means we have to move from thinking to doing.

Every time we change our state of being and begin our day by opening our hearts to the elevated states that connect us to a love for life, a joy for existence, the inspiration to be alive, a state of gratitude that our future has already happened, and a level of kindness toward others, we must carry, maintain, and demonstrate that energy and state of being throughout the day—whether we are sitting, standing, walking, or lying down. Then, when upsetting events occur in our lives or in the world, if we demonstrate peace rather than unconsciously act in predictable, so-called natural reactionary ways (expressing anger, frustration, violence, fear, suffering, or aggression), we are no longer contributing to the world's old consciousness. By breaking that cycle and demonstrating peace by example, we give others permission to do the same. Because knowledge is for the mind and experience is for the body, when we move from thinking to doing—and experience the corresponding emotions of peace and inner balance—the moment we begin to embody peace is when we really begin to change the program.

By tempering those reactive behaviors, and thus no longer creating the same redundant experiences and emotions, we no longer fire and wire the same circuits in the brain. This is how we cease conditioning the body to live in the self-limiting emotions of the mind, and this is how we change ourselves and our relationship to the world around us. Every time we do this, we are literally teaching our body to chemically understand what our mind has intellectually understood. This is how we select and instruct the latent genes that cause us to thrive—not just survive. Now peace is *within* us and we are knocking on the genetic door to biologically *become* exactly that. Isn't that what every great charismatic leader, saint, mystic, and master throughout history has continually preached?

Of course, it's going to feel unnatural in the beginning to go against years of automatic conditioning, unconscious habits, reflexive emotional reactions, hardwired attitudes, and generations of genetic programming, but that is exactly how we become supernatural. To do what feels unnatural means going against how we have all been genetically programmed or socially conditioned to live when we are threatened in some way. I'm sure any creature that has broken from the consciousness of the tribe, the pack, the school, or the herd in order to adapt to a changing environment must have felt the discomfort and uncertainty of the unknown. But let's not forget that living in the unknown means we are in the realm of possibility.

The real challenge is not to return to the level of mediocrity that the prevailing social consciousness agrees on merely because we don't see anyone else doing what we are doing. True leadership never needs confirmation from others. It just requires a clear vision and a change in energy—that is, a new state of being—that is sustained for a long enough period of time and executed with a strong enough will that it causes others to raise their own energy and become inspired to do the same. Once they do raise themselves from their own limited state of being to a new energy, they see the same future that their leader sees. There is power in numbers.

After all my years of teaching people about personal transformation, I know no one changes until they change their energy. In fact, when someone is truly engaged in change, they are less likely to talk about it and more prone to demonstrate it. They are working on living it. This requires awareness, intent, staying present, and constant attention to their inner states. Perhaps the biggest hurdle is not only being uncomfortable but also being okay with being uncomfortable, because discomfort is our challenge to grow. It makes us feel more alive.

After all, if stress and the survival response are the result of not being able to predict our future (thinking or believing that we are unable to control an outcome or that things are going to get worse), then opening our minds and hearts to believe in possibility requires going against thousands of years of genetically hardwired survival traits. We must lay down the very thing that we have always used to get what we want for something much better to occur. To me, that's true greatness.

If we can do it once, disturb those neural networks equated with anger, resentment, and retribution and instead activate the neural networks related to experiences of caring, giving, and nurturing (and so create the corresponding emotions), then we should be able do it again—and the repetition of these choices will neurochemically condition our mind and body to become one. When the body knows how to do this as well as the mind, it becomes innate, familiar, easy, and second nature. Then, thinking and demonstrating peace, which once required focused awareness, becomes a subconscious program. Now we've created a new, automatic peaceful state of being, and again, that means that now peace is *within* us.

This is how we memorize a new internal neurochemical order that's greater than any conditions in our external environment. Now we're not just being peace, but mastering it, as well as mastering ourselves and our environment. Once enough of us can achieve this state of being— once everybody is locked into the same energy, frequency, and elevated consciousness—just like schools of fish or flocks of birds moving as one in a unified order, we'll begin to act as one mind and emerge as a new species. But if we continue to act as a cancerous organism at war with itself, our species will not survive, and evolution will continue its grand experiment.

Take time out of your busy life to invest in yourself, because when you do, you are investing in your future. If your familiar environment is controlling how you think and feel, it's time to retreat from your life and go inward so you can reverse the process of being a victim of life and instead become a creator of it. After reading this book, by now you know that it's possible to change yourself from within and that when you do, it will be reflected in your outer world.

This is a time in history when it is not enough to simply *know*; this is a time to *know how.* According to the philosophical understanding and scientific principles of quantum physics, neuroscience, and epigenetics, we now understand that our subjective mind influences the objective world. Because mind influences matter, we are compelled to study the nature of mind; our understanding then allows us to assign meaning to what we're doing. If knowledge is the precursor to experience, then the more knowledge we have about how powerful we are, as well as understanding the science behind how things work, the more we can understand the limitlessness of our potential, both as individuals and as a collective.

Because we are constantly deepening and broadening our understanding of the interconnectedness of all living systems, and because each of us is a contributor to the Earth's field, I believe we can collectively create and guide a new, peaceful, and prosperous future upon this planet. It all begins by making a habit of practicing leading with our hearts, raising our energy, and tuning in to greater information and frequencies of love and wholeness. With effort and intention, we should begin to produce a coherent electromagnetic signature. Just like dropping pebbles in a still lake over and over, as we continue to raise our energy and open our hearts, we're producing bigger and bigger electromagnetic fields. This energy is information, and we each have the power to direct our energy with intention to produce nonlocal effects on the nature of reality.

When we direct our energy as an observer, a consciousness, or a thought, we can begin to affect a downward causation of matter—in other words, we can literally make our minds matter. When we practice these concepts on a consistent basis—changing our levels of energy from survival states to greater levels of awareness, compassion, love, gratitude, and other elevated emotions—these coherent electromagnetic signatures entrain to one another. The effect should then be that we can unify communities that were once separated by the belief that we are just matter. Once we transition our state of being from survival into love, gratitude, and creation, then instead of reacting to violence, terrorism, fear, prejudice, competition, selfishness, and separation (which, by the way, the media, commercials, video games, and all types of stimulation are constantly reminding and *programming* us to live within), we can come together during crisis. We will have no further need for splintering, assigning blame, or seeking revenge.

Every time we meditate as a global community, we're casting a larger, stronger coherent wave of love and altruism around the world. If we do this enough times, we should be able to not only measure the changes in energy and frequency around the world, but measure our efforts by the positive changes in the events that take place in our future.

To stand up for justice and peace, then, you must first find peace within yourself. You must then demonstrate peace to others, which means you can't make a stand for peace or be peace while you're warring with your neighbor, hating your coworker, or judging your boss.

If everybody (and I mean every body) chose peace, and if we came together at the exact same time, imagine the type of positive change we could create in our collective future. There would be no conflict. What's equally powerful is that when we are the living embodiment of peace, we show up as unpredictable to others and then they pay attention. Thanks to mirror neurons (a special class of brain cells that fire when we see someone perform an action), we are biologically wired to mimic each other's behavior. Modeling peace, justice, love, kindness, care, understanding, and compassion allows others to open their hearts and move from fearful, aggressive states of survival to feeling wholeness and connectedness. Think what would happen if we all understood how interconnected we were to one another and to the field, rather than feeling separated and isolated: We might actually begin to take responsibility for our thoughts and emotions because we would finally understand how our state of being affects all of life. This is how we begin to change the world—by first changing ourselves.

The future of humanity does not rest on one person, leader, or messiah with a greater consciousness to show us the way. Rather, it requires the evolution of a new collective consciousness, because it is through the acknowledgment and application of the interconnectedness of human consciousness that we can change the course of history.

While it appears old structures and paradigms are collapsing, we should not face this with fear, anger, or sadness, because this is the process by which evolution and new things occur. Instead we should face the future with a whole new light, energy, and consciousness. As I have mentioned, the old has to fall apart and fall away before something new flourishes. Integral to this process is not squandering our energy by emotionally reacting to leaders or people in power. When they capture our emotions, they capture our attention, and thus they have captured our energy. This is how people gain power over us. Instead we must make a stand for principles, values, and moral imperatives like freedom, justice, truth, and equality. When we achieve this through the power of the collective, we will unite behind the energy of oneness rather than be controlled by the idea of separation. This is when standing up for truth is no longer personal, but through unifying and building community, becomes universal.

I believe we are on the verge of a great evolutionary jump. Another way to say it is that we are going through an initiation. After all, isn't an initiation a rite of passage from one level of consciousness to another, and isn't it designed to challenge the fabric of who we are so we can grow to a greater potential? Maybe when we see, remember, and awaken to who we truly are, human beings can move as a collective consciousness from a state of surviving into a state of thriving. It's then that we can emerge into our true nature and fully access our innate capacity as human beings—which is to give, to love, to serve, and to take care of one another and the Earth.

So why not ask yourself every day, *What would love do?*

This is who we really are, and this is the future I'm creating—one in which each and every one of us becomes supernatural.

ACKNOWLEDGMENTS

The conception of *Becoming Supernatural* came out of an impromptu conversation with the powers that be at Hay House a few years ago. Little did I know when I was sharing a meal with CEO Reid Tracy, CFO Margarete Nielsen, and vice president Patty Gift that I would be talking about some ideas I had been considering for a new book.

Upon reflection, I think I might have been set up. Hindsight is 20-20.

Something I said must have impressed them because a week later, I agreed to give birth to a book that would be based on new paradigms that I felt would take an enormous amount of effort to write in a simple and coherent manner. The accumulation of continuous research, ongoing data gathering, rigorous measurements and analysis, concise organizational logistics, event planning, scheduling thousands of scientific scans during our events, and tireless hours of intense dialogue with scientists as well as my team about our measurements are not for the faint of heart. Since so much of what we were observing fell outside of scientific convention, it required making a lot of time to meet with me—and a passionate commitment to wrap our minds around such novelty.

It takes a great type of person to stay the course and believe in a vision that exists in the mind of someone else, especially when that abstraction may not even be clear in their own minds. But when there is a steadfast conviction in possibility combined with a passion to make something a tangible reality, magic happens. And that's where I have had the privilege to work with amazing people who have unified as a team. It has been a true blessing for me to be part of such an amazing culture of people.

Once again, I would like to express my sincere thanks to the Hay House family for their trust and confidence in me. It is a joy to be a part of such a community of kindred spirits who demonstrate such kindness, support, and competence. Thank you Reid Tracy, Patty Gift, Margarete Nielsen, Stacey Smith, Richelle Fredson, Lindsay McGinty, Blaine Todfield, Perry Crowe, Celeste Phillips, Tricia Breidenthal, Diane Thomas, Sheridan McCarthy, Caroline DiNofia, Karim Garcia, Marlene Robinson, Lisa Bernier, Michael Goldstein, Joan D. Shapiro, and the rest of the family. I hope that we have all grown from working together.

Special thanks to my Hay House editor Anne Barthel, who lives life with such elegance and grace. Thank you for your endless hours of caring and expertise—and your endurance with me. I am humbled by your humility.

I would like to acknowledge my editors Katy Koontz and Tim Shields for giving so much. Your contribution to my work has been outstanding. Thank you for being so willing to dig so deep.

I would also like to recognize all the people who have participated as my Encephalon team for their ongoing service in supporting me. Thank you to Paula Meyer, Katina Dispenza, Rhadell Hovda, Adam Boyce, Kristen Michaelis, Belinda Dawson, Donna Flanagan, Reilly Hovda, Janet Therese, Shashanin Quackenbush, Amber Lordier, Andrew Wright, Lisa Fitkin, Aaron Brown, Vicki Higgins, Justin Kerrihard, Johan Pool, and Ariel Maguire. I'd also like to recognize the spouses and partners of my staff for being so understanding and unconditional and for allowing your significant others to put so much time and energy into changing people's lives with me.

A special dose of gratitude goes to Barry Goldstein, the fabulous composer of most of our meditation music. Thank you for making me fall in love with music again.

Natalie Ledwell of Mind Movies has given so much to our cause. I appreciate your passion for transformation as well as our friendship. You have helped me change many lives.

I'd like to recognize my best friend, John Dispenza. I appreciate your patience and enthusiasm. I love the interior artwork, the figures, and the fabulous cover design. Your talent is truly stellar.

I'd like to acknowledge our superb and brilliant brain-science team. They are Danijela Debelic, M.D.; Thomas Feiner, the director of the Institute for EEG-Neurofeedback; Normen Schack, OT, I.F.E.N.; Frank Hegger, OT, I.F.E.N; Claudia Ruiz; and Judi Stivers. I want to thank you for your excellent work, your ability to give and to serve with such vital energy, your passion to make a difference in the world, and your open minds and hearts. I am blessed to know all of you. I would also like to thank you for your contribution in providing all the brain scans, for providing state-of-the-art equipment, for your superb analysis, for the accumulation of all the data, and for taking the time out of your busy lives to have long conversations with me about what is natural and what is supernatural. Most importantly, thank you for teaching me and believing in me. You are all a breath of fresh air and belong to the future.

Also, I want to recognize Melissa Waterman, B.S., M.S.W., for your expertise in our GDV and Sputnik measurements. Thank you for giving so much and for making the research so available for me. And for always showing up and being there.

A big shout out to Dawson Church, Ph.D., for your genius and friendship. It was you who also believed that we could change genetic expression in common people in just a few days at our workshops. I am grateful for you being on the team and for being such a resource of scientific practicality. I am blessed to know you.

A very special thank you to Rollin McCraty, Ph.D., Jackie Waterman, Howard Martin, and the entire team at the HeartMath Institute. You have been so instrumental in our research and so selfless in everything you've given. I am blessed by our relationship.

I would like to express my gratitude to the team that manages my corporate training company. They are Suzanne Qualia, Beth Wolfson, and Florence Yaeger. Thank you for maintaining a vision with me. In addition, I have such a special appreciation to the rest of my corporate trainers around the world who work so diligently in becoming the living example of change and leadership for so many.

I would like to thank Justine Ruszczyk, who really took the time to understand this work on a very deep level. Thank you for helping me with the development of some of the coaching program. I'm looking forward to our paths crossing again.

Thanks to Gregg Braden for writing such a heart-centered and powerful foreword. You are a real-life exemplar. Our friendship is so valuable to me.

I cannot express enough gratitude to Roberta Brittingham. You still remain the most wonderful, mysterious, heart-centered person I have ever met. Thank you for your love and support. I would also like to express my appreciation for your work with the creation of the kaleidoscope. No one other than you could have made it into such a work of art.

To my children, Jace, Gianna, and Shen, who are such unique and healthy young adults, thank you for being so generous in giving me the time to follow my passion.

Finally, I would like to acknowledge our community of students who are engaged in this work. I am inspired by so many of you. You are *Becoming Supernatural.*

ENDNOTES

Introduction

1. Global Union of Scientists for Peace, "Defusing World Crises: A Scientific Approach," https://www.gusp.org/defusing-world-crises/scientific-research/.

2. F. A. Popp, W. Nagl, K. H. Li, et al., "Biophoton Emission: New Evidence for Coherence and DNA as Source," *Cell Biophysics*, vol. 6, no. 1: pp. 33–52 (1984).

Chapter 1

1. R. M. Sapolsky, *Why Zebras Don't Get Ulcers* (New York: Times Books, 2004). In addition, emotional addiction is a concept taught at Ramtha's School of Enlightenment; see JZK Publishing, a division of JZK, Inc., the publishing house for RSE, at http://jzkpublishing.com or http://www.ramtha.com.

Chapter 2

1. Also known as Hebb's Rule or Hebb's Law; see D. O. Hebb, *The Organization of Behavior: A Neuropsychological Theory* (New York: John Wiley & Sons, 1949).

2. L. Song, G. Schwartz, and L. Russek, "Heart-Focused Attention and Heart-Brain Synchronization: Energetic and Physiological Mechanisms," *Alternative Therapies in Health and Medicine*, vol. 4, no. 5: pp. 44–52, 54–60, 62 (1998); D. L. Childre, H. Martin, and D. Beech, *The HeartMath Solution: The Institute of HeartMath's Revolutionary Program for Engaging the Power of the Heart's Intelligence* (San Francisco: HarperSanFrancisco, 1999), p. 33.

3. A. Pascual-Leone, D. Nguyet, L. G. Cohen, et al., "Modulation of Muscle Responses Evoked by Transcranial Magnetic Stimulation During the Acquisition of New Fine Motor Skills," *Journal of Neurophysiology*, vol. 74, no. 3: pp. 1037–1045 (1995).

4. P. Cohen, "Mental Gymnastics Increase Bicep Strength," *New Scientist*, vol. 172, no. 2318: p. 17 (2001), http://www.newscientist.com/article/dn1591 -mental-gymnastics-increase-bicep-strength.html#.Ui03PLzk_Vk.

5. W. X. Yao, V. K. Ranganathan, D. Allexandre, et al., "Kinesthetic Imagery Training of Forceful Muscle Contractions Increases Brain Signal and Muscle Strength," *Frontiers in Human Neuroscience*, vol. 7: p. 561 (2013).

6. B. C. Clark, N. Mahato, M. Nakazawa, et al., "The Power of the Mind: The Cortex as a Critical Determinant of Muscle Strength/Weakness," *Journal of Neurophysiology*, vol. 112, no. 12: pp. 3219–3226 (2014).

7. D. Church, A. Yang, J. Fannin, et al., "The Biological Dimensions of Transcendent States: A Randomized Controlled Trial," presented at French Energy Psychology Conference, Lyon, France, March 18, 2017.

Chapter 3

1. N. Bohr, "On the Constitution of Atoms and Molecules," *Philosophical Magazine*, vol. 26, no. 151: pp. 1–25 (1913).

2. Church, Yang, Fannin, et al., "The Biological Dimensions of Transcendent States: A Randomized Controlled Trial."

3. Childre, Martin, and Beech, *The HeartMath Solution*.

4. "Mind Over Matter," *Wired* (April 1, 1995), https://www.wired.com/1995/04/ pear.

Chapter 4

1. Popp, Nagl, Li, et al., "Biophoton Emission: New Evidence for Coherence and DNA as Source."

2. L. Fehmi and J. Robbins, *The Open-Focus Brain: Harnessing the Power of Attention to Heal Mind and Body* (Boston: Trumpeter Books, 2007).

3. A. Hadhazy, "Think Twice: How the Gut's 'Second Brain' Influences Mood and Well-Being," *Scientific American Global RSS* (February 12, 2010), http:// www.scientificamerican.com/article/gut-second-brain/.

4. C. B. Pert, *Molecules of Emotion* (New York: Scribner, 1997).

5. F. A. Popp, "Biophotons and Their Regulatory Role in Cells," *Frontier Perspectives* (The Center for Frontier Sciences at Temple University, Philadelphia), vol. 7, no. 2: pp. 13–22 (1988).

6. C. Sylvia with W. Novak, *A Change of Heart: A Memoir* (New York: Warner Books, 1997).

7. P. Pearsall, *The Heart's Code: Tapping the Wisdom and Power of Our Heart Energy* (New York: Broadway Books, 1998), p. 7.

Chapter 5

1. M. Szegedy-Maszak, "Mysteries of the Mind: Your Unconscious Is Making Your Everyday Decisions," *U.S. News & World Report* (February 28, 2005).

2. M. B. DeJarnette, "Cornerstone," *The American Chiropractor*, pp. 22, 23, 28, 34 (July/August 1982).

3. Ibid.

4. D. Church, G. Yount, S. Marohn, et al., "The Epigenetic and Psychological Dimensions of Meditation," presented at Omega Institute, August 26, 2017. Submitted for publication.

Chapter 6

1. "Electromagnetic Fields and Public Health: Electromagnetic Sensitivity," World Health Organization backgrounder (December 2005), http://www.who.int/peh-emf/publications/facts/fs296/en/; WHO workshop on electromagnetic hypersensitivity (October 25–27, 2004), Prague, Czech Republic, http://www.who.int/peh-emf/meetings/hypersensitivity_prague2004/en/.

Chapter 7

1. D. Mozzaffarian, E. Benjamin, A. S. Go, et al. on behalf of the American Heart Association Statistics Committee and Stroke Statistics Subcommittee, "Heart Disease and Stroke Statistics—2016 Update: A Report from the American Heart Association," *Circulation*, 133:e38–e360 (2016).

2. Childre, Martin, and Beech, *The HeartMath Solution*.

3. HeartMath Institute, "The Heart's Intuitive Intelligence: A Path to Personal, Social and Global Coherence," https://www.youtube.com/watch?v=QdneZ4fIIHE (April 2002).

4. Church, Yang, Fannin, et al., "The Biological Dimensions of Transcendent States: A Randomized Controlled Trial."; Church, Yount, Marohn, et al., "The Epigenetic and Psychological Dimensions of Meditation."

5. R. McCraty, M. Atkinson, D. Tomasino, et al., "The Coherent Heart: Heart-Brain Interactions, Psychophysiological Coherence, and the Emergence of System-Wide Order," *Integral Review*, vol. 5, no. 2: pp.10–115 (2009).

6. T. Allison, D. Williams, T. Miller, et al., "Medical and Economic Costs of Psychologic Distress in Patients with Coronary Artery Disease," *Mayo Clinic Proceedings*, vol. 70, no. 8: pp. 734–742 (August 1995).

7. R. McCraty and M. Atkinson, "Resilience Training Program Reduces Physiological and Psychological Stress in Police Officers," *Global Advances in Health and Medicine*, vol. 1, no. 5: pp. 44–66 (2012).

8. M. Gazzaniga, "The Ethical Brain," *The New York Times* (June 19, 2005), http://www.nytimes.com/2005/06/19/books/chapters/the-ethical-brain.html.

9. R. McCraty, "Advanced Workshop with Dr. Joe Dispenza," Carefree Resort and Conference Center, Carefree, Arizona (February 23, 2014).

10. W. Tiller, R. McCraty, and M. Atkinson, "Cardiac Coherence: A New, Noninvasive Measure of Autonomic Nervous System Order," *Alternative Therapies in Health and Medicine*, vol. 2, no. 1: pp. 52–65 (1996).

11. McCraty, Atkinson, Tomasino, et al., "The Coherent Heart: Heart-Brain Interactions, Psychophysiological Coherence, and the Emergence of System-Wide Order."

12. R. McCraty and F. Shaffer, "Heart Rate Variability: New Perspectives on Physiological Mechanisms, Assessment of Self-Regulatory Capacity, and Health Risk," *Global Advances in Health and Medicine*, vol. 4, no. 1: pp. 46–61 (2015); S. Segerstrom and L. Nes, "Heart Rate Variability Reflects Self-Regulatory Strength, Effort, and Fatigue," *Psychological Science*, vol. 18, no. 3: pp. 275–281 (2007); R. McCraty and M. Zayas, "Cardiac Coherence, Self-Regulation, Autonomic Stability, and Psychosocial Well-Being," *Frontiers in Psychology*; vol. 5: pp. 1–13 (September 2014).

13. K. Umetani, D. Singer, R. McCraty, et al., "Twenty-Four Hour Time Domain Heart Rate Variability and Heart Rate: Relations to Age and Gender over Nine Decades," *Journal of the American College of Cardiology*, vol. 31, no. 3: pp. 593–601 (March 1, 1998).

14. D. Childre, H. Martin, D. Rozman, and R. McCraty, *Heart Intelligence: Connecting with the Intuitive Guidance of the Heart* (Waterfront Digital Press, 2016), p. 76.

15. R. McCraty, M. Atkinson, W. A. Tiller, et al., "The Effects of Emotions on Short-Term Power Spectrum Analysis of Heart Rate Variability," *The American Journal of Cardiology*, vol. 76, no. 14 (1995): pp. 1089–1093.

16. Pert, *Molecules of Emotion*.

17. Ibid.

18. Song, Schwartz, and Russek, "Heart-Focused Attention and Heart-Brain Synchronization."

19. Childre, Martin, and Beech, *The HeartMath Solution*, p. 33.

20. Song, Schwartz, and Russek, "Heart-Focused Attention and Heart-Brain Synchronization."

21. Childre, Martin, and Beech, *The HeartMath Solution*.

22. J. A. Armour, "Anatomy and Function of the Intrathoracic Neurons Regulating the Mammalian Heart," in I. H. Zucker and J. P. Gilmore, eds., *Reflex Control of the Circulation* (Boca Raton, FL: CRC Press, 1998), pp. 1–37.

23. O. G. Cameron, *Visceral Sensory Neuroscience: Interoception* (New York: Oxford University Press, 2002).

24. McCraty and Shaffer, "Heart Rate Variability: New Perspectives on Physiological Mechanisms, Assessment of Self-Regulatory Capacity, and Health Risk."

25. H. Martin, "TEDxSantaCruz: Engaging the Intelligence of the Heart," Cabrillo College Music Recital Hall, Aptos, CA, June 11, 2011, https://www.youtube.com/watch?v=A9kQBAH1nK4.

26. J. A. Armour, "Peripheral Autonomic Neuronal Interactions in Cardiac Regulation," in J. A. Armour and J. L. Ardell, eds., *Neurocardiology* (New York: Oxford University Press, 1994), pp. 219–44; J. A. Armour, "Anatomy and Function of the Intrathoracic Neurons Regulating the Mammalian Heart," in Zucker and Gilmore, eds., *Reflex Control of the Circulation*, pp. 1–37.

27. McCraty, Atkinson, Tomasino, et al., "The Coherent Heart."

Chapter 8

1. E. Goldberg and L. D. Costa, "Hemisphere Differences in the Acquisition and Use of Descriptive Systems," *Brain Language*, vol. 14, no. 1 (1981), pp. 144–73.

Chapter 11

1. A. Aspect, P. Grangier, and G Roger, "Experimental Realization of Einstein-Podolsky-Rosen-Bohm Gedankenexperiment: A New Violation of Bell's

Inequalities," *Physical Review Letters*, vol. 49, no. 2 (1982): pp. 91–94; A. Aspect, J. Dalibard, and G. Roger, "Experimental Test of Bell's Inequalities Using Time-Varying Analyzers," *Physical Review Letters*, vol. 49, no. 25 (9182): pp. 1804–1807; A. Aspect, "Quantum Mechanics: To Be or Not to Be Local," *Nature*, vol. 446, no. 7138 (April 19, 2007): pp. 866–867.

2. D. Bohm, *Wholeness and the Implicate Order* volume 135 (New York: Routledge, 2002).

3. I. Bentov, *Stalking the Wild Pendulum: On the Mechanics of Consciousness* (New York: E. P. Dutton, 1977); Ramtha, *A Beginner's Guide to Creating Reality* (Yelm, WA: JZK Publishing, 2005).

Chapter 12

1. W. Pierpaoli, *The Melatonin Miracle: Nature's Age-Reversing, Disease-Fighting, Sex-Enhancing Hormone* (New York: Pocket Books, 1996); R. Reiter and J. Robinson, *Melatonin: Breakthrough Discoveries That Can Help You Combat Aging, Boost Your Immune System, Reduce Your Risk of Cancer and Heart Disease, Get a Better Night's Sleep* (New York: Bantam, 1996).

2. S. Baconnier, S. B. Lang, and R. Seze, "New Crystal in the Pineal Gland: Characterization and Potential Role in Electromechano-Transduction," URSI General Assembly, Maastricht, Netherlands, August 2002.

3. T. Kenyon and V. Essene, *The Hathor Material: Messages from an Ascended Civilization* (Santa Clara, CA: S.E.E. Publishing Co., 1996).

4. R. Hardeland, R. J. Reiter, B. Poeggeler, and D. X. Tan, "The Significance of the Metabolism of the Neurohormone Melatonin: Antioxidative Protection and Formation of Bioactive Substances," *Neuroscience & Biobehavioral Reviews*, vol. 17, no. 3: pp. 347–57 (Fall 1993); A. C. Rovescalli, N. Brunello, C. Franzetti, and G. Racagni, "Interaction of Putative Endogenous Tryptolines with the Hypothalamic Serotonergic System and Prolactin Secretion in Adult Male Rats," *Neuroendocrinology*, vol. 43, no. 5: pp. 603–10 (1986); G. A. Smythe, M. W. Duncan, J. E. Bradshaw, and M. V. Nicholson, "Effects of 6-methoxy-1,2,3,4-tetrahydro-beta-carboline and yohimbine on hypothalamic monoamine status and pituitary hormone release in the rat," *Australian Journal of Biological Sciences*, vol. 36, no. 4: pp. 379–86 (1983).

5. S. A. Barker, J. Borjigin, I. Lomnicka, R. Strassman, "LC/MS/MS Analysis of the Endogenous Dimethyltryptamine Hallucinogens, Their Precursors, and Major Metabolites in Rat Pineal Gland Microdialysate," *Biomedical Chromatography*, vol. 27, no. 12: pp.1690–1700 (December 2013), doi: 10.1002/bmc.2981.

6. Hardeland, Reiter, Poeggeler, and Tan, "The Significance of the Metabolism of the Neurohormone Melatonin."

7. David R. Hamilton, *Why Kindness Is Good for You* (London: Hay House UK, 2010), pp. 62–67.

8. R. Acher and J. Chauvet, "The Neurohypophysial Endocrine Regulatory Cascade: Precursors, Mediators, Receptors, and Effectors," *Frontiers in Neuroendocrinology*, vol. 16: pp. 237–289 (July 1995).

9. D. Wilcox, "Understanding Sacred Geometry & the Pineal Gland Consciousness," lecture available on YouTube at https://youtu.be/2S_m8AqJ Ks8?list=PLxAVg8IHlsUwwkHcg5MopMjrec7Pxqzhi.

Chapter 13

1. Global Union of Scientists for Peace, "Defusing World Crises: A Scientific Approach."

2. Ibid.

3. D. W. Orme-Johnson, C. N. Alexander, J. L. Davies, et al., "International Peace Project in the Middle East: The Effects of the Maharishi Technology of the Unified Field," *Journal of Conflict Resolution*, vol. 32, no. 4 (December 4, 1988).

4. D. W. Orme-Johnson, M. C. Dillbeck, and C. N. Alexander, "Preventing Terrorism and International Conflict: Effects of Large Assemblies of Participants in the *Transcendental Meditation* and *TM-Sidhi* Programs," *Journal of Offender Rehabilitation*, vol. 36, no.1–4: pp. 283–302 (2003).

5. "Global Peace—End of the Cold War," Global Peace Initiative, http://globalpeaceproject.net/proven-results/case-studies/global-peace-end-of-the-cold-war/.

6. J. S. Hagelin, M. V. Rainforth, K. L. C. Cavanaugh, et al., "Effects of Group Practice of *Transcendental Meditation* Program on Preventing Violent Crime in Washington, D.C.: Results of the National Demonstration Project, June–July 1993," *Social Indicators Research*, vol. 47, no. 2: pp. 153–201 (June 1999).

7. R. D. Nelson, "Coherent Consciousness and Reduced Randomness: Correlations on September 11, 2001," *Journal of Scientific Exploration*, vol. 16, no. 4: pp. 549–70 (2002).

8. "What Are Sunspots?" Space.com, http://www.space.com/14736-sunspots-sun-spots-explained.html (February 29, 2012).

9. A. L. Tchijevsky (V. P. de Smitt trans.), "Physical Factors of the Historical Process," *Cycles*, vol. 22: pp. 11–27 (January 1971).

10. S. Ertel, "Cosmophysical Correlations of Creative Activity in Cultural History," *Biophysics*, vol. 43, no. 4: pp. 696–702 (1998).

11. C. W. Adams, *The Science of Truth* (Wilmington, DE: Sacred Earth Publishing, 2012), p. 241.

12. "Earth's Atmospheric Layers," (January 21, 2013), https://www.nasa.gov/mission_pages/sunearth/science/atmosphere-layers2.html.

13. R. Wever, "The Effects of Electric Fields on Circadian Rhythmicity in Men," *Life Sciences in Space Research*, vol. 8: pp. 177–87 (1970).

14. Iona Miller, "Schumann Resonance," *Nexus Magazine*, vol. 10, no. 3 (April–May 2003).

15. Childre, Martin, Rozman, and McCraty, *Heart Intelligence: Connecting with the Intuitive Guidance of the Heart*.

16. R. McCraty, "The Energetic Heart: Bioelectromagnetic Communication Within and Between People, in Bioelectromagnetic and Subtle Energy Medicine," in P. J. Rosch and M. S. Markov, eds., *Clinical Applications of Bioelectromagnetic Medicine* (New York: Marcel Dekker, 2004).

17. Childre, Martin, Rozman, and McCraty, *Heart Intelligence: Connecting with the Intuitive Guidance of the Heart*.

18. R. McCraty, "The Global Coherence Initiative: Measuring Human-Earth Energetic Interactions," Heart as King of Organs Conference, Hofuf, Saudi Arabia (2010); R. McCraty, A. Deyhle, and D. Childre, "The Global Coherence Initiative: Creating a Coherent Planetary Standing Wave," *Global Advances in Health and Medicine*, 1(1): pp. 64–77 (2012); R. McCraty, "The Energetic Heart," in *Clinical Applications of Bioelectromagnetic Medicine*.

19. HeartMath Institute, "Global Coherence Research," https://www.heartmath.org/research/global-coherence/.

20. S. M. Morris, "Facilitating Collective Coherence: Group Effects on Heart Rate Variability Coherence and Heart Rhythm Synchronization," *Alternative Therapies in Health and Medicine*, vol. 16, no. 4: pp. 62–72 (July–August 2010).

21. K. Korotkov, *Energy Fields Electrophotonic Analysis in Humans and Nature: Electrophotonic Analysis*, 2nd edition (CreateSpace Independent Publishing Platform, 2014).

22. D. Radin, J. Stone, E. Levine, et al., "Compassionate Intention as a Therapeutic Intervention by Partners of Cancer Patients: Effects of Distant Intention of the Patients' Autonomic Nervous System," *Explore*, vol. 4, no. 4 (July–August 2008).

INDEX

NOTE: Page references in *italics* refer to figures.

A

Adrenal gland (energy center), *94*, 96–99
Adrenaline, 47
Advertising, conditioning by, 179–184
Age of Aquarius, 293
Alpha-frequency brain waves
    kaleidoscope video for, 187–189, 192–194
    moving from beta to alpha, 91–93, *92*, 109–110
    present moment and, 52–54, *53*
    quantum field and, 67–69, *68*
Analytical mind
    coherence process and moving beyond, 299
    comparison of conscious, subconscious, and, 184–187, *185*
    entering subconscious mind, 91–93, *92*
Anger, storing, 115–117, *116*
Antioxidants, 271–273
Armour, J. Andrew, 169
Aspect, Alain, 239
Atoms
    classical *versus* quantum models of, *234*, 234–235
    overview and bonding example, *49*, 49–51
    quantum universe concept and, 63
    subatomic level of energy, 104–108, *105*

Attention
    convergent focus for, 91
    energy and place of attention, 126–130, *127–130*
    energy flow for present moment, *35*, 35–36, 44–46, *45*
    on matter *versus* energy, 250–251
Autoimmune disorders (case study), 149–151
Autonomic nervous system (ANS)
    coherence *versus* incoherence, 67
    heart coherence and, 159–161, 167–168
    overview, xxi, 10–11
Awareness. *See also* Tuning in
    superconsciousness as, 19, 23
    tuning in and, 75–76

B

Benzodiazepines, 271
Beta-frequency brain waves
    evolving energy to brain with gamma waves, 131–133, *132*, 269
    moving from beta to alpha, 91–93, *92*, 109–110
    present moment and, 51–54, *53*
    quantum field and, 67–69, *68*
Biophotons, 89, 106

Bio-Well software, 110

Blessing of the Energy Centers, 85–112
    Blessing of the Energy Centers
        meditation exercise, 111–112
    convergent and divergent focus,
        90–91
    drawing from energy field, 102–
        104, *103*
    electromagnetic energy for, 85–90,
        86–88
    energy centers, 92–99, *94*
    energy flow for, 99–102, *100, 101*
    entering subconscious mind for,
        91–93, *92*, 109–110
    example, 11
    increasing energy with, 108–111
    overview, xxvi
    subatomic level of energy, 104–
        108, *105*

Bohm, David, 240

Brain. *See also* Brain-wave frequencies;
        Conscious and consciousness;
        Heart coherence; Mind; Nervous
        system
    body as magnet and, 124–130,
        124–130
    cerebrospinal fluid, 125–130, *126–
        130, 265,* 265–266
    comparing conscious, subcon-
        scious, analytical minds,
        184–187, *185*
    creating mind with, 27–29
    electroencephalograms (EEG), xix,
        69, 165–166
    entering subconscious mind,
        91–93, *92*, 109–110
    evolving energy to, 131–136, *132,
        133, 135*
    "heart-brain," 169
    left/right hemispheres of, 193, 283
    mental rehearsal and, 36–39
    mini-brain of energy centers, 11,
        93–96, *94*, 115
    neocortex, 65, 92, 184–187, *185*, 193
    neural networks, 28, 44, 200
    neurocardiology, 169
    neurogenesis, 137
    neuropeptides, 115
    priming brain for future memories,
        209–211

Brain-wave frequencies
    entering subconscious mind,
        91–93, *92*, 109–110
    evolving energy to brain, 131–133,
        132
    heart coherence and, 166
    kaleidoscope video and, 187–189
    learning to change frequency, xxii
    overview, 51–54, *53*
    quantum field and change in,
        67–69, *68*
    quantum field and coherent/
        incoherent brain waves,
        65–68, *66*, 91
    serotonin and, 257

Breathing techniques
    benefits of, 11
    piezoelectric effect and, 261–265,
        263, 265
    Reconditioning the Body to a New
        Mind meditation exercise,
        140–142 (*See also* Recondi-
        tioning the Body to a New
        Mind)

Buddhism, open focus and, 91

C

Caduceus, 285, *285*
Calcite crystals, 261–265
Carbohydrate metabolism, 260
Cardiac events, stress and, 160–161
Case studies, 143–153, 213–217,
        307–316
    Daniel (electromagnetic hypersen-
        sitivity), 147–149
    Donna (interdimensional beings),
        311–313
    Felicia (severe eczema), 151–153
    Ginny (chronic pain), 144–146
    Janet (depression), 310–311
    Jennifer (autoimmune disorders),
        149–151
    Jerry (medical emergency),
        314–316
    overview, xxvii, xxviii, xxx, 143,
        213, 307
    Sarah (chronic pain), 215–216
    Sasha (Project Coherence), 311

Stacy (headaches), 307–309
Terry (trauma), 216–217
Tim (worthiness), 213–215
Central nervous system, 125
Cerebrospinal fluid, 125–130, *126–130,*
265, 265–266
Chakras, defined, 92. *See also* Energy
centers
Change
as choice, 8–12
creating, 73
Change of Heart, A (Sylvia), 106–107
Chicks/robot experiment, 73–74, *74*
Chizhevsky, Alexander, 293
Chronic pain (case studies), 144–146,
215–216
Chronic stress, 47, 160–161, 167–168
Cilia, of pineal gland, *265,* 266
Circadian rhythm, 273
Cleveland Clinic, 37–38
Coherence
building coherent energy, 109–111
(*See also* Blessing of the
Energy Centers)
coherent heart rate, 12
coherent/incoherent brain waves,
65–67, *66,* 91
incoherence *versus,* 298–300 (*See
also* Project Coherence)
Collapsing the wave function, 63–64
Conditioning, 179–184
Conscious and consciousness
altered state of consciousness as
mystical experience, 16
comparison of conscious, subconscious, and analytical minds,
184–187, *185*
four states of consciousness, 256
oneness consciousness, xxvii, 17,
69, *241,* 242–253, *243, 248*
relationship of time and space to,
219–221, *221*
superconscious state, 52–54, *53,*
131–133, *132*
unconscious mind, 30–33, *32,* 54,
114, 206–209
Constructive interference, 302, *302*
Convergent focus, 90–91

Cortisol
chronic stress and, 47
immune system and, 3, 43, *43*
melatonin and inverse relationship
to, 259, *259*
Creative energy. *See* Flow of creative
energy
Crop circles (Roundway, England),
282, 283
Cymatics, 277–278

D

Delta-frequency brain waves, 52–54,
53, 69, 166
Depression
case study, 310–311
pineal gland and, 260
Descartes, Rene, 155
DHEA, 260
Digestive and pancreatic glands
(energy center), *94,* 96–97
Dimensionalizing process, 201–203
Dimethyltryptamine (DMT), 273–274
Dispenza, Joe
mystical experiences of, 15–26,
188–189
*Reconditioning the Body to a New
Mind* (CD), 142
website of, xxvi
You Are the Placebo, 148
Divine geometry, 277–278
Dreaming, 256, 275. *See also* Pineal
gland

E

Earth, electromagnetic field of, 291–
294, *292*
Eczema (case study), 151–153
Egyptians (ancient)
on heart, 155
pineal gland and, *283,* 283–284
Einstein, Albert, 238–239, 273
Electroencephalograms (EEG), xix, 69,
165–166

Electromagnetic energy. *See also* Blessing of the Energy Centers
  body as magnet, 121–130, *121–130*
  Earth's electromagnetic field, 291–294, *292*
  electromagnetic hypersensitivity (EHS; case study), 147–149
  emotions and, 33, *34*, 34–36, 70–76, *72, 74*
  HeartMath Institute's study of heart's electromagnetic field, 299
  light and frequency of, 85–90, *86–88*
  Schumann resonance and, 294–295

Elevated emotions. *See also* Tuning in
  activating heart center for, 171–173
  as energy in motion, 33
  epigenetics and, 136–139, *138*
  example, 9–12
  heart coherence and, 157
  immunoglobulin A (IgA) and, 42–44, *43*
  intention combined with, 70–76, *72, 74*
  from pineal gland, 279–282
  sustaining heart coherence and, 173–178, *174, 175, 177*

Emergence concept, 296–298
Emotions. *See also* Elevated emotions
  as chemical feedback of brain, 28–29
  as energy in motion, 33, *34*, 34–36
  epigenetics and, 39–44
  linear time and, 227
  negative emotions, 46–49 (*See also* Stress)
  sharing energy and information, *49*, 49–51
  taking energy and power back during meditation, 47

Endowment principle, 139
Energy. *See also* Blessing of the Energy Centers; Energy centers
  attention and energy flow for present moment, 44–46, *45*

calling energy back to present moment, 51–60, *53, 56, 60*
changing, in present moment, *34,* 34–36
elevated emotions combined with intention, 70–76, *72, 74*
overview, xxii
pineal gland and energy delivery to brain, 266–269, *267–268, 270*
quantum field and changes in, 70–76, *72, 74*
as self-organizing intelligence, 61–65
Source energy (oneness), *243,* 251–252 (*See also* Space-time and time-space)
taking energy and power back during meditation, 55–60, *56*

Energy centers
  chakras, defined, 92
  description of eight energy centers, 96–99
  entering subconscious mind for, 91–93, *92,* 109–110
  flow of, 99–102, *100, 101,* 115–120, *116, 118*
  heart as bridge between other energy centers, 158–159
  mini-brains of, 11, 93–96, *94,* 115
  overview, xxii

Entropy, 90
Epigenetics
  embracing elevated emotions, 136–139, *138*
  overview, xxiii
  present moment and, 39–44, *43*
  stress and environmental effects on, 11–12, 14

External imagery, 38
Eye of Horus, *283,* 283–284

F

Fat, 260
Fear. *See also* Survival mode
  changing energy of, 171–172
  present moment concept and, 29
Fehmi, Les, 91

Fibonacci's constant, 284, *284*
Fight-or-flight response
    convergent *versus* divergent focus,
        90–91
    example, 5–6
    present moment and, 47
    sympathetic nervous system for,
        159
Five-dimensional multiverse
    relationship between time and
        space in, *231, 236, 237,*
        238–242
    unified field of, 238, 242–253, *243,*
        248
5-hydroxytryptophan (5-HTP), 258
Flow of creative energy
    between energy centers, 99–102,
        100, 101
    storage of energy and, 115–120,
        116, 118
Frequency
    cymatics, 277–278
    in electromagnetic energy, 85–90,
        86–88
    OM, 295
Future reality. *See also* Mind Movies/
    kaleidoscope
    creating, xix–xx
    imagining, 206–209
    present moment and, 15–22 (*See*
        also Present moment)
    priming brain for future memories,
        209–211
    tuning in for, 82–83

G

Gamma-frequency brain waves
    energy delivered to brain and, 268
    evolving energy to brain, 131–133,
        132
    overview, 52–54, *53*
Gas discharge visualization (GDV), 58,
    110, 111
Genetic expression. *See* Epigenetics
Global Coherence Initiative (GCI;
    HeartMath Institute), 296–297,
    303–304

Global Coherence Monitoring System
    (GCMS; HeartMath Institute), 297
Global community, meditating as. *See*
    Project Coherence
Global Consciousness Project (Princ-
    eton University), 290
Greeks (ancient)
    on heart, 155
    pineal gland and, 284–285, *285*
Guilt, storing, 117–118, *118*
Gut, *94,* 95–99

H

Habits
    developing, 30–33, *32*
    overcoming, in meditation, 54,
        206
    repetition of, 114
Harvard University, 37
Headaches (case study), 307–309
Heart coherence, 155–178. *See also*
    Heart rate variability (HRV)
    analysis
    autonomic nervous system (ANS)
        and, 159–161
    benefits of, 164–167
    brain coherence and, 68
    chronic stress and, 160–161,
        167–168
    coherent heart rate, 12
    defined, 157–158
    examples, 173–178, *174, 175, 177*
    heart as bridge between other
        energy centers, 158–159
    "heart-brain," 169–170, *169*
    heart center, 96, 171–173
    heartfelt emotions, 71
    heart intelligence and, 165
    HeartMath Institute's study of
        heart's electromagnetic field,
        299
    meditation, 178
    overview, xxvii, 155–158
    time-space continuum and,
        229–230
HeartMath Institute (HMI)
    collective coherent field data,
        300–302, *302*

Global Coherence Initiative (GCI), 296–297, 303–304
Global Coherence Monitoring System (GCMS), 297
on heart intelligence, 165–166 (*See also* Heart coherence)
heart rate variability (HRV) analysis by, 162–164, *163*
overview, xx, 156–157
study of heart's electromagnetic field, 299
Heart rate variability (HRV) analysis
communication between brain and heart, 161–164, *163*
example, 173–178, *174*, *175*, *177*
overview, xx
Project Coherence, 303–304, *305*
synchronization with others, 299
Hermes (Greek mythology), 284–285, *285*
Homeostasis, 159–161

I

Imagery, external, 38
Immune system. *See* Case studies; Stress
Immunoglobulin A (IgA), 42–44, 167
Inductance field, *128*, 128–130, *129*, 266–267, *267*
Intention
coherence and, 157
elevated emotions combined with, 70–76, *72*, *74*
energy centers and, 95
example of, 76–80, *78* (*See also* Tuning in)
Interdimensional beings (case study), 311–313
International Institute of Biophysics (IIB), 89
Intrathecal pressure, 135, 264, *265*
Intrinsic muscles, 127, *127*

J

Jesus, 274
Junk DNA, 139

K

Ka, *94*, 99
Kessler Foundation Research Center, 38
Kirlian, Semyon Davidovitch, 88
Known. *See also* Present moment
defined, 46
habits and, 30–33, *32*, 54, 114, 206–209
König, H. L., 295
Korotkov, Konstantin, 58

L

Lead-lag analysis, of peace-gathering projects, 288–290
Lebanon peace project, 289
Ledwell, Glen, 190–194
Ledwell, Natalie, 190–194
Left hemisphere processes, of brain, 193, 283
Light
defined, 33
in electromagnetic energy, 85–90, *86–88*
L-tryptophan, 257–258, *258*

M

Mandalas, 188, 277
Marketing Mastermind Group, 190
Matter. *See also* Energy
attention to, 250–251
influenced by energy, *122*, 122–124, *123*
three-dimensional universe and, 219–222 (*See also* Space-time and time-space)
Matthew 6:22, 274
Max Planck Institute, 295
Mayo Clinic, 160–161
Medical emergency (case study), 314–316
Meditation. *See also* Blessing of the Energy Centers; Brain; Case studies; Energy; Heart coherence;

Meditation exercises; Mind
Movies/kaleidoscope; Pineal
gland; Present moment; Project
Coherence; Quantum field;
Reconditioning the Body to a New
Mind; Space-time and time-space;
Supernatural; Walking meditation
  allowing time for, 58
  benefits of, 9–12, 13
  brain-wave frequencies of, 51–54,
    53, 67–69, 68
  to change internal state, 50–51 (*See
    also* Present moment)
  heart coherence, 178
  for peace as state of being, 317–322
  postures of, 205–206
  stray thoughts during, 54–55
  taking energy and power back dur-
    ing, 55–60, *56*
Meditation exercises
  Blessing of the Energy Centers,
    111–112
  Kaleidoscope and Mind Movie,
    203–204 (*See also* Mind
    Movies/kaleidoscope)
  Project Coherence, 306
  Reconditioning the Body to a New
    Mind, 140–142
  Space-Time, Time-Space, 253–254
  Tuning In Preparation, 80–82
  Tuning In to Higher Dimensions of
    Time and Space, 285–286
  Tuning In to New Potentials, 82–83
  Walking Meditation, 211–212
Melatonin
  ancient symbols about pineal
    gland and, 283–285, *283, 284*
  benefits of, 16, 98, 256–260, *260,*
    270
  inverse relationship between adre-
    nal hormones and, 259, *259*
  late-night production of, 22, 187,
    194, 258
  metabolic effects, 266, 270–274,
    271
  methylation process of, 258, *258*
  piezoelectric properties and,
    261–262
Memory
  music and, 194–197
  pattern recognition and, 200

  repeating past experiences with,
    2–4, 28–29
Mental rehearsal, 36–39
Mesopotamians, on heart, 155
Metabolites, produced from melatonin, 266, 270–274, *271*
Methylation process, 258, *258*
Mind. *See also* Conscious and consciousness; Mind Movies/
  kaleidoscope
  comparison of conscious, subcon-
    scious, and analytical minds,
    184–187, *185*
  creating, 27–29
  entering subconscious mind,
    91–93, *92,* 109–110
  intelligence of heart (*See* Heart
    coherence)
  mini-brain of energy centers, 11,
    93–96, *94,* 115
Mind Movies/kaleidoscope, 179–204
  comparison of conscious, subcon-
    scious, and analytical minds,
    184–187, *185*
  conditioning and, 179–184
  dimensionalizing process, 201–203
  immersion in and uses of, 197–200
  Kaleidoscope and Mind Movie
    meditation exercise, 203–204
  kaleidoscope compared to cymat-
    ics, 278
  kaleidoscope visual for perceiving
    three-dimensional reality,
    187–189, 192–194
  Mind Movies, development of,
    189–194
  Mind Movies case studies, 213–216
  power of music with, 194–197
Muscle training, as mental rehearsal,
  37–38
Music, power of, 194–197
Mystical experience. *See* Supernatural

N

Neocortex
  comparing conscious, subcon-
    scious, analytical minds,
    184–187, *185*

right and left hemispheres of, 193
as thinking brain, 65, 92 (*See also* Analytical mind)
Nervous system
  autonomic nervous system (ANS), xxi, 10–11, 67, 167–168
  central nervous system, 125
  overview, 159–161
  parasympathetic nervous system, 131, 167–168
  peripheral nervous system, 266–267, 267
  sympathetic nervous system, 131, 167–168, 269
Neural networks, 28, 44, 200
Neurocardiology, 169
Neurogenesis, 137
Neuropeptides, 115
9/11 events, collective emotional response to, 290
Noise, of external environment, 90

O

Ohio University, 38
OM, 295
Oneness consciousness
  overview, xxvii, 17, 69
  Source energy, *243*, 251–252
  unified field of, *241*, 242–253, *243*, *248*
Open focus, 91–93, *92*
Oxytocin, 275–276

P

Parasympathetic nervous system, 131, 159–161, 167–168
Pattern recognition, reality perception and, 200
Peace, as state of being, 317–322
Peace-gathering projects, history of, 288–290. *See also* Project Coherence
Peoc'h, René, 73
Perception, 281

Perineum muscles, 126–128, *127*, 134–135
Peripheral nervous system, 266–267, *267*
Photography, in electromagnetic examples, 88–89
Piano exercise, as mental rehearsal, 37, 38–39
Piezoelectric properties, 261–265, *263*
Pineal gland, 255–286
  activating, 260–262
  ancient symbols about, 283–285, *283, 284*
  crowning of the Self and, 285
  defined, 274
  elevated emotions from, 279–282
  energy delivery to brain via, 266–269, *267–268, 270*
  example, 16–17
  melatonin and serotonin, overview, 256–260, *258–260* (*See also* Melatonin)
  metabolites produced from melatonin, 270–274, *271*
  metabolites released by, *265*, 265–266
  overview, 255–256
  piezoelectric effect of, 261–265, *263*
  as transducer, 274–279
  Tuning In to Higher Dimensions of Time and Space meditation exercise, 285–286
Pineal gland (energy center), *94*, 96–99
Pinolines, 271–273
Pisciotti, Frank, 189
Pituitary gland
  as energy center, *94*, 96–99
  function of, 275–276
Popp, Fritz-Albert, 89
Prana tube, *133*, 133–134
Present moment, 27–60
  attention and energy flow for, 33, *34*, 34–36, 44–46, *45*
  calling energy back to, 51–60, *53*, *56, 60*
  epigenetics and, 39–44, *43*
  mental rehearsal and, 36–39
  overcoming stress hormones in, 46–51, *49*

overview, xxiv–xxv, 27–29
unknown and, 29–36, *32, 33, 35*
walking meditation for, 207
Princeton Biofeedback Centre, 91
Princeton University, 290
Project Coherence, 287–306
building collective coherent field
for, 300–301
case study, 311
coherence *versus* incoherence,
298–300
constructive interference, 302, *302*
Earth's electromagnetic field and,
291–294, *292*
emergence concept and, 296–298
events of, 303–304, *305*
history of peace-gathering projects,
288–290
meditation exercise, 306
overview, xxi, xxx, 287–288
Schumann resonance and,
294–295

Q

Quantum field, 61–83. *See also* Atoms
benefits of, 13
biophotons, 89, 106
brain changes and, 65–69, *66, 68*
energy changes and, 70–76, *72, 74*
energy delivered to brain, 269
as inward expression of laws of
nature, 227–230, *228, 229*
overview, xxv–xxvi, 61–65
quantum events, 63–64
time-space, defined, 222
tuning in meditation (example),
76–80, *78*
Tuning In Preparation meditation
exercise, 80–82
Tuning In to Your Future meditation exercise, 82–83

R

RAND Corporation, 289
Random event generator (chicks/
robot) experiment, 73–74, *74*

Rapid eye movement (REM) sleep, 257
Reconditioning the Body to a New
Mind, 113–142
body as magnet for, 121–130,
121–130
embracing elevated emotions for,
136–139, *138*
evolving energy to brain for, 131–
136, *132, 133, 135*
overview, xxvi–xxvii
*Reconditioning the Body to a New
Mind* (CD), 142
Reconditioning the Body to a New
Mind meditation exercise,
140–142
thinking-feeling loop and, 113–114
Resilience, 159–161
Reticular activating system (RAS), 268
Reticular formation, 135
Right hemisphere processes, of brain,
193, 283
Ringer's solution, 161
Romans (ancient), on heart, 155

S

Sacred geometry, 277–278
Sacrum, *124,* 124–125
Schumann, W. O., 294–295
Schumann resonance, 294–295
Schwartz, Gary, 166
Separation, compared to reality of
oneness, 221–222, 227, 230–233,
231, 233
Serotonin, 256–260, *258–260*
Sexual fantasies, 118–120
Sexual glands (energy center), *94,*
96–99
Shingles, advertising example about,
179–184
Sleep. *See also* Pineal gland
overview, 256
rapid eye movement (REM) sleep,
257
Solar cycles, Earth's relationship to,
291–294, *292*
Source energy (oneness), *243,* 251–252.
See also Space-time and time-space

Space-time and time-space, 219–254
    consequences of stress, 222–224
    five-dimensional multiverse, *231,*
        236, 237, 238–242
    overview, xxix
    quantum field construction, *234,*
        234–242, *236, 237, 241*
    quantum laws and, 227–230, *229*
    separation compared to reality of
        oneness, 221–222, 227, 230–
        233, *231, 233*
    space-time, defined, 222
    Space-Time, Time-Space medita-
        tion exercise, 253–254
    3-D space-time reality, 225–227
    three-dimensional universe and,
        219–222, *221*
    time-space, defined, 222
    unified field and, 242–253, *243,*
        248
Special relativity theory, 238–239
Sputnik antenna (sensor), 58, 301
State of being
    electromagnetic energy for, 71
    embodying peace as, 317–322
    present moment concept and, 29,
        34, 42
Stem cells, 41
Stress
    chronic stress, 47, 160–161,
        167–168
    consequences of perpetual state of
        survival, 222–224
    emotional stress as addiction, 6–8
    epigenetics and, 39–44, *43*
    immune system response to, 5–6
    melatonin benefits for, *259,*
        259–260
    memory of stressful events, 2–4,
        28–29
    overcoming stress hormones in
        present moment, 46–51, *49*
    stress hormones, overview, 2–4, 8
    stress hormones in survival mode,
        107–108
Subatomic level of energy, 104–108, *105*
Subconscious mind
    comparison of conscious, subcon-
        scious, and analytical minds,
        184–187, *185*

    entering, 91–93, *92,* 109–110
Superconscious state, gamma-fre-
    quency brain waves and, 52–54,
    53, 131–133, *132*
Supernatural, 1–26
    author's experiences with, 15–26
    evolving energy to brain for, *132,*
        132–133
    mystical experience and kaleido-
        scope video, 188–189
    mystical experiences, examples,
        15–26
    preparation for, xvii–xxx
    transcendental moments of con-
        sciousness, 256
    Willems example, 1–15
Survival mode
    body as magnet and, 123
    consequences of perpetual state of,
        222–224
    energy centers used for, 102–104, *103*
    energy storage in body, 115–120,
        116, 118
    fear, 29, 171–172
    fight-or-flight response, 5–6, 47,
        90–91, 159
    incoherent state of, 165
    stress hormones of, 107–108
Sylvia, Claire, 106–107
Sympathetic nervous system
    energy delivered to brain and, 131,
        269
    heart coherence and, 159–161,
        167–168
Syntropy, 90

T

T-cells, 166
Television, conditioning by, 179–184
Thalamic gate, *135,* 135–136
Thalamus, *268,* 268–269
Theta-frequency brain waves
    kaleidoscope video for, 187–189,
        192–194
    overview, 52–54, *53,* 67–69, *68*
Thinking-feeling loop
    Reconditioning the Body to a New
        Mind and, 113–120, *116, 118*

as state of being, 29, 33, 42 (*See also* Present moment)
Third eye, 269, 279
Third-person imagery, 38
Three-dimensional reality. *See also* Mind Movies/kaleidoscope
overview, 187–189
three-dimensional universe, 219–222, *221* (*See also* Space-time and time-space)
time as linear, 225–227, *226*
Thymus gland
as energy center, *94, 96–99*
heart coherence and, 166
Thyroid gland (energy center), *94,* 96–99
Time issues. *See also* Space-time and time-space
making time for meditation, 58
melatonin production and, 22, 187, 194, 258
Mind Movies and time of day, 199
time as linear, 225–227, *226*
Torus field, 130, *130, 270*
Trance
brain-wave frequencies of, 188
breaking habits with, 208–209
Transcendental moments of consciousness, 256
Transducer, pineal gland as, 261–262, 274–279
Transplant patients, studies of, 106–107
Trapped energy. *See* Flow of creative energy
Trauma (case study), 216–217
Trust experiment, 275–276
Tuning in. *See also* Quantum field
awareness, 19, 75–76
example, 76–80, *78*

Unknown. *See also* Present moment
chemistry alteration and, 279–282 (*See also* Pineal gland)
creating possibility and, 64–65
encountering, 21
present moment and, 29–36, *32, 33, 35*

V

Vasopressin, 275–276
Ventricular system, 265, *265*
Vibration. *See* Frequency
Visualization, dimensionalizing process compared to, 201

W

Wakefulness, 256
Walking meditation, 205–212
example, 12
imagining future with, 206–209
meditation postures, overview, 205–206
priming brain for future memories, 209–211
unconscious behaviors and, 206–209
Walking Meditation exercise, 211–212
Wavelengths, in electromagnetic energy, *87, 88,* 88–90
Wave of energy, 64, 277–278
Wever, Rutger, 295
What the Bleep Do We Know!? (documentary), 22
Willems, Anna, 1–15
World Health Organization, 147
Worthiness (case study), 213–215

U

Unconscious mind, habits and behaviors of, 30–33, *32,* 54, 114, 206–209
University of Arizona, 166
University of Texas at San Antonio, 38

Y

You Are the Placebo (Dispenza), 148

ABOUT THE AUTHOR

Joe Dispenza, D.C., is an international lecturer, researcher, corporate consultant, author, and educator who has been invited to speak in more than 32 countries on five continents. As a lecturer and educator, he is driven by the conviction that each of us has the potential for greatness and unlimited abilities. In his easy-to-understand, encouraging, and compassionate style, he has educated thousands of people, detailing how they can rewire their brains and recondition their bodies to make lasting changes.

In addition to offering a variety of online courses and teleclasses, he has personally taught three-day progressive workshops and five-day advanced workshops in the U.S. and abroad. Starting in 2018, his workshops will become week-long offerings, and the content of the progressive and advanced workshops will be available online. (To learn more, please visit the events section at **www.drjoedispenza.com**.) Dr. Joe is a faculty member at Quantum University in Honolulu, Hawaii; the Omega Institute for Holistic Studies in Rhinebeck, New York; and Kripalu Center for Yoga and Health in Stockbridge, Massachusetts. He's also an invited chair of the research committee at Life University in Atlanta, Georgia.

As a researcher, Dr. Joe's passion can be found at the intersection of the latest findings from the fields of neuroscience, epigenetics, and quantum physics to explore the science behind spontaneous remissions. He uses that knowledge to help people heal themselves of illnesses, chronic conditions, and even terminal diseases so they can enjoy a more fulfilled and happy life, as well as evolve their consciousness. At his advanced workshops around the world, he has partnered with other scientists to perform extensive research on the effects of meditation, including epigenetic testing, brain mapping with electroencephalograms (EEGs), and individual energy field testing with a gas discharge visualization (GDV) machine. His research also includes measuring both heart coherence with HeartMath monitors and the energy present in the workshop environment before, during, and after events with a GDV Sputnik sensor.

As a corporate consultant, Dr. Joe gives on-site lectures and workshops for businesses and corporations interested in using neuroscientific principles to boost employees' creativity, innovation, productivity, and more. His corporate program also includes private coaching for upper management. Dr. Joe has personally trained and certified a group of more than 70 corporate trainers who teach his model of transformation to companies around the world. He also recently began certifying independent coaches to use his model of change with their own clients.

As a *New York Times* best-selling author, Dr. Joe has written *You Are the Placebo: Making Your Mind Matter* (Hay House, 2014), which explores our ability to heal without drugs or surgery, but rather by thought alone. He has also written *Breaking the Habit of Being Yourself: How to Lose Your Mind and Create a New One* (Hay House, 2012) and *Evolve Your Brain: The Science of Changing Your Mind* (2007), both of which detail the neuroscience of change and epigenetics. Becoming Supernatural is Dr. Joe's fourth book. His film appearances include *HEAL* (2017); *E-Motion* (2014); *Sacred Journey of the Heart* (2012); *People v. the State of Illusion* (2011); *What IF – The Movie* (2010); *Unleashing Creativity* (2009); and *What the #$*! Do We Know? & Down the Rabbit Hole*, extended DVD version (2005).

Dr. Joe received a B.S. from Evergreen State College and his doctor of chiropractic degree from Life University, where he graduated with honors. His postgraduate training covered neurology, neuroscience, brain function and chemistry, cellular biology, memory formation, and aging and longevity. Dr. Joe can be contacted at: **www.drjoedispenza.com**.

Hay House Titles of Related Interest

YOU CAN HEAL YOUR LIFE, the movie,
starring Louise Hay & Friends
(available as a 1-DVD program, an expanded
2-DVD set, and an online streaming video)
Learn more at www.hayhouse.com/louise-movie

THE SHIFT, the movie,
starring Dr. Wayne W. Dyer
(available as a 1-DVD program, an expanded
2-DVD set, and an online streaming video)
Learn more at www.hayhouse.com/the-shift-movie

THE BIOLOGY OF BELIEF 10th ANNIVERSARY EDITION:
Unleashing the Power of Consciousness, Matter & Miracles,
by Bruce Lipton, Ph.D.

HEAL YOUR MIND: Your Prescription for Wholeness
through Medicine, Affirmations, and Intuition,
by Mona Lisa Schulz, M.D., Ph.D., with Louise Hay

HUMAN BY DESIGN: From Evolution by Chance
to Transformation by Choice, by Gregg Braden

THE MINDBODY SELF: How Longevity Is Culturally Learned
and the Causes of Health Are Inherited, by Dr. Mario Martinez

All of the above are available at your local bookstore,
or may be ordered by contacting Hay House (see next page).

We hope you enjoyed this Hay House book. If you'd like
to receive our online catalog featuring additional information on
Hay House books and products, or if you'd like to find out more
about the Hay Foundation, please contact:

Hay House, Inc., P.O. Box 5100, Carlsbad, CA 92018-5100
(760) 431-7695 or (800) 654-5126
(760) 431-6948 (fax) or (800) 650-5115 (fax)
www.hayhouse.com® • www.hayfoundation.org

Published and distributed in Australia by: Hay House Australia Pty. Ltd.,
18/36 Ralph St., Alexandria NSW 2015 • *Phone:* 612-9669-4299
Fax: 612-9669-4144 • www.hayhouse.com.au

Published and distributed in the United Kingdom by: Hay House UK, Ltd.,
Astley House, 33 Notting Hill Gate, London W11 3JQ • *Phone:* 44-20-3675-2450
Fax: 44-20-3675-2451 • www.hayhouse.co.uk

Published in India by: Hay House Publishers India, Muskaan Complex,
Plot No. 3, B-2, Vasant Kunj, New Delhi 110 070 • *Phone:* 91-11-4176-1620
Fax: 91-11-4176-1630 • www.hayhouse.co.in

Distributed in Canada by: Raincoast Books,
2440 Viking Way, Richmond, B.C. V6V 1N2
Phone: 1-800-663-5714 • *Fax:* 1-800-565-3770 • www.raincoast.com

Access New Knowledge.
Anytime. Anywhere.

Learn and evolve at your own pace with the world's leading experts.

www.hayhouseU.com

Free e-newsletters
from Hay House, the Ultimate
Resource for Inspiration

Be the first to know about Hay House's free downloads, special offers, giveaways, contests, and more!

 Get exclusive excerpts from our latest releases and videos from *Hay House Present Moments*.

 Our *Digital Products Newsletter* is the perfect way to stay up-to-date on our latest discounted eBooks, featured mobile apps, and Live Online and On Demand events.

 Learn with real benefits! *HayHouseU.com* is your source for the most innovative online courses from the world's leading personal growth experts. Be the first to know about new online courses and to receive exclusive discounts.

 Enjoy uplifting personal stories, how-to articles, and healing advice, along with videos and empowering quotes, within *Heal Your Life*.

 Have an inspirational story to tell and a passion for writing? Sharpen your writing skills with insider tips from *Your Writing Life*.

Sign Up Now!

Get inspired, educate yourself, get a complimentary gift, and share the wisdom!

Visit www.hayhouse.com/newsletters to sign up today!

 HAY HOUSE

 HAYHOUSE RADIO® *radio for your soul®*

 HAYHOUSE online learning